THE PEOPLE NEXT DOOR

T.C.A. Raghavan is a former Indian envoy to Singapore and Pakistan. He has served as Deputy High Commissioner (2003–07) and High Commissioner (2013–15) in Islamabad. He has also had a unique vantage point on India–Pakistan ties as director in the office of the External Affairs Minister (2000–02) and from the Pakistan Desk (2007–09) in the Ministry of External Affairs.

He has a PhD in History from Jawaharlal Nehru University, New Delhi. His first book *Attendant Lords: Bairam Khan and Abdur Rahim, Courtiers and Poets in Mughal India* was awarded the Mohammad Habib Memorial Prize by the Indian History Congress in December 2017.

Praise for *The People Next Door*

'With an insider's confidence, [Raghavan] fleshes out a well-known and oft-documented chronology with stories that illustrate the repetitive pattern of the relationship between hostility and goodwill, and how, with each cycle, the past comes back in new ways to become the present.' – Nirupama Subramanian, *The Indian Express*

'Raghavan's excellent book brings home the necessary truth that in India–Pakistan ties, you must keep inhaling the voices of the past to deal with the present.' – Mini Kapoor, *The Hindu*

'Throughout this most readable book, [Raghavan] keeps a deep, steady but also quizzical gaze on Indo–Pak affairs. He was high commissioner through exceptionally challenging years, but he copes with the ups and downs with composure.' – Saeed Naqvi, *India Today*

'The real strength of the book lies in quietly persuading the reader to develop an unbiased account of a highly complex relationship.' – *The Pioneer*

'Raghavan's well-researched book spans the 70 years of Indo–Pak relationship. The author illustrates its narrative with several anecdotes, events and personalities that revive the hostility, nationalism and nostalgia defining every facet of the relationship.' – *The Times of India*

'Raghavan's book is neither a memoir nor a sweeping look at the history of bilateral relations. It instead focuses on little-known but extremely interesting individuals and episodes to nudge readers towards developing a better understanding of the people living next door and their – in the words of the author – *Rashomon*-like accounts of key events.' – *Hindustan Times*

'Raghavan's book provides us a wide-angle view of India–Pakistan relations and ought to be read by anyone interested in a humanist narration of ties between the two countries, told with a good dose of empathy.' – *The Print*

'Written with both deep personal knowledge and a genuine investment in the India–Pakistan relationship, Raghavan's book is likely to become a classic on this "curious history".' – Wajahat Habibullah, *The Wire*

'Raghavan's is a book that is enjoyable in its style, reliable in its facts, and informed in its tone and substance.' – Manu Pillai, *Mint*

'[A] usefully incisive and informative addition to the considerable literature, of all kinds and approaches, already available.' – *The New Indian Express*

'Former Indian High Commissioner T.C.A. Raghavan charts the ups and downs of neighbourly relations.' – Adil Bhat, *Dawn*

'T.C.A. Raghavan has written with narrative zest, accuracy and an eye for telling detail about India's relations with Pakistan. This is contemporary history as it should be written by a knowledgeable participant in its making ... A welcome, essential and most readable addition to works on India's unhappy relationship with Pakistan.' – Shivshankar Menon, Former Foreign Secretary and National Security Adviser

'This is undoubtedly the best book on India–Pakistan relations. Raghavan writes with the authority of knowledge and experience, with wit and panache ... A very readable book which will be on many bookshelves.' – Meghnad Desai, columnist and political commentator, Member of the British House of Lords

THE PEOPLE NEXT DOOR

The Curious History of India's Relations with Pakistan

T.C.A. Raghavan

HarperCollins *Publishers* India

First published in hardback in India by
HarperCollins *Publishers* in 2017

HarperCollins Publishers India, Cyber City, Building 10-A, Gurugram, Haryana-122002, India
www.harpercollins.co.in

This edition published in paperback in India in 2018 by
HarperCollins *Publishers*

P-ISBN: 978-93-5302-291-4
E-ISBN: 978-93-5277-091-5

2 4 6 8 10 9 7 5 3 1

Typeset in 10.5/14.5 Sabon LT Std
By Saanvi Graphics Noida

Printed and bound at
MicroPrints India, New Delhi

HarperCollins Publishers, Macken House, 39/40 Mayor Street Upper, Dublin 1, D01 C9W8, Ireland

For
Ranjana Sengupta

Contents

Introduction

WHEN HARPERCOLLINS APPROACHED ME to write a history of India–Pakistan engagement for the seventieth anniversary of our Independence, I accepted the commission with some trepidation. Books on different aspects of India–Pakistan relations will easily fill a library. Issues and themes such as the overhang of Partition, terrorism, Kashmir in its different ramifications, sharing of river waters, the 1948, 1965, 1971 and 1998 conflicts and many others have been dealt with in detail many times over and each of these subjects now is perhaps a specialization in itself. Near-conflict situations—1986–87, 1990, 2001–02, 2008–09, amongst others—are similarly the subjects of both research and speculation. Strategic, military and nuclear-related issues form advanced specializations with a large and ever-growing literature. In general, every facet of the relationship has over the decades been scrutinized and commented upon in detail and contemporary events and developments are examined and discussed with knowledge, precision and, of course, passion. Public knowledge about the relationship is considerable. Therefore, the question before me was how much more can possibly be written about a relationship which has been bad in most conceivable ways over the past seven decades.

On the other hand, my own experience of both living in Pakistan and dealing with India's relations with Pakistan had been marked by a near-constant discovery of something new about the past. This was not so much 'new' in terms of factual knowledge as in encountering sentiments and experiences of others who have interfaced with India–Pakistan relations and the connections they have drawn between different events and processes. This, at least for me, often nuanced the known facts and gave a more rounded perspective on viewing an event or set of events. I thought, therefore, of illustrating, to the extent possible, the mainstream chronology of this relationship with these aspects to impart a fuller sense of how and why things developed as they did over the years. So, this is an attempt at writing an animated and anecdotal history with an aim to convey a feel of the relationship at different points of time of its past with all its oddities and curiosities. If nothing else such a treatment may, I feel, make this deeply troubled relationship more accessible and perhaps in the process also help in demystifying it.

In giving a historical overview of how and why India–Pakistan history took the course it did, naturally I also take a great deal of knowledge of this history for granted. Hence, I pass rapidly over seminal and important persons, events and periods while dwelling, perhaps excessively, on others. I also have kept a narrow focus on the broad mainstream of the relationship itself. There are, therefore, many important aspects I am cursory with and leave aside for more specialized reading or study. This includes, for instance, the international context of India–Pakistan relations including, in the early years, Kashmir in the United Nations, third-country relationships important for both countries and how they impacted India–Pakistan relations—the United States of America, China, Afghanistan, the Soviet Union/Russia, and others—the military history of the different wars, internal developments in India and Pakistan and the changing strategic and military balance between the two. Similarly, I am cursory with India–East Pakistan contestations on numerous issues—river water sharing, land boundary demarcation, etc.

In brief, to keep the book to a manageable length, I have discarded trying to be exhaustive. My aim is to bring out a fuller flavour of India–Pakistan relations in terms of a more subjective and selective view of both well- and lesser-known incidents and individuals in the broad context of the principal ups and downs of the relationship. The individuals I have found interesting are from a range of backgrounds—professional diplomats, practising politicians, journalists, academics, writers, peace activists and others. They found themselves in the quirky matrix of India–Pakistan relations and sought to navigate through it with multiple motives and objectives. To me their reflections and reactions provide a point of entry into the curious universe of the India–Pakistan relationship at different points of time.

I have generally followed a mainstream chronology. The first and second chapters deal with the years from 1947 to 1960 and the third and fourth take the story up to December 1971 and the break-up of Pakistan. The fifth, sixth and seventh chapters cover respectively the periods 1972–79, 1980–89 and 1990–99. The eighth attempts to bring the story up to 2008. The reasons for this division are evident enough and I hope will become clearer in the book itself.

I must set out at the beginning two other provisos. This is a 'history' book and not a 'policy' book. In tracing out this history, I do not draw any grand lessons and if there are any takeaways or policy recommendations I leave it to the readers to decipher and extract if they so wish. Secondly, as we come closer to our own times I close the story somewhat abruptly. In my view, the past always needs to incubate before its history can be attempted.

Finally, while I have tried to be even-handed in covering different issues and situations, this is, needless to say, an Indian perspective on a divisive and deeply contested past and present.

1

The Setting of the Mould

BETWEEN AUGUST 1947 AND September 1948 most trends and issues which comprise the current India–Pakistan matrix fell into place.

From June–July 1947 to January 1948 the bulk of the 'ethnic cleansing' in East and West Punjab was completed. Some twelve million refugees had traversed in both directions of the newly plotted part of the Radcliffe Line that divided and defined the newly emerged countries in Punjab. Thus, East Punjab, now falling in India, was largely emptied of Muslims and West Punjab, in Pakistan, of Hindus and Sikhs. The uprooting of Hindus, Muslims and Sikhs was systematic: houses occupied, farms taken over, mosques, temples and gurdwaras desecrated, tens of thousands killed and women targeted for rape and abduction.

This was a demographic upheaval to match the one that had just come to an end in Europe over the territory of Germany, Poland, Hungary and Czechoslovakia. In Europe, although the war had ended in 1945, large-scale displacement and violence had not. What the Poles, Hungarians and the Czechoslovaks did after the World War II with Soviet and Allied (the US, France, the UK) concurrence to the Germans of Europe, the Hindus and Sikhs did to Muslims in East Punjab and the Muslims in West Punjab to Hindus and Sikhs. The magnitude of these population transfers is also similar—about twelve million in both cases of those permanently expelled and with hundreds of thousands killed. But there were differences. In Europe, the movement was largely in one direction: Germans being forcibly moved westwards into a truncated Germany; between East and West Punjab, and elsewhere on a smaller scale, people moved in both directions across the Radcliffe Line. Secondly, in Europe there was a strong policy element inbuilt into this exercise. At Yalta and Potsdam in February and July 1945 respectively, the victorious powers had decided that Europe's nations, to avoid a repetition of the two world wars, had to be made ethnically homogeneous. So, ethnic Germans in Poland, Hungary and Czechoslovakia were driven out to Germany. Germany was at the same time cut down as its borders shrank significantly to what it is today.[1]

In India, the demographic transformation of Punjab was a consequence of its partition—although the movement of population and communal rioting, in fact, began some weeks before the new borders of the new countries were announced. The massive ethnic cleansing that occurred was not, however, an outcome of policy, either of the new governments, or indeed of the parties that formed them—the Muslim League and the Indian National Congress.

If the similarities in the scale of population displacement in Punjab and Eastern Europe is riveting, the analogy can be pushed too far. Neither India, nor for that matter even Pakistan, emerged as ethnically homogeneous entities. While Punjab was homogenized in both directions, Bengal, the other province partitioned in August 1947, was not. In 1951, the Hindu population of East Bengal (East Pakistan post-1947) was at 29 per cent, the Muslim population of West Bengal a similar fraction. Across India, most Muslims, except in Punjab, despite a significant migration, stayed where they were. In the aggregate, about thirty-five million Muslims, about a third of the pre-Partition total Muslim population, stayed back in India.[2] About 10 per cent of the total population of India in the 1951 census was Muslim.

West Pakistan was certainly more homogeneous; nevertheless, even here, in pockets in south-east Sindh, a significant number of Hindus remained where they were. This was in Umarkot, Mithi and Nagarparkar—all Hindu majority, largely rural, areas and where substantial Hindu populations have continued post-1947 up to today. This was despite the wholesale flight of Hindus from all of Sindh's cities which pre-1947 had substantial Hindu majorities or were split almost 50:50 between Hindus and Muslims. Hyderabad—Sindh's second largest city—had a 70 per cent Hindu population and in Karachi, Muslim population figures were only slightly higher than the Hindu (47 per cent to 46 per cent). In a few months after Partition both places were left with very small Hindu populations and the number progressively reduced thereafter.

Similarly, in East Punjab in India there were pockets that bucked the general trend. In tiny Malerkotla, part of the princely state of Patiala, most Muslims stayed put. In the 2011 census, 60 per cent of the town's population was Muslim. Malerkotla can be explained by its own unique history. One of the ancestors of its ruling nawab had, the tradition goes, protested the execution of Guru Govind Singh's young sons in 1705. The Guru had thereafter blessed the family and their estate and this ensured that the furies of 1947 left this small state relatively untouched. There is, however, another and more significant exception. In a small part of the erstwhile East Punjab, now falling in Haryana, the Mewat district today stands out with a 70 per cent Muslim population.[3] This is possibly the highest percentage in this part of India—even if we include districts of UP, Rajasthan and Bihar. Mewat had, in fact, a deep-rooted history of communal strife from the early twentieth century. The Tablighi Jamaat amongst Muslims and the Shuddhi movement amongst Hindus had both originated here and contributed much to the communalization of the political and social atmosphere in north India in the early twentieth century. Despite this history, Mewat remains a contrarian example of the post-Partition ethnic cleansing which swept the undivided Punjab as it was partitioned into two.

The Partition massacres and population displacements were swift, almost surgical. By January 1948, and with the assassination of Mahatma Gandhi, the violence was subsiding. Nevertheless, alongside the Partition massacres and the huge refugee movements other ingredients were also being added to the India–Pakistan crucible. Some were major and, in hindsight, appear now critical. Others look now as being of lesser significance but these cast long shadows too.

Chronologically viewed, the events in Junagadh appear first, initially as a sideshow to the main drama in north and east India, but soon acquired a larger-than-life character. This small princely state in western India, with a Muslim ruling family and a predominantly Hindu population acceded to Pakistan on 15 August 1947. After some dithering, Pakistan accepted the accession about a month later in mid-September. India disputed the accession on the grounds of the state's religious demography (more than 90 per cent Hindu) plus the fact that it was deep inside India with no land border with Pakistan. Pakistan's point was that it was for the ruler to decide whether to join India or Pakistan and Junagadh could access Pakistan through the sea. After furious protests and counter-protests over September and October, the deployment of Indian troops early in November 1947 settled the matter. The nawab of Junagadh, an eccentric of a high order, had flown to Karachi, then the capital of Pakistan, in end-October accompanied by some of his wives, his treasury and his many dogs. Stories about the nawab and his dogs—and there were hundreds, both stories and dogs—were legendary. As the Junagadh state aircraft landed, there was a large ceremonial reception awaiting him, complete with guard of honour, band, etc. This was obviously an important occasion for Pakistan—a princely state deep inside India was joining Pakistan. Those present at the ceremonial reception recall that as the door of the aircraft opened, out charged a pack of yelping dogs thrilled that their confinement had ended.

Some maps of Pakistan to this day show Junagadh as a part of it and to many Pakistanis it was a legal accession undone by brute use of military force by India. For India, a plebiscite carried out to determine the views of the people of Junagadh settled the matter. The plebiscite was held in February 1948 and only some 600 voted in favour of Pakistan. For both Indians and Pakistanis, when Junagadh is discussed, the accusation is made on the other of adopting a 'heads I win tails you lose' approach. Junagadh, for all its small size and relative obscurity, is important because its accession crisis forms the background to the story of the Muslim-majority princely state of Jammu and Kashmir (J&K). In the latter case, facing a choreographed 'tribal invasion' from Pakistan, the Hindu maharaja acceded to India and India accepted the accession. This happened on 27 October 1947 only a few weeks after Pakistan had accepted the accession of Junagadh.

Far away from Delhi and Karachi, another aspect of the Partition of India was being discussed with great concern. Why should, many Afghans wondered in Kabul, the Pashtun in British India's north-western provinces have only the option of India or Pakistan? In this perception, the Pashtun had been unnaturally divided by the British in the nineteenth century through the Durand Line to serve as the boundary between

British India and Afghanistan. As Partition drew closer, increasingly influential Afghans were talking about an independent Pashtunistan to represent those east of the Durand Line, or that the North-West Frontier Province (NWFP) should become part of Afghanistan. In September 1947, these views assumed a formal character as Afghanistan cast the sole negative vote in the United Nations against the admission of Pakistan to the organization. The negative vote was withdrawn three weeks later but the point had been made and it had certainly registered in Pakistan.

Many Pakistanis to this day see in Afghanistan's objection to Pakistan joining the United Nations an Indian hand. India, it is believed, played its cards through the pro-Congress Red Shirts party of Khan Abdul Ghaffar Khan, a strong political force in the North-West Frontier Province and a respected figure in Afghanistan.[4] For Abdul Ghaffar Khan, popularly known as Bacha Khan or Badshah Khan and also the Frontier Gandhi, the division of India was a second tragedy: the Pashtuns had been divided once already through the Durand Line by the British and now India itself was being further divided on religious lines. Whatever were to be the implications of Afghanistan's negative vote in the UN on Pakistan–Afghanistan relations in the future, many doubts about Indian actions through Afghanistan on the western borders of Pakistan were sown at an early date. These doubts only have grown and crystallized with time and circumstance.

Thousands of reams have been written on the accession of J&K and therefore it is unnecessary to reproduce more than the bare bones of the Kashmir chronology. The tribal invaders from Pakistan, led and directed by the Pakistan Army's commissioned and non-commissioned officers reached the outskirts of Srinagar by mid-October 1947. A desperate Maharaja Hari Singh requested Indian military assistance. India made committing its troops conditional on the state's accession to India—how else could the troops be legally deployed? The Instrument of Accession was signed on 27 October 1947. Contingents of the Indian Army were flown to Srinagar reaching just in time to stop the invaders from entering and capturing the city. Pakistan disputed the accession of the state to India on the grounds that the state had a Muslim majority and was geographically contiguous to it. Even as fighting continued in the state,

India referred the matter of the aggression from Pakistan to the United Nations Security Council (UNSC) on 1 January 1948. It has regretted the decision ever since. Pakistan's response to the Indian complaint was one of straightforward denial as also a whole set of general allegations and grievances—of India's genocide of Muslims, the forcible annexation of Junagadh, Kashmir's accession being a fraud, etc. The view in India, almost unanimously, was that the British, enormously influential still by virtue of being the former colonial power and the best informed, persuaded the Security Council to expand India's reference of aggression by Pakistan into a general India–Pakistan question. The Security Council adopted a resolution on 21 April 1948 which did not direct Pakistan to immediately withdraw its proxies and generally treated India and Pakistan as having equal status in Kashmir without considering the fact of the state's accession to India. Both India and Pakistan felt short-changed by the resolution. Pakistan had its own reasons for objecting to the resolution—that it did not recognize Pakistan's right to deploy its forces in the state, that it did not prohibit advances of Indian troops, etc. The April resolution and the generally tardy response of the UNSC to a complaint of aggression were an embittering experience for India. India's representative at the UNSC, N. Gopalaswami Ayyangar, was to comment: 'I will never advise my government to bring any other case to the Security Council. Yes, if you have a bad case, bring it to the Council.'[5] The absence of agreement meant that the fighting continued in J&K.

Every element of the J&K story has two variants—an Indian and a Pakistani. We will encounter these as we progress, but there is one counterfactual that merits a pause. Pakistan was envisaged as a homeland for the Muslims of India. What if Pakistan had not accepted the accession of Junagadh on the grounds that it was predominantly a Hindu territory? The obscure case of the tiny princely state of Dujana near Delhi provides, if not a precedent, a curious contrast. Though it had a predominantly Hindu population, its Muslim nawab migrated to Pakistan in 1947 and offered to accede, only to be turned down.[6]

On Junagadh, there is an occasional debate in Pakistan with the subtext that not accepting its accession would have strengthened Pakistan's case on Kashmir. It is argued that this would also have avoided the initial bitterness imparted to the India–Pakistan relationship by the Junagadh events. But the question is premised on the assumption that post-Partition, newly independent India and Pakistan began on a clean slate. In fact, they did not. All the accumulated differences, tensions and suspicions that had characterized the Muslim League–Congress negotiations from the late 1930s, in fact, carried over after August 1947 and now acquired an international character. This implied a zero-sum mindset which possibly made it impossible for the newly formed government of Pakistan to say no to the nawab of Junagadh.

The communal situation, Partition massacres and refugee movements combined with the Junagadh events and the Kashmir war tended to vitiate every aspect of the India–Pakistan interface at this stage. The war in Kashmir was, however, an undeclared war. The newly established diplomatic relations between the two nascent governments continued, the high commissioners remained in place as indeed did intergovernmental discussions and even cooperation on resolving the administrative debris of Partition—the division of assets, deciding on a framework for trade, separation of currencies, etc. But in the vitiated atmosphere of two armies fighting it out, an obvious issue arose over the partitioning of military assets—spares, armaments, ammunition, etc. Then cash balances of the Reserve Bank had to be divided between the two countries and Pakistan's share of ₹750 million released to it. The details of the divisions had been finalized earlier and the first tranche of ₹200 million paid on 14 August 1947. The balance ₹550 million remained.

By the end of 1947 and early 1948 the question before the new Government of India was a difficult one. Given the ongoing war against Pakistani troops and proxies in Kashmir, was it correct to release Pakistan's balance share of ₹550 million? Release of the finances would straightaway have an impact on the military operations in Kashmir. Most in India at that time saw this as a no-brainer and the cabinet also agreed. Where was the question of releasing funds when it was evident that they would be used by Pakistan for the purchase of arms for the Kashmir war where Indians were being killed?

At this point, Mahatma Gandhi, already distressed by the mayhem in Punjab and the killings still taking place in Delhi, decided to take matters in his hands. To him, the withholding of Pakistan's share was an act of bad faith regardless of the Kashmir situation. He went on a fast—for communal amity, to cleanse a vitiated atmosphere and to persuade the Government of India to release the funds due to Pakistan.

Mahatma Gandhi had no doubt that the military action being taken by the Government of India on the ongoing Pakistan invasion in Kashmir was the right and the merited one. But withholding of the funds was a different matter. Mountbatten's comment to him that this was 'the first dishonourable act' of the free Government of India, also appears to have made a deep impression.[7] His fast began on 13 January 1948, and it lasted five days; the Cabinet backed down and the funds were released.

To many in India, in the supercharged atmosphere of the time, this appeared to be the Mahatma taking his existing pro-Muslim bias to unacceptable limits. To give money to Pakistan when it was at war with India and when defending Indian soldiers were being killed was bizarre and unacceptable. Amongst the hundreds of thousands of refugees in Delhi, sentiment was even stronger: They had lost everything, family members killed, female relatives raped or abducted, ancestral properties confiscated, and here was India financing the very people who had put them through this. Protests began outside Birla House in New Delhi where Mahatma Gandhi's fast had taken place. The reaction was against the government for buckling and even more intensely against the Mahatma. Nevertheless, that a man would kill the Mahatma on 30 January 1948 was inexplicable even to the protesters. The assassin directly linked his act to the grant of funds to Pakistan while its invasion of Kashmir was at its height. The assassination of India's tallest leader on this ground thus provides an early and most dramatic example of how divided views in India about Pakistan can be, as also the moral dilemmas involved in framing a policy towards Pakistan.

In contrast, there is a near-consensus in Pakistan to this day about India holding back Pakistan's share of the cash balances. This was India trying to strangulate Pakistan by doing it out of its rightful share. Memories of this act are, therefore, of an embittering experience—not easily forgotten or forgiven. The context in which this took place and how the funds were finally released is, however, seldom recalled.

The Kashmir war continued all through 1948 A United Nations Commission for India and Pakistan, appointed by the Security Council, meanwhile travelled to the subcontinent in July 1948. In Karachi, it was informed by the foreign minister of Pakistan, Zafarullah Khan, that three brigades of the Pakistan Army had been in operation in Kashmir since May. This disclosure constituted so significant a change in the situation on the ground that some urgent steps by the United Nations were expected by India. Instead, what followed was another resolution in August 1948 that called for a ceasefire, the withdrawal of Pakistani troops and tribesman, following which India should withdraw the bulk of its troops and thereafter the future status of the state would be determined and decided through a plebiscite. While India accepted the resolution—it did after all amount to an implied criticism of Pakistan—Pakistan's response and numerous conditions were tantamount to a rejection. The war in Kashmir continued. In retrospect, some of the reasons which Pakistan gave for the deployment of its regular army in Kashmir are worth pausing over: 'They were moved as an act of self-defence to protect the canal waters'; 'the possibility of India establishing a link for the movement of Pathanistan' and; the possibility of a pincer movement against Pakistan by India and Afghanistan'.[8] However fanciful this may seem now, as possibly it appeared in 1948, these do indicate the dimensions of the Kashmir question in Pakistan. The issues of Pakistani withdrawal of its forces and auxiliaries and plebiscite were thereafter at the heart of all UN efforts in J&K. The inability to agree on the sequencing of the withdrawal and the nature and modalities of the plebiscite meant that these efforts would not yield success through the 1950s.

By the end of 1948, the war had run its course. While the tribal levies and the Pakistan military personnel were evicted from many areas in Poonch, Ladakh and Kargil, a narrow stretch bordering Pakistan and including Muzaffarabad and Mirpur and in the large area of Gilgit and Skardu further to the north remained in Pakistani control. Evicting Pakistan forces from these would require a larger offensive; a move which Prime Minister Nehru and his government, including Deputy Prime Minister Vallabhbhai Patel, had little enthusiasm for. By all accounts the military advice was also not in favour of this, given constraints of logistics and stores.[9] In Pakistan, similarly, Liaqat Ali Khan had no desire to prolong a conflict in which he worried the military balance would ultimately tilt in favour of India. If the military options on both sides by that time had largely exhausted themselves, nevertheless the view has persisted, paradoxically in both countries, that left to themselves the militaries could have finished the job—though of course each defined this differently. By end-1948, a ceasefire had been agreed to and J&K

was de facto divided along where the respective forces stood on 31 December 1948. This was the ceasefire line carefully demarcated as part of the agreement signed in July 1949 by the Indian and Pakistani military commanders and co-signed by representatives of the United Nations. The latter would also monitor the ceasefire on the line through observers known as the UN Military Observer Group for India and Pakistan (UNMOGIP).

The ceasefire line also endured the 1965 war and at its conclusion both armies withdrew to their respective sides. Following the 1971 war this line was modified and realigned, largely at India's insistence, and it was thereafter known as the Line of Control (LOC). Despite the ceasefire line no longer existing the UNMOGIP remains in place, notwithstanding India's view that its mandate ended with the ceasefire line.

The ceasefire line and the Line of Control were, however, identical at their terminal point—known only by a map reference, NJ 9842. This was an inaccessible area with no possible habitation due to high mountains and glaciers. The military commanders meeting in Karachi in July 1949 to finalize the alignment of the ceasefire line agreed that beyond NJ 9842 it would extend *'thence north to the glacier'*. They could not have anticipated that deciphering these five words would lead to further and prolonged conflict in subsequent decades. In the words of a distinguished military historian these five were 'Delphic words' since they encapsulate the core of the Siachen conflict of the 1980s and beyond.[10]

Apart from the 1947–48 war, there were other developments taking place with equally long shadows. The partition of Punjab had meant that the irrigation headworks feeding river waters into canals were in India. The canals themselves, as well as the fields they irrigated were in West Punjab, part of Pakistan. In December 1947, the governments of East and West Punjab reached an agreement to maintain the status quo on the supply of water from rivers in India to canals in Pakistan. The nomenclature used in this agreement was 'standstill', i.e., the status quo would be maintained. The standstill agreement signed was valid up to March 1948, the assumption being that in the interim a more permanent arrangement would be worked out.

This did not happen and on 1 April 1948 the Government of East Punjab stopped further releases of water flowing to Pakistan through the canal headworks in their control. According to some estimates, almost 8 per cent of West Pakistan's cultivable command area of water faced drought.[11] The India–Pakistan water contestation had begun. The chain of events had, even in those early days, more a local and provincial flavour rather than an India–Pakistan character. Both Central governments, harried as they were by numerous other crises, appear to have been taken by surprise: The Pakistan government by the lethargy of the West Punjab authorities in renewing the existing standstill agreement on releases to canals, and the Government of India with the promptitude with which the East Punjab authorities acted on 1 April to close water supplies at the lapse of the standstill agreement. Nehru was to upbraid the provincial government for this: 'Whatever the legal and technical merits may be, there is little doubt that this act will injure us greatly in the world's eyes, and more especially when food production is so urgently needed everywhere,' he wrote to the premier of East Punjab, Gopi Chand Bhargava.[12] The Government of India's responses to Pakistan's complaints about the stoppage of water through the headworks were also prompt and it pushed hard for an early meeting between the two sides to resolve this issue.

The supply was resumed on 30 April after a fresh agreement was reached which provided for payments for the water discharged for irrigation use in Pakistan. In Pakistan, up to this day, feelings run high that this new agreement was concluded under duress, when they had no option but to sign to get water for crops, cattle, city supply, etc. Pakistan Punjab had many characteristics of a 'hydraulic society' as its canal colonies from the end of the nineteenth century defined different aspects of its polity and society. The events of April 1948 are, therefore, permanently etched into the Pakistan psyche as a classic example of India's bad faith and of its intention to undermine Pakistan by all possible means. The security of Pakistan and water security would henceforth be indistinguishable. In India, on the other hand, views on these events of April 1948 have also evolved. It was earlier seen as a local, perhaps misguided, even excessive, reaction by the East Punjab authorities to protect its interests. Now, there is increasingly a view that an opportunity was missed to settle the water issues once and for all by making it clear to Pakistan that it could not claim by right water from rivers that flowed to it from India.

As these developments alongside the war in Kashmir continued, and with both governments fully stretched in dealing with the millions of refugees needing rehabilitation, another accession crisis was looming—this time in the princely state of Kalat, bordering Iran, Afghanistan and Pakistan and comprising a large part of present-day Balochistan province of Pakistan. Here the question was not of religious denomination—both the ruler and his subjects were Muslim. The Khan of Kalat, as its ruler was known, however, contemplated a sovereign state of his own or in any event a state with attributes of sovereignty and autonomy not available to the vast bulk of the princely states in India and Pakistan. If Kalat's resources and wealth were hardly comparable to the major princely states such as Hyderabad, Mysore, Jaipur or Jodhpur, his legal position and political claim was stronger.

Kalat claimed, because of a different history, a status unlike other princely states; in fact, something like that of Nepal.[13] Through the 1930s and 1940s the Khan argued that 'Kalat had never felt part of India' and it should be treated differently as it was a 'non-Indian' state. Kalat bordered Iran and Afghanistan, and that too strengthened ambitions of many in the Khan's circle of advisers. In some accounts, Kalat's accession to Afghanistan was part of an agreement being negotiated between the Khan of Kalat and the Afghan king in case the Kalat–Pakistan negotiations did not fructify.

As the British exit approached, the Khan of Kalat hired the services of an eminent British lawyer, William Monckton, to advise him on how to press his case with Pakistan. William Monckton incidentally was also, many in India believed, the evil legal genius of the Nizam of Hyderabad as he pursued a similar claim with the Government of India. The Khan of Kalat was, till as late as August 1947, also encouraged in his independence claims by Muhammad Ali Jinnah. On 11 August following meetings between the Khan and Jinnah a communique issued says:

> The Government of Pakistan recognizes Kalat as an independent sovereign state in treaty relations with the British Government with a status different from that of Indian states. After legal opinion has been received, further meetings will take place between representatives

> of Pakistan and the Khan of Kalat at Karachi. Meanwhile a standstill agreement has been made between Pakistan and Kalat.[14]

After the emergence of Pakistan, Jinnah's—as the country's first Governor General—perceptions changed very quickly and in the negotiations that followed, the Khan was told he had no option but to sign a treaty of accession as other princes were doing.[15] Jinnah pressed the point personally with the Khan who said that he would have to consult his newly constituted 'Houses of Parliament'. The latter came out against accession but advocated friendly relations with Pakistan based on a treaty as between two independent states. The Government of Pakistan and Jinnah were exasperated at this obduracy and contemplated options like those exercised by India in Junagadh. Tensions built up till by March 1948 it was clear that something dramatic was going to happen. In Pakistan, suspicions grew that the Khan was secretly intriguing with India and Afghanistan. Pakistani troop consolidation near Kalat reinforced the view that military action was imminent. At this stage, on 27 March 1948, the All India Radio from New Delhi reported that Kalat had approached the Government of India in January 1948 for accession and that India had refused the request. In one version V.P. Menon, then the secretary in the Department of States and a key person in securing the accession of different princely states to India, had said to a news reporter that:

> Kalat approached us ... one or two months ago through one of the agents but we refused to have anything to do with Kalat, because we stand by our commitment that we will not touch a single State which rightly belonged to Pakistan. In the sense that it is geographically situated inside Pakistan directly or indirectly.[16]

This was possibly the basis for the All India Radio broadcast. The report was denied but the damage was done. A wave of protest in Pakistan followed and the Khan immediately announced his accession to Pakistan. In April 1948, this matter came up in the Constituent Assembly of India and Prime Minister Nehru sought to clarify the position further. The question of Kalat's accession to India did not arise at all because of the 'geographical position of the state'. What had happened, he explained, was that:

> In August last, soon after the declaration of independence in India, the Government of Kalat drew the attention of the Government of India, to a press communique in which it was said that the Government of Pakistan had recognized Kalat as an independent sovereign state, in treaty relations with the British Government, with a status different from that of the Indian States. They invited the Government of India to make a similar declaration. Sometime later a request was received from the Kalat State for permission to establish a trade agency of the state in Delhi.[17]

Nehru went on to explain that the Government of India had, in fact, not replied to either of these approaches. Yet regardless of the position India took, many in Balochistan saw, and still see, the accession to Pakistan as an act of betrayal of the decision of the Balochistan parliament. The first of the many insurgencies in Balochistan that have taken place began largely dovetailing with the formal accession. In Pakistan, however, the 'role' of India in this chain of events has again seldom been forgotten and periodically resurfaces in our own times.

A fourth—after Junagadh, J&K and Kalat—accession crisis was also to take place. These were the events in the princely state of Hyderabad, which was a mirror opposite of J&K in some ways: a Muslim ruler with a predominantly Hindu population. It was, however, not geographically contiguous to Pakistan and being without a coastline did not possess the Junagadh argument of connection by sea, although a connection through Goa (not Indian territory till 1961) enabled access to the Arabian Sea. Besides, Hyderabad was rich enough and large enough to nurture the idea of being neither in India nor in Pakistan. For Pakistan, even if a formal accession to it was unrealistic, an independent and sovereign Hyderabad appeared plausible. This had enormous symbolic significance. Hyderabad was one of the great medieval kingdoms of South Asia. For many dreamers of the 1920s and 1930s of separate Islamic spaces in South Asia, Hyderabad would form a sovereign Osmanistan, part of a confederation of different Islamic states in India.

For India, the issue was a simple and pragmatic one. The state had a large Hindu majority and notwithstanding what its prince and its ruling elite wanted, it could not be allowed to form a large gaping hole in the middle of India. Hyderabad held out against accession till September 1948. This period was a story of internal decay and strife in Hyderabad as the law and order situation deteriorated and increasingly more radical Islamic elements took control of the state administration. They were often belligerent, not just with the local Hindu population but also with Indian security forces at the borders of the state. The final accession followed only after a surgical military intervention by the Indian Army, though the term employed was 'Police Action'. Although at no stage had the ruler of Hyderabad contemplated accession to Pakistan, there were numerous signs that he sympathized with the idea and he received subtle and not so subtle encouragement from Pakistan to hold out to achieve some measure of sovereign status.

On 21 August 1948, the Nizam of Hyderabad appealed to the UN Security Council for assistance, complaining of a crippling economic blockade and numerous intimidatory tactics by India. The commencement of the Indian military action on 13 September 1948 largely coincided with the death of Jinnah in Karachi on 11 September. The action had, however, been imminent for some weeks but the coincidence is further proof to this day to many in Pakistan of India's perfidy in taking advantage of its grief and distraction over the demise of its leader. A large protest mob, for instance, which gathered around the Indian high commission in Karachi accusing India: 'You cowards; you attacked us just when our father had died.'[18]

Although the accession of Hyderabad is now part of history, memories of the Indian action remain and surface periodically in Pakistan as part of an accumulated stock of grievance. But here again the same questions as are raised vis-à-vis Junagadh occasionally surface. Why did Pakistan not recognize the Hindu majority that existed in Hyderabad and consistent with the two-nation theory focus instead only on Kashmir?

In the first eighteen months after Partition, thus piece by piece an atmosphere of mistrust came into being that forms the bedrock of the India–Pakistan interface to this day. The Partition massacres and ethnic cleansing; the division of assets; Junagadh; the choreographed tribal infiltration amounting to an invasion and then the war in Kashmir; Afghanistan's initial non-recognition of Pakistan in the United Nations; Hyderabad; the distribution of river waters; and Balochistan—these are the layers of the bedrock even as debates about this tangled history continue.

The accessions of Junagadh and Hyderabad have receded substantially from public memory in India. In Pakistan both issues remain alive, even if ritually so. It would be rare to find a commentary on India which will not mention these two along with other injustices done to Pakistan. The Government of Pakistan as an annual exercise presses the UN Security Council not to delete these items from its agenda. The descendants of the erstwhile nawab of Junagadh in Karachi occasionally emerge from the woodwork to make a claim to their abandoned state. Junagadh is often shown as part of Pakistan in official maps. Most Indians when confronted with Pakistan's position are surprised or even shocked at such irredentism. Prime Minister Indira Gandhi is believed to have been presented a coffee table book on Pakistan in 1980 by its then president, General Zia-ul-Haq, during a meeting at Harare commemorating the independence of Zimbabwe. Flipping casually through it, she was surprised to see the map of Pakistan showing Junagadh as a part of the country. She is believed to have sent the book back.[19]

Hyderabad, on the other hand, remains in Pakistani consciousness not so much as a territorial claim but as an example of Indian perfidy and deviousness. If Kashmir's Hindu maharaja could accede to India, why was the Nizam's inclination towards Pakistan or independence dealt with by military force by India? Howsoever dormant and forgotten elsewhere, in many circles in Pakistan, Hyderabad evokes a sentimental and emotional response of being the wronged party.

The dogged persistence with which Pakistan has maintained its position on a curious legal tussle emanating from the accession of Hyderabad is illustrative. On 20 September 1948, a sum of UK £1 million was transferred into an account opened that very day in the name of the Pakistan high commissioner to the UK, Habib Ibrahim Rahimtoola. The amount was transferred from another account, thereafter closed that day, in the name of the Nizam of Hyderabad. The instructions to the bank which was to carry out the transaction were in a letter dated 16 September and signed by Nawab Moin Nawar Jung, a minister of the Nizam. The transfer took place on 20 September. In the meantime, the Indian military action, begun on 13 September, had ended with the surrender of the Hyderabad forces on 17 September. The Government of India protested the transfer of funds and the Nizam himself sought to reverse it and insisted that it was carried out without his permission. The UK bank, however, declined to oblige him and took the position that the account holder himself must agree to the reverse action. The Government of Pakistan and Mr Rahimtoola refused and claimed immunity from proceedings because of their diplomatic status. The Government of India took the bank to court in 1954 and the case went up to the House of Lords, which upheld the claim of immunity of the Government of Pakistan. Both bilateral discussions between India and Pakistan and litigation has continued since. The original amount of £1 million has now increased to over £30 million. Depending on the state of the India–Pakistan relationship, the original case has been fiercely contested, lain dormant or headed towards an out of court settlement that India and Pakistan divide the balance in an agreed formula.

From prime ministers downwards, different levels in both governments have engaged themselves with the nitty-gritty of the legalities or to find a pragmatic way out on the grounds that only lawyers and the bank are benefiting from this long stalemate. No substantive step forward has been possible—perhaps largely because the principles at stake supersede in significance the amount of money on the table. Given the size of both the Pakistani and the Indian economies, the quantum of funds is obviously no longer a material consideration. For Pakistan, the issue is of Hyderabad's forced accession following a military intervention when its ruling Muslim prince wanted independence and a closer relationship with Pakistan. The fund thus represents that symbolic relationship. The legal claim which Pakistan makes is not unrelated: the money was no more than the payment due to Pakistan for arms and ammunition it had purchased from third countries on behalf of Hyderabad to enable it to resist the Indian military invasion and the economic blockade that had preceded it. For India, equally, the issue is of principle—what possible claim can Pakistan have to the funds of the erstwhile Hyderabad state?

So, the case has persisted—as a curiosity to some, principle to others and a reminder of the layered history of the India–Pakistan interface for most. Over time, its complexity has grown with the demands and claims being made by the now numerous heirs and their descendants of the Nizam clamouring for some share of the corpus. For Indians, this case can be understood and explained only in terms of an inability in

Pakistan to concede that Hyderabad became part of India because the clear majority of its citizens would not have had it in any other way. For many Pakistanis, the question was, and is, also of the Islamic dynasty which ruled Hyderabad for centuries and therefore of the Muslims who remained in India after August 1947 and with whose fate the idea of Pakistan as conceived could not engage with.

It is well known that the name Pakistan emerged or was coined as an acronym by Rahmat Ali, usually described as a student in Cambridge in the 1930s. He was, in fact, older than most students at the time, being in his mid-thirties. The term used was PAKSTAN in a pamphlet titled 'Now or Never' brought out by Rahmat Ali in 1933. The immediate context was the ongoing Round Table Conference in London convened to deliberate upon and frame a federal structure for India. An Indian federation was an idea that filled Rahmat Ali with the deepest anxiety—it would be 'an inexcusable and prodigious blunder'. What he proposed instead was a homeland for thirty million Muslims comprising the 'five northern units of India, viz., **P**unjab, North-West Frontier Province (**A**fghan), **K**ashmir, **S**ind and Baloch**istan** '.

The idea of a Muslim state in north India was not in itself a novel one. In a biography of Rahmat Ali, the Pakistani historian K.K. Aziz has counted some 70–80 occasions when a suggestion from prominent figures for a separate Muslim state in north India had appeared from the mid-nineteenth century to the 1930s.[20] Nevertheless, Rahmat Ali's acronym caught on and captured public and media attention in a way that its predecessor ideas had not. Rahmat Ali lived to see his acronym become the name of a real country. Indeed, he came to live in Pakistan in April 1948 but it was an embittering experience as dreams confronting reality often can be. He had to leave Lahore and Pakistan, never to return, in October that same year.

Lahore, teeming with refugees from India with stories and grievances of what they had had to go through in the months before and after Partition, was then hardly a pleasant place to be in. Yet Rahmat Ali was bitter about the partition of Punjab and Bengal as also the loss of Assam.[21] His own ancestral village in Hoshiarpur was now in India and that part of his heritage was also lost forever. If the partition of the two major Muslim provinces was to him the real betrayal, an even greater betrayal was the Muslims left behind in India. He, therefore, set the future task for Pakistan as being the 'sovereignization of Muslims of India in National States' by the launching of a 'Pakistan National Liberation Movement'.[22] These states—in a federal system—would form the 'Continent of Dinia'. The Bay of Bengal would be the Bang-i-Islam Sea and the Arabian Sea as the Pakistanian Sea. In Rahmat Ali's dreamy meanderings, Pakistan would be only one of the many Muslim states in South Asia—Bang-i-Islam (Bengal and Assam), Osmanistan (Hyderabad and the Deccan), Haideristan (for the Muslims of the United Provinces or Uttar Pradesh), Siddiqistan (for the Muslims of the Central Provinces later called Madhya Pradesh), Faruqstan (for the Muslims in Bihar and Orissa), Muinstan (for Muslims in Rajasthan), and Maplistan (for Muslims in South India).[23] In addition, there was the immediate need to bring the ongoing war in Kashmir to a successful closure. He was asked whether the plan for 'sovereignization of Muslims in India in National States' would not increase the difficulties for the Muslims in India. His reply was, 'To begin with yes, it would. But in the end, such a determination would be the best shield for their defence.'[24] His criticism of the government for its timidity and indeed of M.A. Jinnah for the same reason, did not make him popular. Rahmat Ali was told to go back to England, failing which he would be arrested.

This drastic act of forcing him out has never been sufficiently explained in Pakistan. The most plausible explanation is that the Government of Pakistan had enough on its hands in the immediate aftermath of its creation to add a potentially disruptive dreamer to that portfolio. Rahmat Ali's view that the terms of the Partition had been unfair to Muslims and that they were victims of a 'British–Hindu alliance' was shared by many. In the words of K.K. Aziz, an admiring, but not uncritical biographer:

> One major reason for Rahmat Ali's banishment from Pakistan in 1948 was the fear that he would exploit this feeling, thus bringing a bad name to the Muslim League and to Jinnah. This feeling of having been dealt an unfavourable deal grew with years and continual reports of suppression of Muslims in India intensified it. Pakistani thoughts went back to Rahmat Ali's suggestions and for a few 'national homes to accommodate the Muslims scattered all over Hindu India'.[25]

Rahmat Ali died in Cambridge virtually a pauper and remains buried there. After his return, he used to refer to Jinnah as 'Quisling-i-Azam Jinnah' and to Pakistan as Pastan 'because it does not include even East Punjab, Delhi Division, Jammu and Kashmir, West Bengal and Assam'.[26]

Rahmat Ali retains in Pakistan a certain appeal represented in the voices heard from time to time that his grave be shifted to Pakistan for a more appropriate burial in Lahore or Islamabad as part of a national memorial of how Pakistan came into being. This act will yield some political dividends for whoever achieves it but is not without its own risk. This is largely because of the bitter polemic Rahmat Ali deployed against Jinnah and this has so far come in the way of attempts to move his grave to Pakistan. For others, Rahmat Ali's 'impossible dreams' propelled by memory, nostalgia and desire to regain a lost glory mean that it is better to 'let the visionary rest in peace in Cambridge'. [27]

Rahmat Ali's sense of injustice at the Radcliffe Award which demarcated the boundaries of India and Pakistan in the west and the east is shared by many in Pakistan. Nehru's 'manipulation' of the Mountbattens is the subject both of polemics in seminars as also half-humourous late-night dinner party jokes. In the Radcliffe demarcation of India–Pakistan boundaries, it is the award of the larger part of Gurdaspur district in Punjab to India which is regarded as the greatest injustice. This implied that Pathankot, a vital connection to Jammu and onward to the Kashmir Valley through Jammu, fell to India. In this view, with the Gurdaspur award, the pieces were in place by August 1947 for the Indian takeover of Kashmir. The Gurdaspur award is, for many, a double blow—the loss of a Muslim-majority area which had been the centre of Muslim culture for a millennium, and then that it was a part of the conspiracy to snatch Kashmir from Pakistan. To this day the subject draws innumerable comments and impassioned analyses.

There is an interesting sidelight to this issue. In the summer of 1947, Hindus, Muslims and Sikhs got ready their respective cases on the division of Punjab to present to the Boundary Commission chaired by Sir Cyril Radcliffe. The Muslims on one side and Hindus and Sikhs on the other prepared maximalist positions for their share of the territory of the undivided Punjab. In this situation, the Australian geographer O.H.K. Spate received an unusual commission. He was employed as a technical adviser by a Muslim sect—the Ahmadiyas. The headquarters of the Ahmadiyas was in Qadian in Gurdaspur district. Spate's brief was to make the strongest possible case to the Boundary Commission that Gurdaspur should belong to Pakistan. In this capacity, therefore, Spate became in effect an informal adviser to the Muslim League.[28] As he immersed himself in the passionate claims and counterclaims of each side and prepared the best possible case for Qadian and Gurdaspur, Spate perceptively recalled this verse of the English romantic poet Swift:

And shew'd by one satyric Touch,
No Nation wanted it so much.

In the final award, Gurdaspur went to the Indian side. The reasons were, however, not a Kashmir-related conspiracy as many Pakistanis suspect. Adjoining Amritsar which had the Sikh's holiest shrine, Gurdaspur had a certain locational importance. If it fell on the Pakistani side of the border, Amritsar would be almost surrounded by Pakistani territory—perhaps virtually indefensible. The award of Gurdaspur to India was, therefore, an extra consideration to the Sikh faith for the enormous loss they had suffered because many of their principal religious sites—Panja Sahib, Kartarpur Sahib and Nankana Sahib—would fall in Pakistan. It was much for this reason that Lord Wavell, the viceroy preceding Mountbatten, in a draft partition plan he had made a year earlier had also awarded Gurdaspur to India. For similar reasons the district of Khulna with a Hindu majority and the Chittagong Hill Tracts with a Buddhist majority, both in Bengal, became part of East Pakistan.[29]

But the Gurdaspur case casts other shadows as well. In India–Pakistan relations, it is frequently the case that what begins as a bilateral issue often ends up as an internal one. So, it is with Gurdaspur, which was awarded to India despite all the efforts of the Ahmadiyas who, in turn, found themselves in an environment in their new homeland far from what they had imagined. Almost from the beginning they faced an orthodox backlash about their provenance as Muslims culminating in major riots in Lahore in 1953. Ironically enough, the principal protagonist of the anti-Ahmadiya agitation was the Majlis-i-Ahrar, an outspoken opponent of the Muslim League and the demand for Pakistan before 1947. Discrimination and violence against Ahmadiyas have been characteristic of Pakistan's history since then, and from 1976 they have been officially characterized as non-Muslims. But if Ahmadiyas are not counted as

Muslim, Gurdaspur may not have had even the slender Muslim majority claimed in 1947. This was the question posed somewhat rhetorically by a Pakistani historian recently.[30] This is, therefore, another Partition paradox best understood if the creation of Pakistan is seen also as a division of the Muslim community of South Asia.

Yet, Rahmat Ali's anguish about the large Muslim population left behind does not encapsulate the entire South Asian Muslim experience post-1947. Staunch Muslims such as Abul Kalam Azad, a major Indian National Congress leader, and Husain Ahmad Madani, the head of the famous seminary in Deoband, did not give importance to the two-nation theory and remained convinced that a large Muslim minority in a predominantly Hindu country would find its rights secure. If this is well known—although debates around this continue in Pakistan, and occasionally even in India—there is another, if more marginal, dimension to Muslims in India, post-1947. The two-way religious displacement between India and Pakistan from mid-1947 had a predictable quality to it. Millions of Muslims crossed from India into West and East Pakistan; Hindus and Sikhs in similar magnitudes moved in the opposite direction. Despite the violence and trauma of this process, most Muslims chose to remain in India; in East Pakistan too, most Hindus did not leave. Of the Muslims who stayed behind in India, it was likely that many families would have split. Such cases ranged from the highest princely families in the land to ordinary middle-class, working-class and peasant households. But overall, if a person or a family was on the move in 1947 or 1948, their religious persuasion would almost invariably indicate in which direction the movement was taking place. But this was not always the case. Less well known are the instances of Muslims who would, in the normal course, have been the pillars of the new Pakistan but who moved in the opposite direction.

The first of these stories is of Azim Husain (1913–2007).[31] He came from a distinguished family in pre-Partition Punjab. His father, Sir Mian Fazl-i-Husain (1877–1936) was one of the founders of the Unionist Party—a combine of well-established Muslim and Hindu agriculturists and landlords—determined to keep both the Muslim League and the Congress out of Punjab and thereby keep it united. Azim Husain joined the Punjab cadre of the Indian Civil Service in 1937. Posted in Delhi in 1947 he faced the choice, given to all civil servants at the time, of opting for either India or Pakistan. Azim Husain took the decision to uproot himself from Punjab and the majority of his family and move in a direction opposite to his co-religionists. He was by no means the only Muslim ICS officer to opt for India. There were others including Badr-ud-Din Tyabji (also known by his initials, i.e., B.F.H.B. Tyabji), also in the Punjab cadre. But Tyabji, although Muslim, was not from Punjab but from Bombay. This was also a family choice—he was a descendent of the first Muslim president of the Indian National Congress and Badr-ud-Din Tyabji's wife, Surayya, is believed to have designed the Indian national flag.

A related but still different case is of E.N. Mangat Rai, a Christian Punjabi from an eminent Lahore family who joined the ICS in 1941 and was also in the Punjab cadre. At Partition, the choice before him as a Christian was genuine as he did not 'by virtue of his religious label fall within one fold or the other'.[32] Mangat Rai thus became an Indian citizen 'by choice'. His sister, on the other hand, did not and staying on in Lahore, chose Pakistan. She later became the principal of Kinnaird College—one of Pakistan's most distinguished educational institutions. Some other Christian officers in the ICS in Punjab also opted for Pakistan—most notably A.R. Cornelius who went on to become the chief justice of Pakistan, and Samuel Martin Burke, diplomat, professor and author.[33]

Nevertheless, Azim Husain's case stands apart and is on a different footing. In 1947, he had the option of choosing one or the other of the two countries. In terms of what was happening all around, the choice should have been straightforward—he was a Punjabi Muslim, an ICS officer in the Punjab cadre and from a family with considerable status and material assets in what was to be Pakistan. But Azim Husain agonized over the question and finally opted for India, convinced that this is what his father would have wanted him to do. His brother, on the other hand, stayed on in Lahore and was to join the Pakistan Foreign Service. Many other relatives also were in Pakistan and his choice of India was to continue to surprise many over the years. For instance, on a visit to Lahore in 1957, Azim Husain was introduced at a family wedding to Iskander Mirza, then the president of Pakistan. In one account, Mirza had 'a bit of a shock when he found that Azim Husain, son of Fazl-i-Husain and nephew of Afzal Husain, was a joint secretary in the Indian Foreign Office and not an officer in the Pakistan High Commission'.[34]

After Partition, Azim Husain joined the Indian Foreign Service and served in it with great distinction. From time to time his career also intersects, as we shall see, the tangled history of India–Pakistan relations. At one stage both he and his brother were simultaneously Indian and Pakistani ambassadors to Lebanon. Azim Husain last served as deputy secretary general of the Commonwealth Secretariat and died in London in 2007. For students of modern Punjab history, the inscription on his gravestone captures in its entirety the unusual chosen trajectory of his life as it records him as 'Ambassador of India' and 'Son of Mian Sir Fazl-i-Husain'.[35]

The second story is of Mohammad Yunus (1916–2001), a Yusufzai Pathan from the Frontier. His reputation—posthumously but also when he was alive—has suffered due to his close association with the Emergency in India (1975–77), but the course of his life has a constant contrarian current to it in the context of the principal trends of India–Pakistan history. Born in Peshawar in a family deeply influenced by nationalist aspirations, he was drawn to Badshah Khan's politics in the NWFP and thereafter became close to many leaders of the Congress including Jawaharlal Nehru. He was jailed on more than one occasion during the freedom struggle. He was a close friend of Indira Gandhi, Sheikh Abdullah, Feroze Gandhi, Krishna Menon amongst others and had an intimate knowledge of what was happening in the corridors of power of the Indian National Congress.

In July 1947, Badshah Khan advised him to leave Peshawar and the Frontier as his opposition to the impending Partition and to the Muslim League made him a political risk and a liability. The Partition in August 1947 meant that he finally had also to choose, and he writes: 'Freedom brought partition and, for no fault of mine, I became a refugee in my own country. Torn from my roots in the North-West Frontier, Delhi became a forced home.'[36]

Mohammad Yunus was also to join the Indian Foreign Service, served as ambassador to three countries and retired as commerce secretary. Partition and exile from the Frontier was nevertheless a searing experience and is a recurrent theme as he progressed in his career. His memoirs published in 1980 are 'dedicated to my friends in Pakistan whom I had not seen in 32 years'.

In the late 1950s, just before leaving for Spain he recounts an encounter with an old resident of Delhi, Haji Mohammad Saleh, who said to him:

> You are going to Spain. Please look out for one thing. The Muslims came to India in the same century as they went to Spain. They ruled well in both places. But I hear there is not a single Muslim left there while there are millions milling around here. Please find out what the mistake was; by letting them live on here or eliminating them there.[37]

Yunus went on to write:

> The Haji was not far wrong, as I actually did not find trace of a Muslim in Spain, living or dead. There was not even a mausoleum of a dead Muslim king to be seen anywhere. The old forts and palaces of the Moorish Kings have been greatly altered in shape and design and decorated with the insignias and Coats of Arms of the subsequent Christian Kings.[38]

Notwithstanding his many detractors in India, Mohammad Yunus's presence close to those in power was a testimony also to the links between the Indian National Congress and Badshah Khan's secular politics in the Frontier as equally a reminder of the many Muslims remaining in Pakistan who had opposed Partition to the end. He remained throughout a perceptive observer of the India–Pakistan scene and one whose observations we will encounter from time to time.

The third story is both poignant and the most curious. K.L. Gauba is largely forgotten today, but from the late 1920s up to the 1960s he was a celebrated lawyer, author, public figure and a genuine sensationalist.[39] Son of a prominent businessman-cum-politician of Lahore, Lala Harkishen Lal Gauba, K.L. Gauba, after studying law in England, set up practice in the Lahore High Court. This conventional setting was interrupted by a public stir when he married a Muslim in 1923. This was a civil marriage and in Gauba's words, 'There was a furore in the city as the word leaked out. The newspapers commented divergently, according to they were Hindu or Muslim. The Associated Press, however, looked upon it as the triumph of love over communal prejudices and cabled the news to all corners of the country. From distant corners came congratulatory letters and telegrams. Cupid had hit the bullseye.'

It says something about Lahore's cosmopolitan atmosphere then that notwithstanding initial public indignation, Mr and Mrs Gauba were accepted as such in Lahore high society. Lala Harkishen Lal too reconciled himself to his son's marriage although the rest of the family did not. In any event, Gauba made his reputation thereafter as a man of letters—and it was an all-India reputation—when he wrote a response to the American author Katherine Mayo's book on India and Indians, *Mother India*. India was outraged by the book which Mahatma Gandhi called a 'drain inspector's report'. Others had also attempted a riposte but without much success—there was C.S. Ranga Iyer's *Father India*, the nationalist leader Lala Lajpat Rai's *Unhappy India* and, in Gauba's recollection, a 'Sister India' and a 'Brother India'. Gauba's book was about the United States, which he had never visited, and was titled *Uncle Sham*. He wrote it in about ten weeks. Gauba recollected that he had advised Lala Lajpat Rai that 'it is no good writing about "Unhappy India" because India is then likely to be unhappy for a considerable length of time' and then 'it occurred to me that I might try myself replying to Katherine Mayo by writing about America'.

Khushwant Singh was to summarize *Uncle Sham:* '... as Mayo had maligned India, Gauba maligned Mayo's motherland, the United States of America'. *Uncle Sham* consisted largely of 'incest, juvenile prostitution, dope and drink and all that was seamy in American life'.[40] A review in the prestigious US journal *Foreign Affairs* by the historian William L. Langer noted that while the book dealt with the working of democracy in America and 'the treatment meted out to the Negro', but 'by far the larger part is given over to a consideration of the sex problem'. Langer had possibly not read Katherine Mayo as he hoped in his review that it was more accurate than Gauba who had 'no difficulty in drawing a lurid, grotesque and extremely uncomplimentary picture of our civilization' and that 'the book shows once again that with a few quotations and the right spirit one can prove almost anything'.[41] Possibly K.L. Gauba would have agreed for he inscribed on the copy he sent to Katherine Mayo: 'To one Drain Inspector from Another'. The gifted jurist and later foreign minister of India, M.C. Chagla, reviewed the book in the *Bombay Chronicle* and said, 'So far no one has met Miss Mayo at her own level except K.L. Gauba ... Mr G is an artist of the first order.'[42]

In Gauba's account, the book was a 'hit overnight'. Priced at ₹6—not a small amount in 1929–30—*Uncle Sham* went through twenty printings in the space of a year and, in Gauba's recollection, sold 'more than six figures, several times over'. The nationalist press loved it and their reviews marketed it all over the country. According to Gauba, some 20,000 paperback copies were sold during the Lahore session of the Indian National Congress in 1929. The proceeds from the book made Gauba's first fortune and he built a large bungalow for himself by the canal in Lahore. *Uncle Sham* inaugurated a successful writing career and Gauba was soon to emerge as a successful author with an assured market.

But more sensational acts followed: a love–hate relationship with his father and differences over business decisions are possibly what led to the next public drama when K.L. Gauba converted to Islam on 1 March 1933. For Lahore, this was K.L. Gauba's most outrageous act and, not surprisingly, given his father's stature and his own growing profile, it created a public sensation of a high order. Quite literally the who's who of Muslim Punjab made it a point to be present at the conversion ceremony: they included Chaudhry Mohammad Ali, Sir Mohammad Iqbal, Sir Feroz Khan Noon, Zafarullah Khan and the nawab of Mamdot amongst others. When he went to the Badshahi Mosque later, in the company of many of these notables, there was a congregation of ten thousand to greet him.

The reaction of the Hindus and especially in the Hindu press can be imagined. Bhai Parmanand, an important leader of the Hindu Mahasabha, for instance, ascribed the conversion to there being 'something wrong' in K.L. Gauba's 'mental condition'. The *Milap* had a headline '*Musalman larki ke saath shadi karne ka natija*' (The consequences of marrying a Muslim girl) and 'they were selling thousands and thousands of copies on the subject of my conversion'. The result was that 'the bitter articles that were written against me in the Hindu press only emphasized my importance and welcome among the Muslim press' and 'I became an important figure in the Muslim world overnight'.

But, and in brief, although Kanhaiya Lal Gauba became Khurshid Latif Gauba, since he used only his initials, K.L. Gauba remained K.L. Gauba. As a Muslim, he was never a devout one but he was nevertheless sincere and committed to his new faith and he says that 'my whole life was thereafter directed, as far as possible, in as small or as big a way as it lay within me to render service to the Muslim community'. His next book was again a success—a biography of the Prophet Muhammad titled *The*

Prophet of the Desert. K.L. Gauba's reputation as a leader of the Muslim community grew and in a number of Hindu–Muslim and Sikh–Muslim contestations in Punjab which went in for legal redress, he appeared on behalf of the Muslims. He won consequently a Muslim seat in a strongly contested election in 1933 to the Indian Legislative Assembly, defeating the Muslim League candidate.

Gauba's next public controversy was taking on the chief justice of the Punjab High Court, Sir Douglas Young. Young had ordered a judicial investigation, bordering on a vendetta, against the business concerns of Gauba's father whose business was, in any case, under stress because of the great depression of the early and mid-1930s. Both father and son lost heavily in the process. His father died, in and out of jail, and Gauba retaliated as only he could with a book, titled *Sir Douglas Young's Magna Carta*, on Douglas Young's misdeeds and how his decisions against the Gaubas were not above board.[43] The book was written in 1941 when he writes, 'my fortunes had fallen to their lowest level' and being declared an insolvent was inevitable. The book was proscribed and never sold as a priced publication but copies circulated secretly. He was conscious of the risks—'the price to be paid was never in doubt' but 'while I had survived the judgment of Douglas Young and his judges would they survive my indictment?' Gauba was jailed for contempt but the book found its way to the Secretary of State for India in London when Gauba filed an appeal in the Privy Council against his conviction. The appeal was not admitted but the chief justice was quietly advised to resign by the viceroy. Gauba left jail as a hero all over India for unseating a British chief justice.

As the Muslim League gained traction in Punjab and Partition began to be a distinct possibility, Gauba was in a dilemma. That he was a Muslim leader of prominence in Punjab was not in doubt. He was nevertheless no friend of the Muslim League and in elections had defeated its candidates often with support from the most orthodox sections of the Muslims such as the Khaksars and the Ahrars who were themselves opposed to the League. By 1945, however, the tide had turned. The idea of Pakistan 'swept Muslim thinking from Punjab to Bengal, Kashmir to Madras'. In the 1945 general elections 'Muslim middle of roaders like Unionists, Khaksars, Ahrars and others including myself were swept away in ignominious defeats'.[44]

In 1946, Gauba set out his objections to the Pakistan idea—typically in a best-seller titled *The Consequences of Pakistan*.[45] His differences with the idea of Pakistan stemmed from the fundamental point that 'it was based on an inferiority complex' for 'the Muslims in India had always been a minority ... when the Mughals were ruling the country, they were in a minority, yet they ruled the country'. There were also more specific issues that Pakistan as a concept had not clarified or answered: What would happen to the millions of Muslims left behind in India? A partition of the Punjab would be inevitable and a civil war would follow. What would happen to the Ahmadiyas in Pakistan? Pakistan would mean the liquidation of Osmanistan (Hyderabad state) and war with the Dogras of Kashmir. Howsoever prescient all this may sound now, it was hardly likely to endear him then to the Muslim League. Incidentally, Gauba held the Hindu leaders of the Congress and other parties primarily responsible for the traction the Pakistan idea got. 'I do not exempt Muslims from the charge of giving way to communalism. But that is by way of retaliation. The main responsibility for the communal hatreds and passions that sweep the country I would, however, lay at the door of the Hindus. It is the Mahasabha and not the Muslim League that has laid the foundations of Pakistan.'[46]

August 1947 found Gauba holidaying in Simla with his second wife (also a Muslim) and her children from an earlier marriage. With some difficulty, disguising their religious identity, they made their way to Delhi and then flew back to Lahore. Once in Lahore, Gauba agonized over the future and in the end decided to go to India feeling that his differences with the Muslim League would hinder him in Pakistan even though he had a lucrative practice in Lahore. That his children from his first marriage were in Bombay was also an important consideration. The Bombay bar also held out promise when he reached there in November 1947. He says he did not 'consider himself a refugee, did not register as one and did not file any claim for property'. He also recollects that 'the three weeks in Pakistan had been hot and suffocating' and arriving in Delhi 'was like the opening of a window—the air was fresh and friendly'. Early in 1951 his wife returned to Pakistan—largely to ensure that the children from *her* first marriage did not lose their claim over properties owned by their father. Gauba's practice flourished in Bombay till the 1960s as did a series of sensational books on different legal cases or whatever would sell most. Nevertheless, he never attained the heights he had in Lahore—either in his practice or in notoriety. His books, however, continued to sell and there are some who say that the much more successful Khushwant Singh modelled his style on Gauba.

Gauba visited Pakistan in 1975 at Prime Minister Bhutto's invitation. He was received there as a minor celebrity. Both the invitation as also his celebrity status was not because of his Lahore achievements or legal reputation but followed from his most recent book—*Passive Voices*—a study of Muslims in India, post-1947.[47] This is an anticipation of sorts of the Sachar Committee Report by some three decades, focusing on under-representation of Muslims in different walks of life and the discrimination they faced. Published in 1973, the book made little impact in India but was soon reprinted in Pakistan and an Urdu edition of some 15,000 copies was sold out in a few days. The book remains an often-cited text in Pakistan today and Gauba during his month-long stay there in 1975 was courted by the media and politicians as its author. Characteristically, he wrote a book about this month in Pakistan ending on a note of hope that after the Simla agreement relations between the two countries would improve.[48]

Sadly, Gauba's last years were spent in penury as his practice eroded and age took its toll. It was left to Khushwant Singh to write his epitaph when he died in Bombay, forgotten and unsung: 'Fifty years ago, K.L. Gauba's cortege would have been followed by half the city of Lahore; last week he did not have a dozen to mourn his departure.'[49]

Each of these three individuals reappears occasionally in the pages that follow. It is self-evident that they defied the logic of the population movements accompanying Partition, which make up so much of what we know and remember of 1947. So, they are not representative of the general picture in any sense. But, equally, they do convey a sense of the appeal of Indian secularism and pluralism even at a time when it was most under stress as the two-nation theory scored heavily against it. These cases also underline how much Partition of India was the partition of the Muslim community of undivided India. But the appeal of pluralism is evident elsewhere too. The journalist, and now politician, M.J. Akbar recounts a story of his father who left West Bengal for Dacca but returned after three months to his village near Calcutta. Akbar later asked his father why he had returned from Pakistan in 1948. 'His answer told a long story in a few words. "There are too many Muslims in Pakistan," he answered.'[50]

2

Working Together?

THE KASHMIR WAR, KALAT, Afghanistan, the Punjab violence and the intergovernmental tussles between Delhi and Karachi gives to the India–Pakistan story in the immediate aftermath of Partition a largely northern and north-western flavour. Hyderabad and Junagadh add a southern and western dimension. Given this background of crisis, mistrust and anger could the two new governments do anything together at all, howsoever minimally? It was a crisis emerging in the east that would answer this question.[1]

The partition of Bengal in August 1947 had left the two parts with significant—and proportionately similar—minority populations. West Bengal in India had five million Muslims in a total population of twenty-one million; East Bengal in Pakistan was left with some eleven million Hindus in a total population of thirty-nine million. How to prevent a repeat of the Punjab experience—bloodbath and ethnic cleansing—was an obvious enough preoccupation of both governments in the two national and state capitals. The atmosphere was supercharged and the steady stream of Hindu refugees from East Bengal into India and a smaller number of Muslims from West Bengal into East Pakistan was a regular feature figuring prominently in public and official discourse.

In April 1948, following a meeting in Calcutta, the two governments agreed to do whatever they could to avoid a repetition of the Punjab situation in Bengal.[2] The agreement reached had a number of high-minded statements of principle and intent: 'The responsibility for protecting the lives and properties of the minority communities and for ensuring that they receive justice and their civic rights are fully safeguarded rests on the

Government of the Dominion in which the minorities reside'; and 'there shall be no discrimination against the minorities whose cultural rights shall be fully safeguarded'. The agreement also had similar statements regarding hostile propaganda: 'Propaganda for the amalgamation of Pakistan and India or of portions thereof including East Bengal on the one hand and West Bengal or Assam or Cooch Behar or Tripura on the other shall be discouraged,' etc. The substance of the agreement was the creation of a Provincial Minorities Board in East and West Bengal and below these District Minorities Boards with: '... the express object of protecting the interests of the minorities, removing fear from their minds and inspiring confidence in them. These Boards shall ensure that the grievances of the minorities are promptly brought to the notice of the authorities and that they are satisfactorily and promptly dealt with.'[3]

The precariousness of the situation in both halves of Bengal being self-evident, the agreement also stipulated that the premiers (later to be termed chief ministers) of both East and West Bengal meet once every month and senior officials once a fortnight. The hope obviously was that this high-level attention would impart confidence to the minority populations in both halves of the now divided province and induce them to stay where they were. The aim of both sides was thus clear—prevent large-scale refugee flows to avoid a recurrence of a Punjab-like situation.

Even as war in Kashmir continued and, as the year progressed, an already tense relationship acquired added bitterness with the disputes over the accession of Kalat and Hyderabad; the Bengal situation remained one in which both India and Pakistan had an obvious convergence of interest. But the situation was fragile and there were many voices calling for stringent measures. Deputy Prime Minister Vallabhbhai Patel in a speech in November 1948 was blunt:

> There are 125 lakhs of Hindus in East Bengal. In the Punjab, we could put the Hindus and Sikhs in place of Muslims who had left. What are we going to do about the Hindus from East Bengal? Think of the vast problem that has presented itself to us by this question. Do you feel we have any time to get involved in narrow provincialism, while this problem is increasing in its dimensions? How can we solve this problem? We have to tell Pakistan plainly that the problem should either be solved amicably or it is likely to prove a source of trouble

> between the two Dominions. We are ready for all eventualities. If you are determined to turn out Hindus, you must part with sufficient land to enable us to settle them. We cannot take things lying down.[4]

Prime Minister Nehru in a letter to the West Bengal premier, also in November 1948, summed up his slightly different approach:

> [L]arger interests of West Bengal and India require us to take a long distance dispassionate view and not be pushed about by Pakistan misbehaviour. Any claim for territory is completely unreal. It only means, not only in eyes of Pakistan but of the world, that we are thinking in terms of war with Pakistan. This must necessarily add to the exodus greatly apart from other unfortunate consequences.[5]

And a few months later in another letter to the West Bengal Premier:

> The whole question of East Bengal is tagged on to larger issues concerning India and Pakistan. I do not myself see any swift solution of these issues ... we have to hold on in East Bengal and try to prevent minorities from coming away. It is obvious that any further emigration of minorities to West Bengal will be a calamity for all of us.[6]

Matters came to a head in early 1950 as violence against minorities led to large-scale migrations in both directions. What triggered the crisis is now less material and both governments put the onus for the initiation of the migration on the other. Retaliatory violence and forced expulsions in equal measure in both East and West Bengal exacerbated the situation. At the height of the crisis and in the eight-week period between 7 February and 8 April 1950 almost a million and a half people crossed the borders: about 850,000 coming into India from East Pakistan and a little over 650,000 in the other direction.[7]

The scale of the crisis was dramatically illustrated in the grounds of Dacca secretariat on 10 February 1950 when an Indian delegation led by the senior-most civil servant of West Bengal was the target of a large and hostile demonstration made up of Muslim refugees from West Bengal and numerous sympathizers. The Indian delegation, ironically enough, was in Dacca as part of regular meetings to oversee the implementation of the April 1948 agreement on minorities. The Indian deputy high commissioner reported that subsequently 'Muslim mobs began killing the Hindus and looting and burning Hindu offices simultaneously in all parts of the city. More than five thousand refugees took shelter in our mission and attached offices and at the residence of the Deputy High Commissioner. ... For three days, there was a complete breakdown of the entire communication and transport system in the city of Dacca'.[8]

He also referred to events of February 1950 as constituting a 'Holocaust':

> The fact that mob attacks on Hindus broke out almost simultaneously in eight of the biggest districts of the province showed a well-organized plan initiated and executed by influential sections of Muslims leaders with the active connivance of the authorities.[9]

The Government of East Pakistan on the other hand blamed radical right wing groups as well as speeches by mainstream politicians in India for communal rioting in Calcutta in January and February, which then led to retaliatory rioting and violence in East Bengal. The premier of East Bengal wrote to his counterpart in Calcutta on 18 February about these events:

> It is quite obvious and has been for some time past that certain organizations in India, notably the Hindu Mahasabha with its 'storm troopers' the RSS ... are now reliably training their own 'irregular army' without any interference from Government, have been engaged in deliberately whipping up communal passions. ... It was not until as late as February 10th that communal rioting broke out in this province for the first time since the partition and was directly the result of an almost continuous series of widespread riots that had been taking place in West Bengal, according to your own Government's admission, since January 24th...[10]

The failure of the April 1948 agreement was now too evident to be ignored. Both Nehru and Liaqat Ali Khan faced a full-blown crisis which had the potential to escalate into military action. The latter was being increasingly spoken of in India as the only way to secure protection for the Hindus in East Bengal. As the crisis mounted, both prime ministers came under tremendous pressure and embarked on a frenzied correspondence exchanging some forty-odd letters and telegrams between mid-February and mid-March 1950. These exchanges, full of mutual recriminations and accusations, nevertheless also reveal the view of both that while the earlier agreement had failed the only real option was to negotiate a new one.

To diffuse the situation, Nehru initially suggested joint commissions at ministerial level for both East and West Bengal to inquire into what was happening as a means of restoring minority confidence. Liaqat Ali Khan disagreed—he felt a fact-finding commission would become a fault-finding commission. In his view, what was required was mutual acceptance of the fundamental principle 'that we should create in the minds of the minority community on either side the conviction that it is to their own Government that they should look for the redress of their wrongs and not to the Government across the border'.[11]

In fact, as Liaqat Ali Khan was to explain, issues of sovereignty were naturally ever present; anything 'joint' would be difficult to market in Pakistan politically even if the substance of the commission—to restore confidence in the minority community—was not disputed. But while the elements of a draft declaration were being exchanged, as the correspondence progressed, recriminations also grew. Pressure on Nehru steadily increased to take steps to protect minorities in East Bengal and stop their influx into India. Continuing violence on both sides of the border added to the heat of the polemical exchanges between the two governments and to the rhetoric of a supercharged media. Nehru in a speech on 23 February to the Indian parliament said that '... if present methods and proposals fail, we shall have to adopt other methods'. Liaqat Ali Khan reminded him of this while referring to a press statement of Nehru's in which he had not explicitly and categorically ruled out military action. He wrote on 6 March:

> Reports have also been coming for some time of troop carrier concentrations on borders of East Bengal. A whispering campaign originating from Calcutta is afoot that India would soon invade East Bengal...[12]

The possibility of a military solution to the continued inflows from East Bengal was, in fact, being widely discussed in India. As the crisis mounted, others in New Delhi were concerned at the growing tensions.

There is an unusual letter to Prime Minister Nehru from President Rajendra Prasad, with his views and advice on the prevalent situation. He wrote on 18 March:

> In any negotiation that we may have with Pakistan, we must try to avoid a repetition of what has happened on our western border ... We must do our best to avoid armed intervention. Even if it is forced on us its objective cannot be anything more than securing ... an agreement. In our own interest, we cannot afford to have large territories with sullen and hostile majority ever anxious to revolt and ever plotting against our Government. Conquest is thus out of the question, whether we look at it from the point of view of international repercussions or our own interest involved in effecting it which will not be any easy affair on the whole, and then even if we succeed, in maintaining our position and getting anything out of it.[13]

In brief, the object of use of military force, if it came to that as a last resort, would only be to secure an agreement from Pakistan on security for its minorities. The view that an Indian military build-up was what pressurized Pakistan had a widespread credibility among many Indians at the time. The Indian deputy high commissioner in Dacca was later to write: 'On receipt of troop movements on the Indian side of the border, the Government of East Bengal sent frantic wires to Karachi which brought Liaqat Ali Khan to this province.'[14] This view continues to have a certain currency and is seen as an early example of coercive diplomacy in Nehru's India.[15] Nevertheless, the tenor of the Liaqat–Nehru correspondence as also the number of Muslims entering East Pakistan suggests that the Pakistan government was equally keen to come to a workable arrangement. In any event, both sides stepped back from the brink. Liaqat Ali Khan, after touring East Pakistan, visited Delhi and, after intensive meetings spread over a ten-day stay, a fresh agreement on minorities was concluded on 8 April by both governments at the level of the prime ministers.

Much like the April 1948 agreement, the April 1950 agreement on minorities is a mixture of lofty aims and specific detail. Declaring that minorities have equal rights and opportunities, the agreement also had specific provisions about the amount of cash migrants could carry, custody of properties left behind, recovery of looted movables, rehabilitation of returning migrants, recovery of abducted women, etc. Both governments undertook to appoint a Central minister to tour and remain in the riot-affected areas. The provincial governments concerned were to include in their cabinets a minister from the minority community. It was also decided that both governments would set up minority commissions for each of the affected provinces to be chaired by a provincial minister, and these commissions would include representatives of both the majority and minority communities. The 1950 agreement was intended to supersede the 1948 agreement by giving the structures being created more political weight. The official-level minority boards of the 1948 agreement were replaced by minority commissions headed by ministers.

The immediate impact of Liaqat Ali Khan's visit to Delhi, the agreement itself and a return visit by Nehru to Karachi shortly thereafter was a reduction in tension. Nevertheless, criticism of the agreement was also strong, both in East Pakistan and in West Bengal, with important ministers on both sides resigning in protest. In India, Syama Prasad Mookerjee and K.C. Neogy resigned from the cabinet. Mainstream politicians, however, stepped in with support, especially Deputy Prime Minister Vallabhbhai Patel who was at one stage at the forefront of the need to take strong action against Pakistan. He had, however, played an important role in seeing that the agreement was concluded and afterwards travelled to Calcutta at Nehru's request to 'sell' the pact to West Bengal. He spoke there candidly about the need for pragmatism:

> I know that in the light of past history of agreements which have fallen in disuse, or pledges which have been broken, people approached the latest agreement with sceptical cynicism and even convinced disbelief. The researches in such past made by critics have yielded no new discoveries or facts which were not known to those who undertook upon themselves the burden of implementing the agreement. Human nature, as far as I am aware, places no limit of time on its capacity to change. ... One thing that has made a profound impression on me in accepting the Pakistan Prime Minister's assurances at their face value was the earnestness and visible sincerity with which he laid stress on the need for bringing the two countries closer in our life time ...

And he went on to say:

> I regard it pointless at this stage to enter into any disputation of respective responsibility for the tragedies that have occurred on both sides of the border. I can tell my West Bengal friends quite candidly that it is the ugly and deplorable incidents which happened on our side of the border that made a world of difference to our capacity and freedom to deal with the problem more effectively and expeditiously. To counsel firmness and consistency in such circumstances or to charge Government with weakness, hesitation or inconsistency, is to ignore the elementary rule of prudence that one can act correctly only when one's own conscience is clear and not clouded by one's own guilt. Those who demand more heroic remedies may do well to ponder over this simple fact.[16]

B.K. Acharya who was deputy high commissioner in Dacca was to reflect later, on the unusual nature of the agreement—for India–Pakistan relations as also in international relations. 'It had', he felt, 'an entirely new principle, as far as I know, that the representative of India would have certain responsibilities towards the Pakistani Hindus, and the representative of Pakistan in India would have certain responsibilities towards the Muslims living in India.'[17]

The domestic politics over the agreement and its novel features aside, how effective was it in providing any reassurance to minorities? In its immediate aftermath, migration increased—people could now leave in an environment of greater security and carry some movables and cash. At the same time, some migrants started returning. Figures about the magnitudes were notororiously hard to compile but some do exist with numerous qualifications. In the period of about ten weeks (9 April 1950 to 25 July 1950) after the agreement was signed, an estimated 1.2 million Hindus left East Pakistan for India but this was balanced to an extent by some 600,000 returning from India to East Pakistan. Muslim migration from India to East Pakistan in this period shows about 450,000 leaving but about 300,000 coming back.[18] By the end of the year, a dispatch from the Indian deputy high commissioner in Dacca reported that from 'September onwards the outward rush of migrants from East Bengal began to slow down' as the 'joint tours of the Minority ministers in terms of the Agreement also allayed to some extent the panic of the Minority community'. The opposite flow 'began from June and gradually gained in volume. It is estimated that about ten lakhs returned to East Bengal by the end of December.'[19]

Clearly, the agreement did have some impact. A review meeting of the Central ministers and the minority commissions that took place in August 1950 made a detailed list of prescriptive administrative measures to deal with communal incidents and deterrent action against offenders including officials and police officers, measures to ensure return of properties to returning migrants and recovery of abducted women, etc. Mutual complaints and recriminations, however, continued about the other side not honouring the agreement. Complaints from both sides were, not unsurprisingly, similar: that the minority commissions of the other governments were ineffective; requisitioned houses and properties were not being returned and little or insufficient attention was being paid to rehabilitation of returning migrants. The agreement, however, provided a channel for a bureaucratic and political interface which itself acted as a restraint in tensions building up even when events on the grounds were far from satisfactory.

Bengal, the focus area of the India–Pakistan agreements of 1948 and 1950 on protection of minorities, does not, therefore, show a comparable picture of the elimination of the minority population as took place in Punjab. By that minimal standard, the minority regime designed by India and Pakistan in the early years after Partition seems at least partially successful. Nevertheless, the changing demography of East Bengal, first as East Pakistan and then as Bangladesh portend a grim reality, far from the lofty aspirations of the 1950 Nehru–Liaqat Agreement. The minority Hindu population of East Bengal as a percentage of total population fell steadily from decade to decade from the 1950s.The Muslim population of West Bengal on the other hand does show a stable and upward trend.

Hindus in East Bengal, would migrate in large numbers during periods of bilateral crisis such as during a flare-up in tensions in Kashmir in 1964 or the 1965 India–Pakistan war. The 1971 war leading to the creation of Bangladesh and the demolition of the Babri Masjid in India in 1992 again were situations which saw very large migrations of Hindus into India. Yet, to put the onus of each of these subsequent seismic events and shifts in South Asian politics on the Nehru–Liaqat pact on minorities of 1950 would be to miss the contingent nature of the agreement intended to stabilize the post-Partition crisis in the east.

The resolution of the Bengal crisis is a good point to stand back and look at emerging trends. Evidently, there is the all-encompassing bitterness associated with the violence and displacement of Partition. In addition, Junagadh, Kashmir, Hyderabad, the division of financial resources, canal waters and Kalat made for a politically charged atmosphere. By any standards and for any period of history, India and Pakistan started with a background and an inheritance which could not have been worse. In general, the post-Partition period left a burning sense of injustice and betrayal that to this day evokes strong responses on both sides of the Radcliffe Line. Over the years these responses have not changed but their intensity has abated with the passage of time. Nevertheless, during times of heightened tensions, all and each of these and other related events and developments between the summer of 1947 and the first quarter of 1950 resurface, and old wounds and grievances acquire a fresh relevance.

So, if one concludes that contestation and conflict are the most visible characteristics of India–Pakistan relations from day one, it is not surprising. Nevertheless, there were other oddities to the relationship right from the beginning. Through this period, political and diplomatic contacts continued—often supercharged and polemically intense, but on other occasions placid, almost prosaic as if everything around was normal. Both sides tacitly seemed to agree that no matter how important or divisive the issue of the day may be, no single aspect should so dominate relations that everything else became subject to its satisfactory conclusion.

Through Junagadh, Hyderabad, the Kashmir war, the water crisis and the Bengal crisis, there was hardly a day when the two governments were not engaged with each other. This engagement was on matters believed to be so pressing and of daily relevance that civil servants and politicians on both sides felt that they could not be left untended till such time as the overall atmospherics changed or the major political issues were resolved. So, amidst the Partition massacres and all the other political crises, a silent intergovernmental engagement continued, concentrating on disentangling India and Pakistan from each other and in the process also putting down the building blocks of a future relationship as separate, sovereign entities. This was, in fact, a vast bureaucratic and administrative exercise which had been initiated a few months before Partition.[20]

On 12 August 1947, the Partition Council of India and Pakistan was constituted along with the Bengal Separation Council, the Punjab Partition Committee and the Assam Separation Committee to decide on the minutiae of the caesarian section. If after 15 August it was the communal mayhem that took precedence, bilateral meetings on numerous administrative issues took place amidst joint appeals for peace and mutual recriminations. For instance, among the many meetings taking place, we have Prime Ministers Liaqat Ali Khan and Jawaharlal Nehru meeting in Ambala on 17 August, then in Lahore on 15 September and then again in Delhi on 22 September 1947 appealing for communal peace. In between, there was a constant stream of letters and telegrams of allegations and complaints as also practical suggestions. Neither side considered the other as being even-handed or fair in maintaining communal peace; 'who started it' was a familiar argument with both usually blaming the other for the greater excesses.

If the communal mayhem seemed to engulf both sets of leaders and civil servants, it was not the only issue the new governments had to address. Trade and economic issues were an area more amenable to administrative remedies. Amongst the earliest agreements signed by India and Pakistan was on 'Avoidance of Double Taxation' and this was concluded as early as December 1947 even as they were engaged in the Kashmir war. There were numerous other practical issues. How was the flow of goods between the two countries to be regulated? There were questions of currency, banking and a host of related issues arising from separated sovereignties arising from a single entity. In these matters, a sense of pragmatism was the guiding principle, which usually prevailed as civil servants on both sides proved adept at handling the broad framework of policy. Amongst the first orders issued by the Pakistan government was on 14 August 1947 stipulating that the Reserve Bank of India (RBI) would carry out central banking functions on behalf of Pakistan also till 30 September 1948. Similarly, Indian currency notes would remain legal tender in Pakistan till that date. This required, naturally, that the Government of Pakistan give up the right to issue its own currency till that date, and this too is clearly specified in that order.

These arrangements had been worked out with the RBI and the Indian Ministry of Finance in advance. But this manner of limited pragmatic cooperation was overshadowed comprehensively by the question of the release of Pakistan's share of the RBI's cash balances. Nevertheless, the scope for pragmatic decision making is evident in other areas also. As far as customs duties were concerned, it was agreed that till March 1948 status quo would continue and India and Pakistan would be treated as a single unit. For postal stamps and stationery, a rough-and-ready solution was found. The only security press then operating—in Nasik in India—agreed to fix an overprint 'Pakistan' on existing postal stamps. These overprinted stamps started circulating from October 1947.

A large part of the India–Pakistan intergovernmental interface consisted of such small but vital factors. But there were more contentious issues which were less amenable to administrative planning and action—for instance, how to deal with the media in either country. This question does have a contemporary ring to it and it existed with equal resonance in the early 1950s with the major difference that media then meant the print media. Newspapers, and especially the vernacular newspapers—Urdu, Hindi and Bengali in the main—were baying for blood and corroding further a deeply vitiated atmosphere. In Pakistan, the English daily *Dawn* was a leading protagonist in the charge against the deviousness and insincerity of 'Hindu India'. This was too important and explosive an issue to be ignored. Both governments were to focus on the print media, finding ways to temper and moderate it, using legal remedies wherever possible. This was a process attended to with a considerable degree of bureaucratic attention from the earliest days after Partition and was finally a factor leading to the first amendment to the Indian Constitution. A joint consultative machinery, a joint press code, meeting between editors, etc., are the numerous bureaucratic terms and initiatives that litter the record of the period. After the Liaqat—Nehru pact on minority protection, these measures acquired greater momentum.[21]

In India, the legal difficulties in curbing a newspaper were, however, considerable and difficulties were encountered not just regarding the virulent criticism and warmongering with respect to Pakistan from the right-wing press but also from the left, from publications with communist sympathies on other issues. In the former, it was the *Organiser* from New Delhi which was the most resolute in resisting attempts at censorship. When served with orders that its articles be shown to the government before publication, it appealed to the Supreme Court. This was the case filed by the publisher of *Organiser*, Brij Bhushan, and its editor K.R.

Malkani against the chief commissioner of Delhi challenging his orders that they 'submit for scrutiny before publication all communal matter and news and views about Pakistan including photographs and cartoons other than those derived from official sources or supplied by the news agencies'. The Supreme Court was to rule on 26 May 1950 that 'imposition of pre-censorship on a journal is a restriction on the freedom of the press which is an essential part of the right of freedom of speech and expression'.[22] The Supreme Court struck down the chief commissioner's order and the relevant sections of the East Punjab Public Safety Act on which it was based. In this case, the court was following the precedent it had set in a similar case involving the communist magazine *Cross Roads*, edited by Romesh Thapar, and the Government of Madras.[23]

The Union government responded with enabling laws that were included in the first amendment to the Indian Constitution in June 1951. The amendment to Article 19 of the Constitution thus provided for imposition of reasonable restrictions in the interest, inter alia, of 'friendly relations with foreign states'.

It is a moot point, notwithstanding this legal change, whether the situation improved very markedly. In April–May 1954, an advisory from the Directorate of Public Relations of the Delhi administration to the daily *Pratap*—described as a 'minor communalist paper'—that it curb the hostility of its articles received in reply a response termed as 'unfortunate' by the official. The editor of *Pratap* wrote in response to the government advisory:

> We are surprised to see its contents. The only thing we can say in reply to it is that you are presuming too much about yourself. We are not prepared to have any instructions or advise from you with regard to our editorial policy and we would only request you to mind your own business.[24]

Protests and counter-protests between the two foreign offices and diplomatic missions at the vilification pouring out in the newspapers remain a staple of the diplomatic discourse of the time. The positions adopted were mirror opposite, of course. Thus, in the Ministry of External Affairs while there was an internal acknowledgement that the Indian media was sometimes equally guilty, the reaction to a Pakistan protest was:

> The Pakistan press has been hurling insults and abuses on respected leaders of this country, not excluding the Prime Minister. *Dawn* which is considered the foremost English daily of Pakistan referred to Prime Minister as 'Greatest Primitive' in its leading article of 21.1.1954 and the *Morning News* of Dacca called him 'demented Maniac' in its issue of 9.1.1954.[25]

The *Organiser* in Delhi provided similar ammunition to the Pakistan high commission but it was only one of many publications in Urdu, Bengali or Hindi. A protest note from the Pakistan high commission in New Delhi reads:

> The editor has transgressed all bounds of journalistic ethics and the various agreements between the two governments by his uncalled-for attack on the Government of Pakistan which he calls 'criminals centred in Karachi' and 'a murderous party elevated to a sovereign statehood'.[26]

In this case the Ministry of External Affairs was to convey its regret but also advised that no importance be attached to the *Organiser* as it was 'a minor weekly of a political party having hardly any influence in the country'. If the target in these newspapers largely remained the Government of Pakistan and the Muslim League, actions or statements of Indian leaders also could lead to polemical outbursts. One such occasion was Prime Minister Nehru's visit to Karachi in July 1953 when he also laid wreaths at the graves of Muhammad Ali Jinnah and Liaqat Ali Khan. The *Pratap* was to ask in an editorial:

> Many Indians would question Pt Nehru's placing of wreath on the grave of Mr Jinnah on the ground that he was the worst enemy of India. ... How could an Indian lay wreath on the grave of Mr Jinnah who was responsible not just for the partition of India but for the killing of lakhs of innocent people? ...[27]

How to deal with the incendiary reporting of the print media remained the great unanswered question. Privately, there was greater concurrence between Indian and Pakistani ministers and officials about the problem than public positions across the India–Pakistan divide would ever suggest.

There was also the occasional case when the two ministries would privately coordinate action to deal with particularly difficult journalists. Yet most of the time the only corrective seen to be possible was a longer-term one—a change in public opinion and a putting aside of the bitterness of the past. It is interesting to find that cricket as an instrument to bring this about was thought of and used almost from the start of the India–Pakistan relationship. The first India–Pakistan cricket series took place in October–December 1952 with Pakistan touring India for a five-Test series. India won 2–1 but the result appears less significant than the fact that the series took place at all.

Were intergovernmental efforts through dialogue and discussion succeeding at all? With Kashmir unresolved, frequent cross-border firing incidents across the Punjab and Sindh–Rajasthan border, sustained pressure on minorities in East Pakistan despite the Liaqat–Nehru pact, and an overall adversarial atmosphere to which the print media in both countries contributed with energy, it looked as if the bureaucratic and political class were engaging more and more over less and less. Nevertheless, however suboptimal and despite frequent and massive upsets, a minimum stability was becoming visible. That this minimum stability and effort to establish some form of a cooperative relationship had its limitations was obvious enough. How these limitations worked could still be surprising and, in this respect, dealing with cross-border crime provides a graphic illustration.

Since the early 1990s extradition has been an issue that has been debated and disputed threadbare between India and Pakistan. A criminal from India either in hiding or getting sanctuary in Pakistan is inevitably something that draws attention and focuses minds. As terrorism moved to the centre stage in the India–Pakistan interface, this matter steadily grew in importance. The most prominent case is that of Dawood Ibrahim—a mafia don who organized a major terrorist attack in Bombay in 1993, when multiple bomb blasts targeting prominent institutions led to a very large number of fatal casualties. He ranks the highest in India's 'most wanted' list, while Pakistan on its part has steadily denied that Dawood Ibrahim is in Pakistan. For public opinion in India, exposed to the mounting evidence of Dawood's residence in Karachi—in 2005 his daughter married the son of Javed Miandad, one of Pakistan's best-loved cricketers—this denial is the litmus test of Pakistan's mindset and real intentions towards India. Dawood's life has inspired many Bollywood characters in feature films and is a media and political issue of great intensity. The extradition of Dawood Ibrahim is a hardy perennial in the India–Pakistan dialogue and over the years has climbed up and down the ladder of political importance depending on the overall state of the relationship.

There are other cases of this kind—Hafiz Sayeed and Masood Azhar, for instance—of Pakistani nationals who have carried out or inspired major terrorist attacks in India. The Dawood Ibrahim case is different because he is, or at least was, an Indian national when the terrorist attacks were carried out.

One of the earliest cases for potential extradition was of a character like Dawood Ibrahim, though he was an old-fashioned and straightforward outlaw or dacoit. He had achieved considerable notoriety in the early 1950s, especially in Gujarat and Rajasthan. Between July 1949 and February 1952, 'Bhupat Dakoo' and his gang were held responsible for eighty-two murders. The last of these was in February 1952 after which, facing considerable pressure from local police, Bhupat and two associates crossed into Sindh in Pakistan. He was arrested for illegal entry, possession of firearms and sentenced to a year's imprisonment. In his native Saurashtra, his stay in Pakistan was followed with great interest and as his imprisonment term came to an end speculation mounted about what would happen to Bhupat once he was out of a Pakistani jail.[28]

The matter was sufficiently important to be considered by the Government of India at high levels. No formal extradition treaty existed between Pakistan and India, so there was no legal framework to work within. In the internal examination of this question, the view that emerged was that the problem with working out a legal arrangement, such as an extradition treaty, would be that Pakistan would insist on excluding Junagadh, Hyderabad and Jammu and Kashmir from its application. This was the earliest appearance of an objection, variants of which are encountered to this day. The Indian Ministry of Home Affairs was indignant—this was not a question of extradition of a Pakistan national but the return of an Indian, wanted for crimes committed in

India. The Indian high commissioner in Pakistan was less sanguine about this argument and apart from the technical problems of extradition pointed out that the Pakistan government was simply too weak politically to ignore public opinion and simply hand over Bhupat to India.

Pressure from Saurashtra politicians and non-stop speculation in the media continued and Bhupat was sufficiently important to figure in a conversation in July 1956 between Prime Ministers Jawaharlal Nehru and Mohammad Ali Bogra, Nehru recorded the gist of this conversation later:

> The Prime Minister of Pakistan mentioned the case of Bhupat to me. I think that this was done at his own instance. ... Mr Mohammad Ali said that he entirely agreed that Bhupat should not be encouraged and he had been surprised and a little shocked at the way it had been proposed to give various facilities to Bhupat, apparently just to annoy India.
>
> As for sending him back to India, there was, he said, unfortunately no extradition agreement between India and Pakistan. But arrangements could be made to release him on the border, presumably after informing the Indian authorities.[29]

Some effort was made to see if a quiet, informal arrangement—a 'gentlemen's agreement'—could be arrived at. Bhupat could be handed over at some agreed point on the border. Somewhat predictably, this got leaked to the media in India and this idea dried up. The case had attracted too much public attention to be handled in a quiet 'pragmatic' way.

Bhupat's continued stay in Pakistan led to feverish speculation in India's tabloid media. The redoubtable *Blitz* of Bombay carried an article in April 1953 titled 'Bhupat Recruits Indian Dacoits for Pakistan Army?'. The article was, presumably for greater effect, bylined and attributed to 'Blitz's intelligence in Pakistan'![30] According to this report, Bhupat was recruiting bands of Indian dacoits for Pakistani military intelligence and touring the India–Pakistan border on this 'top secret' mission. The article had a photograph of a most distinguished-looking Bhupat adorned with various (presumably Pakistani) military medals. This agreement with the Pakistan Army, the article continued, was reached in a meeting Bhupat had attended at its General Headquarters. US intelligence and military officers had also attended but they were in disguise and dressed as 'Pathan Chieftains'. The US interest arose, the article informs us, because Bhupat had close links with 'counter-revolutionary elements and vested classes like Princes, Zamindars, Jagirdars' in India. The US 'whose hand was apparent in some post-1947 Princely efforts at rebellion in India' was keen to make Bhupat 'a point around which Indian counter-revolutionary and fascist forces' can be rallied.

As public and media speculation continued, Bhupat was obviously working out his defensive strategy to avoid deportation to India where the gallows awaited him for certain. At one stage, we find him and his associates staging dramas and in one of them collected some ₹1,500 (not a small sum in those days) by the sale of tickets. So, enthused was Bhupat by this success that he considered becoming a film producer, and his first venture he felt could be on the forcible takeover of Junagadh by the Indian Army. Such a film, he argued, would help the Government of Pakistan in its propaganda against India.

How much of this was real and how much totally fanciful is difficult to say, but for the public in India the fact that Pakistan was not deporting a criminal to face justice was proof that its government was determined not to agree to anything India asked for. Bhupat, possibly on his own or perhaps he was tutored, realized that his best defence would be to become a cog in the India–Pakistan imbroglio. Adopting the role of a freedom fighter then came easily and his affidavit to a local Sindh court seeking release from detention contains precisely such a defence. Bhupat, or perhaps his lawyer, places him in the context of a mythical struggle of the Saurashtra states which, notwithstanding their predominantly Hindu populations, wished to join Pakistan. The Congress (Indian) government used force to incorporate them. The ruler of Junagadh had in this situation no option but to resist. Bhupat's defence statement reads:

> When his state which acceded to Pakistan was attacked by the Bharat Army it added insult to injury and the Princely states of Sorashtra and its peoples and others decided in their own defence to fight against force with force. The people of these states contributed men and money to raise an army in self-defense and trusted its command to me to fight against the tyranny of the Congress, which I successfully carried on for three and a half years but eventually we were overpowered ... (and) ... I was forced to leave Bharat and take refuge in Pakistan. ... I am ever loyal and faithful to Pakistan who has given me refuge and saved my life. I will give my last drop of blood for the maintenance of Pakistan.[31]

Bhupat's self-appointed role as a freedom fighter for Junagadh evidently worked. He was to stay on in Pakistan till his death, which took place, according to some reports, in 2006. He converted to Islam, remarried and had several children but lived quietly. The story in his native Saurashtra is that people came to know of his death when they noticed that his first wife, still living in her old village, had stopped putting vermilion on her head. The Government of India, after the publicity of 1953 subsided, also let the matter rest. In India, Bhupat's reputation grew as did that of the police officers who had hunted him and a full-length feature film was made about him in 1960. Bhupat, however, is important not so much for his notoriety and the drama associated with his stay in Pakistan but for the parallels his now obscure case provides for other individuals in the decades to come.

Malik Ghulam Muhammad as Governor General of Pakistan (October 1951–August 1955) and Mohammad Ali Bogra as prime minister (April 1953–August 1955) represented to many in India the emergence of a spirit of pragmatism in Pakistan. But events were moving faster than the speed diplomacy could muster. In June 1953, Syama Prasad Mookerjee died in a Kashmir jail in circumstances that are disputed to this day. Shortly before, he had set up the Bharatiya Jana Sangh. The full integration of J&K into India was a priority for this charismatic leader of the political right. He was arrested while he was in Kashmir to launch an agitation against the state and Central governments. His supporters blamed both Sheikh Mohammad Abdullah and Jawaharlal Nehru for his death in custody. At the time, the relationship between Abdullah and Nehru was strained and many in India, including some in Nehru's inner circle, had strong doubts about the Sheikh's real intentions as far as Kashmir's political future was concerned. *The Times of India,* for instance, in an editorial on 26 June 1953 warned:

> Evidence is not wanting to suggest that certain external elements have recently been canvassing the idea of an independent enclave within Kashmir. It may be that some of this seed has fallen on receptive ground. Time will tell. Meanwhile both India and Pakistan, as also Kashmir, would do well to remember that a stable Kashmir is not built on the shifting loyalties of a single man.

The problem was also that Nehru was squeezed between the maximalist demands such as those of Syama Prasad Mookerjee—full integration—and Sheikh Abdullah—full autonomy. To Nehru, it would have been, as his foremost biographer notes, a 'tragedy ... that the internal situation had deteriorated just when, for the first time since 1947, there was a real chance of a settlement with Pakistan.'[32]

Nehru visited Karachi on 25 July 1953, about a month after Syama Prasad Mookrjee's death. In his own words, he received 'extraordinary friendliness' and he wrote to Governor General Malik Ghulam Muhammad later: 'I can truly say that I felt among friends and completely at home. The tragedies of the past few years seemed to fade away.' Prior to his return, in a press conference in Karachi he said that both he and PM Bogra were 'actuated' by the 'desire to do the utmost to remove the cause of unfriendliness or suspicion between the two people'.[33] Badr-ud-Din Tyabji accompanied Nehru to Karachi as Commonwealth secretary in the Ministry of External Affairs and recollects this time as the 'golden period of Indo-Pakistan relations' and that there was 'a great upsurge of emotional longing for reconciliation'.[34] He recollects telling Nehru in Karachi that 'you should consider Pakistan as your constituency in which you have yet to get elected; where you could get elected if you tried. You have to win them over. You should treat the Government of Pakistan as the opposition whose popular support you have got to win over. Your reactions to Pakistan should be entirely those of one who was standing for election from there.' He was also to recall: 'There was a kind of feeling in the air that anything might happen.'[35] Nevertheless, many storm clouds were forming. Sheikh Abdullah in Kashmir had drifted away, both from Nehru as also from his own party. He was dismissed from office and arrested on 9 August just a few days after Nehru's visit to Karachi and when a return visit by Prime Minister Mohammad Ali Bogra was being planned.

If Nehru's visit to Karachi was backgrounded by Syama Prasad Mookerjee's death in jail, Mohammad Ali Bogra's return visit on 17–18 August 1953 had similar problems. Sheikh Abdullah's dismissal and arrest meant that in Pakistan, from being an Indian quisling he had suddenly become the poster boy of Kashmiri freedom and nationalism. The arrest had ignited high-intensity rhetoric in Pakistan with loud talk of jihad and exhortations to the people of Pakistan to 'keep their swords shining and their horses ready'.[36] This irritated Nehru and he was to complain to Bogra about it. But the visit turned out to be more successful than Bogra could possibly have imagined. Nehru agreed to a plebiscite in the whole of J&K; a plebiscite administrator would be appointed by April 1954. Tyabji recalled, 'I remember Panditji remarking, "If we cannot win the plebiscite under these conditions we do not deserve Kashmir."'[37]

But neither Prime Minister Bogra nor Governor General Ghulam Muhammad were politically strong enough to harness wider acceptability in Pakistan for the Delhi agreement. Instead of being hailed as a step forward, the agreement was strongly denounced in Pakistan as a sellout. Nehru's insistence that the UN appointed (in March 1949) plebiscite administrator, Admiral Chester Nimitz (from the US), be replaced by one from a smaller country was initially accepted by Bogra, but he changed his mind on returning to Pakistan. But Nehru too began to have doubts about the agreement. For one thing, the Constituent Assembly of Pakistan decided around this time that the name of the country should be the Islamic Republic of Pakistan. To Nehru, this was a retrograde step; but he was equally concerned about its implications for the minorities in East Bengal. What weighed with him most, however, were the clearly visible moves of Pakistan to join a military alliance led by the United States. His letter to Mohammad Ali Bogra in November 1953 summed up this position:

> If such an alliance takes place, Pakistan enters definitely into the region of cold war. This means to us that the cold war has come to the very frontiers of India. This is a matter of serious consequence to us, who have been trying to build up an area of peace where there would be no war whatever happens elsewhere. It must also be a matter of grave consequence to us, you will appreciate, if vast armies are built up in Pakistan with the aid of American money. ... All our problems will have to be seen in a new light.[38]

Badr-ud-Din Tyabji, recounts a conversation illustrating the atmosphere of the time and the strongly held views amongst many in Delhi about Pakistan as it drew closer to the United States. In a meeting in the prime minister's room, there was speculation about what concessions Pakistan had made to the US in return for the arms it was receiving. The prevailing view was that some airbases may been made available in

Gilgit and thereabouts to enable the US to monitor activity in the USSR.[39] Krishna Menon then had interjected in his most dramatic style: 'It is not just a question of granting a base here or a base there; the whole of Pakistan has now become an American base.'

Tyabji relates that he had felt this to be a 'grossly exaggerated statement' but the phrase appealed to Nehru and he was to use it often. Tyabji goes on to say how this: 'illustrates how Krishna Menon could often, by putting a striking demagogic phrase in Panditji's mouth, give acceptable shape to a mere suspicion that Panditji might otherwise dismiss in the light of his own rational thinking, and thus tip the scales in favour of belligerence at critical moments.'

Under these circumstances and amidst mutual recriminations, the momentum generated by the high-level visits in July–August 1953 was lost. Many in Pakistan attribute this to India's bad faith: that it used the US–Pakistan alliance as a pretext to wriggle out of the commitment made for a plebiscite during the visit by Bogra in August 1953. After the commitment had been repudiated by Nehru following the announcement of the US–Pakistan military agreement, a young Pakistani diplomat Afzal Iqbal posted in New Delhi recalled the Indian education minister Maulana Abul Kalam Azad telling the Pakistan high commissioner: *Yeh aapne kya kiya? Kashmir paka hua phal ki tarah aapke god me gir raha tha.* (Why did you do this? Kashmir was falling on your lap like a ripe fruit.)[40]

Elsewhere, describing his high commissioner Raja Ghazanfar Ali Khan, Iqbal notes that 'it was during his tenure that the two countries reached agreement on holding a plebiscite in Kashmir ... the diplomatic triumph was, however, frittered away by the timing of our acceptance of US military aid which Nehru used as a pretext for wriggling out of his commitment. The High Commissioner was most distressed.'[41]

Is there some truth to this view that Nehru conceded the point during the Bogra visit for tactical reasons only because he needed to consolidate things in Kashmir after Sheikh Abdullah's arrest? These debates will continue but the truth is that many in Pakistan and in India knew that the Pakistani leadership had failed to grasp an opportunity.

Real opposition to the Delhi agreement on a plebiscite arose not in India but in Pakistan. In retrospect, we can see more fundamental reasons for Pakistan not being able to move forward with India despite wanting to. Its internal politics after the assassination of Liaqat Ali Khan in October 1951 simply lacked enough coherence. After the assassination, Governor General Khawaja Nazimuddin became the prime minister and Malik Ghulam Muhammad, a civil servant, was made the Governor General. A massive and violent anti-Ahmadiya agitation in March–April 1953 saw Nazimuddin's dismissal and Mohammad Ali Bogra, the then Pakistan ambassador in the United States appointed as prime minister. He was, in one careful historian's description, 'a confirmed political nonentity from East Bengal'.[42] Behind the intrigues and manoeuvrings of these musical chairs was the growing influence of the Pakistan Army and its push for an alliance with the United States both for its own sake to counterbalance India and as the most effective instrument for securing and bolstering Pakistan's position on Kashmir. In Tyabji's recollection, 'Mohammad Ali's efforts were completely stymied by the West Punjabi political leaders. ... They took advantage ... of his being a non-Punjabi when he made this agreement with Panditji in Delhi about Kashmir. When he went back there was loud uproar in Lahore about his having sold the pass.'[43]

The US on its part saw Pakistan as a convenient building block for its most pressing preoccupation—the red scare. More ominously for Pakistan, a paranoia in West Pakistan about the growing influence of Bengali politicians, Bogra included, was quietly pushing many to support the army. Nazimuddin's dismissal and then that of Pakistan's Constituent Assembly in October 1954—in effect a bureaucratic-cum-military coup—were only the manifestations of all these tensions.[44] Under these circumstances, any major agreement with India was predestined to fail.

Yet, the initiatives to normalize, even improve, relations also continued. The Indian cricket team toured Pakistan in 1955, a follow-up on the Pakistan tour of India in 1952, beginning with the first match in Dacca. Afzal Iqbal in Delhi recalled how the return series came about and gave credit for the initiative to his high commissioner Raja Ghazanfar Ali Khan:

> The holding of the match was entirely Raja Saheb's idea. When he mentioned it for the first time in a meeting of his officers, no one displayed any enthusiasm. He rang up Gurmani, who did not think

> it a good idea for he feared a law and order problem in Lahore. He rang up Firoz Khan Noon, who was the Governor at Dacca, and told him that Gurmani was having cold feet. Firoz Khan Noon, in order to down Gurmani, offered to hold the match in Dacca. Raja Saheb then rang up Gurmani and told him that Noon had all the confidence to host the Indians, but Gurmani would not suffer to be outwitted by Noon and agreed quickly to have a match in Lahore. He then rang up the Governor General, who too, agreed after some initial hesitation. After having cleared the decks, the High Commissioner, made a formal proposal to the Foreign Office. J.A. Rahim, the Foreign Secretary turned it down out of hand, not knowing that the High Commissioner had already obtained the Governor General's clearance.[45]

The Test match in Lahore in January 1955 saw thousands—in some accounts about ten thousand—of Indians visiting Lahore, some to watch cricket, many to see their old houses, even perhaps friends. In one account, it was described as 'the biggest mass migration across the frontier since Partition'.[46] If this struck many as being extraordinary, there were other occasions too with even larger movements. Some weeks later in April 1955, matches were held in East and West Punjab between the hockey teams of the respective police forces of the two provinces. The Indian deputy high commissioner in Lahore reported issuing 54,000 short duration visas to enable travel to Jullundur and Amritsar to see the games. A few days later some 30,000 Indians visited Lahore and Montgomery to see the return matches.[47] If this suggests forward movement, even more striking in hindsight at least is the presence of Malik Ghulam Muhammad, Governor General of Pakistan, during the Republic Day celebrations of 1955 in India, which also provides the background to another Kashmir initiative. For Ghulam Muhammad, in very bad health and partly paralysed, this was an emotional and nostalgia-filled visit and he obviously felt some burden of responsibility in trying to do everything in his power to salvage a bad relationship and resolve the widening differences over Kashmir. In Delhi, apart from the attendant ceremonial of a state visit he found time to visit old friends:

> The governor general created a sensation by diverting the official motorcade to a block of buildings where an old friend of his lived.

This was the wife of a professor of chemistry at the Delhi University. But the problem was that the lady lived on the fourth floor; there was no lift and the governor general could not walk one step! A resourceful lady rushed upstairs and the professor's wife came down and the reunion was emotional as such events in the India–Pakistan lexicon always are to this date. She sat between the governor general and the high commissioner in the car and the motorcade proceeded to Rashtrapati Bhavan where the distinguished guest was staying. On the way Raja Saheb (the high commissioner) asked her name. The governor general muttered, 'People call her Mrs Puri; the name I have given her is Sada Bahar—eternal spring.'[48]

Ghulam Muhammad was also to go privately to the Deva Sharif shrine near Lucknow: 'He wept like a baby when he touched the grave and ate later with the management sitting on the ground, although it was an ordeal for him to squat for the meal.'[49]

But Ghulam Muhammad's visit was not only for ceremony, sentiment and nostalgia. At the departure ceremony at Palam airport on 28 January 1955 he handed over to Nehru a small slip of paper with proposals regarding Kashmir and a plebiscite. Nehru recognized the impulse behind this:

> I recognize and feel that Ghulam Muhammad is anxious to have a settlement and is prepared to go some distance for it. That is a welcome approach. But to suggest that a plebiscite should be held in J&K in the autumn of this year is manifestly not possible. The other suggestion which he made about my representing Pakistan's interest and Chaudhry Mohammad Ali, Finance Minister, representing India's interests is also rather odd. I realize both his desire for a settlement and his own difficulties.
>
> At the same time, there are obvious difficulties on our side. Personally, I really see no way out except a recognition by both parties of the status quo, subject to minor modifications. Also of course, if there is an agreement, many mutual privileges might follow. At the same time, I am very reluctant naturally to say that we will not have a plebiscite. That might appear as a breach of faith and I do not want to be guilty of that.[50]

Nehru's reply to Ghulam Muhammad encapsulated this view without saying so:

> I liked your approach to this question in the sense that you wanted to leave out outside interference in this problem, casting the burden of solution on ourselves. I liked the approach of mutual trust. All this is to be welcomed. At the same time, the four points that your paper contained seemed to me not to be very helpful as they were and appeared removed from present facts. They did not bear much relation to what had happened thus far and the suggestions made in them did not seem to be feasible.[51]

Ghulam Muhammad, however, persisted and did so relying on an intermediary whom we only know as Mulraj, a resident of Karachi and obviously well known to him and with some acquaintance with Nehru. Through this channel the offer communicated to Nehru was 'that a large piece of territory in Jammu, north of the Chenab, should be transferred to Pakistan. Also, that Kashmir proper should be under some kind of a joint control of a joint army.'[52] What was conveyed back to the Pakistani Governor General by Mulraj we do not know but certainly he felt there was a basis for proceeding further. Prime Minister Bogra and Defence Minister Iskander Mirza were sent to Delhi to follow up. Over three days of intense discussion in mid-May 1955 with Prime Minister Nehru, Abul Kalam Azad and Govind Ballabh Pant, it became clear that messages had been deliberately garbled because of Mulraj's own keenness to make sure that both principals were satisfied.

In the meeting Nehru disclosed that his response to Mulraj was clearly that: 'It was quite impossible for us to transfer these large areas to Pakistan. No government in India could do it, apart from this involving huge political and social upheavals in these areas which were settled and progressing satisfactorily. ... As for joint control of Kashmir, this was unthinkable, and such a thing had not happened anywhere before with success.'[53] He also said: 'It appeared to me that this way of doing business was most unsatisfactory and was bound to create misunderstandings as, in fact, it appeared to have done.'[54] The Pakistani ministers pressed for some idea of the Indian position: 'What was the least or the most that we would accept?' Nehru and his ministers responded with what was the only feasible option for them—the status quo with adjustments along the ceasefire line. The Pakistani response was equally predictable: 'If they accepted my proposals of the previous day, they would be blown sky-high in Pakistan.'[55]

As this initiative, if it can be called that, petered out, time had also run out for both Prime Minister Mohammad Ali Bogra and Governor General Malik Ghulam Muhammad and by August 1955 both made way for new incumbents Chaudhry Mohammad Ali and Iskander Mirza respectively. The political flux in Pakistan since the assassination of Liaqat Ali Khan was now entering its final phase.

3

Highs and Lows

IN A SPEECH IN Patna in April 1956, Prime Minister Nehru referred to Pakistan's rulers as 'Daftaries'.[1] The reaction in Pakistan was a mixture of indignation and amusement. Indignation because who was the prime minister of India to comment on Pakistan's rulers; the remark was hardly likely to be helpful and was poorly judged. But the use of the term also enjoyed some popularity because of its accuracy.

That Pakistan was ruled by civil servants seemed clear enough. Following Liaqat Ali Khan's assassination in October 1951 the then Governor General Khawaja Nazimuddin assumed charge as prime minister. In his place the civil servant Malik Ghulam Muhammad was appointed as Governor General. About a year and a half later, in April 1953, the prime minister was dismissed by the Governor General. This was for all practical purposes a coup with the governor general (a Punjabi), the army chief (Ayub Khan, a Pathan) and the defence minister (Iskander Mirza, a former civil servant and army officer, a Bengali) coming together to oust the prime minister. Mohammad Ali Bogra, then serving as ambassador to the United States was appointed prime minister. His tenure was akin to his predecessor's. He survived till mid-1955 but only just. In September 1954, the Governor General dismissed the Constituent Assembly and Bogra was now made prime minister of a technocratic cabinet. Many in it had never been elected to public office, but the member who drew the most attention was the new defence minister—General Ayub Khan who was also to continue as commander-in-chief of the army.

Amidst all this intrigue some major political and constitutional engineering was also under way. West Pakistan's different provinces—Sindh, NWFP, Punjab, Balochistan—and the princely states were merged into a single unit in 1955. The main aim was to balance the numerical strength of East Pakistan's population in Pakistan with a single province for the western wing as well. A new Constituent Assembly was set up—its members being elected by the provincial assemblies. The dubious legality of all this was upheld by a pliant judiciary. Legal principles from ancient Rome and British common law such as *salus populi suprema lex* (the safety of the people is the supreme law) and *salus republica est suprema lex* (the safety of the republic is the supreme law) were invoked.[2]

Bogra himself was replaced in August 1955 by Chaudhry Mohammad Ali—a former civil servant who had been serving as finance minister. Meanwhile, Ghulam Muhammad was replaced by Iskander Mirza as Governor General. Bogra returned to the United States as Pakistan's ambassador for a second time. Chaudhry Mohammad Ali's main contribution to Pakistan was the installation of the 1956 Constitution. In September 1956, he made way to H.S. Suhrawardy whose tenure lasted just over a year. The next year and a half saw two more prime ministers dismissed by Governor General Iskander Mirza who, in turn, was dismissed by General Ayub Khan in a coup in October 1958.

Within eleven years of its establishment, Pakistan had had seven prime ministers and four Governors General. The consensus is that for at least half this time, it was General Ayub Khan and the army which was in charge. So, when Nehru spoke of 'daftaries'—politely translated as civil servants but actually suggesting low-level clerks—there was clearly an implied comment on the frequent constitutional and political changes in Pakistan. Inside Pakistan, in any case, there were few regrets at Ayub Khan's coup with many, perhaps most, seeing the step as overdue, hoping that it would restore some direction to Pakistan's external and internal policies. In some senses, Ayub's tenure did mark the end of the instability that had characterized Pakistan since Liaqat Ali Khan's assassination.

Ayub Khan's long tenure began well and some of his early statements were forthright on the importance of a better India–Pakistan relationship. Manzur Qadir, a lawyer from Lahore, was appointed foreign minister and he made no secret of his own desire to improve relations with India and resolve outstanding disputes and problems. Manzur Qadir incidentally was and remained through his life a close friend of the writer and journalist Khushwant Singh whose life he had saved during the 1947 Partition violence in Lahore. He was married to a sister of Azim Husain—the civil servant who opted for India despite his family's considerable assets and deep roots in Punjab and in Lahore.

Coincidentally, a new Indian high commissioner, Rajeshwar Dayal, arrived in Karachi soon after Ayub Khan's coup. Both Manzur Qadir and Ayub Khan made a good impression on him—realistically pointing out that Kashmir and the canal waters issue were the two outstanding problems that were of real importance. The Pakistan foreign secretary Ikramullah, whose younger brother Mohammad Hidayatullah was then the chief justice of the Madhya Pradesh High Court, similarly appeared forward-looking and positive. Rajeshwar Dayal's appointment boded well for the future and, in his view, there was 'a fortunate conjunction for India in the Foreign Office of Pakistan'.[3]

Most of all, he knew Ayub Khan from pre-Partition days when in 1940 he was deputy commissioner in Mathura and Ayub Khan was posted there as a captain. Throughout Dayal's tenure in Pakistan, Ayub Khan made much of this older association and acquaintance—always a good sign for a foreign ambassador. This older relationship was not unusual as far as high commissioners in either country was concerned in those early days. Rajeshwar Dayal's predecessors were previously acquainted with one or the other of Pakistan's top leaders. Sita Ram, India's second high commissioner, had been president of the UP Legislative Council and Liaqat Ali Khan had been his deputy. C.C. Desai, Dayal's predecessor, was a friend of Iskander Mirza from their Cambridge days.

In a conference at the Karachi Press Club in January 1959, Manzur Qadir spoke on lines which could not but be liked in India. A record note of the Indian high commission reads:

> Manzur Qadir chided local newspapers for calling India 'Bharat' and referring to Indians as *Bharatis*. He said this was a cheap way of gibing at India. Some newspaper men defended the use of the word 'Bharat' by pointing out that this was the name found in the Constitution of India and that vernacular papers were using the words 'Hindustan' and 'Bharat' in place of India. Manzur Qadir said that this was alright so far as the vernacular papers were concerned and that the use of the word 'Bharat' in English newspapers was obviously meant to express contempt and that this was not the way newspapers should behave.[4]

Manzur Qadir's reference was to the English daily *Dawn*—a constant thorn in the flesh for the Indian high commission. According to Dayal, a presidential order was also issued at this time to the press that India was to be referred to as India.[5]

Even more direct were General Ayub Khan's overtures. He accepted Rajeshwar Dayal's invitation to attend the high commission's Republic Day function and did so with three ministers in tow. A few weeks later, an Indian Air Force (IAF) Canberra which had drifted into Pakistan territory was shot down by the Pakistan Air Force (PAF) but this did not halt the momentum being built up and pushed along by Manzur Qadir. A suggestion that Ayub Khan make a stopover in Delhi, en route to Dacca and meet Prime Minister Nehru at the airport was accepted and this took place on 1 September 1959. This provided the opening for more futuristic ideas to be discussed. Among these, for instance, was the supply of gas from the recently discovered Sui gas fields in Bugti, Balochistan to Gujarat and East Punjab. That Dayal's older acquaintance with Ayub Khan stood him in good stead is suggested by conversations such as these:

> Remarking that in Sui Gas, Pakistan had a valuable asset, I informed the President that we were examining his offer of supply of Sui Gas to Gujarat. The President said that he had in mind the extension of the pipeline to Multan and Lahore and he thought that Sui gas could be supplied in bulk to East Punjab as well. I mentioned that there had been some doubts, which I personally did not share, regarding the wisdom of dependence on a foreign country for fuel supplies which could be vulnerable to changes in political relations. Ayub immediately interjected with the retort that such fears should be immediately dispelled as Pakistan could never adopt such a suicidal policy.[6]

Rajeshwar Dayal was, in fact, pushing Delhi hard in favour of Ayub Khan, using arguments that would be repeated over the decades by other Indian high commissioners in Pakistan—that this was a good time and that the present incumbent was a good bet. Nehru should also visit Pakistan, he argued, and discuss Kashmir and other issues with Ayub Khan: 'I feel that Ayub realizes that Pakistan would be dragged down unless it mends its fences with India and comes to practical arrangements.'[7]

Recalling his old association with Ayub Khan, Dayal added: 'One impression which has persisted through the years is of Ayub's patriotism, generosity and sense of fair play. ... [H]e has not undergone any basic change in his psychology and thinking since that time.'

He went on to argue:

> Ayub occupies a position of eminence in Pakistan and there is no sign of any challenge developing to his overriding authority. Should however a change take place—and it can only be from one military dictator to another—one thing is certain and that is that his successor will not be a man of the same breadth of understanding and tolerance ...
>
> There is of course very little that is new in all this, but since one is constantly encountering psychological hurdles in dealing with the Pakistanis, it is as well to remind oneself occasionally of what might appear to be so obvious—the present is perhaps the most opportune moment ever since partition for grappling seriously with our mutual problems.[8]

But not all shared Dayal's assessments. He was himself conscious of the resistance that was there in the Ministry of External Affairs to many of his recommendations. On occasion, he took recourse to subterfuge, taking up issues directly with Prime Minister Nehru after first having convinced Ayub Khan and getting his agreement. This, for instance, was the tactic he employed on getting an agreement on demarcating, to the extent possible, the actual course of the Radcliffe Line on the ground—both on the east and in the west. This was essential because 'the very first problem was to fix on the ground where India ended and Pakistan began'. The Radcliffe Line was still in many areas no more 'than a blue pencil line drawn on a map which intersected villages even houses in two'. There were daily disputes and often border firings over perceived infringements. To secure this, Dayal was to employ the tactics many disapproved of. He was later to write that he '... deliberately short circuited our Ministry, as the Commonwealth Secretary ... had highly coloured views about Pakistan and an almost pathological aversion to it. He poured cold water over any suggestion to try and do business with Pakistan ... strongly under the influence of Krishna Menon.'[9]

Krishna Menon was first a minister without portfolio and then defence minister but he had Nehru's ear and a considerable say in all matters relating to foreign policy and, according to Dayal, his aversion to Pakistan also verged on the 'pathological'.[10] He, Dayal recounts, 'would point a warning finger at me whenever I ran into him in Delhi and say that I was on the wrong track and no good would come of whatever I was trying to do in Pakistan.'[11]

This is, in fact, the familiar tale of hawks and doves, each with assessments and recommendations derived from experience and evidence, but also a sign of preconceived notions and prejudices. In this process, some issues did get resolved; with others, there was less success. Rajeshwar Dayal's pushing had led to Swaran Singh, a cabinet minister, being appointed to lead the negotiations for resolving the disputed areas in the India–Pakistan boundary demarcation. Ayub Khan, in turn, appointed General Khalid Sheikh, then an important member of his presidential cabinet. These two undertook a pragmatic operation of 'Pakistan giving up here, India giving up there'.[12] For Y.K. Gundevia, who was a few months later appointed as Commonwealth secretary in the Ministry of External Affairs, this was an entirely successful exercise across the Radcliffe Line dividing Punjab as 'the empirical Sikh ... celebrated the resolution of the disputes with the even more empirical Musalmans across the borders ... '[13] The Swaran Singh–Khalid Sheikh negotiation was, therefore, an example to Dayal of what was achievable. He remained bitter that this approach was not extended further west to the Sindh–Kutch (Gujarat) border. For Dayal, leaving this segment unattended was a mistake and finally led to the serious clashes in the Rann of Kutch in 1965 which were to be resolved only through international arbitration.

There were, however, more serious problems on the eastern border, especially between West Bengal and East Pakistan. Here the peculiar case of the Berubari Union illustrates better than any other all the latent tensions of Partition and the complexities of the Radcliffe Line in the east which left numerous enclaves on both sides. The Berubari case also got complicated by legal issues of Centre–state relations and the powers of the prime minister and the government versus the limits placed or believed to be placed by the Constitution of India. In brief, give and take with Pakistan was not always feasible. More importantly Pakistan policy and domestic policy could not be separated from each other.

The dispute arose because Berubari, comprising 8.75 square miles (22.66 sq. km), was described in the Radcliffe Award as falling in West Bengal. The map attached to the award, however, showed the area as part of East Bengal. The last prime minister of Pakistan before Ayub Khan's coup and the onset of military rule, Feroz Khan Noon, had signed an agreement with Prime Minister Nehru on resolving issues of enclaves of the other country in East and West Bengal respectively. The Nehru–Noon Agreement of September 1958 was premised on a pragmatic give-and-take policy and divided Berubari into two parts—one to remain in India and the other to go to East Pakistan. Surgery of this kind was, however, easier said than done. The West Bengal Legislative Assembly declared that the whole of Berubari was and would remain part of India and soon a Berubari Defence Committee came into being.[14] Y.K. Gundevia recalls that so inflamed was public opinion in West Bengal over the cession of half of Berubari that 'shoes were exchanged on the floor of the West Bengal Legislative Assembly for the first time'.[15]

The matter soon reached the Supreme Court, which in a landmark judgment ruled that while the Government of India had the power to cede territory to another country, it could only do so by means of a constitutional amendment. This was the background to the ninth amendment to the Constitution of India which was enacted finally in December 1960. Litigation over the transfer, however, continued and Berubari was never divided as through the 1960s local protests and then a steady deterioration in bilateral relations with Pakistan prevented movement on this front. Gundevia was later to recollect that the impasse, a 'breach of an international agreement ... hurt Jawaharlal Nehru's conscience as long as he was alive'.[16]

In the 1970s and with the creation of Bangladesh, not only Berubari but also the larger problem of enclaves passed out of the India–Pakistan realm into that of India–Bangladesh. The India–Bangladesh Land Boundary Agreement of 1974 settled the Berubari issue as far as India was concerned but the enclaves matter would persist till 2015 when the 100th amendment of the Constitution brought an end to this long-standing boundary issue that had begun with Berubari in 1958. Changing cartographic realities was not going to be easy and this fact silently underpinned the next India–Pakistan summit which was, however, pegged on another division—that of the Indus waters.

Nehru's visit, for which High Commissioner Dayal kept pushing, took place finally in September 1960. The occasion was the signing of the Indus Waters Treaty (IWT)—in itself a considerable achievement. The April 1948 crisis, when water flow into some canals in West Punjab in Pakistan had been shut off because their headworks were in India, had been relatively expeditiously resolved. Yet the temporary stoppage has had a long afterlife in terms of the shadow it has cast on sharing of river waters between India and Pakistan. The May 1948 agreement through which water supplies were restored was denounced by Pakistan shortly after it was signed on the grounds that it was an agreement under duress. The agreement had provided for Pakistan to pay seigniorage charges for the water released into its canals from the rivers in eastern Punjab, now in India. It also recognized that India had the right to develop its upstream potential which could in the future adversely affect water flows into Pakistan. In Pakistan's view, the levy of a charge for water supplied upheld India's ownership while ignoring Pakistan's rights as lower riparian user. The water charges were never paid and, in fact, not insisted upon by India.

The May 1948 agreement is, therefore, significant in Pakistani perceptions as an example of India's bullying. On the other hand, for some in India it is an example of the right approach that should have been followed but was ultimately discarded in favour of the softer option of 'appeasement' by negotiating a bilateral treaty through the good offices of the World Bank. From 1948 onwards terms and slogans such as 'riparian aggression', the 'existence of Pakistan being imperilled as India sought to turn it into a desert', 'water wars' or predictions of military conflict if water supplies were interrupted, now permanently entered Pakistan's vocabulary and political lexicon. In India, if there was some talk of appeasement of Pakistan, the more dominant sentiment was of concern at Pakistan's often irrational posturing. At the same time the water requirements of east Punjab and increasingly of Rajasthan had also to be considered and, therefore, any talk of Pakistan's inherent downstream rights countered.

After three years of inconclusive bilateral meetings, both governments agreed to use the good offices of the World Bank to resolve the issue. The Bank initially worked with the idea of an integrated Indus basin approach. In this, the hope was that engineering and economics would prevail over politics and nationalism and the canal and river systems would be jointly managed by both countries. It soon gave up the idea as difficult to implement, given levels of mistrust between the two governments and equally between engineers on both sides. Early in 1954, it proposed a division of the eastern and western rivers. The eastern rivers—Beas, Satluj and Ravi—were to be allocated for the exclusive use of India. The waters of the western rivers—Indus, Jhelum and Chenab—were allocated to Pakistan with two important qualifications. These were: India could extract hydroelectricity from the western rivers but not dam their flow and, secondly, the existing use of these rivers for irrigation could continue.

If the division of rivers was accepted, for Pakistan it meant that new canal networks would have to be constructed to divert water from the western rivers to feed existing canals in western Punjab, hitherto dependent on flow from the eastern rivers. Financial assistance was to be provided to Pakistan by India for these replacement works that amounted to over £62 million.[17] Additional assistance to Pakistan would also come from the World Bank, the US and others amounting in all to $1.121 billion. These were, for the times, substantial sums of money, the idea being that shifting from dependence on the eastern to the western rivers should not be a burden for Pakistan; the financial assistance would also be an incentive. This World Bank–recommended agreement was accepted by both countries after stiff bargaining not least over the amount of money India would pay for the replacement works in Pakistan.

By 1960, the final treaty was ready for signature with its provisions detailing in a precise and quantifiable way the different rights of the two signatories. The treaty was and has remained a considerable achievement of engineering precision married to political pragmatism and a landmark in the field of international river waters' sharing. It was also stridently criticized politically in both India and Pakistan. Given the controversies over it later, nevertheless, the criticism in the early days seems, at least in hindsight, milder.

In Pakistan, the fact that it was a military regime meant that criticism was in any case muted. An early critic, however, was Fatima Jinnah, Muhammad Ali Jinnah's sister and a vocal critic of General Ayub Khan. She accused the general of 'frittering away our permanent water rights'.[18] Others too felt that Pakistan had not got a sufficiently good deal or that there had been a sell-out to India. Over the years, and especially during the long periods of military rule in Pakistan, criticism of the treaty is also an implied critique of military rule. A democratic dispensation, this argument goes, would have consulted more widely and negotiated harder and more effectively than an autocratic general bent on quick-fix solutions.

In India, the Nehruvian consensus on foreign policy meant that such criticism as there was never amounted to a serious threat to the treaty itself. Nevertheless, there was much criticism of the government for the payments to be made to Pakistan and in general for its policy of 'appeasement and surrender'.[19] There was also resistance from some within the system. B.K. Nehru, then the Indian ambassador in the US, describes a crucial meeting where the final proposals of the World Bank were explained to Prime Minister Nehru. Defence Minister Krishna Menon was present and 'he was deadly opposed to this proposed treaty as he was opposed to any kind of step which lessened tension between ourselves and Pakistan or the distance between the United States and India'.[20]

What was most galling to many was the payment of compensation made to Pakistan for building the replacement canals and works. In Kuldip Nayar's recollection, Morarji Desai, then a cabinet minister, had organized opposition from political quarters and the then home minister G.B. Pant too was unhappy over the financial payments; he wanted that they 'be adjusted against the value of the property that Hindu refugees had left in Pakistan'.[21] During the 1965 war, Prime Minister Lal Bahadur Shastri had to explain in parliament that the payments being made to Pakistan through the World Bank would not find their way into buying armaments.[22]

In India, defending the treaty, then as now, has remained a complex and hazardous undertaking. The arguments used to convince Pakistani interlocutors that it had not just been fair but in fact generous could, and would, then and even more in the future, be used against the government as evidence of excessive 'appeasement'. Thus, the fact that the treaty assured for Pakistan the use of 80 per cent of the total water of the Indus rivers is highlighted as proof of India's misconceived upper riparian generosity, overlooking, of course, the complex topographical and hydrological issues involved and arising from the natural flow of the rivers.

Nevertheless, and for the time being, pragmatism had prevailed. Both sides got something substantial out of the agreement. Nehru, in going ahead with the Indus Waters Treaty, overruling such objections as they were, may well have been influenced by other factors, apart from wanting to give a fillip to relations with Pakistan. For one, relations with China had started worsening and therefore this agreement with Pakistan appeared sensible. But India now also had unfettered rights to the eastern rivers. Their potential was in the coming years to be exploited thoroughly and fully for the hydroelectric and irrigation needs of Punjab and Rajasthan. Pakistan, on its part, was freed of its dependence on the eastern rivers and thereby on India to feed its canals. It received very substantial sums of external finance, which was one of the principal factors that helped Ayub Khan's 'decade of development', as his tenure was often called. Further, its rights to the western rivers were safeguarded by a robust treaty regime.

Over the years, criticism of the treaty in both countries has increased and expectedly there has been a spike in this criticism in periods when relations are already bad for some unconnected reason. Since the 1970s, the central question which has agitated the most has been the treatment of the western rivers in the treaty as we shall see in the case of the Salal Hydroelectric Project in the 1970s, the Tulbul Navigation Project in the 1980s and 1990s, the Baglihar Project in the early years of this century and the Kishanganga Project, which is the subject of the latest contestation. The fact that the western rivers flow into Pakistan through Jammu and Kashmir, and these and future projects are all located in that state, has added an even greater intensity to Pakistan's territorial claims and demands on Kashmir and thereby make the India–Pakistan terrain even more of a minefield.

Nehru's visit to Pakistan in September 1960 was unusual for its duration—almost five days, covering Karachi, Muree, Nathiagali and

Lahore including a brief visit to the site of Ayub's new capital, Islamabad. For many in Pakistan's officialdom, with the settlement of the canal waters issue and progress being made on the settlement of the West Pakistan–Punjab–Rajasthan and East Pakistan–Assam–West Bengal residual boundary issues, the stage was now set for a final settlement on Kashmir. In India too, the perception was that the conclusion of the decade-long and complex negotiation on water sharing and the resolution of border alignments both in Punjab and Bengal augured well for the future. And who better—the votaries of India–Pakistan normalization felt—than a strong president-cum-commander-in-chief to deliver it, after the long period of political instability in Pakistan.

This was certainly the subtext of the conversations Ayub Khan and Nehru had, often alone, during the five-day visit. It is not as if Kashmir was the only item on the agenda. Despite thirteen years of intergovernmental grinding, numerous residual issues—some new, others a carry-over of the Partition agenda—remained: taxation, customs duty evasion, division of defence assets, evacuee properties, the Hyderabad funds, the Bengal boundary demarcation, pensionary liabilities of civil servants, visas, etc. But all this was minor compared to Kashmir.

Rajeshwar Dayal was absent from Pakistan during Nehru's visit; he was on deputation to the UN mission to the Congo from August 1960. When he left Pakistan, things had appeared to be looking up—Ayub's stopover in Delhi, the settlement of the pending Indus waters issues, Nehru's forthcoming visit to sign the treaty, progress in the boundary demarcation and some substantive discussion at the ministerial level on how the hostile media on both sides could be handled and tempered. Rajeshwar Dayal's view of this thaw in Karachi, almost a moment of hope, may be overenthusiastic but is nevertheless worth recalling:

> We had reached a peak in relations between the two countries. At the official and personal level, we found that we had suddenly become popular. Even the normally hostile press spared us undue attention. The general public too responded to the new mood and our flagged car when passing in convoy was greeted by clapping instead of boos.[23]

Some months later, things were changed completely and Dayal writes about the situation when he returned. 'I was to discover to my dismay how sharp was the decline in Indo-Pakistan relations.' He had, in fact, received notice of this during a meeting when both he and Ayub Khan happened to be in London:

> Ayub Khan was cold and distant—he upbraided me for leaving my post in Pakistan at such a critical juncture, remarking caustically that Pandit Nehru seemed to think that the Congo was more important to India than Pakistan. When I ... pleaded that an envoy was not a prime mover but only a conveyer belt, Ayub Khan bristled. ... Lapsing into Urdu he said with much bitterness, '*Woh mujhe hiqarat ki nazar se dekhte hain*', Mr Nehru looks down upon me with contempt.' I was flabbergasted and tried vainly to assuage his hurt feelings. He went on to say that he expected better of Pandit Nehru, adding that he too was the head of a large state and should not have been treated thus.[24]

Back in Karachi, Dayal tried to figure out what exactly had gone wrong. Manzur Qadir, who had since been replaced as foreign minister, gave Dayal a graphic account of the visit:

> The President and the Prime Minister drove up to Muree in an open car with Manzur Qadir in the front seat. There was no conversation between the two leaders throughout the hour-long drive. Manzur Qadir made some attempts to start a conversation but met with deafening silence.[25]

Ayub Khan apparently also told Manzur Qadir that in Muree itself when the subject of Kashmir was broached, Pandit Nehru 'shut up like a clam' and gazed out of the open window at the panorama of the mountains of Kashmir'.[26]

Another version of this encounter is provided by Ayub Kahn's biographer and is closer to Nehru's record of what happened. 'Nehru merely repeated the old offer of the ceasefire line, with minor modifications, as the international border. With this proposal, presumably on a take-it-or-leave-it basis, the talks concluded.'[27]

Prime Minister Nehru himself wrote a detailed account of what transpired. Ayub Khan's position was that the present status quo was an ad hoc ceasefire line with no real justification—political, strategic or religious—to being a border. Ayub Khan agreed to difficulties on both sides to any change—in Pakistan and in north India there were strong feelings but 'South India did not care about it' and this made it easier for Nehru to look for practical solutions. Nehru's point was the mirror opposite—given the passage of time, national feeling in India, the integration of Muslims in India and views in Kashmir itself, there was no other basis to proceed than to respect the reality of the status quo with minor adjustments. Given the storm over a small issue such as Berubari, Nehru pointed out, the difficulties could be imagined over 'any larger issue'. Nehru also wrote in his personal record of the meeting:

> As was inevitable, we were constantly repeating the same arguments and not getting anywhere. The talk was friendly and at no time was there any heat or excitement to it. The only result that came out of it was that we should keep this matter in mind and think again over it.[28]

Rajeshwar Dayal was to agonize over this failure to achieve a breakthrough and which contributed to an overall decline in relations. For him the disappointment was also a personal one especially as the failure led to a worsening of relations and finally to the conflict of 1965. The scenario he had hoped for was that both leaders would agree to a process of talks without preconditions. The decade-long Indus water negotiation was, in fact, the model since 'talking about Kashmir would help drain it of emotional content ... the very process of discussion could produce its own solution'.[29] As far as Kashmir went, the process of talking 'would at least have given some assurance to Ayub Khan's constituency, the army, as well to the people at large, that the regime was not neglectful of a problem which had excited such high emotions'.

But whatever the reasons, the opportunity and opening created by the Indus Waters Treaty was missed. An insufficiently prepared summit leaving too much for the leaders to resolve given widely divergent positions, Pakistan's irredentist claims and possibly a martyr complex vis-à-vis India are also factors at play and there may well be others too. With the benefit of hindsight, we can also dwell further on this failure. Confident of his own abilities, Ayub went further than seeking an open-ended discussion on Kashmir and sought to impress upon Nehru the strength of Pakistan's case and the advantages for India too of an early settlement. Nehru, on the other hand, was going over Kashmir with a

Pakistani leader for the fifth or sixth time within a decade. What would have appeared to Ayub Khan to be a novel approach, pragmatic and forward-looking, would be to the Indians old hat. Perhaps with the eighteen-year difference in age, Ayub appeared no more than a brash and cocky general catapulted to power by Pakistan's weak politics. By the same token, Ayub would have been hypersensitive to any real or imagined condescension.

In any event, the India–Pakistan equation was now getting further muddied as India–China relations deteriorated sharply. In October–November 1962, in a border war with China the Indian forces were comprehensively worsted. The country was left demoralized and disheartened. Nehru was a much-diminished man after the defeat—personally and politically.

During this crisis, Pakistan made no major military moves to derive any advantage from this situation. To this day there are those, especially in the Pakistan Army, who believe that this was the real 'strategic opportunity' Ayub Khan missed.[30] It is not unusual to encounter the half-wistful 'what if there had been a determined push by the Pakistan military across the ceasefire line in Kashmir when Indian morale was low and its military had its back to the wall'. Kuldip Nayar has recounted a conversation with Zulfikar Ali Bhutto in 1972 wherein he was told: 'If Pakistan had attacked India at that time, we could have gone up to Delhi.'[31] Bhutto also used to say that 1962 was a great opportunity but Ayub developed cold feet. In another account, the conflict was a 'tempting chance' and 'on face value Pakistan could up the military ante in Kashmir'.[32]

Many in India expected a Pakistan thrust at this time to use the China war to its advantage. The then chief of the army staff General K.S. Thimayya had complained to Nehru in August 1959 about Defence Minister Krishna Menon's 'war psychosis against Pakistan' as compared to apathy regarding Chinese moves.[33] Rajeshwar Dayal recounts a bizarre episode late in August 1962—just a few weeks before the Chinese attack—which shows that Defence Minister Krishna Menon was expecting an attack from Pakistan. Dayal was in Delhi and was summoned to Krishna Menon's office for a meeting. There he found the service chiefs and the foreign secretary also present and equally bemused by the urgent summons. In Dayal's account:

> Opening the meeting the Minister observed that he was glad the High Commissioner was present to give a first-hand account of the vast preparations being made in Pakistan to launch a professedly non-violent massive infiltration of so-called volunteers across the ceasefire line in Kashmir. Taken aback, I said that I was not aware of any such plan. ... [V]ague second-hand rumour seemed to be just what the Minister was driving at .... [he] thereupon directed that all leave be cancelled and the armed forces put on alert.[34]

This account in largely confirmed by Y.K. Gundevia, the Commonwealth secretary in the Ministry of External Affairs, who was present in the meeting.[35] 'I have never been able to fathom why this nonsense about Pakistan troop movements in Muree was fabricated in that crucial week in October. ... Did Krishna just think up this meaningless diversion on the spur of the moment on hearing that Rajeshwar Dayal was in Delhi?'[35]

But it also appears that through 1962 attention remained more focused on possible Pakistan actions elsewhere too. Nehru's biographer notes, for instance, that Nehru viewed through the summer of 1962 'all questions of India's armaments in the context of Pakistan rather than China'.[36]

The border with Pakistan stayed quiet throughout the course of the border war with China. Some have suggested that pressure from President Kennedy prevailed on Ayub not to get involved in the India–China situation in return for India purposefully engaging Pakistan on Kashmir later. For most Pakistanis, Ayub 'did not take advantage of India's weakness' and 'stab India in the back'. In such tellings, it remains an open question 'whether Ayub succumbed to US pressure or he was too honourable a person to hit his adversary below the belt'.[37] His son writing about the time, however, perceptively notes that 'while it is true that the Indian forces were demoralized, not a single Indian soldier or aircraft positioned for operations against Pakistan had been withdrawn'.[38] After the border war with China, there was considerable pressure on India from the UK and the US to begin a discussion with Pakistan on Kashmir. These pressures were not new but, after the military defeat to China, were far more effective. The subtle and often not so subtle leverage used was India's now urgent requirement of arms to enhance military capabilities against China. President Ayub on his part kept 'insisting that if the US was arming India, they should also nudge Delhi towards a settlement on Kashmir'.[39]

India and Pakistan began a series of discussions on Kashmir, led respectively by Swaran Singh, then the minister of railways, and Zulfikar Ali Bhutto, who in his thirties was already the rising star in Pakistan and in Ayub Khan's cabinet as minister of industries. That the UK and the US were the main force behind the entire negotiations was clear enough—in the words of J.K. Galbraith, the US ambassador in Delhi, he and his colleague in Karachi haunted the negotiation sites 'like the ghosts of Banquo'.[40] These talks continued for over five months, from December 1962 to May 1963 and six meetings were held in Rawalpindi, New Delhi, Calcutta and Karachi. They achieved nothing. Pakistan's approach, at least as perceived by the Indians, was summed up by Bhutto's comment: 'You are a defeated nation, don't you see.'[41] If the defeat by China had led many in India to see the desirability of some settlement with Pakistan, the failure of the negotiations was evident in the first round itself. As the Indian delegation settled into their guest house in Rawalpindi, they heard the news on Radio Pakistan that an agreement on demarcation of 'their' border had been reached between China and Pakistan. For the Indians huddled around the radio set, the meaning was clear: 'a good chunk of the north-western frontier of Kashmir had been gifted away to China'.[42]

In India, this was the clearest evidence required of a Pakistan–China collusion. It also meant to many—especially in the US, the main pusher for these negotiations—that a joint Pakistan–India position against China was not feasible. China apart, the differences in the respective positions of the two sides were too wide to be bridged despite days and days of non-stop discussions. The maximum India was prepared to offer—relatively major adjustments along the ceasefire line—was far short of what Pakistan expected—the Kashmir Valley and the Muslim majority areas at the minimum and the rest of the state to be negotiated. During the meeting in Karachi in February 1963, Bhutto was asked what Pakistan's expectations were. In Gundevia's account, 'Bhutto said, "of course, of course", and leaned over the table and pointed to the little town of Kathua on the Kashmir-Himachal border, drew a circle somewhere there with his forefinger and said, "You can have this part of Kashmir. We want the rest."'[43]

As the talks dwindled down, many in Pakistan felt that 'as the danger of a further flare up on the border with China receded, Nehru had no incentive in giving even an expression of interest in a settlement with Pakistan'.[44] For the public at large in Pakistan, the line given was that India had sold an exaggerated notion of the border clash with China to the world and to its own people to extract arms from the West, playing on its paranoia of communism. Speaking in Pakistan's National Assembly in November 1962 the foreign minister (and earlier PM) Mohammad Ali Bogra said:

> The rushing of large-scale arms to India at an extraordinary speed instead of first exhausting all possible means to ensure a negotiated settlement is a matter of concern to us. ... [T]he conflict arose out of a border dispute. ... It was therefore crystal clear to us that India was making a mountain out of a molehill and was raising Cain in order to bamboozle the Anglo-American Powers into giving her military supplies.[45]

For the Indians closely involved in these protracted negotiations, the conclusion was self-evident: Pakistan was overreaching. The final round of talks ended in Delhi in May 1963. If the failure to make progress was evident for some time, neither side wanted to be blamed for it. The UK and the US had also kept pressing both sides and this further prolonged the negotiations till the stalemate was not sustainable. At one stage this weighing in had seen visits by the US Secretary of State, the British foreign secretary and Mountbatten himself to see if his presence could convince Nehru. The inability to reach any agreement was finally announced in May 1963 and Swaran Singh and Bhutto held separate press conferences in New Delhi in Rail Bhavan and Vigyan Bhavan respectively to give their points of view. Gundevia went to see Bhutto off at the airport and recounts:

> After saying a host of nasty things about us in the press conference, having got it off his chest, with no holds barred, he was perfectly

> affable at the airport. I had my last chat with him while we were standing around and then walking to the waiting aircraft. ... 'No one will give you more on Kashmir than what we are giving you this time,' I said. 'Isn't that a pity'? said Bhutto. ... As we reached the aircraft I said, 'Goodbye Mr Bhutto. Don't fight for it.'[46]

As in the case of the failed summit after the Indus Water Treaty was signed, this time around too the failure of the talks contributed to an overall decline in atmospherics. Mutual recrimination was loud, public and on a wide range of issues—Kashmir, minorities, accusations of espionage, etc. If this was by now par for the course, other events were looming that were to alter the state of the relationship even more markedly.

The disappearance in December 1963 of an important religious relic, believed to be a hair of the holy Prophet, from the Hazratbal Mosque in Srinagar it was housed in, led to widespread protests in the Kashmir Valley. While the relic was located intact, the situation took time to stabilize and many in the government in Srinagar and in Delhi were shaken at the scale of the outburst of public anger. The Kashmir situation was accompanied by some serious communal clashes in other parts of the country. There was, in parallel, an outburst of rioting and victimization of the Hindu minority community in East Pakistan with a large volume of refugees moving into West Bengal and Assam. The Government of Pakistan had its own counter-accusations that Muslim residents were being forced out of Assam and pushed into East Pakistan.

Amidst all this, Nehru, shaken by the Kashmir situation and seriously ill himself, decided that Sheikh Abdullah must be released and brought back into the picture. He had been in detention now for ten years. Abdullah was released and on coming to Delhi stayed with Nehru at the prime minister's residence. Thereafter, at Ayub Khan's invitation, he visited Pakistan. Audiences there were disappointed when the Sheikh, painted by many in India for a decade as a Pakistani quisling, spoke in terms of a solution for Kashmir arising only in the framework of India–Pakistan friendship and of the importance of safeguarding the secular fabric of India. He secured agreement with Ayub Khan for a summit with Jawaharlal Nehru. But Prime Minister Nehru's time had by now run out and he died when Abdullah was still in Pakistan. A year later Abdullah was back in custody.

Nehru's successor, Prime Minister Lal Bahadur Shastri, visited Pakistan in October 1964, a brief transit halt but significant nonetheless. Shastri in his first public address, as also Ayub Khan in a broadcast after Shastri's election, had spoken in conciliatory terms about India–Pakistan relations. The stopover in Karachi had been Shastri's idea, which was immediately accepted by Ayub Khan. But in an atmosphere thoroughly vitiated by the Kashmir situation and by distressing reports coming in on the plight of minorities in East Pakistan, it was events on the ground and not summits that were the driving agents.

The years 1964 and 1965 are crowded and eventful in India–Pakistan relations and not least in terms of assessments being made in Pakistan about future strategy with respect to India. In Pakistan, the failure of the Swaran Singh–Bhutto talks, the Hazratbal events and Nehru's death in May 1964 were linked to two seemingly unrelated but optically very powerful constitutional changes in J&K in December 1964. These suggested to Pakistani public opinion, and to its government alike, that India was now moving to complete its integration of J&K and make it no different from any other of its states. The designation Sadr-i-Riyasat, hitherto used in J&K, was replaced by the more conventional governor in line with the one in other Indian states; similarly, the term chief minister would now be used instead of prime minister of J&K.

In Pakistan, the Hazratbal incident and consequent disturbances were analysed as being a clear sign that Kashmir was ripe for an insurrection, but only firm steps on the ground would dislodge India from its position on the Kashmir negotiations. For these strategists, Nehru's death raised for the first time the spectre of real political instability in India while Pakistan under Ayub Khan provided a favourable contrast. In this line of thinking, the assessment was that 'the Indian Union with its diverse population was vulnerable to break up. The cry of the Madras based Tamiz [sic, Tamil] party for independence, the Maharashtra Mysore dispute and the Sikh demands for a Punjab province were taken as further evidence.'[47] Bhutto in an article wrote:

> How long will the memory of a dead Nehru inspire his country and keep alive a polyglot India, the vast land of mysterious and mighty

> contradictions, darned together by the finest threads ... the key to Indian unity and greatness has not been handed over to any individual. It has been burned away with Nehru's dead body.[48]

The border war with China, in Pakistani assessments, had showed up the serious Indian military weaknesses. These weaknesses were, however, believed to be temporary since US and Western arms transfers had begun after the defeat and in a finite period, the gap between Indian and Pakistani military capability would become very large. For such military and strategic thinking in Pakistan, there was therefore a window of opportunity to shake loose the status quo in Kashmir by direct and calibrated military action. From early 1964, serious military and political planning began in Pakistan in the army headquarters and the foreign ministry on how Kashmir could be 'defrozen'. Such few doubts as existed about this approach were whittled down by April–May 1965 on account of developments in the Rann of Kutch.

Beginning from April 1965, there were serious but relatively limited skirmishes on the Gujarat–Sindh border around the Rann of Kutch—a largely un-demarcated area on the India–Pakistan border with both sides having a differing perception of where the boundary lay. These differences go back to British India, with the princely state of Kutch and the commissioner of Sindh having differing perception of their borders. In some accounts, these differences predate the British and in others that they were fanned by the British to generate a territorial dispute between the Mirs of Sindh and the Raos of Bhuj (Kutch).

In any case, post-1947, these now acquired an India–Pakistan character. Not unexpectedly, we have widely varying explanations of how the clashes started on 9 April 1965. In Pakistani accounts, the Kutch clashes were on account of aggressive patrolling by the Indian Army, keen to salvage its reputation after the mauling by the Chinese. In India, the assessment has been that the clashes were a result of calibrated probing tactics by the Pakistan Army to test the new weaponry it had received from the United States and to ascertain Indian capabilities as an input to the planning under way on how to 'defreeze' Kashmir.

By the end of April, both India and Pakistan had agreed with British mediation to refer the boundary dispute to an international tribunal. The Kutch Agreement was signed on 30 June. Apart from procedures to ensure that the ceasefire held, it provided for a three-member international tribunal to go into claims and counterclaims; its decision would be binding on both parties. In Pakistan, the agreement was welcomed as a victory for common sense but also because it set a precedent for settling Kashmir through international arbitration.[49] For many in Pakistan, the agreement that the award of the Kutch Tribunal would be binding on both sides was the real clincher.[50]

The agreement was signed by two close relatives in Delhi—Azim Husain, now secretary in the Ministry of External Affairs and Mian Arshad Hussain, his cousin and brother-in-law (Mian Arshad Hussain was married to Azim Husain's sister), who was then the Pakistan high commissioner in India. Another curiosity that was to emerge later pertained to the final award of the tribunal. It demarcated most of the length of the Kutch–Sindh border but did not do so for the last stretch near the coast along the Sir Creek. This part was believed to have been demarcated in 1914 by an agreement between the princely state of Kutch and the Sindh province of British India. It was only subsequently to emerge that there were different interpretations regarding the 1914 agreement and therefore in whose territory the Sir Creek lay was unresolved. The Sir Creek as a dispute has persisted and got further amplified from a border demarcation issue into something larger. The creek flows into the sea and the location of the border now has implications for the maritime boundary and the exclusive economic zone of both countries in the Arabian Sea under the UN Convention on the Law of the Sea of 1982.

The Kutch clashes were platoon- and company-level engagements without any major battle. Nevertheless, the lesson drawn from them by the higher military command in Pakistan was consistent with their own thinking after India's China debacle—that the Indian Army lacked the will to fight. In one Pakistani post-mortem, it is noted that our 'minor tactical successes ... in the Rann of Kutch assuaged all hesitations and perhaps gave impetus to the launching of guerilla operations in Indian-held Kashmir'.[51] If the military lesson drawn was of Indian weakness, the political lesson was that armed clashes would invite international intervention and arbitration and then the status quo would become negotiable. Older racial memories and myths that one Muslim soldier was equal to ten Hindus were reinforced—even at senior levels, normally expected to be more immune to such thinking. The pieces for a Kashmir war had fallen in place. By the time the Kutch ceasefire agreement was formally signed by Azim Husain and his brother-in-law, focus had already shifted to Kashmir.

The 1965 war has been much studied on both sides—by military experts, historians and journalists. In its essence, the Pakistan plan was to secretly infiltrate guerrillas into J&K to catalyse a mass insurgency and uprising against Indian rule. The attacks by guerrillas would be described as a Kashmiri uprising to the world. This, code-named Operation Gibraltar, was launched on 5 August 1965. Indian retaliation was anticipated but expected to be defensive, confined to J&K against the infiltrators. Over August this was how it played out but with significant variations to what the Pakistan planners had anticipated. The Indian Army first concentrated on tying down and neutralizing the guerrillas but then began undertaking more aggressive operations against the bases and passes across the ceasefire line they entered from. A key infiltration route—the Haji Pir Pass—was captured on 27 August.

Operation Gibraltar was now heading for a disaster. At this point, Pakistan, to retrieve what was looking like a lost cause, launched a major tank offensive on 1 September in Chhamb towards Akhnur. The idea was to cut off all supply routes into Kashmir from Jammu. This in its essence was Operation Grand Slam and the war had started widening. Operation Grand Slam had, in fact, been planned as the final act to complete the task Operation Gibraltar initiated—it was anticipated that as Indian forces would struggle to contain the guerrillas and the insurgency they catalysed, an armoured thrust through Chhamb, Akhnur and Jammu would cut off Kashmir from its supply routes. As it happened Operation Grand Slam, when launched, was not the final coup de grace of the operation as planned but an improvisation to save as many of the Gibraltar guerrillas from being hunted down and killed and to reduce Indian retaliatory attacks across the ceasefire line.

As Pakistan's massive armoured thrust overran the surprised Indian ground forces in Chhamb by the evening of 1 September, the Indian Air Force was carrying out attacks against the Pakistani tank columns. Even if the Pakistan offensive was slower than it should have been, it was, however, evident to the Indian Army commanders that pressure on Pakistan could more effectively be mounted if another front was opened. The risk otherwise was of the road to Srinagar and the Kashmir Valley being breached at Akhnur. This new front would be most effective across the international border—the old Radcliffe Line—in Punjab and towards key Pakistan cities: Lahore and Sialkot. By the evening of 3 September, the Indian cabinet had approved this course of action. Early on 6 September, the Indian Army crossed into Pakistan. The war in Kashmir was now an India–Pakistan war.

In military terms, the conflict ended on 23 September and is known by various names—the 1965 war, the 18-day war, the Monsoon war, etc. The Pakistan strategy that caused it was premised on three assumptions: the people of Kashmir would rise to support the Pakistani infiltrators; the Indian Army would not have the nerve to take major retaliatory action across the ceasefire line and into what they called 'Azad Kashmir'; there was no possibility of India widening the war by attacking across the international border. As it happened, each of these assumptions turned out to be wrong.[52] Within the Kashmir Valley, the situation remained far from the insurgency Pakistan had expected. E.N. Mangat Rai, now chief secretary of Jammu and Kashmir, recalled that through the conflict, 'We had practically no internal security problem in Kashmir Valley' and 'not a single arrest of a political nature was made during this entire period'. For him at least, 'We could hardly have had a clearer plebiscite from the people of the valley.'[53]

India–Pakistan curiosities during and after the war, however, abound. During combat, opposing units on either side discovered old regimental friends, colleagues and acquaintances and even noted manoeuvres of old subordinates or superiors with some pride. Lieutenant General Gul Hasan, later the chief of the army staff in Pakistan, was to recollect:

> '... the Poona Horse was commanded by Colonel Tarapurwala and he commanded it in textbook fashion. I was told ... that it was quite an education to listen to Tarapurwala's wireless intercepts. He maintained a total grip over his command.[54]

This reference was to Lieutenant Colonel A.B. Tarapore, commanding officer of the Poona Horse who was killed and posthumously awarded the Param Vir Chakra. Many such accounts have survived. The son of

India's first (non-British) commander-in-chief, General K.M. Cariappa was a fighter pilot shot down during the conflict. Ayub Khan is believed to have sent a private message to General Cariappa that his son would be released. General Cariappa's reply is said to have been: 'I have thousands of my sons fighting in this war. Every Indian prisoner of war is my son. There is no need for any special gesture regarding my son. No exception need be made.'[55] Similarly, there is the tale of a Pakistani brigadier sending a message after the ceasefire was in place to the Indian Army unit facing him asking if there were any Doon School alumni amongst them and if so he would like to meet them! [56]

Even more striking was the familiarity and connections between civil servants and politicians. In the Tashkent summit in the USSR after the war, Lal Bahadur Shastri and Ayub Khan spoke in chaste Urdu, elaborately courteous to each other. The record of one snippet remains:

> President Ayub: '*Kashmir ke mamle men kuchh aisa kar deejiye ki main bhi apne mulk men munh dikhane ke qabil rahoon.*' (Please do agree to some arrangement about the Kashmir question so that I may be able to show my face to my people.)
>
> Prime Minister Shastri: '*Sadar Saheb, main bahut muafi chahta hoon ki main is mamle men apki koi khidmat nahin kar sakta.*' (Mr President, I apologize profusely that in this matter I cannot be of any service to you.)[57]

Yet for all this, there are other examples illustrating that this was a real war and treated as such with no quarter given. The small aircraft of Chief Minister Balwant Rai Mehta of Gujarat strayed closer to the border than its pilot possibly realized. It was shot down by a Pakistan Air Force jet, possibly mistaken for a reconnaissance aircraft. Chief Minister Mehta, his wife, staff members and the aircraft crew all died.[58] Almost five decades later in 2011, the pilot who shot them down was to send a message of explanation and apology to Balwant Rai Mehta's daughter: 'I did not play foul and went by the rules of business but the unfortunate loss of precious lives, no matter how it happens, hurts each human and I am no exception. I feel sorry for you, your family and the other seven families who lost their dearest ones.'[59]

There are, however, also examples of older relationships surviving in a climate of conflict and suspicion. Mangat Rai in Srinagar recalls the 'unique distinction of housing two Pakistani nationals, in freedom, with me, during the crisis. Those were my sister Priobala, caught up in Kashmir on holiday from Kinnaird College, Lahore, and my mother-in-law Mrs S.P. Singha also from Lahore. ... I felt sorry for my sister, as she was cut off from her beloved college, and restive in inactivity, while the two countries fought.'[60]

How older relationships interfaced with the realities of tension and war is illustrated also in the tenure of Kewal Singh, the Indian high commissioner in Pakistan during the 1965 war. His account of the time is a classic rendering of the quandaries an envoy faces in a situation of high tension and conflict and in an environment that was both fundamentally hostile yet seemingly full of possibilities.

He arrived in Pakistan on 5 August 1965, the day Operation Gibralter was launched. Strangely, at least in retrospect, it was a time that he felt 'when all the signs seemed to be propitious for better Indo-Pak relations'. The agreement to end the Rann of Kutch clashes had seemingly created the impression that peaceful settlement of disputes was the only way forward. He was received with elaborate courtesy and felt further reassured by the very large number of cross-border friendships and linkages. The Kutch ceasefire agreement had been, he noted, signed by two cousins; the brother of the chief of protocol in Delhi was till recently the foreign secretary of Pakistan; and there were many other such examples. Kewal Singh was further reassured when he was informed as soon as he arrived that Ayub Khan had, as a special gesture, advanced the date of presenting his credentials to the very next day, so he must fly to Rawalpindi straightaway. In the ceremony, Ayub Khan was warm and overall left a positive impression on Kewal Singh. But, as there are always buts in India–Pakistan relations, Kewal Singh was later to write: 'What we had mistaken for unusual courtesy with which the presentation of my Letters of Credence had been arranged was nothing but inordinate haste to have done with it before the news spread about the large-scale guerilla skirmishes in Kashmir.'[61]

From his very first week, Kewal Singh was receiving increasingly stronger instructions to convey to Ayub Khan and the Government of Pakistan India's strong protest about the infiltration into J&K. As the fighting to repel the invaders intensified, so did the blanket denials in Pakistan of any involvement on its part. In a meeting with Kewal Singh,

Bhutto, the foreign minister, reacted very strongly to his remarks and said '... it was absurd to point a finger at Pakistan when what was happening was an open revolt by the people of Kashmir. ... The meeting ended on a harsh and un-conciliatory note.'[62]

We have the flavour of these meetings from the Pakistani side as well:

> The High Commissioner, Mr Kewal Singh, spoke fluent, literary Urdu and recited verses of Ghalib and Iqbal to make his points and he did so with exquisite courtesy ... Earlier the High Commissioner met Foreign Secretary Aziz Ahmed—a man not given to making his points in Urdu couplets. Aziz Ahmed told Kewal Singh bluntly that Indian actions in Kashmir had virtually destroyed all hope of settling the Kashmir dispute and if the people of Azad Kashmir decided to cross the ceasefire line to go to the help of their brethren on the other side, the Pakistan Government could not be expected to use force to stop them. ... For good measure, he added, 'Besides, infiltrations are occurring both ways and people from Indian-held Kashmir have also crossed into Azad Kashmir'. Kewal Singh smiled at this and said with mock sympathy, 'So I see we are facing a common problem.'[63]

But amidst all this, Kewal Singh was struck also by the contrasting set of emotions and sentiments he encountered. 'What continued to surprise and hearten me was the genuine goodwill and friendly feelings which I was receiving from Pakistanis at all levels. The Ministers, in spite of the hostile press propaganda, could not have been more considerate, informal and reassuring to me of their friendly feeling and cooperation.'[64]

The finance minister of Pakistan, Mohammad Shoaib, possibly an old friend or acquaintance, in fact, pressed Kewal Singh till he committed to attending the wedding reception of his son in Rawalpindi in the first week of September.

Kewal Singh, although he had been in Pakistan as high commissioner for only a few days, was no stranger to the country or the people. Pre-1947, he was in the Punjab cadre of the ICS and originally was from Lyallpur (now Faisalabad). He had studied in Lahore and after joining the ICS in 1940 had served in different Punjab districts. He, therefore, had a wide range of acquaintances in Pakistan and was familiar with the lay of the land. Nevertheless, for a newly arriving ambassador, his first month was an unusual one for any diplomat. He would have been naturally keen to have a successful tenure, possibly hoping against hope that in his time as high commissioner a real change may take place or at the least, even as reports of infiltration mounted, a larger conflict would be avoided.

Should he attend the wedding reception on 3 September as he had promised the finance minister? Inadequate details and briefings from Delhi due to initially faulty and then non-existent communications and a constant propaganda barrage in Pakistan that the situation in Kashmir was an internal uprising made the situation even more opaque. As he pondered over this, his colleagues advised him against going to Rawalpindi to attend the wedding. The situation as it developed can, however, best be described in Kewal Singh's own words:

> With the tension approaching the outbreak of war any minute and the first shots having already been fired, it certainly appeared rash for the Indian High Commissioner, the representative of the enemy country, to try to mingle with some 200 members of the Pakistani elite at this wedding reception in honour of the Finance Minister's son and his bride. But I was using all the arguments to support my own decision. After all I had given my solemn promise to Shoaib and the news did not indicate that the final die had been cast. ... I wish I had known even a fraction of the reality on the ground that evening. ... Both because of ignorance and goaded by personal goodwill and undue optimism I decided in favour of the reception. I seem to have been spurred by a strange impulse of willing suspension of disbelief.[65]

When he reached the venue at the Rawalpindi club, Kewal Singh immediately 'sensed the folly of my decision'. From his host downwards, everyone present in the gathering was hostile. 'The war I could sense was on and I was the representative of the enemy country barging into the reception.' Cut dead by everyone except two old ICS colleagues who carried out a desultory conversation despite hostile remarks and looks, Kewal Singh worried now about an 'untoward incident by one of the other guests'! At this stage, Kewal Singh was spotted by another old colleague from pre-Partition days— Syed Fida Hussain, now Pakistan's defence secretary.

> I saw Fida Hussain, with his wife Zeenat and two daughters looking aghast at me. ... Standing there they realized my shocking indiscretion and predicament. While Fida thought it wise not to make any move because of his official position, Zeenat and the two daughters hurriedly walked over, warmly greeted me and surrounded me as if to shield me... (they) talked vivaciously to keep my spirits up and to show the other guests that I was a welcome guest.[66]

After a very quick dinner, they escorted him back to his car in good order. Kewal Singh reflected on 'the stupidity of his decision' and on the 'grace, courtesy and culture of my Pakistani friends'. He goes on to note that 'I seriously doubt if any senior Indian officer would have such courage. I myself, with all my goodwill for Pakistan and its High Commissioner in New Delhi, might have miserably failed to display that decency and courage.'

We shall incidentally encounter Fida Hussain again in New Delhi in the late 1970s as Pakistan's high commissioner in India. The Rawalpindi story has, however, a sad ending. Kewal Singh had sent in advance of his attendance a Benarsi sari as a wedding gift. After the war, while in Delhi, Kewal Singh learnt of media reports that the sari he had gifted to the finance minister's daughter-in-law was being auctioned and the money raised deposited in the Pakistan Defence Fund! For Kewal Singh, 'what was particularly galling was that those he had regarded as men of culture and international stature could stoop to such a decision' but he had no doubt 'that even the intelligentsia of Pakistan would have found this antic nauseating.[67]

For Pakistan, the war was the defence of Pakistan against an attack on Lahore by India on 6 September 1965 and 6 September is inscribed as the 'Defence of Pakistan Day' in Pakistan's political calendar. Following one such anniversary observance of the war, there was a protest lodged by the Indian high commission, by then shifted to Islamabad, that such commemoration was against good neighbourly relations. It was rejected by Pakistan on the grounds that the 'aggression against the borders of Pakistan which occurred on 6 September is part of the history of this country'.[68]

The 'Defence of Pakistan Day' remains a solemn occasion in Pakistan, a ritual to pass on to the next generation the memory of Pakistan standing up to the perpetual aggression from India. That Lahore was defended successfully meant victory. In India, memories of 1965 have also continued to be strong although for many years, commemorative functions were low-key and largely military affairs and then usually regiment- and unit-centred. The fiftieth anniversary commemoration of the 1965 war in India was, however, different—with the Ministry of Defence and the Government of India taking the lead to recall the past with books, seminars, exhibitions and numerous events commemorating battles, soldiers and the political leadership.

Nevertheless, what was the duration of the conflict and how to date it were and are an unresolved issue in memories of the war in India. In Pakistan, the chronology is definite—to the extent that no other explanation is possible—the war began on 6 September with the Indian attack on Lahore and it ended on 23 September with a UN-declared ceasefire, accepted by both India and Pakistan. In India, there is greater ambiguity about when the war began. The fiftieth anniversary celebration of the Ministry of Defence began on 28 August—the day that Indian forces, to choke off further infiltration, crossed the ceasefire line and captured the Haji Pir Pass, the principal infiltration route. Yet others place the date to 3 September when Lal Bahadur Shastri addressed the Nation and said, 'What is at stake in the present conflict is a point of principle. Has any country the right to send its armed personnel to another country with the avowed object of overthrowing a democratically elected Government?'[69]

But to the majority in India, the war really began on 5 August when Operation Gibraltar was launched by Pakistan. For Mangat Rai in Srinagar, heading the civil administration in J&K, when the war began is a no-brainer and the real question was why the Government of India hesitated for a whole month till 6 September:

> It has always seemed incongruous that the 1965 invasion by Pakistan has been described as the 'twenty-one days' war' dating it from the attack on the international border. In fact, the invasion started, or at least became definitely known, about a month earlier, on 5 August 1965 and the integrity of our borders was in crucial jeopardy during that month.[70]

In Jammu, Commissioner T.C.A. Srinivasa Varadan had been touring the border villages in late July 1965 and recalled informing the state home minister D.P. Dhar of the gaps in border security and 'massive infiltration from across the border was possible and would remain undetected until it was too late'. Nevertheless, the news when it came was like a 'cloudburst' and 'the entire ceasefire line had become active'.[71] To Mangat Rai and his gallant team of officers in J&K, this one month period was of 'avoidable and dangerous delay'. As they coped with well-armed infiltrators with poorly equipped police forces, Mangat Rai recalled an apt comment of the J&K chief minister G.M. Sadiq: 'India will fight this war to the last policeman'.[72]

Much of the questioning about when the war began is because the 1965 war—as indeed the first Kashmir war in 1947–48 or the India–China border war of 1962—was an undeclared war. Diplomatic relations were not formally broken and no formal state of war declared. However, whether a state of war existed was, for the high commissions of India and Pakistan, not an academic or historical issue but one on which a pressing administrative decision rested. Standing instructions to all diplomatic missions are to destroy cipher codes and secret documents in the event of war breaking out to prevent these falling into the hands of the enemy government. But had war broken out? Neither high commissioner wanted to be in the position of having acted prematurely and later blamed for destroying top-secret documents and ciphers, having panicked under pressure.

On 6 September 1965, back in Karachi, from his ill-advised Rawalpindi trip, Kewal Singh had to take a decision on destruction of records and cipher codes. By then President Ayub Khan had already made his famous radio broadcast announcing to the people of Pakistan: 'We are at war'. But was this an actual declaration of war? Should the high commission proceed with destruction, in the absence of any news from India? In the absence of any clear information, the high commission decided to ask the Pakistan Foreign Office—did a state of war exist or not? The grand reply received was that Islamabad would be consulted and the reply given to the high commission later! As hostile mobs gathered outside the high commission, Kewal Singh decided that enough was enough and the risk of his records being left undestroyed was too great.

The Pakistan high commission in New Delhi faced a similar quandary and question: although fighting had begun, did a state of war exist? And should the cipher codes be destroyed? The deputy high commissioner improvised his way out of these questions and he relates:

> I slipped out of the High Commission in a hired taxi. Our most precious possession was the bundle of top secret cypher pads. ... Now that all communications had been abruptly ended with the undeclared war and the High Commission had been converted into what became a refugee camp under siege of an alien and hostile power, my first impulse was to seek a safe vault for the cypher documents. I ... drove straight to the residence of the Iranian Ambassador. ... The poor man came down in a dressing gown ... and was not aware that India had attacked Pakistan that morning. There was no time for niceties. The Ambassador was shocked and stunned but he did not have a word of sympathy. He refused to accept the cypher documents. ... I threatened him with dire consequences in the event of his failure to comply with my request for that, I pointed out, would mean an instant dismissal. The Ambassador relented ....[73]

Another set was deposited with less trouble with the Turkish ambassador.

While the choice of the Iranian and Turkish embassies to deposit the documents with was a deliberate one, the 1965 conflict was largely a bilateral affair with only limited international engagement. China, however, kept up steady diplomatic pressure on India throughout the duration of the conflict. While it made no substantial military moves to open an actual front, in India itself such a move could not be discounted. At one stage, on 7 September, China condemned India's 'criminal aggression' and charged it with trying to 'bully its neighbours, defy public opinion and do whatever it likes'. This war of words was kept up by the Chinese thereafter but on 16 September the Indian charge d'affaires was summoned (at midnight) and informed of Indian aggressive tactics on Chinese territories. The obvious aim of the accusation and threat was to keep the pressure on India at a stage when the war was clearly not going well for Pakistan. There was alongside some material support to Pakistan in terms of ammunition and spares. The UK, mildly reproachful of Pakistan at Operation Gibraltar, was almost openly partisan with it after 6 September when India widened the war into Punjab. The US decided to remain strictly neutral. Its weaponry supplied to Pakistan was used in the conflict, which triggered a wave of condemnation in India. There was similar condemnation in Pakistan when on 8 September, the US placed an embargo on arms supplies to both countries. This, it was felt, affected Pakistan more since the Indians had a bigger armament production industry. The Soviet Union also saw no reason to get involved although it offered its good offices to end the fighting.

Both superpowers thereafter largely left it to the UN to broker a ceasefire as quickly as possible. From the Islamic countries, Pakistan had considerable expectations and Turkey and Iran weighed in with support—in terms of arms, ammunition and oil. But perhaps the most forthcoming in terms of moral, political and material support was Indonesia. It pledged naval and air assistance and, howsoever stage-managed, there was also public sympathy and support—so much so that mobs attacked Indian embassy properties in Indonesia. Consequently, India–Indonesia relations touched their lowest level ever at this time. By contrast, for Indonesia–Pakistan relations, 1965 has been a high point and something which is recalled with great warmth in Pakistan to this day. For instance, it is mentioned with great sentiment and emotion by whosoever is the chief guest at the diplomatic reception on the Indonesia national day in Islamabad.

But even more curious was the fallout of the war on Pakistan–Malaysia relations and this goes against the trend of Islamic countries supporting Pakistan uniformly. In the UN Security Council in New York on 18 September while debating an immediate ceasefire, the Malaysian ambassador spoke against Pakistan, pointing to the reports of UN observers of large-scale influx from Pakistani to Indian territory as having caused the conflict. India's reaction, the Malaysian ambassador said, was therefore 'defensive' and Pakistan's denials were 'vague'. Pakistan thereafter protested to Kuala Lumpur that the ambassador 'being of Indian origin' had favoured India. Malaysia rejected these protests—their ambassador was acting under instructions and not voicing personal opinions. This position had also much to do with the bitter Indonesian–Malaysian rivalry of the mid-1960s. But for Pakistan, a fellow Islamic country taking such a position was both a betrayal and, at the very least, a severe embarrassment.

The outcome of this duel was equally bizarre with Pakistan breaking off diplomatic relations with Malaysia on 4 October 1965. This somewhat drastic act is, nevertheless, revealing of how high emotions ran on this issue in Pakistan. It also led to a wry comment from the Malaysian foreign minister Tunku Abdur Rahman that Pakistan's decision was astounding, all the more so 'given her determination to maintain diplomatic relations with India', a country with which it was at war. This was, he said, an act 'unprecedented in the annals of diplomatic history for its apparent lack of rational motivation'.[74]

For most people in India and Pakistan, 1965 is the memory of a glorious and heroic war. People in both countries were participants to the fullest. The enduring memory of soldiers on both sides is of the public acclaim their units received as they moved towards combat. Old-fashioned patriotism ruled and to this day 1965 was and remains a good war fought for a noble cause. Extolled in poetry and in song, the images of 1965 remain as enduring landmarks both in India and in Pakistan. In Pakistan, Begum Noor Jahan singing '*Ai vatan ke sajeelay jawano*' is the most poignant national memory of 1965 as the country came together against its great enemy.[75] As an iconic song in Pakistan it has much the same status as Lata Mangeshkar's *'Ai mere watan ke logo'*, composed and sung soon after the 1962 war with China, has in India.

An area where the 1965 conflict reflected itself most dramatically on both sides was in Urdu poetry. If the response of poets in both countries to the war was vigorous and spirited, there were also differences in the two treatments. Urdu poets in India drew a line between the people of Pakistan and their rulers suggesting 'that the latter misled the masses into this war, allegedly either because of their own Fascist motives or at the instigation of some outside powers'. In Pakistan, by contrast, the position is more unambiguous: Pakistan is the victim of Indian—government and people alike—aggression. A careful analysis of 1965 Urdu war poetry in both countries explains the difference:

> The Indian side emphasized the common heritage of Indian Hindus and Muslims, the so-called Ganga-Jamni culture that developed in North India and Hyderabad. The Pakistani poets begin with two separate nations and completely ignore any common past. Needless to say, all the Pakistani poets involved are Muslims, while on the Indian side there are non-Muslims as well. Indian poets invoke the spirit of patriotism and old nationalism and ask for sacrifices in the name of the motherland. They also refer to their peaceful heritage of ahimsa, to the teachings of Buddha and Gandhi, although, of course, they add for good measure the names of such warriors as Maharana Pratap, Shivaji, Siraj-ud-daulah, and Bhagat Singh. The Pakistanis raise the slogan of jihad, refer to what seems to be a newly discovered fiery past, and invoke the names of Muhammad Qasim, Mahmud Ghaznavi, Babar, and Nadir Shah.[76]

What should be the role of the intellectual, the artiste or the poet in a time of national crisis with Pakistan? If the question has a contemporary ring to it, it also arose very pointedly in India after the 1965 war. In common with debates half a century later, the specific point of issue then was the attitude poets in India should adopt over the role of progressive Pakistani poets such as Faiz Ahmad Faiz in the 1965 war.[77] The controversy began with an article in the Hindi magazine *Dharmayug* by the noted Urdu poet Ali Sardar Jafri in October 1965 extolling Faiz for his poetry that sent out a message of peace and revolution. Sardar Jafri argued that Indian writers should have friendship and sympathy for the people of Pakistan even as they wait for the conditions there to change. Jafri's article 'Pakistan under the shadow of Ayubdom' drew a strong and critical response from the well-known Hindi writer Kamleshwar who himself was sceptical about Jafri's claims regarding Faiz and 1965. Faiz, if he disagreed with the Pakistani regime, Kamleshwar argued, could have chosen to keep silent. He did not do so and instead participated in war mushairas. His verse, Kamleshwar said, was an attack on India rather than, as Jafri had suggested, on the Pakistani regime. Kamleshwar's article was titled 'Indian intellectuals under the shadow of Faizdom'. Jafri himself did not respond but the debate spread to different Urdu magazines, apart from drawing several articles in subsequent issues of *Dharmayug*.

Kamleshwar had based his criticism in part also on what the accomplished film-maker and writer K.A. Abbas had written about Faiz in the Bombay tabloid, *Blitz*: '"F" is also for Faiz Ahmad Faiz, the Pakistani poet and intellectual, who should now reject the Lenin Peace Prize (which he received on the recommendation of India's Progressive writers) for tacitly supporting Ayub–Bhutto's war-mongering against India.'

On Faiz and the 1965 war, possibly both Kamleshwar and K.A. Abbas were too harsh and perhaps even unfair, given the trajectory of his life and his politics. Nevertheless, the debate was a wider one with many subtexts. These questions have continued to surface in the India–Pakistan framework in the decades since. In the context of the 1965 war, what they also bring out is the hardening of attitudes on both sides. After the war, a great deal had changed and especially for people who had reason to keep in touch with the other country.

4

From One War to Another

SOME OF THE CHANGES after the war were obvious enough. Travel became more difficult especially from Karachi to Bombay as the steamer service came to an end and has not resumed to this day. Although the Delhi–Lahore train through the Punjab border at Wagah–Attari resumed after about a decade, the train from Karachi to Barmer through Khokhrapar and Munabao—the border crossing points in Sindh and Rajasthan—did so only after four decades. Getting visas became a more cumbersome and prolonged process and the somewhat laid-back administrative procedures through which cars of the well connected could be occasionally driven through crossing points at the Punjab border also came to an end and have not been reinstated. Some Indian business concerns had continued in Pakistan post-1947 and in fact up to 1965. Easily the most prominent of these were the hotels owned by the Oberoi family in India—Flashman in Rawalpindi and Falettis in Lahore. The architect Piloo Mody—a great friend of Z.A. Bhutto and subsequently a politician himself—recalls visiting Pakistan in the early 1960s as a consultant in their renovation. After the 1965 war, all these businesses were closed and properties acquired by the government and then auctioned.[1]

Trade, when restored after a long gap, was increasingly through sea freight, and banks on either side no longer existed. But more than problems of travel logistics and trade infrastructure there was a developing psychological gulf. Indian films were banned in Pakistan and the ban remained in place for over four decades. Magazines, books and newspapers of each country increasingly became rarities in the other. Intellectual contacts and cultural links became progressively more difficult. In the reflections of Aitzaz Ahsan, a prominent lawyer and public intellectual of Pakistan today, it was only in 1965 that from 'a less than friendly neighbour, India was converted into a hostile enemy'. Till the outbreak of the war, he argues,

> Relations between the two states remained far better than they are now described as having been. Visas were easy to come by. Indian films were box office hits in Pakistan. Madhubala, Nargis, Dilip Kumar and Raj Kapoor adorned massive billboards and were household icons several decades before sitting-room video viewing reintroduced them. Sports competitions were frequent. Cross-border matches in cricket, volleyball, hockey, kabbaddi, football drew substantial crowds.[2]

The Indian journalist S. Nihal Singh lived in Lahore for about six months after the 1965 war and noticed that the conflict created an environment which assisted those whose effort was to separate the two countries intellectually and culturally: '... the conflict of 1965 became the great divide, and it became easier to impose the official view that for West Pakistan, the starting point of Pakistani culture was 1947, except for those who had supported the concept of Pakistan or belonged to the Muslim past.'[3] The Pakistani poet Fahmida Riaz, whom we shall encounter later living in India as an exile in the 1980s, similarly described how in Pakistan Urdu literature 'suffered a patriotism so imbecile, so sloppy and so infantile as could never find a worthy place in print at any other time'. The war, in fact, she says, 'successfully generated an ambience of self-righteous militancy that was not to be easily appeased'.[4]

Yet for all this, some things could occasionally go on unchanged especially for the elite in both countries, even more so if they were well connected. Rikhi Jaipal held charge briefly as head of the Pakistan Division of the Ministry of External Affairs after the war. He describes his first meeting with Arshad Hussain, the Pakistan high commissioner. Hussain 'expressed the curious hope that I would deal with Pakistan as a foreign country'. Jaipal found that this had to do with his predecessor who 'spoke Urdu, had been in Pakistan, and like many others had found it odd to look upon Pakistanis as "foreigners"'. Jaipal, in turn, assured the high commissioner that 'I was a barbarian from the south ... unfamiliar with Urdu culture and Pakistan was an unknown entity

... and he could count on me in treating Pakistan in all respects as just another foreign country.'

Sometime later Arshad Hussain came to Jaipal with a request 'that we grant permission to a marriage motorcade of some 200 cars to come to Delhi by road from Lahore bringing a Pakistani bridegroom and his large party to marry an Indian bride here. ... He made out a convincing case for a special dispensation on the ground that the political division of the country should not be allowed to come in the way of observance of common cultural traditions of relations separated by the Partition.' To Jaipal this meant that, 'I was being asked to forget temporarily that Pakistan was a foreign country.' He turned down the request since other neighbouring countries had similar situations and there was nothing special about India and Pakistan. Arshad Hussain was regretful but 'was good enough to prophesy' that Jaipal would be overruled by his superiors. This, in fact, is exactly what happened. Jaipal concludes that he did not stay long enough in the Pakistan Division to understand the psychology of this love-hate relationship! [5]

The war had ended with a UN sponsored ceasefire on 23 September 1965. The Soviet Union, thereafter, undertook to bring Ayub Khan and Lal Bahadur Shastri to Tashkent for a summit in January 1966. The Tashkent Agreement essentially went back to the status quo before the launch of Operation Gibraltar. In a tactical and military sense the war was a stalemate. Neither side had anything tangible to speak of—at least in terms of territory gained. India had captured approximately 700 sq. km of Pakistani territory in the Sialkot and Lahore sectors apart from the Haji Pir Pass and some key heights across the LOC in J&K. Pakistan had around 400 sq. km of Indian territory around the Chhamb area.[6] But intangibly, a great deal had changed.

On the Indian side the positives abounded. Pakistan as the aggressor had been deterred as none of its war aims had even remotely been realized. Thus, the stigma of 1962 faded, to some extent. Communal peace had held in J&K and for that matter all over India. The intense internal conflicts of the mid-1960s—regional, economic and linguistic—were temporarily set aside and in a very real sense the nation had come together. On 6 September in an all-party meeting the government conveyed details of the military operations that had been launched by the Indian Army. One observer recalled: 'Mohammad Ismail, president of the Muslim League, affirmed that the 'people will make all sacrifices in fighting the enemy. The DMK chief Annadurai urged that there should be a moratorium on all controversies. It was heartening for Shastri to hear every opposition leader speaking with strong feelings of nationalism and patriotism.'[7]

On the other side also, the big positive was the wave of nationalism and patriotism that consolidated West Pakistan. If similar sentiments were there in East Pakistan too, reactions there were not as homogeneous but, as we shall see, more complex. In the West, however, '... the establishment simply declared victory and set about remaking the war to its desires. Thus, the war had not been over Kashmir. 'It was an Indian war of aggression to destroy Pakistan and victory was ours because we prevented India from taking Lahore.'[8]

If this line could be sold convincingly enough to a domestic opinion eager to believe, there were two consequences of the 1965 war which were to prove disastrous for Pakistan—one in the short term and the second over the next six years. The Tashkent Agreement was seen by most people in Pakistan as a sell-out. This was so even for those aware of the ground-level realities or understanding that 'not that Pakistan lost anything at or through Tashkent that hadn't been lost already'. Nevertheless, Tashkent was galling and a member of the Pakistan delegation has this recollection of the signing ceremony: 'The signing took place amid much clapping and handshaking. ... The Soviets wore the triumphant look of a midwife emerging from the delivery room to announce 'It's a boy'. The Indians looked smug, the Pakistanis grim.[9]

Part of this grim exterior was because the discussions in Tashkent were divorced from public opinion in Pakistan, which had been fed on the elixir of victory. In one account, hundreds of thousands of Pakistanis had wept openly as they heard Bhutto's tear-choked voice in a speech to the UNSC on 22 September that '(w)e will wage war for a thousand years'.[10] In contrast, 'Tashkent was soon to become a bad word, used by opposition politicians to revile and embarrass the Government.'[11] Tashkent thus became in Pakistan a diplomatic sell-out of the 'victory' on the battlefield. What had begun as a national undertaking to fulfil the destiny of Pakistan had ended with an insult, given the barest of reference to Kashmir in the Tashkent Agreement. In one account, 'after deafening world forums for eighteen years on the rights of the Kashmiri people, that Pakistan was willing to fight for barely sixteen days seemed like a bad joke'.[12] Further the text of the agreement itself was dynamite since all it said was that Jammu and Kashmir 'were discussed'. 'There was no reference to Kashmir as "an issue", "dispute" or "problem".'[13]

S. Nihal Singh, living in Lahore after 1965, described the reactions there. 'Tashkent remains a dirty word,' he found, 'because once in the thick of fighting, people wanted to go on fighting.'[14] A short story by the great Pakistani writer Intizar Hussain similarly described a Lahori, who like many others had dug a trench close to his house during the war. With the ceasefire, others filled in their trenches but he did not, keeping it ready. As news of Tashkent came in he found a dead rat inside the trench and in disgust decided to fill it up.[15]

The going was not easy for India too and most difficult was the agreement to return the Haji Pir Pass—a key infiltration route into J&K—then as now. As Pakistan infiltration began in the 1990s and later continued and expanded, the decision has been much regretted and criticized. The decision itself was certainly something that was agonized over but many did, in fact, see it as no more than inevitable. Rikhi Jaipal, present during the Tashkent talks as a member of the Indian delegation, writes:

> There was a great deal of fuss over our hanging on to Haji Pir, because in the political mind in India it had assumed an importance far beyond its real military significance. Pakistan's view was that we should quit Haji Pir but it would stick to Chhamb. ... Eventually under the principle of both reverting to positions antebellum, Haji Pir was exchanged for Chhamb.[16]

B.K. Nehru similarly recalls a discussion with Prime Minister Shastri before the departure for Tashkent in which he (Nehru) said that we would have to return all the territory we had conquered. 'Shastri asked me, "Even Haji Pir?" I said, "Yes, even Haji Pir."'[17] Prime Minister Shastri's death in Tashkent itself meant that criticism on this issue, post-Tashkent, was muted, although there is the view that the stress due to this very decision may have led to his heart attack the night after the signing of the agreement.

President Ayub Khan had, however, to face the full force of public odium as he became the focus of all criticism: the public blamed him for the sell-out in Tashkent when victory was in hand; the more discerning for embarking on such a misguided venture in the first place. On returning to Pakistan, his silence on Tashkent exacerbated the situation even more. To remedy this, he began meeting select groups of 'opinion makers'. A description of one such meeting captures the flavour of the time:

> Ayub spoke cogently and with irrefutable common sense about the hows and whys of the war and of the Tashkent declaration; he described in detail the disparity between India's military strength and ours. He concluded, 'I simply don't understand what all the fuss is about.' Although the group was 'select', there was at least one forthright question. 'Sir,' a mild-looking individual rose to ask, 'you have spoken of the disparity between our strength and India's and other such facts. But this situation prevailed also on the fifth of August....' A hush fell on the gathering. For, on that day Operation Gibraltar was launched. Ayub waited, seemingly for the man to finish and then said with a touch of impatience, 'Well go on man, ask your question, don't be afraid!' In a small voice the man replied, 'The question is self-evident, Sir!' Later over tea and cakes while the President sat in a corner ... the room buzzed with malice and gossip against him. Ayub was the scapegoat for a failure that was not his alone but the cumulative result of the many errors and illusions of the past.[18]

Why did General Ayub Khan get so carried away by the talk of India's weakness—military and political—that he abandoned common sense to embark on this venture? We get as near a real answer from a close confidant of Ayub Khan who apparently had once put the same question to the president. The answer he received was, 'My error was not to have established a counter syndicate.'[19] As any army officer will know, what this referred to was a training technique in military staff colleges the world over—one set of officers would propose a course of action and an opposing set, forming the counter syndicate, would pick holes in this strategy and demolish it. In brief, Ayub Khan had let only one set of like-minded people do all the thinking and the enterprise was, therefore, doomed from the start. In an internal meeting prior to Tashkent, Ayub Khan had commented, 'I know of people who want to risk Pakistan for the sake of Kashmir.'[20] This was clearly a reference to the hardliners who had bought Pakistan to the brink of disaster which the loss of Lahore to Indian forces would have been in September 1965.

The bad odour in Pakistan around the Tashkent Agreement coupled with Ayub Khan's growing weakness meant that its substantive clauses regarding normalization through restoration of links of trade, travel, etc., remained a dead letter. A year after the agreement was signed, the Indian Ministry of External Affairs wrote to its Missions in a briefing message:

> It is clear now—a year after the Tashkent Declaration—that in signing it, Pakistan's immediate interest was to secure withdrawal of the Indian forces, the repatriation of Pakistani prisoners of war, the resumption of overflights to and from East Pakistan and the restoration of full diplomatic relations. Since securing these principal gains, Pakistan has been tardy in taking any additional major steps towards complete normalization of relations.[21]

A Pakistani may not have disagreed with this assessment—where was the question of full normalization if the Kashmir question was not resolved as a prelude to embarking on the Tashkent agenda. That was in substance the position taken by Pakistan in the few discussions that did take place between the two governments post-Tashkent. Sardar Swaran Singh as foreign minister had visited Pakistan in March 1966 to discuss the implementation of various normalization measures listed in the Tashkent Agreement. Foreign Minister Bhutto spoke only on Kashmir. The talks led nowhere. Kewal Singh as high commissioner was, in fact, blamed by some in the Indian delegation for having obtained Prime Minister Indira Gandhi's approval for overflight rights to East Pakistan. As the talks failed and Swaran Singh headed back to India, one of the delegation members told Kewal Singh: 'This is the result of your ill-conceived insistence on the resumption of overflights. Pakistan is no longer interested in any dialogue.'[22]

One of the items under discussion was also the properties seized by the Pakistan government owned by the few remaining Hindus and Sikhs in Pakistan or belonging to companies whose owners had left for India.

These were acquired under ordinances termed 'Confiscation of Enemy Property', which had been introduced both in India and Pakistan after the 1965 conflict. Iqbal Akhund relates how the Pakistan position was finalized in an internal preparatory meeting:

> In the very first meeting the lines were drawn between the hawks and the doves. Foreign Secretary Aziz Ahmed led the hawks and S.M. Yousef who would succeed him shortly, was the most vocal of the doves. Aziz Ahmed said he knew the Hindu mind and what would count most with it, wanted to retain seized properties as a means of putting pressure on the Indian delegation. I said to Agha Shahi after the meeting, 'Surely Aziz Ahmed doesn't really think that we can swap Faletti's hotel for Kashmir'.
>
> As it happened the brief approved for the Pakistan delegation was that 'the talks with India not be broken off in any circumstances, but at the same time the world was not to be given the impression that Pakistan had acquiesced in the status quo; our own people were not to feel that the Government would agree to the normalization of relations without a Kashmir settlement'.

Akhund concludes:

> So, the Indians flew back to Delhi nicely wined and dined, but with nothing in their pockets. One of them said wryly that of their twelve working hours, they had spent more at the dining table than around the conference table.[23]

The idea of a glorious victory by the defence forces against a larger enemy in 1965 is zealously guarded in Pakistan. Perhaps the most detailed account of the war in either country is by a Pakistani, Lieutenant General Mahmud Ahmed. His study of the 1965 operation is also a critique of the Pakistani higher command and the political leadership and is titled *Illusion of Victory*. It goes into every aspect of the different engagements in the 1965 conflict. The fact that its author had been an instructor at the Military Staff College in Quetta and of the National Defence College (apart from having served as DG, Military Intelligence and DG, Inter-Services Intelligence [ISI]) meant that he had access to virtually all records as also to officers at different levels in different combat units. The book published in 2002 was, however, never ever sold in Pakistan through the simple expedient of the army buying all its printed copies. Amongst the reasons for this was the title which questions the notion of a Pakistani victory but General Ahmed was also candid in his overall conclusions:

> The greatest casualty of the 1965 War was perhaps our modesty. We prided ourselves over achievements which were doctored for public consumption to boost the national morale. We began to believe what was meant only for the sake of propaganda, namely, that we had won the war, when actually it had ended in stalemate. While we basked in the glory of tactical success of Chhamb, Jaurian, Sialkot and Lahore, the enemy learnt from his mistakes and graduated into the realm of Grand Strategy. The price of undeserved glory was paid barely six years after the 1965 war; the seeds of defeat had been sown on the banks of River Tawi on 2 September 1965 and the bitter harvest of humiliation was reaped in East Pakistan in December 1971.[24]

The second and more fatal consequence of the 1965 war for Pakistan was, therefore, in its eastern wing and not just for military reasons. Many there felt that during an India–Pakistan war, they were left undefended and to their own devices. Did the defence of Pakistan mean only West Pakistan—this was the troubling question that many in the East were posing.

One night, well past midnight, during the height of the September war, Kewal Singh, in effect a prisoner in his own house, received a summons from the Pakistan foreign secretary Aziz Ahmed. In Pakistan, Aziz Ahmed along with Zulfikar Ali Bhutto are believed to have been responsible for convincing Ayub Khan that Operation Gibraltar and Grand Slam would not invite an Indian response outside Kashmir. Among Indians who dealt with Aziz Ahmed, his reputation was that of being aggressive to the point of boorishness on anything to do with India. What transpired in the midnight meeting bears repetition:

> He started by shouting about the treacherous aggression launched by the 'rabid Hindu leaders' who had been planning their evil designs against Pakistan for a long time. For too long had they watched the Hindu atrocities against the Muslims in India and the reign of terror in

> Kashmir by the Indian army. Unable to suppress the people's uprising in Kashmir the Indian leaders had gone mad and launched aggression against Pakistan. Their reckoning had come. ... He continued in the same vein, more aggressive than coherent and aimed more at offending than communicating.[25]

After hearing this harangue for some time, Kewal Singh decided to leave. He was seen off by an officer who had been present during the meeting. As Kewal Singh got into his car he said: 'Sir, if this is Pakistani culture I am thoroughly ashamed of it. Please forgive me that I had to be a witness to this scene. May I also say that I felt proud of you.'

Kewal Singh was later to write that this snippet would have disappeared from the historical record but for it being disclosed by the officer concerned himself. This happened in 1972 when the officer, then posted in the Pakistan high commission in New Delhi, defected to the government in exile of Bangladesh and sought asylum in India. The narratives of 1965 and 1971, therefore, flow from one to the other in many ways.

It was, however, internal developments in Pakistan that dominated both the foreground and the background and provided the stage for the next India–Pakistan contest to play out. Contrary to the position of most West Pakistan politicians for whom condemnation of Tashkent Agreement was the most convenient way to beat Ayub Khan, Sheikh Mujibur Rahman, emerging as the undisputed leader of the east wing, supported the agreement. He was to shortly also announce his six-point programme of autonomy: Pakistan should be a parliamentary democracy, have a federal constitution and the federal government's ambit should be limited to defence and foreign affairs, the two wings should have separate currencies, independent fiscal policies including separate foreign exchange accounts and a separate force for the defence of East Pakistan.

The internal situation between East and West Pakistan, unfolded rapidly after this. The predominant view in ruling circles in Pakistan was that India was the factor behind the East Pakistan situation. The more astute were struck by another parallel—difficult to absorb for those who had internalized the logic of the two-nation theory to the full. Some of the fundamental points of disagreement between the Awami League and the Government of Pakistan concerned fiscal and federal issues; here the Awami League's position was close to what the Muslim League took against the Indian National Congress in the 1940s as the endgame began on British withdrawal from India. Positions had thus been reversed in the quarter-century that had passed as the Awami League wanted constitutional autonomy with a very limited role for the Central government.[26]

Beyond Mujibur Rahman's six-point autonomy proposal were accumulated grievances—old and new—of East Pakistan. Amongst the old grievances, festering for years, was the cultural superiority all West Pakistanis were felt to assume in the East. This combined with a vast cultural disparity was represented best by the primacy accorded to Urdu over Bengali. Many introspective accounts from Pakistan point to the psychological feeling of superiority West Pakistani civil servants displayed while serving in East Pakistan; 'they adopted a haughty, colonial attitude towards the public ... considering themselves the successors of the British rulers'.[27]

There was inevitably an India angle also. At its most benign, this was reflected in the attitude among many in the western half of the country that Bengali culture was insufficiently 'Pakistani', being far too influenced by India. More strident views saw Indian conspiracies as being the engine driving Bengali aspirations and politics. Mujibur Rahman's own statements of support of the Tashkent Agreement and in favour of stronger economic and cultural relations with India raised the spectre of the India angle further. In this perception, implementing the normalization provisions of Tashkent at a time of strong demands for autonomy from East Pakistan would be disastrous. Kewal Singh, writing about the post-Tashkent period, noted:

> Restoration of cultural, commercial and economic relations, always considered as risky for the authoritarian regime, now raised the spectre of East Pakistan establishing close relations with India in these fields and distancing itself from West Pakistan. ... I have little doubt that a major factor in Ayub going back on his solemn commitments in Tashkent was the challenge posed by East Pakistan's demand for autonomy.[28]

But it is also useful to recall how low an ebb the India–Pakistan relationship was at in the late 1960s. The war left a deep residue of bad blood on both sides. The stalemate over the implementation of the normalization provisions of the Tashkent agreement continued. Azim Husain found himself at the centre of a small India–Pakistan contestation, important now only to illustrate how India and Pakistan found it difficult to agree even on small things. He was then the Indian ambassador in Switzerland and proposed by India to be deputy secretary general of the Commonwealth in 1970. To avoid an election, Kewal Singh, now foreign secretary in Delhi, suggested to his Pakistan counterpart that Pakistan support Azim Husain in return for Indian support for a Pakistani candidate for an equivalent post in the future. To his surprise this was not agreed to and Azim Husain found himself pitted against a Pakistani candidate whom he beat by a wide margin.[29]

If this was a minor episode, it took place after something which had caused great fury in India and is still occasionally remembered as a deliberate and gratuitous insult to India by the Pakistan ruling elite. The setting was in Rabat where an Islamic summit was held in September 1969 following an incident at the Al Aqsa Mosque in Jerusalem. India was formally invited to the summit—the invitation being conveyed to the Indian ambassador Gurbachan Singh. By then the summit had already begun but the ambassador was asked by the Moroccan foreign minister to request a high-level participation from India. On being specifically asked whether this was a consensus decision in which Pakistan had agreed, he received an unambiguous 'yes' in response. This position was, in fact, reiterated publicly by the foreign minister in a press conference too. In Delhi, it was decided to send Fakhruddin Ali Ahmed, a Union cabinet minister, to lead the Indian delegation.

It is relevant, but often forgotten, that the summit coincided also with large-scale Hindu–Muslim rioting in Ahmedabad, Gujarat, with communal violence of a magnitude not seen since the Partition. By the time the Indian minister arrived in Morocco, Pakistan had a change of heart and President Yahya Khan refused to leave his villa and attend any meetings if India were to participate. Following repeated entreaties by the hosts as also other participating countries to India to withdraw—which was not agreed to—the summit finally went ahead without Indian participation. Naturally in India—both for officials as also for the public—this was a public snub contrived by Pakistan, which blackmailed other Islamic countries into going along.[30]

Clearly, Yahya Khan, while first agreeing to India participating in the summit, subsequently changed his mind on being advised about the domestic repercussions of this when communal rioting was taking place in Ahmedabad in India. The received wisdom in Pakistan is that it had agreed to the participation *not* of the Government of India but of the 'Muslims of India'. This understanding was breached when a Sikh (Ambassador Gurbachan Singh) attended the first meeting: 'by sending a non-Muslim envoy, India failed to observe the distinctions between the Muslims of India and India as a state'.[31] That this was no more than a gloss is something many in Pakistan acknowledge. Another account by a seasoned Pakistani diplomat is more on the mark:

> President Yahya at first had sort of agreed to let India come in, but when the Indian delegation showed up in Rabat ... Yahya realized what India's admission into the Islamic Conference would mean in diplomatic terms and to public opinion in Pakistan. So, he dug in his heels and threatened to walk out if India was let in. The explanation we offered for Yahya's apparent volte-face was that he had agreed only to India's Muslim community being represented. Other Conference members were annoyed at the incident and at the diplomatic ineptitude exhibited by Pakistan. At any rate, they could hardly afford to let Pakistan walk out.[32]

Through the last week of September 1969, India's 'humiliation' in Rabat appeared as headlines in India along with the news of continued rioting in Ahmedabad with increasing number of fatalities. The diplomatic consequences were strong. India downgraded diplomatic relations with Jordan—seen as Pakistan's vanguard—and Morocco, the host. But this was hardly likely to assuage public opinion and an editorial in *The Times of India* captured the spirit:

> Seldom has this country put up with the kind of insult it had to suffer at Rabat. ... There is no point in wondering why President Yahya Khan worked so zealously to get the Indian delegation excluded. ... After 22 years of dealing with Pakistan, the Indian Government should have the sense to know that he would not miss any opportunity to malign and isolate this country. ... Even if the Ahmedabad riots had not taken place he would have found some other excuse to embarrass India.[33]

Incidents such as these and a public opinion aggrieved at an international put-down did not bode well for the future.

Over the years, post-mortems on the break-up of Pakistan have accumulated—principally by Pakistanis themselves. In hindsight, the 1971 crisis can be seen to transform itself from an internal federal crisis in Pakistan to an India–Pakistan crisis and finally to a great power crisis. This was the globalization of a regional issue in a manner that had not taken place earlier in the subcontinent. The principal actors on both sides recognized this evolution even as it unfolded before their eyes.

The milestones in this chronology of events during the year-long crisis are well known: Pakistan's first general election in December 1970 in the wake of a major cyclone in East Pakistan gave to Mujibur Rahman's Awami League an absolute majority to form the government in Pakistan; the reluctance of the Pakistan Army and the West Pakistan political elite led by Zulfikar Ali Bhutto to hand over power to a powerful Bengali leader riding on his six-point agenda for provincial autonomy was followed by a military crackdown with widespread brutality from March 1971; a Bangladesh government in exile came into being in India in April 1971—it was recognized by none, had no territory in East Bengal but was to become the focal point of Bengali resistance to Pakistan and of Indian assistance to what was increasingly seen internationally as a Bangladeshi freedom struggle; refugee inflows into India to escape Pakistani brutality became a flood by May–June 1970 as numbers swelled to over five million and thereafter continued increasing on a daily basis; India's concerns mounted as a US–China axis cemented by a Pakistan fulcrum crystallized and was dramatically announced by way of the US Secretary of State Henry Kissinger's using a meeting in Pakistan for a secret visit to China in July 1971; India's concerns were matched by those of the Soviet Union and the Indo-Soviet friendship treaty followed in August 1971. All this took place amidst mounting concern internationally but particularly in the Western capitals at the scale of the carnage unleashed by the Pakistan Army on its own citizens in East Pakistan. This sense of outrage bolstered Indian diplomacy giving it a moral high ground while simultaneously isolating Pakistan outside of the support to it from China and the US president and Secretary of State. For the Pakistan Army, the defence of East Pakistan both from the Bengalis and from India was a nightmare which was never envisaged, planned or trained for. Following the hijacking and destruction of an Indian passenger aircraft to Lahore, India announced a ban on Pakistani overflights to East Pakistan in early 1971. Provisioning and manning the troops in Dacca became in itself a logistical feat. In one analysis of Pakistan's misjudgement and folly in its eastern wing: 'The distance from Karachi to Chittagong by sea is the same as that from Karachi to the south of Europe. We had, therefore, launched ourselves on a military adventure with impossible odds ...'[34]

The final acts of the break-up of Pakistan played out in December 1971 with Pakistan's desperate but seriously misjudged attempt to reduce Indian pressure on it in the east through pre-emptive strikes on Indian Air Force bases in north India. This heralded the formal start of the India–Pakistan war. Why did General Yahya Khan embark on this, in retrospect, suicidal course? One answer is provided by Air Chief Marshal Asghar Khan who commanded the Pakistan Air Force from 1957 to 1965. He had visited Dacca in October 1971 and returned depressed and concerned. He had a chance encounter with General Gul Hasan Khan, then the chief of the general staff and described as someone with an 'odd sense of humour'. There was an exchange of views on the situation in East Pakistan in which Gul Hasan agreed that the situation was grave but that 'the only answer is to start a war'. In Asghar Khan's telling:

> Why? I asked. 'In order to have a ceasefire', he replied.
>
> In retrospect, I think that perhaps Gul Hasan was voicing the thoughts of the Junta and Yahya Khan. In the desperate situation they had got themselves in, they had begun to believe that should open hostilities start with India, they would be bailed out by the United States.[35]

Regardless of what actually were the calculations behind the pre-emptive air strikes, one legacy of the war that followed is Pakistan's acute sense of victimhood and of being let down at critical moments by those it had helped.

The 1971 war was a fourteen-day long conflict and ended with the surrender of the Pakistan Army in Dacca on 16 December and the coming into being of a new nation, Bangladesh. The last days of East Pakistan were marked also by a systematic killing by the Pakistan Army or proxies on its behalf of many Bengali intellectuals and public figures. The support of the Soviet Union to India, both in the United Nations as also politically, meant that any US or Chinese moves in support of Pakistan were checked. In any case, all the major powers realized that the ground situation in East Bengal had changed so much so that the old Pakistan no longer existed.

Jamsheed Marker, the Pakistani ambassador in Moscow was distant from events on the ground, but nevertheless had a ringside seat as he describes the rapid change in the political atmosphere in Moscow with the news of Kissinger's visit to Beijing and of Nixon's forthcoming visit to China:

> In the closed atmosphere and society of Moscow the reaction had no dramatic manifestations, but was a much more menacing one of muted fury and concern. I reported at the time that we must expect a hardening of Soviet attitudes towards us, but I hoped that we might be able to keep Soviet Pakistan relations 'on an even keel'. This hope unfortunately proved to be far too optimistic. ... In my meetings with Soviet officials there was almost no emissions of sound and fury, but there was instead a disquieting attitude of deep suspicion bordering on betrayal. No awkward questions were asked of me, and I was reminded of Andre Malraux's incomparable description of a difficult meeting that he once had with the formidable General De Gaulle: 'His silence was an interrogation.'[36]

Marker received a blunter feedback from a friend who was also connected with the Soviet foreign minister: 'The turning point in our relations was when Kissinger went to Peking from Pakistan. My dear Marker, why did he have to go from Rawalpindi? He could have gone from Hong Kong, or from Bangkok, or from anywhere else, but not from Pakistan.'[37] In retrospect, what thus emerges is the confluence of the internal situation in Pakistan, a bilateral breakdown with India and a changed external environment resulting in the breakup of Pakistan and the emergence of Bangladesh.

For the West Pakistan elite, the break-up of Pakistan was an agonizing trauma which relives itself every December. December is the month when the dull ache of an old wound transforms itself into a raw pulsating agony. Since 1971, there have been other tragic events contributing to making December the cruellest month in the calendar for Pakistan. Benazir Bhutto was assassinated in December 2007; more recently, in December 2014, over a hundred school children were killed in a terrorist attack in a school in Peshawar. Yet, 1971 remains the year when the dream of a Muslim homeland was jointly shattered by the Indian Army and the Bengali Muslims of East Pakistan.

Over the years, all the major actors in Pakistan have written their accounts of what transpired during those fateful months. The list includes the president and commander-in-chief General Mohammad Yahya Khan, the commander-in-chief of Pakistani forces in East Bengal Lt General A.A.K. Niazi as also numerous other military commanders. Each of these accounts was a cathartic and painful exercise. The result was summed up in an introduction to one of these many books: 'History it is often said, "is written by victors". In the case of East Pakistan, it has been written by the losers.'[38]

Most Pakistanis of a certain age group retain some particularly painful memory of December 1971. For the diplomat Iqbal Akhund, posted then in New York in the United Nations, a memory that remained was of the Indian commanding officer bringing his wife to the surrender ceremony at Dacca; '... to savour his triumph, and she stood by his side as Niazi made his submission.'[39]

Elsewhere, there are bitter memories and recollections of the behaviour of General Niazi. The charge sheet against him was long, detailing various acts of omission and commission. What incensed many in Pakistan the most were acts such as:

> (t)hat he displayed a shameful and abject attitude in agreeing to surrender when he had himself offered a cease-fire to the Indian Commander-in-Chief; in signing the surrender document agreeing to lay down arms to the joint command of the Indian forces and the Mukti Bahini; in being present at the Dacca Airport to receive the victorious Indian General Aurora; in ordering his own ADC to present a guard of honour to the said General; and in accepting the Indian proposal for a public surrender ceremony which brought everlasting shame to the Pakistan Army.[40]

Then in the United Nations, Akhund describes his own experience and sentiments:

> The Pakistani delegation had stayed away from the Council meeting to avoid the indignity of listening to India's unilateral promulgation of a ceasefire in the Western theatre announced by Indira Gandhi the previous evening. Some of us sat in the Security Council lounge just off the Council chamber in order to keep track of what was going on there. An Indian delegate, then another, walked by on their way to the meeting. Neither could resist the temptation of turning around to stare at the representatives of the now humbled age-old foe—a gesture human enough, but as inelegant as that of the Indian general in bringing his wife to the surrender ceremony.[41]

Perhaps the circumstances were such that there was nothing an Indian could do, which would reduce the burden of shame and humiliation a Pakistani felt. In the United Nations, Swaran Singh, at the time leading the Indian delegation, had given strict instructions to each delegate to avoid any posture of triumphalism. Swaran Singh said:

> No Indian delegate should be seen at the bar in the delegates lounge in the coming 48 hours. He also cautioned us not to be boastful or jingoistic in our conversation with other delegates about the victory of the Indian Army. ... He said we should limit ourselves to responding to inquiries ... our response should underline that the breakup of Pakistan was a tragedy, that the cause of the tragedy was entirely due to the unreasonableness of the Pakistan military regime, that India's support to the liberation struggle was unavoidable and that India's declaration of a unilateral ceasefire in the western theatre of war was proof it had no aggressive designs.[42]

The creation of Bangladesh posed fundamental questions for Pakistan. The Indian view was that it disproved the two-nation theory. The Muslim League was after all born in Dacca in 1906. In Pakistan, many felt, or at least consoled themselves, that a separate Muslim nation, Bangladesh, did not question the validity of the two-nation theory as originally envisaged: Hindus and Muslims were separate nations and Pakistan's difficulties arose in grouping the eastern and western wings into a single state. For instance, in the aftermath of the break-up, Bhutto, then the president of Pakistan, used to refer to the new state as 'Muslim Bengal'.[43] But aside from these larger issues there were more pressing and troubling questions that remained: the Urdu speakers or the Biharis left behind in Bangladesh despite their professed desire to live in Pakistan; the large-scale massacre and rape of innocent Bengalis; and, most of all, the conduct of state policy to deny power to the party elected with a popular mandate.

The creation of Bangladesh is then a painful subject to discuss in Pakistan and will remain so. The 1971 defeat, of course, obviously also eroded the self-image of the Pakistan Army. An American scholar had noted: 'Pakistan's warrior image was ... tarnished and the pride that Pakistanis had so enthusiastically nurtured seemed to evaporate.'[44] The acceptance that failure of policy and Pakistan's own acts of commission and omission led to Indian intervention and the break-up of Pakistan has been easier to accept. Denying power to the Awami League when it had won in the election is now accepted as the root of the problem. The military crackdown, in Iqbal Akhund's elegant turn of phrase 'was, to paraphrase Talleyrand, a mistake as well as a crime'. Most difficult of all has been dealing with or accepting the charges of rape and genocide against the Pakistan Army.

In Pakistan a conversation on this subject today will invariably lead to a book published in 2011 by an Indian scholar, Sarmila Bose, whose treatment of 1971 applied a much-needed salve and reinforced the view that the Pakistan Army was a victim of false propaganda and vilification carried out by the Indians, Bangladeshis and sections of the international community.[45] In Bose's telling, the events of 1970–71 are not a straightforward story of a West Pakistani—largely Punjabi—army using brute force against East Pakistani and principally Bengali civilians. Bengali secessionism, represented by the Awami League, was not universal in East Pakistan and many Bengalis, apart from the Urdu-speaking Biharis did support a United Pakistan. The Awami League secured 75 per cent, she acknowledges, of the popular vote in the 1970 election and won 160 of the 162 seats in East Pakistan. But in her view, this is not incontrovertible evidence of support for the creation of Bangladesh since voter turnout was only 56 per cent, which meant that the Awami League had support of only 42 per cent of the total population of East Pakistan.[46] Violence in East Pakistan, moreover, was also not simply in one direction—the Pakistan Army against the civilian Bengalis. A significant amount of the violence was also inflicted by armed secessionists on other Bengalis, on the minority Hindus, on Biharis and on the army itself. In any event, Indian and Bangladeshi accounts have exaggerated the extent of violence by giving a figure of three million or at the least one million fatalities. This is 'an exaggeration so gross as to be absurd', 'nothing more than a gigantic rumour'.[47] In Bose's evaluation, a figure of 50,000–100,000 can be used with reasonable justification 'including combatants and non-combatants, Bengalis and non-Bengalis, Hindus and Muslims, Indians and Pakistanis'. Finally, Bose portrayed the Pakistan Army not as one of occupation but as a disciplined force, let down by its higher command, leaving officers on the ground to deal with an impossible situation of restoring order in their own country with a hostile population and in the absence of a political process. There is more on these lines which minimizes the widespread brutality, rape and targeted killings unleashed by the Pakistan Army.

The rage and anguish in Bangladesh at this 'genocide' or 'holocaust' denial, the anger in India at 'a pro-Pakistan Army' treatment did much to enhance the popularity of Bose's book in Pakistan. More objective scholars were to pose doubts about Bose's flawed methodology, deliberate and exaggerated revisionism and excessive generalization based on limited samples. Nevertheless, for Pakistani readers this was immaterial and the book is seen as a vindication of the conduct of its army in a difficult situation. The authorship itself made a big difference: Sarmila Bose is an Oxford don, an Indian and most of all from the family of Subhas Chandra Bose. Her credentials, therefore, have made her arguments even more persuasive in Pakistan. For most Pakistanis, she is the corrective to the 'edited narratives of the victorious side'. In India and Bangladesh, hers is an account permeated by a pro-Pakistani bias and an effort to whitewash what were a deplorable set of actions and policies of the West Pakistan elite and army. The debate will not only continue but will gather intensity as the fiftieth anniversary of the fall of Dacca draws closer. What is striking, however, is how one single book by a scholar becomes such a palliative to many in Pakistan today.

In Karachi and Islamabad, one can very occasionally hear Bengali even today if you eavesdrop into a private conversation. These are the rare isolated cases of Bengalis who chose to stay on in Pakistan post-1971—

for reasons of marriage, employment or just habit. Some possibly did so because they had no real roots in East Pakistan at all and no prospects even if they went there. There is also the even rarer case of those who disagreed with the creation of Bangladesh and consciously chose not to live there after 1971.

The Awami League had won 160 out of 162 seats in the November 1970 elections. The two non-Awami League victors were Nurul Amin, an old Muslim League stalwart and Jinnah associate and Raja Tridiv Roy, the Chakma raja. Nurul Amin had been chief minister of East Bengal immediately after 1947 and in the early years of the Bengali movement he was on the side of the Urdu protagonists. His political career had thereafter dwindled—a combination of the Muslim League fading away in East Pakistan and the onset of martial law regimes. The 1960s saw him opposing both Ayub Khan and Mujibur Rahman's six-point programme for autonomy. During the December 1971 war, General Yahya Khan in a characteristically eccentric move appointed Nurul Amin as prime minister of Pakistan on 6 December 1971. He held the post for fourteen days till Yahya Khan's resignation and Zulfikar Ali Bhutto taking over as the new president. He was then appointed as vice-president—the only time Pakistan has had the post—continuing till April 1972. The history of his opposition to the Bengali language movement and to the Awami League possibly meant that he had no future in the new Bangladesh. He stayed on in West Pakistan till his death in 1974.

More poignant is the case of the Chakma raja Tridiv Roy—bitter about the second partition of the subcontinent which shrunk even more the political space for his indigenous Chakma people of the Chittagong Hill Tracts. This was predominantly a non-Bengali but Buddhist/Hindu-majority area and its inhabitants in 1947 may well have thought that their area would fall in India. The larger issues surrounding the Radcliffe Line meant otherwise: the only major port falling in East Pakistan was Chittagong and the Chittagong Hill Tracts went to Pakistan largely as a hinterland of the port. From the 1950s onwards, this area saw substantial migration and settlement of Bengalis from the plains into the traditional Chakma areas with the tribals being gradually marginalized by the recent migrants. For this indigenous people, success of the Awami League's struggle for autonomy or independence meant 'the Hill Tracts would be thrown open to Bengalis who would grab their land and dishonor their women and turn them into slaves in their own habitat'.[48]

This view led Tridiv Roy to see a distant Islamabad rather than a proximate Bengali-dominated Dacca as being more in his people's interest. A centrally guaranteed autonomous status for the Chittagong Hill Tracts and the indigenous people there, much like the Federally Administered Tribal Areas (FATA) of West Pakistan, became his principal political aim rather than sympathy for autonomy for East Bengal, which he feared will erode his people's traditional rights. During the 1970 election, apparently Mujibur Rahman tried to get the raja to contest for the Awami League. He did not agree and comfortably won his election in the Chittagong Hill Tracts in the face of the Awami League landslide.

In the insurgency and military crackdown that followed, we find Tridiv Roy more concerned at the violence the Chakmas faced from the Awami League and the Mukti Bahini than with what was happening in the rest of East Pakistan. Around this time Yahya Khan offered full autonomy for the Chittagong Hill Tracts binding him closer to the military regime. Tridiv Roy was appointed a special envoy and sent to Sri Lanka, Myanmar (then Burma) and Thailand to lobby support for Pakistan's position. This assumed that as a Buddhist he would be able to better reach out to the leadership in these countries. While in Thailand he heard of the surrender of Pakistan forces and started receiving overtures to join the Bangladesh government. His recollection of his sentiments bear repetition:

> I thought about my successful efforts at obtaining the special status for the Tracts under direct central administration in the forthcoming Pakistan constitution. ... It meant that the tracts would be totally outside the purview of the exploitative provincial government in Dacca. Now that Pakistan seemed on the verge of being torn asunder, all this was nullified. I nursed no illusions about Sheikh Mujib and his Awami League. ... Could I serve the Hill Tracts' cause as a henchman of Mujib? ... (E)verything within me revolt(ed) at the idea of defection ... owing my allegiance to Pakistan ... that was discredited, vanquished, down in the dust, I could not let the side down. It was not cricket.[49]

Tridiv Roy now undertook the long journey back to Pakistan via Tehran, Kabul and then by road to Islamabad. He was soon thereafter sworn in as minister of minority affairs in Zulfikar Ali Bhutto's new government. He abdicated as Chakma raja in favour of his son who along with the rest of the family continued in Bangladesh.

In the new Pakistan, Tridiv Roy had a certain optical value and he was a cabinet minister in Bhutto's government. Zia-ul-Haq appointed him as ambassador to Argentina where he lived for many years. On his return in the 1990s, he was appointed as a 'minister for life', but was increasingly a sad and forlorn figure given a certain ritual and nostalgic deference by those who knew him and his history, but regarded with bewilderment and impatience by those who did not. For the Bangladeshis, he was the playboy ruler enticed into betraying his people by the comforts and continuities life in Islamabad provided. For himself, the choice was made because he did not see himself being able to protect his tribal people in any way in the future in a Bengali-dominated establishment.

Tridiv Roy's story is then a movement contrary to the general trend that followed the break-up of Pakistan in December 1971. But it was fundamentally different in character from those traced earlier in 1947: Azim Husain, Mohammad Yunus or K.L. Gauba in choosing to move in an opposite way across the Radcliffe Line were nevertheless to become part of the larger Muslim narrative in India, post-1947. For Tridiv Roy, there was no such larger framework in post-1971 Pakistan to embed himself in. His was therefore a sad and incomplete life in exile till his death in 2012.

5

Picking Up the Pieces

WITH THE MILITARY VICTORY in December 1971, the story now shifts to the diplomatic field and specifically to Simla in June–July 1972 as India and Pakistan met to decide on the future. In Simla, diametrically opposite to the situation in Tashkent, Pakistan did not want to discuss Kashmir at all; the return of its territory in West Pakistan in the Indian Army's control and the return of POWs and other Pakistani nationals captured in East Pakistan were its priorities. The big achievement from an Indian point of view that finally emerged on 2 July was an agreement that J&K would be settled bilaterally and that demarcating Pakistan-Occupied Kashmir (POK) from Jammu and Kashmir would be a new line—termed the Line of Control—to replace the old ceasefire line.

From the Indian perspective, there were then—and have remained to this day—many detractors of the Simla Agreement. To them the Pakistanis had been let off too easily and a last-minute softening of position by Indira Gandhi meant that the moment to secure a clear and unambiguous agreement on the status quo in J&K with the LOC/old ceasefire line being clearly recognized as an international border, was lost. After all, with substantial areas including rich agricultural lands of West Pakistan and more than 90,000 POWs and Pakistani nationals in Indian control, Pakistan would have had no option but to agree. Another variant to this view is even more fundamental: that a mistake was made in bringing about a formal separation between East and West Pakistan; a weakened but single Pakistan would have served Indian interests better in the long term. Prime Minister Morarji Desai told Javid Iqbal, son of the poet Sir Mohammad Iqbal who was visiting India for the poet's centenary in 1977, 'Indira has brought into existence two Pakistans and multiplied our difficulties.'[1] Curiously, Girilal Jain, then the editor of *The Times of India*, said much the same to the Pakistan charge d'affaires when diplomatic relations were re-established in 1976: 'What did India get out of the War? Instead of one Pakistan, now we have got two Pakistans.'[2]

A further variant is added by those who say that there was a secret, informal agreement between Indira Gandhi and Zulfikar Ali Bhutto on gradually converting the LOC in Jammu and Kashmir into an international border, but this understanding was not subsequently honoured by Pakistan. This view was held by many in India and, some two-and-a-half decades after the Simla Agreement, the secretary to Prime Minister Indira Gandhi, P.N. Dhar, had written about this in detail. He did so first in an article in April 1995 in *The Times of India*, then in the *Mainstream*, a weekly magazine from Delhi and thereafter in a book on Indira Gandhi and politics in India in the 1970s.[3] Indira Gandhi's 'mistake', protagonists of this view held and indeed still hold, was to have presumed that Bhutto would consider himself bound by this verbal personal understanding once he had returned to Pakistan with an agreement on the POWs and the return of West Pakistan territory. Thus, 'India had lost on the negotiating table what its armed forces had won on the battlefield.'[4] These lines were written in 1995 and India had faced a serious crisis from Pakistan-sponsored infiltration and an insurgency stoked by Islamic extremism in Jammu and Kashmir for over five years. Naturally, the past was being relooked to see how things could have been handled differently.

In this analysis, Indian keenness to be benevolent in victory led to a flawed negotiating strategy, which the Pakistani negotiators saw through and exploited. The blame for this is often laid at P.N. Haksar's door. Eloquent and widely read, Haksar was the principal secretary to the prime minister and was convinced that India should not end up taking the position the victorious powers did against Germany at the end of World War I. He felt India should not force a 'Versailles' upon Pakistan. Indira Gandhi implicitly respected Haksar's judgement. P.N. Dhar was to write that confirmation of India's flawed approach was given to him during a chance meeting with Aziz Ahmed, the civil servant leading the Pakistani delegation in Simla. They happened to be on the same flight while returning from an international conference in

Paris in 1975 and this provided the opportunity for long conversations. Dhar writes:

> I complimented him on the diplomatic skills he displayed in Paris and earlier at Simla. At the mention of Simla his expression suddenly changed. With an undisguised sneer that distorted his face, he said it was not Pakistan's skills but India's strong desire for positive results that made the summit a success. I would have taken this as a compliment but for the sarcasm of his tone, which made a strong impression on my mind at the time.[5]

But it is possible that Dhar mistook Ahmad's attempt to retain some shreds of a tattered dignity as triumph. In any event and somewhat naturally, the idea of a 'secret' understanding is rejected in Pakistan. In this view, Pakistan negotiated under 'duress' in Simla, but managed to defend at least some of its core interests in Kashmir. A rejoinder to Dhar's original articles by Abdul Sattar, a member of the Pakistani delegation in Simla and subsequently twice high commissioner in India, foreign secretary, and twice foreign minister of Pakistan, was also published in the *Mainstream* in August 1995. In this, Sattar argued that '... neither Pakistan escaped unscathed in safeguarding its interests nor did India succeed fully in securing its aims'. There was also no secret understanding: 'Dhar's account was hearsay. If Indira Gandhi told Dhar that Bhutto had made the statement, it is not uncommon for negotiators to claim self-reconstructed accounts of conversations to embellish their own performance and denigrate that of the adversary.'[6]

We also get a glimpse of the principal actors in Simla from a longer account of the negotiations from Abdul Sattar. In this, Simla was 'a veritable drama in which superb actors played skilful roles using words and gestures, that masked, but did not conceal real aims and intentions...' Indira Gandhi was 'intensely nationalistic and probably never felt happier and more self-fulfilled than on the day India humiliated Pakistan'. She was 'petite and seemingly frail' but 'robust in mind' and though 'deceptive in her inarticulate speech' no one could 'miss the thrust of her remarks'.

D.P. Dhar, special envoy of the prime minister, was 'a charmer' presenting his demands 'as requests and recommendations' and one who 'seldom thought to score points'. P.N. Haksar, principal secretary to the prime minister, was 'without a peer in knowledge and erudition' and blessed with 'lucidity of expression'. T.N. Kaul, the Indian foreign secretary, in contrast was one whose 'unctuous speech' contained 'unmistakable hostility towards Pakistan'. In general, the Indian approach was guided by a 'visceral antagonism towards Pakistan' and one not content with 'cutt(ing) it into two'. On the Pakistan side, according to Sattar, while Bhutto must have hated having to negotiate from a weak bargaining position, he comprehended the country's predicament and the traumatized nation's need to be spared further humiliation.[7]

We also have an Indian account of the Pakistani delegation from K.N. Bakshi, then in the Pakistan Division of the Ministry of External Affairs. Bakshi was posted in Karachi in 1970 and through the December 1971 war was under 'house arrest' in his office. A key figure in his account of the summit was Aziz Ahmed, Secretary General for foreign affairs, and leader of the Pakistani official delegation. He was well known to many Indian officials since the 1965 war for his role in planning Operation Gibraltar as equally on account of bruising encounters with different Indian high commissioners over a period of time. He is described in the Simla drama as 'totally negative, inflexible, arrogant and typical of how Pakistanis have always behaved ... his nose was always at 45-degree angle from the ground. He spoke little. But, when he spoke, he said the same thing in different ways.'[8]

Bhutto, on the other hand, played the good cop; '... all sugar and honey, peace and prosperity. All this was music to our ears. ... He kept emphasizing his democratic credentials. He needed an agreement he could sell to his people, etc.' In this account, a major role was played by a third group of actors: '... (ZAB) brought along an 84-member delegation comprising politicians, civil servants, intelligence officers, journalists, intellectuals. ... He brought in Wali Khan who had several friends and admirers in India. ... And all the time the messages kept coming through this cast of "extras" that we must help Bhutto.'[9] Others in the delegation included Arbab Sikander Khan Khalil, governor of the North-West Frontier Province, and Ghaus Baksh Bizenjo, governor of Balochistan, Mohammad Hayat Khan Sherpao, etc. Some of these had been associates of Jawaharlal Nehru and members of the Congress before 1947 and Mrs Gandhi, in a Pakistani account, 'held them in high esteem'.[10]

We have another first-hand dissenting Indian view of the proceedings at Simla from, strangely enough, Mohammad Yunus.[11] Although not an official member of the Indian delegation, he was present and had a ringside view of events. Yunus differed from the prevailing assessment of some in decision-making circles in India that Bhutto's rise meant the erosion of the role of the Pakistan Army. For Yunus, '... reliance on extreme options has been the accepted practice in Pakistan. High politics has been the monopoly of a small group. No one ever encouraged a broad-based party in the Punjab, which has controlled Pakistan since its creation'. In this view, 'We should not have any truck with Bhutto ... it was as clear as daylight that Bhutto was keen on a settlement and was in no position to go back empty-handed.' The problem, as he described it, was that 'a Kashmiri Ensemble, popularly known in the political and bureaucratic elite of the time as the Panj Pyare or the Five Musketeers, felt otherwise'. The five were, in Yunus's account, apart from Haksar, the two Dhars (D.P. Dhar and P.N. Dhar), Foreign Secretary T.N. Kaul and the secretary of the Research and Analysis Wing (RAW), R.N. Kao. Yunus also gives some details of the personal interactions he had with Bhutto. He was 'arrogant, sarcastic, cunning, and self-centred' and someone who 'could revel in gutter politics'.

Yunus would have been regarded by the main delegation members as an upstart interfering in the high politics of India–Pakistan diplomacy. But he did have Indira Gandhi's ear and was, therefore, involved in some of the informal back-room discussions. Indira Gandhi had possibly asked him to be present to act as a conduit with the politicians who had accompanied Bhutto. They certainly pressed him to advise Indira Gandhi of Bhutto's sincerity. But according to Yunus 'our common background and my familiarity with their thinking and the topics involved, helped me fathom the true political reality' and it was 'not difficult to see through the game'.[12] Yunus's account also reveals the intense stresses and strains amongst the Indians:

> I had a row with P.N. Haksar for the first time. ... We had been colleagues for 25 years. ... The Simla Summit certainly put an end to that. Though our quarrel was over the political issues involved, Haksar's arguments became so personal that it was impossible to return to our former camaraderie.[13]

The debates about Simla are thus not new and, apart from their resurfacing in the mid-1990s, were also present in India in 1971–72. They have been continued by historians and strategic analysts but the passage of time and the benefit of hindsight have added greater weight to present-day analysis, which presume that the Government of India possessed greater freedom of options than may in fact have existed. There was an international context to the 1971 crisis and war, which is generally overlooked in the process. For instance, about the discussions in the Security Council in December 1971, it has perceptively been observed that the most 'virulent exchanges' were not between India and Pakistan but between the Soviets and the Chinese.[14] A dramatic moment in the fourteen-day war was when the United States dispatched a task force led by the aircraft carrier USS *Enterprise* to the Bay of Bengal as a coercive instrument to deter India. The argument advanced by the US Secretary of State Henry Kissinger then was that India had to be stopped from the complete destruction of the Pakistan Army in the West. The United States also tried very hard with China to make some military moves on its borders with India. All this had made the Soviets apprehensive of a wider escalation of the crisis in which they would be drawn into the conflict.[15]

Too rigid a stand by India in Simla, or the failure of the negotiations, would have raised the spectre of external intervention again. The creation of Bangladesh through military action by India was the first time that a member of the United Nations had been dismembered and a formal secession of a country brought about. India was seen as the unequivocal gainer from all of Pakistan's mistakes in its eastern wing. There were, therefore, limits on how much more India would be allowed to extract from what remained of Pakistan on the west. In the discussions about the failure at Simla and the consequential polemics, however, then as now, the specific context of Simla is incidental. The real issue is of differing philosophical approaches to dealing with Pakistan and on that there is hardly ever likely to be one view in India.

The view that prevailed was that Bhutto should have something he could go back with and on which basis a new relationship with Pakistan could be built—or at least the attempt could be made. Notwithstanding the numerous debates on what happened in Simla and the import of the agreement signed on 2 July 1972 between Zulfikar Ali Bhutto and Indira Gandhi, what is also striking is how very slowly things changed post-Simla. According to Rafi Raza, a close associate of Bhutto, although 'the accord was really a victory of common sense' the 'so-called spirit of Simla died soon after the ink was dry on the accord.'[16] The return of the POWs only began a year later in September 1973. Pakistan's recognition of Bangladesh was in February 1974 and Bangladesh gained entry into the United Nations in September 1974. Only in May 1976 was the formal re-establishment of diplomatic ties between India and Pakistan completed as two new ambassadors simultaneously presented their credentials in Delhi and Islamabad; the resumption of air links also took place then along with goods and passenger traffic by rail across the Punjab border at Wagah–Attari.

Why did the entire process stretch out so long, given the broad agreements reached in Simla in July 1972? In hindsight, it may appear that this long period was inevitable given the trauma Pakistan had gone through—its people had to come to terms with the loss of half the country, a humiliation caused by its traditional opponent. But at that time there appeared to be seemingly insurmountable differences holding things back other than the inevitable catharsis Pakistan was internally going through. There were numerous complicating factors arising out of the triangular Bangladesh–Pakistan–India situation of 1971. First was the question of war crimes with the new Government of Bangladesh intent on trying at least the most culpable—at one stage this was a shortlist of 195 Pakistani soldiers. This was a non-negotiable point for Pakistan—Bhutto told an Indian delegation visiting Pakistan: 'I simply cannot take the risk.'[17] Then there was the question of Pakistan recognizing Bangladesh, which, although implicit in many of Bhutto's statements, was nevertheless dragging on and was also linked to the war crimes issue. Finally, there was the question of significant numbers of Pakistani nationals stranded in what was now Bangladesh. Some of these were families of POWs, others family members of West Pakistani civil servants or in related categories. The vast majority were those who had lived in East Pakistan since 1947. These were the Urdu-speaking 'Biharis' whose natural allegiance was to Pakistan. Many of them had supported the crackdown by the Pakistan Army and certainly they shared none of the aspirations of the Bengalis for an independent Bangladesh.

Each of these issues was an emotionally and politically charged point for the new Bangladesh government. The fact that Pakistan did not recognize the new state meant that these discussions were formally carried out between Indians and Pakistanis. Bangladesh made an application to join the UN in August 1972, which was vetoed by China adding more bad blood to this cocktail. Eleven of the fifteen UNSC members supported, three abstained and China vetoed the move. China had been admitted into the United Nations as a permanent member of the Security Council only ten months earlier. This was China's first veto in the Council cast at Pakistan's request although the Chinese, predictably for the time, blamed 'Soviet social imperialism' and its 'most insidious role in South Asia'.[18]

Then there were purely India–Pakistan issues. The most important and seemingly most easily doable was the restoration of diplomatic ties. The process, however, took almost four years. In the interregnum, the Swiss embassy in both countries acted on behalf of the respective governments. The absence of diplomatic relations did not mean that there was no dialogue and discussion on all these issues—there was but formal communications were usually routed through the Swiss. But there was no trade, travel or any normal contacts. The respective foreign offices and the political leadership may have been in touch but hardly anyone else was.

There were also specific issues to be resolved. Optically the most important was the restoration of air links suspended by India when an Indian Airlines aircraft was hijacked and blown up in Lahore in January 1971. The hijackers were two young Kashmiri men belonging to a group seeking Kashmiri independence. India had then placed a ban on flight of Pakistan aircraft over Indian airspace. The absence of a direct route to East Pakistan over India placed a heavy burden on Pakistan through the entire East Pakistan crisis in 1971 till war finally settled the issue. Many in Pakistan to this day, including at its highest levels, hold that the hijacking was a conspiracy of Indian intelligence to isolate West from East Pakistan in anticipation of the military action that was going to follow.[19] This view attributes a power of foresight to Indian strategists for which there is little evidence, but it is unlikely that this view will ever be given up in Pakistan.

The fact is that the hijackers, when the aircraft landed in Lahore, were lionized in Pakistan and treated like heroes. Bhutto, then head of the Pakistan Peoples Party and the most important politician in West Pakistan, went to the tarmac to greet them. In some accounts, he had just landed at Lahore airport and was taken to the hijackers on the shoulders of boisterous and supercharged supporters who insisted that he meet them; 'he shook their hands, exchanged a few pleasantries but then beat a hasty retreat'.[20] In another Pakistani account, the government was paralysed—'too proud to concede to pre-emptory Indian demands and too weak to control the emotional outburst of popular opinion'.[21] The destruction of the aircraft took place without any real effort to stop it and India consequentially announced a ban on overflights. Pakistan had approached the International Civil Aviation Organization (ICAO) against the stoppage of overflights and there the matter had pended. Post-Simla, India insisted that the case in the ICAO be withdrawn before overflights or direct air connections between India and Pakistan were resumed. Biting this bullet took Pakistan longer than possibly anyone had anticipated.

Then the delineation of the new Line of Control (LOC), as distinct from the ceasefire line of 1949, was itself a sensitive issue. The Pakistan military and political leadership was conscious that India was in effect trying to legally close the chapter of its Security Council reference of the first Kashmir conflict following the 'tribal' invasion from Pakistan. The Security Council had created after the J&K ceasefire of 1948 a United Nations Military Observer Group for India and Pakistan (UNMOGIP) for overseeing the ceasefire line. A new line—the Line of Control—created through a bilateral treaty between India and Pakistan did not make the UNMOGIP totally irrelevant. Pakistan still swears by it but India can more effectively ignore it because the line it was meant to oversee has itself been erased and replaced by a new line and formally recognized as such in the Simla Agreement. The leverage India had was that at the time of the ceasefire in December 1971, it was in control of some 5,000 sq. miles (12,950 aq.km) of West Pakistan territory.

As it happened, the first point to be accomplished was the delineation of a new line in Jammu and Kashmir, the Line of Control, and then the withdrawal of both armies to the international borders and to the Line of Control. This gave back to Pakistan its territory but also gave to India a new line in J&K, not referred to in the old UN Security Council resolutions. The new Line of Control was formally agreed to by both sides in December 1972 but had also required a protracted discussion with two meetings between the respective army chiefs.[22] The then Indian chief of the army staff General S.H.F.J. Manekshaw had, in fact, been one of the Indian military representatives that had finalized the ceasefire line under UN aegis on 27 July 1949. He was then a brigadier. That he presided over its erasure too as army chief was a cause of some satisfaction to his many admirers, especially because the new line was demarcated bilaterally without UN involvement.

Virtually all other issues went through more prolonged negotiations and wrangling, additional unanticipated twists and consequentially long delays. Much of this arose, even Pakistani officials conceded privately, because of the delay in recognizing Bangladesh as a separate country. As the months turned into a year and beyond, pressure on India also increased—how long were these POWs to be kept in India. The repatriation process finally began in August 1973 with other issues still unresolved.

Pakistan's recognition of Bangladesh too was a sensitive and explosive issue. Rafi Raza, describes an incident in December 1972 which illustrated the problem:

> [T]he public was not yet ready for the recognition of Bangladesh. At a rally at Liaqat Bagh, Rawalpindi, to commemorate the fifth anniversary of the founding of the PPP, ZAB for the first time specifically raised the question of recognition. The meeting was immediately disrupted. Ambassadors and other dignitaries who had been invited scurried away along with everyone else in total confusion. ZAB was taken from the ground under heavy escort. This major reversal delayed normalization with Bangladesh.[23]

A resolution of the recognition issue came about in February 1974. An Islamic summit in Pakistan provided a platform for reconciliation between Pakistan and Bangladesh. This was, of course, carefully choreographed in advance. The summit was co-chaired by the king of Saudi Arabia. President Mu'ammar Gaddafi of Libya, considered a heroic figure in Pakistan, was present and praised Bhutto's decision to recognize Bangladesh in response to which Mujibur Rahman agreed to attend the summit. In the words of Rafi Raza, 'Most important, this was achieved with dignity and without India.'[24] Thereafter, in a tripartite India–Pakistan–Bangladesh deal, the Government of Bangladesh agreed not to try the identified 195 Pakistani POWs for war crimes. Pakistan on its part 'condemned and deeply regretted any crimes that may have been committed'.[25] If this agreement did not address the repatriation of Biharis to Pakistan, it was now left to Pakistan and Bangladesh to resolve this issue, India having removed herself from the equation.

The resolution of the Bangladesh-related issues seemingly cleared the way for a fuller India–Pakistan normalization. This, however, was to not happen for some more time and three other seminal events, quite unconnected to the 1971 war, occurred. As is often the case, each event cast an unintended 'dark shadow' on India–Pakistan relations.[26]

On 18 May 1974, India exploded an underground nuclear device. A 'peaceful nuclear explosion' (PNE) to develop nuclear energy for peaceful purposes was the term employed by Indira Gandhi in a letter to Bhutto just four days after the test. The latter was in response to Zulfikar Ali Bhutto's statement in a press conference a day after the test that India's nuclear explosion was a 'dangerous development' and a 'threat to Pakistan'. Pakistan, he said, would never submit to 'nuclear blackmail'.[27] Bhutto's response to Indira Gandhi's letter, in turn, said: 'How is it possible for our fears to be assuaged by mere assurances ... the acquisition of a capability, which has direct and immediate military consequences, becomes a permanent factor to be reckoned with.'[28] Kewal Singh, now the foreign secretary, wrote about the strong public reaction in Pakistan to the PNE:

> So far as the strong public reaction in Pakistan was concerned, I found Bhutto's arguments quite persuasive. He said: 'When Pakistan's attempts to obtain even spare parts under treaty commitments cause an outcry in India not only unjustified but totally disproportionate, it would be unnatural to expect public opinion in Pakistan not to react to the chauvinistic jubilation widely expressed in India at the acquisition of nuclear status.'[29]

Pakistani concerns and assessments are worth pausing over. That the reaction in Pakistan to the PNE would be negative now appears inevitable. The question, however, is whether such a negative reaction was factored in. According to Kewal Singh, and given that his own background of dealing with Pakistan made him conscious of the sensitivities involved, 'utmost efforts were made to allay Pakistan's anxieties'. This obviously did not work and shortly thereafter Pakistan cancelled a planned series of talks and normalization measures agreed to. Equally predictable was that in the wake of the strong rhetoric from both ends, the momentum generated by the tripartite Bangladesh–India–Pakistan agreement was vanishing quickly. If there was some understanding in India of the predicament that the peaceful nuclear explosion had put Bhutto in, in Pakistan, there was little that could be done about it. 'If India makes an atomic bomb' Bhutto had said as far back as 1965, 'then we will also do so, even if we have to eat grass.'[30] Despite these older ambitions it was 1974 and the memory of the military defeat of 1971 which gave Pakistan's own nuclear programme a momentum which no other factor could have produced.

While some limited moves were made in late 1974 to revive trade and shipping links, the recovery was not easy. In February 1975, there was another development, more directly concerned with Pakistan and which had a disproportionately negative reaction. Prime Minister Indira Gandhi and Sheikh Abdullah signed a historic accord in February 1975. This provided for several constitutional changes in the relationship between J&K and the Union government. More specifically, it led to Sheikh Abdullah becoming chief minister of J&K with Congress party support in the state legislature. Pakistani protests both to India and in terms of strike calls and demonstrations, were strong. Hostile propaganda at both ends ruled the media.

K.L. Gauba, visiting Pakistan a few months later, was asked by Prime Minister Bhutto why Indira Gandhi had appointed the Sheikh as chief minister. Gauba surmised, 'maybe she thinks he will be able to deliver the rest of Kashmir to her on a platter'. Bhutto in response, according to Gauba, 'clenched his fist and brought it down on the table. "That can never be—Never, Never, Never."'[31] In Pakistan itself, perceptions about Sheikh Abdullah were coming full circle—from quisling in 1947 to imprisoned Kashmiri freedom fighter of the 1950s and '60s to quisling again in the '70s. In India, on the other hand, there was concern on another count. By one of those quirky coincidences, the US announced the end of its decade-long arms embargo on Pakistan (and India) on the same day as Sheikh Abdullah's swearing in as CM which had a naturally adverse impact on many in India with a long memory of US–Pakistan collusion.[32]

Further fuel was injected by another set of events—wholly unconnected to Pakistan but having a bearing on perceptions of India. This was the final act of the merger of the formerly quasi-independent kingdom of Sikkim into India. In April 1975, the thirty-sixth amendment to the Indian Constitution made Sikkim the twenty-second state of India. The reaction of the Government of Pakistan on the occasion referred to the 'grave news of annexation' as being a 'matter of great concern' and of India's predilection 'for resorting to the use of force in ordering its relations with its neighbours'. Bhutto in an interview to the *New York Times* had also employed language hardly likely to please. India should not, he said, 'aspire to control the destiny of the region' and 'pretend to be the Mother India feeding her children'.[33] Whom this would offend the most is as evident now as it was then.

All these accumulated tensions and frustrations were illustrated by a direct India–Pakistan contest for a UN Security Council seat in October 1975. Now largely forgotten, it was at the time a sustained and bitter contest. India had announced its candidature earlier and for this reason, although it saw all the pitfalls of a direct contest, did not withdraw when Pakistan also threw its hat into the ring. The Pakistani claim was that while India may have announced its candidature earlier, it had already served on multiple occasions in the Security Council. All other candidates withdrew leaving the field for a direct India–Pakistan contest. The election rules required that the successful candidate get a two-thirds majority. Neither could do so in the initial round of voting and the contest was on. There were seven more rounds over the next four days. To Foreign Secretary Kewal Singh, the contest made 'both the countries the laughing stock of the rest of the world (and) setting unedifying examples of bickering'.[34]

There were various forces at play in the election. The US did not want India to win—India's nuclear test was no doubt one reason but it also did not want a stronger non-aligned voice in the Security Council and thus make it more difficult 'for the US to deal with, or arrange things with the USSR'. This was the message clearly given to Rikhi Jaipal, then India's ambassador to the UN, by his US counterpart.[35] The Islamic bloc rallied around Pakistan as did others keen to pull India down a notch or two after the PNE. Possibly, the declaration of the Emergency in India in June 1975 also contributed. There may also have been in many a private sympathy for Pakistan, post-1971.

In any event, as the rounds of voting progressed, Pakistan drew ahead but was still short of the two-thirds mark. Some sixty countries consolidated around India making for a logjam. After the seventh round of voting with no clear outcome, the UN General Assembly decided to adjourn for two days as under its procedures the agenda first required the completion of the electoral process. The president of the General Assembly said that it was necessary because, this '... to put it mildly, unpleasant and indeed unattractive spectacle does not redound to the prestige of the Assembly or do it honour'.[36] During the adjournment, pressure was on India to withdraw and finally it did so with the compromise that it would be elected the following year. For Pakistan, or at the very least for its diplomats, this victory against India in the Security Council was a step out of the morass of humiliation of 1971 and the 'consecration of Pakistan's reinstatement to the world community'. This sentiment is reflected in Iqbal Akhund, then the Pakistani ambassador to the UN who writes recollecting a New York paper's headline about the victory: 'Pakistan Bombs out India':

> I don't know if this was so but it was a fact that ... after the euphoria of the Bangladesh victory, India seemed dispirited and in disarray, whereas Pakistan had emerged from defeat to play a more active and prominent role in the world stage ... at home too Bhutto's vigorous leadership and reforms had created the image of a dynamic country that had turned its back on the past and was trying to return to democracy. The Indians themselves were conscious of the relative decline in India's position. On one occasion when India's Defence Minister Chavan came to lunch at my residence and I escorted him down to his car afterwards, the car would not start. ... It took only a few moments to jump start it from the battery of the Pakistan mission's car. I said, 'Mr Minister here is a practical demonstration of what we can do through peaceful coexistence!' He replied with a grin, 'I know, but Pakistan likes to coexist only when India's battery is down.'[37]

Others too have pointed to the brief but unexpected buoyancy in Pakistan under Bhutto in the mid-1970s. The break-up of Pakistan and India's military victory were not forgotten or forgiven but there was the hope of a new Pakistan. In contrast to the situation in India in the throes of political agitation and unrest because of the growing opposition to Indira Gandhi and the Congress, in Pakistan 'during the first few years of the Bhutto regime, the nation's mood had successfully transformed'. Discontent in Balochistan did grow into a full-scale armed insurgency from 1973 but this remained tangential to mainstream Pakistan in the cities of Lahore, Rawalpindi and Karachi. Cultural observers of the period have pointed to a surprising effervescence in Pakistani cinema then and that nightclubs, bars, horse racing and cinemas continued to thrive and mushroom at least in these cities: 'Pakistanis had decided to settle down and do whatever they could do to restore their pride after the East Pakistan debacle.'[38]

In another account, what Pakistan lost was made up seemingly by 'the relatively homogeneous character of the West Pakistan population'—the 'Aryan Pakistan' an American newspaper called it. Once the shock of the military defeat and the break-up of Pakistan had subsided 'most people realized, perhaps subconsciously, that the operation had not been an amputation but rather the separation of Siamese twins'.[39] What helped also was the contrast with India, which saw a suspension of civil liberties following the declaration of an internal emergency by Indira Gandhi as a means of reducing pressure on her government following an adverse court verdict in an electoral malpractices case. 'India's discomfiture gave pleasure to Pakistan, enhanced by the fact that, for the first time since 1948, the nation could glory appearing more free than India.'[40]

At around this time, an ageing K.L. Gauba was invited to Pakistan by Z.A. Bhutto. He travelled there through the Wagah–Attari border and spent about five weeks in Lahore, Karachi, Rawalpindi and Islamabad. The invitation had to do with his latest book—*Passive Voices*—about the backwardness of Muslims, the discrimination they faced and their under-representation in public life in independent India, which was published in 1973. The book had largely disappeared without a trace in India 'where only 1,500 copies could be sold by our publishers in two years'. A copy, however, reached Pakistan 'where it found spontaneous appreciation and became a best-seller overnight'. The book was translated into Urdu and possibly sold even more copies consequently. Gauba's visit was, therefore, in his capacity as the author of *Passive Voices* and he was lavishly entertained and feted throughout his stay for his exposure of the poor conditions of Muslims in India. Typically, he wrote a book about his visit and stay in Pakistan—in part a travelogue but in the bulk a compendium of facts and figures about Pakistan to show that it was not doing too badly in comparison to India. Towards the end of his stay he writes: 'The *Pakistan Times*, Pakistan Radio, Pakistan TV, the *Nawai Waqt* and other papers have all prominently featured my visit to Pakistan after 28 years, a once non-believer in the viability of the two-nation theory, who has come to Pakistan to find that he could be wrong.'[41]

Since he is a committed sensationalist, it is difficult to gauge K.L. Gauba because he quite possibly concealed as much as he revealed about his assessments Pakistan since the creation of Bangladesh. Nevertheless, he encountered a sense of optimism about the future amongst many Pakistanis and this bolstered his own feeling that after the Simla agreement, relations with India were poised for an upswing.

Despite Simla and despite the breakthrough in Bangladesh–Pakistan relations, some four-and-a-half years after the ending of the 1971 war, relations between India and Pakistan had remained static. The break-up of Pakistan had not also solved India's problems on the eastern border. The assassination of Mujibur Rahman in August 1975 (by coincidence on 15 August, India's Independence Day) meant an immediate deterioration in relations with that new country in which India had invested so much. Not surprisingly, Bhutto 'virtually hailed this as a victory for Pakistan, a vindication of the idea of one Pakistan' indeed almost as if 'we had regained the ground lost in 1971'.[42] If such hopes were exaggerated for Pakistan, for India the difficulties with Bangladesh were only beginning. In 1976 in the United Nations, India suddenly found itself confronting Bangladesh when it bought a resolution for UN intervention on the question of sharing of river waters flowing from India into Bangladesh. For Ambassador Rikhi Jaipal in the UN, this was Bangladesh acting in 'an extraordinary state of amnesia'.[43] In Pakistan, the India–Bangladesh friction was the cause of some satisfaction if not glee and the vindication of an older truth: '... it was not long before the geopolitical algebra asserted itself and the equations changed again with Bangladesh at odds with India and looking to Pakistan for support.'[44]

Change in the India–Pakistan logjam was, however, to come from a direction perhaps neither side had anticipated. Internal situations always have a bearing on external postures and Jagat Mehta, foreign secretary in 1976, wrote about the situation as it had changed since the signing of the Simla Agreement:

> [T]he Simla agreement incorporated commitment to a step by step process of normalization. But Simla was nearly 4 years earlier. We could still rejoice in the laurels and triumph of military victory and had reason to be diplomatically self-confident. In 1975 however we had suspended our Constitution and proclaimed an Emergency. Many correspondents of the international media had been expelled or withdrawn and the world had become critical of India. Even well-known friends of India had been denied visas. Our international reputation as a democracy stood sullied and, for the first time, Pakistan could boast of being a working democracy, while India was imposing strict censorship and throttling human and political rights. In any case, I thought we should be ready with a more imaginative approach so that Pakistan could be brought on to a less hostile and more reciprocally friendly wavelength so that our image abroad improved.[45]

A letter from Zulfikar Ali Bhutto to Indira Gandhi in March 1976 provided an opening. Pakistan agreed to withdraw its case in the International Civil Aviation Organization against India for denial of overflight rights. A meeting in Islamabad followed in which restoration of diplomatic relations, civil aviation links and rail connections across the Punjab border were agreed to. Rail connections on the Wagah–Attari border crossing in Punjab and the Khokhrapar–Munabao crossing on the Rajasthan–Sindh border had remained suspended since 1965.

Thus, after five years of standing still, things moved quickly as both the Indian and Pakistani ambassadors presented credentials on 12 July 1976. Fida Hussain who had stood by Kewal Singh during his embarrassing trip to Rawalpindi in September 1965 was incidentally the new Pakistan ambassador in Delhi. The normalization process finally seemed to be on track. This changed context meant that developments that would have otherwise been a severe setback were taken in their stride. We get a graphic instance in the hijacking of an Indian Airlines aircraft to Pakistan just two months later, on 10 September 1976. The last hijacking incident in 1971 had seen the hijackers feted in Lahore as heroes and the aircraft destroyed on the tarmac. This time around the hijackers were taken into custody to be tried under Pakistani law, the passengers treated with great courtesy and the aircraft returned.

Evidently, the context had changed. Further proof came from the opposite direction, when the hijackers were released in December. While the Government of India protested that this was against the understandings reached earlier, it let the matter rest at that. The Pakistani position was quietly explained: the hijackers were from Kashmir and they claimed the hijacking was to draw attention to the Kashmir cause; it was, in the circumstances, impossible for Bhutto either to continue their detention or to hand them over to India. What the Government of Pakistan could do was to see that the hijackers, after being released, were not given publicity or a platform. With some complaining, the Government of India went along. Clearly, there was no appetite to embark on any steps that would retard the recently begun normalization process. Foreign Secretary Jagat Mehta explains the context and the thinking in the Government of India:

> The critical situation for us in Delhi was to understand the dilemma in Pakistan of not wanting to betray its sympathizers and at the same time, not cause a major incident with India. Shah Nawaz (the Pakistan Additional Foreign Secretary who handled the situation in Lahore) understood the implication when I told him on the phone that the hijackers should be 'seen' to be taken into custody when they left the aircraft. I was certain that asking for the repatriation of Pakistani hijackers for trial in India would only invite a rebuff. But seeing them arrested was likely to satisfy Indian public opinion. When the hijackers were released a few months later, it really caused me no surprise or offense.[46]

The changed context could thus withstand the crisis of a hijacking and the release of the hijackers. Essentially, this demonstrates that context is everything. A hijacking in one context could, and would in the future, trigger a bilateral crisis, in another it hardly caused a ripple.

Possibly, with Sheikh Abdullah back in charge in J&K, the mood in India was sufficiently confident to ignore the occasional provocation, although Indira Gandhi herself remained sensitive to what Pakistan said. If Pakistan predictably continued to make statements on the UN resolutions, her reactions were tough and frequently designed to leave her interlocuter at a loss. One episode is frequently recounted in Islamabad in which Fida Hussain, Pakistan's newly appointed ambassador, got a taste of Indira Gandhi's fury during his introductory call on her in early September that year. In the words of a colleague accompanying him:

> The conversation started with the expression of good wishes which Mrs Gandhi briefly reciprocated. For the next few minutes, there were comments of a general nature. Turning to bilateral relations, the Ambassador expressed the hope that the two countries would be able to establish friendlier ties. He then said there was need to resolve the Kashmir dispute in accordance with the UN resolutions. This comment produced a visible effect on Mrs Gandhi. She more or less froze. The atmosphere suddenly became tense and there was an uncomfortable silence lasting at least a couple of minutes. I thought that perhaps the meeting had come to an end. Then Mrs Gandhi spoke in a low voice. 'This is not what President Bhutto had told me at Simla,' she said, looking peeved and a little angry. There was again a silence. Looking rather uneasy, Fida Hussain thanked the Prime Minister for receiving him and took his leave.[47]

The same account informs us that Fida Hussain did not receive a clear reply from Islamabad on Indira Gandhi's contention but also that 'he never again referred to the Kashmir dispute during his stay in India'. [48]

The changed context also explains the equanimity with which Indira Gandhi replied to a letter—seemingly innocuous from a Pakistani perspective but bound to raise hackles in India—from Bhutto in August 1976. It concerned an issue which was of some sensitivity in India at that time. The background was the jailing, during the Emergency, of a socially prominent politician—Maharani Gayatri Devi of Jaipur. She was a member of parliament and her arrest was on the grounds of tax evasion and smuggling. Simultaneously, there was an orchestrated outcry about vast Mughal treasures lying buried in different Jaipur forts and palaces. These were, the accounts went, what Raja Man Singh of Amer (the medieval capital of Jaipur state) had brought from Afghanistan when he was the Mughal governor. The Archeological Survey of India was tasked with locating and recovering these treasures from the different properties of the old Jaipur maharajas. Bhutto's letter requested that Indira Gandhi 'remain cognizant of Pakistan's claim to its due share of this wealth ... an asset which was not known at the time of partition (but) the historical provenance of this treasure, regardless of the location of its physical discovery, makes it the joint patrimony of our two nations ... and with an approach based on equity, we will discountenance any usurpation and amicably arrive at a formula for the division between us'.[49]

The letter appears to have been Bhutto's own initiative—not raised otherwise through official channels although it was delivered by Fida Hussain, the high commissioner who also was given specific instructions on what to say while delivering it.[50] It would have been received with some degree of irritation in India but PM Gandhi's reply was matter of fact and designed not to upset the recent normalization measures. Our legal experts, she wrote, were asked to give careful consideration to Pakistan's contention and they were of the clear opinion that the claim had no legal basis. 'Incidentally', the letter concluded, 'the treasure has turned out to be non-existent'.[51]

Normalization reflected itself most in symbolic gestures outside the realm of politics. In December 1976, the centenary of Muhammad Ali Jinnah, the Qaid-i-Azam of Pakistan, was observed in Pakistan. The Government of Pakistan decided as part of the commemoration to present gold medals to world leaders. In Delhi, Ambassador Fida Hussain was pleasantly surprised when he was informed by the Ministry of External Affairs that a presentation to the president of India had been arranged. A Pakistani diplomat Shahid Amin then posted in Delhi recalls: 'Ambassador Fida Hussain went to the Rashtrapati Bhavan to present the medal to President Fakhruddin Ali Ahmed. I thought there was a certain irony in the situation as the Qaid-i-Azam medal was being presented to a Muslim leader who had strongly opposed the creation of Pakistan.'[52]

In the first half of 1977 an even larger contextual change was taking place. Both India and Pakistan had elections at about the same time, in March 1977. Both elections were announced in January 1977 within eleven days of each other. Possibly both prime ministers were equally surprised at the capacity of their respective oppositions to sink ideological differences to unite. Nevertheless, the elections had astonishingly different results. In Pakistan, the elections were notoriously rigged in Bhutto's favour, unleashing a chain of events that led to his overthrow in a military coup in July 1977. In India, the election was in effect a referendum on the Emergency, and Indira Gandhi was decisively defeated. The two March elections were a dramatic demonstration of the different trajectories of India and Pakistan some thirty years after 1947 and their coincidence is another of those India–Pakistan oddities that surfaces from time to time.

The massive rigging of the March 1977 election led to a Bhutto majority the size of which stunned even his supporters and, by some accounts, even embarrassed him. He and his party had been expected to win but the near-total decimation of the opposition made the election results lose credibility. 'Why did you do this to me?', he is widely believed to have rhetorically asked a group of senior civil servants as the results came in. In any event, the loss of popularity and personal legitimacy was swift. This mirrored in some ways the trajectory followed by Indira Gandhi when she had imposed the Emergency to deal with political dissent in June 1975. If the mid-1970s showed the common authoritarian streak in Gandhi and Bhutto, the similarities between the two polities ended there but these different trajectories should not disguise how one influenced the other. As Bhutto's personal stock plummeted, a close associate has described how he was 'further weakened by the catastrophic defeat suffered by his old adversary Indira Gandhi in the Indian elections in the third week of March'. The Indian election result 'gave the Pakistani opposition a further valuable boost, and the feeling was widespread in Pakistan that the Indians could not be allowed to gain a greater reputation than the far less docile Pakistanis for the removal of dictatorial government'.[53]

For Bhutto then, Indira Gandhi's defeat was a 'body blow' and many were to reflect 'that Indira Gandhi had now done Pakistan two grand disfavours. She had been responsible for finalizing the break-up of Pakistan in 1971 and now she had taught her neighbour Bhutto another lesson by withdrawing from office with good grace.'[54] Domestic dissent and political agitation over the election's rigging led in Pakistan to military intervention by the chief of the army staff, General Zia-ul-Haq, in July 1977 with the prime minister, his principal cabinet colleagues and the leaders of the opposition jailed and martial law imposed. In India, the search for legitimacy had led Indira Gandhi to end the Emergency and call a general election in which she and her party were comprehensively defeated and the first non-Congress government came to power.

The India–Pakistan normalization process survived both the change of government in India and the coup in Pakistan. The coming to power of the Janata Party government in India was initially seen as an ominous sign in Pakistan. The Janata Party was, in this assessment, 'a motley group of mostly right wing parties' with the Bharatiya Jana Sangh, no friend of Pakistan, a critical part. Atal Bihari Vajpayee's appointment as foreign minister, in particular, was seen as especially harmful—he was the prominent face of the Hindu fundamentalist Jana Sangh with its 'record of hostility towards Muslims in general and Pakistan in particular'.[55] Vajpayee was conscious of these fears and views in Pakistan and went about addressing them in his own characteristic way. For instance, when the Pakistan ambassador Fida Hussain came to call on Vajpayee, shortly after he became foreign minister, he disarmed the ambassador by receiving him at the entrance to his office with a well-known verse of Ghalib:

Wo a-ain ghar mein humaray Khuda ki qudrat hai
Kabhi hum unko, kabhi apnay ghar ko dekhtay hain[56]

(It is a miracle of God that I see you in my home.
Astonished, I sometimes look at you and sometimes at my house)

A few months later, in December 1977, Fida Hussain died suddenly. Vajpayee went to the Pakistan embassy and wrote in the condolence book:

Zamana baray shouq say sunn raha tha
Tumhi so gaye dastaan kahte kahte.[57]

(We were engrossed in what you were saying,
But you chose to go to sleep while relating your engrossing story)

All this was noted with appreciation by those in the Pakistan government who were trying to decipher what the new government in Delhi meant to do in terms of its Pakistan policy.

A year after the Quaid centenary in December 1976, another landmark anniversary, in both India and Pakistan, was that of the greatest of Urdu poets of the first half of the twentieth century—Mohammad Iqbal—in December 1977. Here, Pakistan rolled out the heavy artillery. The great ghazal singer Mehdi Hasan was sent by the Government of Pakistan on a tour of India accompanied by the poet's son, Dr Javid Iqbal, an eminent Pakistani jurist of the future. The first concert was hosted by the Pakistan embassy in New Delhi. Foreign Minister Vajpayee agreed to be the chief guest. The embassy was, however, careful about the speakers for the function—choosing scholars of literature rather than Vajpayee or any other politician. The charge d'affairs Shahid Amin explains:

> I did not invite FM Vajpayee, who was the chief guest to speak on the function. I suspected that, firstly, he would claim that Iqbal was an Indian poet (which was technically correct since Iqbal died in 1938, nine years before Pakistan came into being). I also thought Vajpayee would advance the Indian argument that, culturally, Indians and Pakistanis were the same people. Of course, the sting in this line of thinking was that Indians used this as a subtle argument to deny the rationale for the very creation of Pakistan.[58]

In any event, the embassy was soon flooded with requests for invitations for the concert from all quarters. At the concert, the hall was packed beyond capacity with people sitting on the floor and even on the stage. The embassy had, out of courtesy, sent a card to Indira Gandhi and to its surprise she attended and stayed on till the end.

Some three-and-a-half decades later, Iqbal's grandson, Waleed Iqbal, who was part of the Pakistani cultural delegation recalled his father Javid Iqbal being seated between Indira Gandhi and Atal Bihari Vajpayee. Those were the days when the Janata Party government was also trying to fix responsibility and accountability for the numerous excesses committed during the Emergency, and Indira Gandhi was the subject of inquiry by a judicial commission. Javid Iqbal, possibly out of courtesy or just to make conversation, invited her to visit Lahore, Iqbal's city. In his recollection,

'She looked at Vajpayee and sarcastically commented, "First, please ask him to return my passport."'[59]

Then, as now, these high-profile initiatives and symbolic gestures were intended to lighten the atmosphere and facilitate political interactions. If the Janata Party government sought to show that it would manage relationships with neighbours better than the Congress, General Zia-ul-Haq—the military dictator of Pakistan—needed to have an even keel in relations with India for his own reasons. The coup and the overthrow of a civilian government, howsoever tainted and unpopular domestically, meant some extent of international opprobrium, and forward movement with India was one way of dealing with this.

Chance encounters at heads of government level also played a role in improving relations. One such stands out. A surprised Indian high commissioner in Nairobi found that the funeral of President Jomo Kenyatta in August 1978 had become the platform for an unscheduled India–Pakistan summit engagement. At the funeral, Prime Minister Morarji Desai and President Zia-ul-Haq were seated on the same row with the Aga Khan between them. The funeral was long and:

> ...the obsequies continued for several hours. The distinguished foreign mourners at first sat in dignified silence. But then they began to engage in discreet chit chat. The Aga Khan could be seen making small talk with Desai and Zia. ... Gradually their banter included all the three. To the distant but watchful eyes of India's resident envoy, the first exchanges between Desai and Zia seemed cursory. After sometime they got into a conversation and soon were talking directly, across the Ismaili chief between them.[60]

As the ceremony ended, Prime Minister Desai informed his ambassador that 'the General Sahib would be coming with them'. As the car proceeded 'the envoy sitting in the front could discern that an India–Pakistan summit had begun at the back'. At the hotel, the meeting continued in Desai's suite with nobody in either delegation any the wiser what was being talked about. But a personal chemistry was evident as they emerged and 'a smiling Desai accompanied a beaming Zia to the lift and saw him off with great aplomb'. In keeping with 'subcontinental traditions, Zia extended a courtly deference to his eighty-two-year-old Indian counterpart addressing him frequently as "Sir" with a toothy smile. On his part, Prime Minister Desai shed his usually dour demeanor and responded with unexpected warmth.'

If this seemingly unplanned meeting augured well for the future, a more planned engagement had been the visit of Foreign Minister Vajpayee to Pakistan in February 1978. This was by no means the first visit by a foreign minister from India but it took place after a long time—Sardar Swaran Singh had last visited in 1966, post-Tashkent. Foreign Minister Vajpayee's visit is still recalled in Pakistan today as being a landmark, because it was termed as a goodwill visit and Vajpayee conducted it as such. He had visited all other South Asian capitals—although these were prior to the formation of the South Asian Association for Regional Cooperation (SAARC)—and saw no reason to exclude Pakistan. The naysayers were many—especially in Pakistan where the perennial question of 'what value of normalization without Kashmir' and Vajpayee's Jana Sangh background received much prominence. Jagat Mehta as foreign secretary describes his nervousness before the visit:

> For months before Vajpayee's actual journey in February 1978, the Pakistan media, especially the Lahore papers, wrote critically of the old Jana Sanghi, who had opposed the creation and existence of Pakistan, and led a demonstration against the Simla Agreement in 1972, was being allowed to come to the country. I was myself nervous that hostile demonstrations might mar the visit.[61]

But Vajpayee, in a remarkable diplomatic performance during the visit, turned public opinion by 'a mixture of non-denial of his anti-Pakistani past and the sincere promise of friendly relations'.

Jagat Mehta recalls: 'Vajpayee started by taking the wind out of the sails of curiosity and criticism by reading a statement honestly confessing to his political past and his earlier deep hostility towards the very existence of Pakistan and then went on to affirm a new faith in friendship and sincere wishes for the well-being of Pakistan.'[62] An amusing account has survived of the official banquet hosted by Foreign Minister Agha Shahi in honour of Vajpayee. Just before the dinner the Pakistani protocol discovered with 'some consternation' that Vajpayee intended to speak in Urdu. Agha Shahi's speech had been prepared in English but this 'necessitated that Shahi too must speak in Urdu'. A translation was hurriedly arranged but it used highly Persianized Urdu and in the banquet Agha Shahi struggled through it and the 'speech lacked flow'. Vajpayee on the other hand 'spoke extempore' interspersing his speech generously with Urdu verses and the 'contrast with Shahi was rather telling'. A Pakistani diplomat present concluded: 'Urdu was Pakistan's national language but Vajpayee seemed much more at ease with this language than his Pakistani counterpart.' [63]

Two outcomes of significance from Vajpayee's Pakistan visit were the resumption of India–Pakistan cricketing ties and an agreement on the construction of a hydroelectric project by India on the Chenab in J&K. Cricketing ties thus resumed after a gap of eighteen years when the Indian team toured Pakistan in 1978–79. Virtually a whole generation was seeing India and Pakistan play each other for the first time—these were still pre–World Cup or any multilateral tournament days. For many Indian cricket aficionados, what stood out in the series was the biased umpiring in the three-Test series which Pakistan won 2-0. In the return tour, in 1979–80, Pakistan lost by the same margin and Pakistan fans had similar complaints but perhaps of a lesser order.[64] There were other discordant notes. For many in India, the series in Pakistan was the first cricket telecast seen live and this was also their first view of Pakistan—or at least its crowds and cricket stadiums. 'Three wars and the loss of East Pakistan', recalls Shaharyar Khan, a scion of Bhopal and later foreign secretary of Pakistan, 'had filled the Pakistani psyche with bitterness and anger which were reflected in the surreal atmosphere of the cricket matches. Politics and cricket were not separate but part of a whole.'[65]

If both governments could agree on the larger picture that the resumption of cricketing ties was a big step forward, the internal tensions were also evident. Vajpayee bitterly complained to the Pakistani ambassador about President Zia declaring a national holiday in Pakistan when Pakistan defeated India in the second Test in November 1978. What was more galling was the Pakistan captain Mushtaq Mohammed saying on television that all Muslims had prayed for the Pakistani team. Vajpayee said to the ambassador, 'These are small things, we should forget them but the public here notices.'[66] Whatever may have been the governmental impulses in restarting cricketing ties, the age when this competition would be an aid to diplomacy was still in the future.

In terms of substantive agreement, what also stands out in this period was the compromise reached on the Salal Hydroelectric Project on the Chenab river in Udhampur district in J&K. The waters of the Chenab, a western river, were allocated to Pakistan under the Indus Waters Treaty (IWT). India could not interfere in these flows although it had certain rights to build hydroelectric projects that could use the flow of the water but not store it. A hydroelectric plant in Salal had been envisaged from pre-Independence days but it was only in 1968 that a project design was ready. According to the IWT, the design needed Pakistan's concurrence. For Pakistan, then as now, any Indian activity on the western rivers was both an implied and actual threat.

There were many who noticed that following the IWT and Pakistan's greater dependence now on the western rivers, its concerns about Kashmir and Indian capacities and control over the upstream areas were also growing. The Salal project was therefore objected to on many grounds—some stated, others not. For one, even the limited storage in a relatively low dam was in Pakistan's view a possible flood threat to its agriculture, if the water was suddenly released. Then it was feared that the dam could be used to store and hold back water at times when agricultural operations needed it most. Equally important, but usually unstated, were military-related fears. Water releases would be a defensive weapon to halt a Pakistan offensive to capture Kashmir. Some theories were even more ludicrous but after 1965 and 1971 military-related concerns were deeply rooted in public opinion in Pakistan.[67] That India has a well-thought-out, diabolical plan to starve Pakistan of water and thereby into submission was, as indeed it is today, a widely held notion.

For Foreign Secretary Jagat Mehta, leading the Indian negotiating team, resolving Salal was important if the normalization process was to have substance. The project had been discussed innumerable times by engineers on both sides and by the foreign secretaries over the past decade without any real breakthrough. The option India was now contemplating was to go in for arbitration by an external neutral expert as provided for in the Indus Waters Treaty. For many in the government, this was hardly the preferred solution—involving foreigners in India–Pakistan issues went against the grain after the Kashmir experience in the UNSC. It also went against the basic spirit of the Simla agreement—at least as it was understood then. Nevertheless, after years of fruitless negotiation this seemed the only viable course left. Jagat Mehta was one of those who was against using the treaty mechanism of an outside expert to resolve the issue.

> It did not require much perspicacity to foresee that even though the process of adjudication would take a long time but in the meantime the atmosphere would become so vitiated that it would complicate the resolution of other issues. Anyway, the construction of the hydel project would remain deferred and the delay could extend into years. ... I feared the hazard of another 'Kashmir' that is, a bilateral problem being internationalized.[68]

In the event, more bilateral talks were proposed by India and accepted by Pakistan. By October 1976, some additional concessions by India such as reducing the height of the dam had a greater impact on the Pakistani position. An agreement was reached before the 1977 elections but at Zulfiqar Ali Bhutto's suggestion its formal signature was deferred till after the Pakistan election in March 1977.

The understanding reached survived both the change in the government in India and the military coup in Pakistan and a formal agreement on the Salal Hydroelectric Project was concluded in April 1978. Thus, something agreed to by Indira Gandhi and Z.A. Bhutto was formally cemented under Morarji Desai and General Zia-ul-Haq. For Jagat Mehta, the key in this successful conclusion lay in three factors: assuaging unwarranted suspicions, 'measured unilateralism in small concessions' such as the dam height reduction, and finally, avoiding 'public relations one-upmanship' and not being triumphalist.[69]

Successful India–Pakistan negotiations are rare, so the Salal Agreement does stand out as a milestone in a sensitive area such as river waters sharing and in which many in Pakistan are firmly convinced that India has a strategic game plan with respect to the Indus rivers. The 'Salal Approach', if it can be called that, however, also meant that the hydroelectric potential of the dam was downsized considerably and the project's life reduced because a lower dam height also meant higher silting. In the opinion of some power engineers, then and now, this was too high a price to pay for a bilateral agreement. Nevertheless, it was the view that prevailed then. In private conversations in India, this would be somewhat derisively termed the 'Salal complex', representing the lengths to which India could go to avoid involvement of foreign experts even when provided for under the Indus Waters Treaty. As we shall see the so-called 'Salal complex', prevailed for a quarter-century before it was finally exorcised.

There is, however, a final footnote to the Salal Agreement that illustrates how the present and the past often come together in the case of India and Pakistan. These events occurred late in December 2001. There was a mood of intense public anger in India following the attack on the Indian parliament by a terrorist group from Pakistan, which had made its way to Delhi through the LOC in J&K. Prime Minister Vajpayee and his government were under pressure to respond. The parliament attack took place soon after the 9/11 attack in New York, and the US military response in Afghanistan was an implicit benchmark for many in India, exasperated and exhausted by Pakistan's use of terrorist proxies through the 1990s. Suggestions and options were pouring in from all over the country on what would be an appropriate response. One that was gathering some traction was that India abrogate the Indus Waters Treaty. There were powerful voices supporting this course of action—for them the IWT was an extreme example of upper riparian generosity and Pakistan's present and past behaviour hardly merited such large-heartedness. A group of cabinet ministers was to meet to discuss different options on the table and the one point on which there was unanimity across India was that some strong response was required.

It was at this juncture in late December 2001 that Jagat Mehta, past eighty but still his old self, found his way to the office of the minister for external affairs and demanded to see Jaswant Singh. On finding that the minister was out, he left a message for the external affairs minister and asked that it be conveyed also to the prime minister: Abrogating the treaty would be a mistake for various reasons, including the fact that we were a lower riparian of China; but even more so we had not discarded the treaty either in 1965 or in 1971 in the face of equally grave provocation. Jagat Mehta's clinching argument was a more personal one: the prime minister was to be reminded that it was he who, putting aside political considerations, had signed the Salal Agreement reached by the Congress government and thereby had vindicated the Indus Waters Treaty. The message certainly reached the prime minister. Whether it was the reason cannot be said with certainty, but in the final menu of sanctions and measures decided against Pakistan, there was no reference to the Indus Waters Treaty or of using river water flow as part of a package of coercive diplomacy.[70] For Jagat Mehta, the decision was vindication that 'diplomacy has to have a long-term vision and, at times, override public opinion'.

Answering a question in the Lok Sabha in September 1980, P.V. Narasimha Rao, the foreign minister in the newly returned-to-power Congress government said regarding Jinnah House—a property in Bombay owned in the past by M.A. Jinnah: 'The property is at present leased out to the British High Commission and on expiry of the lease in December 1981 it is proposed to lease out this property to the Pakistan Embassy for use by their consulate.'[71]

Amongst the package of measures agreed to in the 1976 normalization 'breakthrough' was that India and Pakistan would open consulates in Bombay and Karachi respectively. While restoration of diplomatic relations and air links had been agreed to, the consulates were, to Jagat Mehta, a real step to 'gild the lily'.[72] His counterpart did not disagree but thought this step could wait a little. Possibly he also conveyed the expectation of getting M.A. Jinnah's old house in Bombay for their consulate or the residence of the consul general. During Vajpayee's visit to Pakistan in October 1978, opening of the consulates was announced. India's first consul general (CG) was in place in Karachi soon thereafter in December 1978.

Mani Shankar Aiyar was the first CG in Karachi from 1978 to 1981. At a time when public diplomacy was not a term used as frequently as it is now, he personified it in many ways. He was articulate, charming, considerate of Pakistani sentiments and indulgent, to a fault his detractors say, of their insecurities. With the passage of time his tenure as consul general has acquired for many in Pakistan a larger-than-life character as he attempted to meet the pent-up demand—in effect since 1965—for visas from the vast mohajir—the refugees from India—community in Sindh. He did so with consideration and good humour that is recalled with warmth to this day. No greater testimony to his functioning with great elan in an adverse environment can be provided than by the fact that even some three-and-a-half decades later any Indian diplomat occasionally visiting Karachi from Islamabad will first be asked about M.S. Aiyar and then be regaled with stories about him.

In retrospect, M.S. Aiyar's tenure exemplified an India–Pakistan moment during the tenure of the Janata Party government and Vajpayee's and Morarji Desai's initiatives as foreign minister and prime minister respectively.[73] If India's experience of the early years of the consulate in Karachi is a happy one, for Pakistan the Bombay experience is less so. Unlike the Indians, the Pakistanis in Bombay had to stay in a hotel and their efforts to purchase properties for staff and officers were unsuccessful. Jinnah House, contrary to the earlier understanding reached during A.B. Vajpayee's visit, was never leased to Pakistan. Pakistan's then ambassador to India, Abdul Sattar, recounted: 'After the house was vacated by the British High Commission, Indira Gandhi decided to refuse its lease to Pakistan.' He adds somewhat bitterly: 'Not for the first time was Pakistan to rue acceptance of an Indian undertaking on trust'.[74]

Why did Indira Gandhi reverse the decision regarding Jinnah House? Clearly, she would have been consulted on this from the start since the issue had first emerged during Jagat Mehta's visit in 1976 when she was the prime minister. We get a hint from the writer and journalist Khushwant Singh, a member of parliament in the early 1980s. 'Suddenly the Indian Government decided to go back on its word. ... That was Mrs Gandhi's personal decision and based on the fear that the house would become a place of pilgrimage for Pakistanis.'[75]

The Bombay consulate of Pakistan never had the same prestige as the Indian consulate in Karachi through the 1980s. For one, it lacked the infrastructure, in terms of office and residential space. The Indians moving into properties used to house the high commission from the 1950s, for instance, used to host a weekly Bollywood film in their in-house auditorium to packed audiences—hugely popular because Indian films were banned in Pakistan. But most of all, the Pakistani foreign office and its diplomats posted in India could never fully reconcile themselves to not operating from Jinnah House and anything else was seen as a let-down. It is not, therefore, surprising that despite years of searching they could never locate suitable alternative accommodation in Bombay for their consulate or the consul general.

Both consulates existed till 1994, when they were finally closed—Pakistan closed its consulate voluntarily and then ordered India to wind up from Karachi. Throughout their existence both remained vulnerable to the vicissitudes of the relationship. The Indian consulate had, primarily because of the demand for visas, a high profile in the social and cultural life of Karachi. It faced progressively more stringent constraints till its final closure. In 1992, after the demolition of the Babri Masjid in India, its personnel faced the full fury of local mobs as the consul general's residence was attacked and ransacked and his family barely escaped with their lives.

The simultaneous opening of the consulates was for divided families in both countries a visible sign that pragmatic arrangements between India and Pakistan were possible. The limitations on their working and the constant pressure under which both consulates worked, however, illustrated that this opening too was vulnerable and fragile. Perhaps, residence in Jinnah House may have created for the Government of Pakistan stakes in Bombay it never developed.

So, what was so special about Jinnah House? Built by Jinnah in 1936 with no expenses spared, it was his favourite residence although he had other houses too. Perhaps for this reason it strikes a chord in Pakistan in a way Jinnah's many other residences—in Delhi, Lahore, and Karachi—do not. Post-1947, Jinnah had even spoken of returning to Bombay to live in it, most famously to the then Indian high commissioner in Pakistan.[76] This is taken as evidence by many in Pakistan that Jinnah never anticipated that in the future India–Pakistan relations would take the path they did. The property was declared evacuee property—belonging to those who had left the country and therefore now vesting in the state—in 1948 as were hundreds of thousands of others in both countries. Its legal status was not a live issue till Vajpayee travelled to Pakistan in 1978 and embarked on an ambitious agenda of normalization.

But it would be too easy to see the Jinnah House issue as simply one of intergovernmental differences, for in so doing its metaphorical value would be misunderstood. M.A. Jinnah had left a will in 1939 in which he bequeathed Jinnah House to his sister Fatima Jinnah who later also accompanied him to Pakistan. In doing so, he deliberately overlooked the claim of his daughter Dina Wadia who did not go to Pakistan. His daughter was not disinherited and the will handsomely provided for her. But he did not leave his beloved Bombay mansion to her—possibly a sign of his displeasure that she had married outside the faith. In any event, Fatima Jinnah was allotted another property in Karachi in lieu of Jinnah House. This was the procedure followed in the tens of thousands of similar cases of persons who moved in either direction and then sought compensation from their new country for properties left behind.

Once the lease of the British high commission had ended in the early 1980s, Dina Wadia also staked a claim to the house. Indira Gandhi, no doubt familiar with the whole background, said the property now belonged to the Government of India and these matters could not be decided on grounds of sentiment. After the matter lay dormant for two decades, Dina Wadia pressed her case again and the matter is now with the Bombay High Court. There are some in India who feel that restoring the property to her is an appropriate riposte to Jinnah's two-nation theory: his only daughter chose not to be a Pakistani national and his only grandson is an Indian citizen and owner of one of India's prominent corporate houses.

Others feel that Jinnah's last wishes, as expressed in his will, should be respected. He was categorical that the property must not pass to his daughter. The Government of Pakistan is not a party to these proceedings but is evidently a careful observer. If the property passes to Dina Wadia and her descendants, the chances of Pakistan ever being able to use it will recede even further. As long as it is with the Government of India, the possibility, howsoever remote, remains that at some stage something else can still be worked out.

The matter of reopening of the Mumbai and Karachi consulates resurfaced in 2004 during a major thaw in the India–Pakistan relationship. President General Musharraf then revived the older request for Jinnah House for use of their consulate. Given the past background, he did not get a positive reply. Although a formal decision on reopening the two consulates was agreed upon, as in the 1980s, without the symbolism of Jinnah House in Mumbai, there was not enough on the plate to whet Pakistan's appetite for opening a consulate. The initiative, therefore, petered out when Pakistan finally did not accord permission to the reopening of the Indian consulate in Karachi.

The Jinnah House case has similarities to the parallel case of the properties of the raja of Mahmudabad in India, although the legal framework of each is different. Mohammad Amir Ahmad Khan, the raja of Mahmudabad, was one of the principal supporters of M.A. Jinnah and the Muslim League in the 1930s and '40s. Post-Partition, he left for Pakistan although his wife and infant son stayed back or were left behind in India. His properties in India were taken over by the 'custodian of enemy property' after the 1965 war but litigation has continued since then as his son, the legal heir and an Indian national, has claimed them back from the state. Both cases thus pertain to claims by progeny, who remained in India or chose not to go to Pakistan, of two leading protagonists of Partition.

The commonsensical question that arises is whether the act of persons leaving India for Pakistan extinguishes all their rights—and those of their children—to property in India. Posing the question in this manner may lead to one set of answers. On the other hand, the question also is of the burden of responsibility of the leading advocates of Partition for its intended or unintended consequences. There were also many others who left India in 1947 and consciously did not make any claims on their properties left behind, either for themselves or for their relatives. Two conspicuous examples stand out. The first prime minister of Pakistan, Liaqat Ali Khan, left behind a large estate in Uttar Pradesh and does not appear to have sought compensatory allotments from his government in Pakistan. He gifted his house in Delhi to the Pakistan government for use as their high commission. It—*the Gul-i-Rana*, named after his wife Rana—remains the residence of the Pakistan high commissioner in Delhi. The eldest daughter and legal heir of the nawab of Bhopal similarly consciously chose Pakistan—leaving behind, incidentally without any regret, the claim of being the begum or ruler of Bhopal and a large personal estate. She too did not strongly pursue compensation in Pakistan either for herself or for her son—the future foreign secretary of Pakistan, Shaharyar Khan—and was awarded a bare fraction of what was possibly due to her.[77] India–Pakistan property tangles, thus, have many dimensions—much like the relationship itself. At one end is a straightforward intergovernmental conflict as in the case of the Hyderabad Funds Case. There are, however, other more personal claims such as those over Jinnah House or the Mahmudabad Estate, and these are more difficult to take a final or definite view on; and this perhaps explains the long and inconclusive litigation that has continued over them.

The 1977–79 period stands out for positives, which had been missing for a long time: the resumption of cultural events, the better atmospherics, the resumption of cricketing ties, the opening of the consulates and, finally, the Salal Agreement. There were, of course, recurrent discordant notes: statements on Kashmir emanating from Pakistan being one. But there were even stronger views in India regarding the continued Pakistani statements on the condition of Muslims and the communal situation in India. Speaking to a special envoy of President Zia in May 1979, Morarji Desai commented in exasperation on the Pakistan foreign secretary Agha Shahi: 'He never seems to open his mouth without condemning India.'[78] The discordant notes, seemingly serious momentarily, were however, limited in impact because of the larger process of normalization that was under way. After receiving a clear signal that India would not object, Pakistan successfully applied to join the Non-Aligned Movement (NAM) and President Zia attended its Havana summit in September 1979. To the disappointment of many in India, but not unexpectedly, he referred in his formal speech at the summit, to a settlement of Jammu and Kashmir in accordance with the resolutions of the United Nations but also threw in the spirit of the Simla Agreement for good measure.

How do we evaluate the thaw from 1977 to 1979—the Pakistan policy of India's first non-Congress government? To its supporters, a new political leadership in India meant more balanced, perhaps less hawkish, perceptions of Pakistan. Pragmatism and greater understanding certainly guided both governments, notwithstanding perceived provocations in both directions—but especially from Pakistan.

However, other views in India, over the years, on the Janata Party government's Pakistan policy have been less charitable. This was only a 'surrealistic thaw' as both went through a 'minuet of manifesting good intentions and giving some content to it at the public level' while in terms of realpolitik nothing had changed. The thaw was, therefore, an illusion—misplaced optimism of India and a tactical exercise by Pakistan to deal with the isolation consequent to the Zia coup and then the execution of Zulfiqar Ali Bhutto.[79] Implicit also in this view is that the Janata Party government was superficial and assumed that with good intentions and transparency things may actually improve.

So, is this a fair assessment? In contrast, it is useful to see how Jagat Mehta, the then foreign secretary, recalled the period.[80] In his view the thaw was an example of successful bipartisanship in India—initiated by the Congress and Indira Gandhi and continued by the Janata Party, Atal Bihari Vajpayee and Morarji Desai. The process, therefore, dated not to 1977 but began in 1976 and was inherited by the Janata Party government, which took it forward. The Salal Agreement was reached during Indira Gandhi's tenure as prime minister and adhered to by the subsequent government. As such, the change in government in India may well have made some difference but the substance of the approach was already there.

Such debates are a variant of the perennial hawk-vs-dove syndrome and approach, and will continue about the 1977–79 'thaw' and indeed about other periods of India–Pakistan history. Howsoever one analyses the bilateral moves begun in 1976, both countries were by 1979 moving into turbulent times. In India, the wobbly Janata Party coalition lurched from one crisis to the next and increasingly lacked conviction. The appeal of the Congress and especially of Indira Gandhi grew as the excesses of the Emergency appeared remote when compared to a government which appeared unable to function. Morarji Desai's resignation in July 1979 was the final act of the drama as elections loomed ahead.

Pakistan's polity and society was undergoing even more fundamental changes and Bhutto's execution in April 1979 was the most dramatic illustration of this. In a decision that was controversial then and remains so up to this day the Government of India under Prime Minister Morarji Desai remained silent as Bhutto was hanged. Indira Gandhi, then only the leader of the Congress party and in the opposition, had written to President Zia that Bhutto's life be spared, but the official silence in India through the final proceedings and after the execution was deafening.

These developments in India and Pakistan were accompanied by larger changes in the region. The overthrow of the Shah and the Shiite revolution in Iran in January–February 1979, and the Chinese attack on Vietnam in February 1979 meant that in West and South-East Asia there were new realities impacting South Asia. These new realities manifested themselves in various ways. One dramatic illustration was the seizure of the grand mosque in Mecca in Saudi Arabia in November–December 1979 by Sunni radicals. The siege ended after two weeks with hundreds of fatalities. Ayatollah Khomeini, the new revolutionary supreme leader of Iran, predictably blamed the US. This contributed to the wave of anti-Americanism that swept through large parts of the Islamic world and especially in Pakistan. The US embassy in Islamabad was attacked and burnt by a mob. At this very time, the Soviet invasion of Afghanistan changed the situation in South Asia even more fundamentally.

All these factors impacted on India–Pakistan relations directly and indirectly. The Chinese invasion of Vietnam had followed the installation of the Heng Samrin government in Kampuchea (Cambodia) after Vietnamese troops had thrown out the murderous Pol Pot regime. The Soviets supported the Vietnamese action, the Chinese and the US opposed it. These developments and the Soviet invasion of Afghanistan coincided in India with strong criticism by the Congress that under the Janata Party government the close ties with the Soviet Union, India's traditional friend, had eroded. The Soviet invasion of Afghanistan on 25 December 1979 coincided with the mid-term general election process in India and was barely a week before Indira Gandhi was declared elected. She formed her government a few days later. Whatever may have been her and her government's internal doubts about the Soviet invasion, her public position was seen as tilting towards, even if not being fully supportive of, the Soviet Union and in the opposite camp as far as the United States was concerned. Thereafter, in July 1980, India recognized the Heng Samrin government in Kampuchea—again putting it on the same side as the Soviet Bloc. Pakistan was arrayed on the opposite side, the Soviet invasion giving it a new primacy in US policies. The cold war had re-entered the subcontinent much as it had in 1971 although it would take a few years for its effect to be fully manifest.

But setting aside the political and the diplomatic, and beyond the fast pace of events from the late 1970s, was there some more significant process at work? Many in India then certainly thought so, believing that in the decade-and-a-half since 1965 something fundamental had changed in Pakistan. In this view, the long process of even partial restoration of pre-1965 linkages, military defeat and the loss of East Pakistan in 1971, the reversion to military rule in 1977, the execution of Zulfikar Ali Bhutto and the changed international and regional context had all cumulatively led to a change in Pakistani perceptions—both about itself and about India. This view formed the parameters of what appears to be, in hindsight at least, a debate of some intensity in India about Pakistan.

The re-establishment of diplomatic relations since 1976 and a greater frequency in intellectual contacts catalysed this introspection and discussion. It was, overall, Delhi-led and Delhi-centred—a wider national debate was still in the future. What also contributed to it was President Zia's evident intention to be accessible to visiting Indians, which also had the effect of making the Government of Pakistan appear more open to Indian views and questions. Relatively larger number of Indians also travelled to Pakistan at this time, often for longish periods, and pondered over the question of whether something had changed and if so, what had. Certainly, a real effort was made to invite prominent intellectuals and writers to visit Pakistan to see for themselves the changes which had taken place. Many did so and candidly recorded their views later, contributing to this debate in Delhi.

Some who did, like Pran Chopra, knew Pakistan well. Hailing from pre-1947 Lahore, he personally knew many people in Pakistan, and as an accomplished and respected journalist and editor had closely followed developments there for years. He wrote in 1981: 'India's more intimate neighbour whose life intermeshes with India's life as capillaries do in living tissue, is making basic revaluations about itself.' What this meant was that 'Pakistan in a very healthy sense', has 'turned its thinking process upside down'.[81] Pran Chopra's view also was that 'Indian recognition of this change in Pakistan is incomplete as yet'.

Such views found resonance among other scholars and journalists who travelled in Pakistan around this time. The academic Bashiruddin Ahmed spent some two weeks there in September–October 1980.[82] In trying to understand the prevailing public mood and attitudes, Ahmed realized that he had no 'benchmark to help me assess the degree of change in Pakistan today' as his last visits were as far back as 1948 and 1949. But he had been in touch with some Pakistani academics and scholars when he met them in conferences and universities abroad. So, what were the attitudes he found changed? The first change was in the confidence which the Ayub decade had bestowed in the Pakistan elite, a sense of triumphalism on account of the 'victory in 1965' and, along with it, a 'condescending sympathy' for post-Nehru India. This was a view Bashiruddin Ahmed was familiar with and expected to encounter again. He says he came across instead a 'deep sense of disappointment and strong sense of alienation' with the direction Pakistan had taken and with the present regime. He found also a 'widespread desire for friendship with India' and this sentiment coexisted with 'the fear and suspicion that India has not yet abandoned its desire to undo the partition, or at least to further weaken Pakistan'.

Another highly regarded scholar, Bimal Prasad, stayed in Karachi for a month in December–January 1981.[83] The dominant impression left in his mind was one of a 'widely felt desire among its people for friendly contact with India'. He also noted that 'it is paradoxical but true that the emergence of Bangladesh has given a considerable push to this tendency'. A journalist, Ajit Bhattacharjea, visiting Pakistan in 1981 had, as the good reporter he was, perceptively prepared himself against being misled by his own subjective assessments: 'Nostalgia can be mistaken for a desire for political union. Politeness can be misinterpreted similarly for agreement. The common cultural inheritance of the subcontinent makes it impolite to express a sharply contrary opinion; at best, it is indicated by a turn of phrase or gesture.' Nevertheless, his conclusion was 'the change in Pakistan is unmistakable especially to those who have visited the country before'. Comparing his fortnight-long stay in September–October 1981 with a visit in 1967, he commented: 'The only thing in common between my visit then and my later visit was the hospitality of my hosts and the nostalgia expressed by those I met. For Pakistani attitudes, official and private, even in 1967 were the same as those that had led to the conflict of 1965' and 'there was no mistaking the determination one found in Pakistan to seize Kashmir, by force if necessary'. For Bhattacharjea then '... a historic change had occurred in Pakistan and has been reported by visitors from India in the face of scepticism and hostility from those who cannot, or find it inexpedient to, visualize an altered political relationship between the two countries.' The break-up of Pakistan, the revolution in Iran and the Soviet forces in Afghanistan meant a 'moment of truth for Pakistan'. This was a 'gut change'—and a logical outcome of the agonizing reappraisals Pakistanis had been forced to undertake of their place in the subcontinent in the past decade. It was to him precisely why 'so many Indians, with varying political views come to conclusions that differ from those propagated by their Government'.[84]

Another veteran journalist's point of comparison in a 1981 visit was a two-month stay in Pakistan in 1962. Inderjit's visit after nineteen years had him describe a military dictatorship as milder than what he had witnessed in Indonesia or Egypt, and Islamization as 'unpopular with the liberal and educated classes and the rich', but an overwhelming section of women and the common people 'seemed to appreciate Gen. Zia's efforts to subscribe to moral and ethical values...' But most of all, for Inderjit it was the 'popular mood' that showed a heart-warming change. In 1961 'every Pakistani' not only asserted his separate nationality but also language, culture and heritage. 'Hindu India' was shunned in talk. This time, however, the contrast Inderjit found was 'they talked freely of a common culture, common background and common heritage. Some prominent public men even talked of a common destiny.'[85]

Mani Shankar Aiyar, India's first consul general in Karachi from 1977 to 1980, writing in December 1981 similarly noted:

> Whereas before 1971 the votaries of armed conflict with India were in an overwhelming and vocal majority at all levels of Pakistan society, today they are in a small and muted minority. ... while the best definition of a Pakistani still remains 'one who is not an Indian', the prospect of conflict with India generates not excitement and the conviction of victory but fear and apprehension of the certainty of defeat.[86]

These views were grounded in the specific context of President Zia's outreach to public and political opinion in India as those who advanced them recognized. They have also as background the 1977–79 'thaw' in India–Pakistan relations. Nevertheless, the originators of these views saw them as also having a general validity and they possibly had also received some larger resonance in India even as they were contested by others. How this squared with emerging realities as the 1980s progressed is what we will see next.

6

Dissidents and Crisis

THE YEAR 1979 SAW the re-entry of the cold war into the subcontinent. The coincidence of the Soviet invasion of Afghanistan and the return of Indira Gandhi as prime minister is striking but the end of the Janata Party interregnum did not imply an immediate change in India–Pakistan relations. On the contrary, both governments tried hard to maintain the earlier momentum set during the Morarji–Vajpayee period. Special envoys from Zia-ul-Haq to Indira Gandhi and vice versa, ministerial visits and official-level meetings were numerous. President Zia, with Bhutto's execution to put behind him, had the most reason to reach out. But Indira Gandhi and the Congress government, aware of the high marks scored by their predecessor on the 'relations with Pakistan' test, also did not want to be accused of letting things regress. So, in the period after early 1980 there was no dearth of contacts, discussions and planning towards moving forward.

But there were several underlying problems. First and foremost was Afghanistan where differing political assessments and a deep residue of suspicion meant a further hardening of lines between India and Pakistan. For Pakistan, the Soviet invasion meant it was now squeezed between an unfriendly Soviet Union and an old enemy. In one account, Pakistan was now exposed 'to the nightmare of an Indo-Soviet nut cracker' and reaction to the invasion was 'visceral'.[1] Less than a decade after Bangladesh, this appeared as a real threat. To many others its psychological ramifications were even greater with the memories of Afghanistan refusing to recognize Pakistan's entry into the United Nations and its refusal to accept the Durand Line. The good relations between India and the political forces that Badshah Khan represented in the North-West Frontier Province of Pakistan added to this sense of insecurity. There was, in addition, the burden of a million refugees from Afghanistan and the number increased steadily to about three million by the end of the 1980s.[2] As a burden, incidentally, this was in proportionate terms more than, or at least equivalent to, the burden of refugees from East Pakistan in India in 1971.

Secondly, there was the accumulation of evidence in India that the supporting roots of a spreading militancy in the Indian state of Punjab lay in Pakistan. On the other hand, growing US assistance to Pakistan, especially fighter aircraft and armaments, added to Indian concerns that Pakistan would use Afghanistan to leverage its new relationship with the Western alliance to build up military capabilities for eventual use against India. As militancy and terrorism in Punjab grew, very few in India harboured illusions that Pakistan was going to simply walk away from the 1971 humiliation. Finally, there was Kashmir, quiet otherwise, but with Pakistani statements and Indian rejoinders always having the potential for upsets elsewhere.

Pakistan's fear of another India–USSR combination like in 1971 and Indian distrust of Pakistan arming itself with US largess were formidable hurdles. Sardar Swaran Singh was in Islamabad in April 1980 as a special envoy of Indira Gandhi's new government and he tried hard to reassure President Zia that India had its own difficulties with the Soviet invasion. Why seek US assistance to shore up its western borders with Afghanistan when India had no desire to act in concert with the Soviet Union to squeeze Pakistan? He then went on to make the following offer to President Zia:

> We know, as a matter of fact, that in 1965 and 1971 when things were boiling you withdrew your divisions from your western frontier. Zahid Shah told us and later Daoud told us the same thing. Now a situation has arisen when we can do for you what the Afghans then did for you. If your eastern front is secure you will get much more security than what $200 million can buy ... Cannot the same strength be achieved by talking to us? You can remove your Divisions from our frontier.[3]

President Zia's response was equally candid:

> It is (an) idea but it is (a) question of basic confidence ... We are reminded of the connivance with the Soviet Union which halved Pakistan. That is history which is difficult to forget even though we are trying to do so but there are bitter memories. How can Pakistan go to India and say that as we have been attacked by Afghanistan and we would like to draw Divisions then from the Indian frontier?[4]

Clearly in Zia's eyes the suggestion was impractical. Later in April 1980, General Zia and Indira Gandhi met in Salisbury, Rhodesia. By most accounts, the meeting did not go well. Before the meeting some newspapers had published some, possibly uncharitable, remarks about India by President Zia. One account of the meeting which gained a certain currency at the time goes: 'Indira Gandhi, however, was all smiles and courtesy when he arrived. "Madam, please do not believe everything that you read in the newspapers" was Zia's opening gambit. "Of course not," replied Mrs Gandhi. "After all, aren't they calling you a democrat and me a dictator?"'[5]

Apparently during the meeting President Zia also spoke frequently of his 'understandings with Desai Sahib' leading to Indira Gandhi commenting: 'You do not seem to realize that Mr Desai is no longer in charge of our government.'[6]

President Zia was later to say to the Indian ambassador, Natwar Singh, 'I succeeded in breaking the ice with Morarji Desai, but I am sorry to say, I have not been able to establish rapport with Mrs Gandhi. When I met her at Salisbury, I tried to explain to her, but she has continued with her suspicions and reservations.'[7]

If a large part of the differences was related to Afghanistan, support to terrorism in Punjab, Kashmir and Zia's references to communal rioting in Moradabad in India were other factors that were at play. The flow of arms to Pakistan from the US was also the cause of much alarm in India especially seen in the context of, and with memories of, the 1965 conflict. Indira Gandhi's dramatic return to power and the larger-than-life space she occupied then in Pakistan's perceptions of India had also a role in this growing cocktail of mistrust and suspicion. Her reputation in the Pakistan foreign office on Kashmir was of a person who was single-minded and not open to discussion. Thus, comments made by President Zia to an Indian journalist in March 1981 comparing Vajpayee, Morarji

Desai and Indira Gandhi were hardly likely to endear him to her. On the issue of Kashmir, Zia described Vajpayee as 'very understanding', one who 'accepted that there was a problem'; and, 'Mr Desai, I must say is a very able statesman. Also, merciful and sympathetic.' Zia described Indira Gandhi, in contrast, as 'very allergic' and someone unable to understand why, despite the Simla Agreement, Pakistan raised the Kashmir issue in international platforms. Zia thus described his meeting with Indira Gandhi in Salisbury as warm but 'interjected by a few bouts of allergies here and there'.[8] Indira Gandhi on her part, in an interview with visiting Pakistani journalists in July 1980 had cryptically commented while conveying good wishes to the people of Pakistan that 'I feel concerned about their welfare'.[9] When asked about a meeting with President Zia her response was: 'In the near future I am not going anywhere at all. For the time being our foreign minister has accepted the invitation to visit Pakistan.'[10]

Despite these less than auspicious signs, both governments tried, through 1980 and 1981, to introduce and strengthen normalization measures. Indian foreign minister Narasimha Rao visited Pakistan in June 1981 and in substance said much the same things as had been articulated by Vajpayee during his visit in 1978. In a speech in Karachi he spoke of India and Pakistan's destinies being 'interlinked' and the need 'to undertake a deliberate and conscious transformation of our respective psyches'.[11] The intention was clearly to try and reassure Pakistan that India was not going to pile up pressure to add to the difficulties it faced because of the Afghanistan situation. The Pakistan foreign minister Agha Shahi also visited India in February 1982. Both foreign offices exchanged draft agreements on a 'Treaty of Peace and Friendship' and decided on setting up a joint commission—a normal diplomatic forum for exploring cooperation between countries. This was a routine step as far as most bilateral relationships go but in the India–Pakistan context was and is seen by optimists as an important first step in at least thinking about a more 'normal relationship'.

These steps could signal to the diplomatic world the beginnings of a process. But there were other signs that showed many differences which would not be so easily papered over. Pakistan had left the Commonwealth in 1972 protesting Bangladesh being admitted as a member. After the Soviet invasion of Afghanistan, the Commonwealth's Western members led by the UK expectedly sought to get Pakistan back in the organization. Zia and his government were understandably keen as this would be a further step in burying 1971 and, more significantly, the sense of international isolation that had followed the execution of Bhutto. There was as element of anticipation that just as Morarji Desai had facilitated, or at least not obstructed, Pakistan's entry into the Non-Aligned Movement in September 1979, Indira Gandhi would act similarly in this case. It was, however, not to be.

The Indian put-down was, in fact, almost brutal and the Ministry of External Affairs in stating India's official position only paraphrased and repeated what Indira Gandhi said a little earlier in a press interview. There had to be set criteria for countries wishing to re-enter—this was an obvious enough procedural ploy to prolong consideration of this matter. More to the heart was her view that 'membership of the Commonwealth is based on an expression of public opinion. There is no forum in Pakistan which can express itself on this question'. And finally was the fact that 'it has been India's experience that Pakistan has used all such international forums repeatedly to raise bilateral issues'.[12]

Notwithstanding this snub, discussions and visits continued. Some positive expectations focused on the two specific areas in hand—the joint commission and a non-aggression and non-use of force agreement, in other words, a peace and friendship treaty. While differences between the two sides on the latter were numerous, it at least appeared that there was scope to think of a formal agreement of this kind to supplement the Simla Agreement. During Agha Shahi's February 1982 visit, it was agreed that a draft agreement would be discussed by the foreign secretaries and the Indian foreign secretary would visit Pakistan for the purpose.

If all this appeared to suggest a situation of stability, appearances can be deceptive. In a Human Rights Commission meeting in Geneva, also in February 1982, the Pakistan ambassador Agha Hilaly, a former Pakistan high commissioner in Delhi and brother of the foreign minister Agha Shahi, made critical comments about India and J&K, equating Kashmir with Palestine. Indira Gandhi, seething in any case at Zia's occasional comments on Kashmir which she felt violated the spirit of Simla, now was convinced that some line had to be drawn. Possibly she felt that the Janata Party government had not been firm enough with Pakistan in this regard, although such statements in the UN and other international fora had been made by Pakistan even in the 1973–76 period when the Congress was in power.

In the event, the scheduled foreign secretary's meeting was postponed: India was trying to lay down a red line or at the minimum was sending a strong signal where it came to Pakistani statements on Kashmir in international fora. In Pakistan, the reaction was that India had used the statements made in Geneva as a pretext since these points had been made before; it was uninterested in normalizing the relationship in any manner. The setback was, however, only temporary. By May, the foreign ministers were again in touch and in June an Indian delegation was in Pakistan to pick up the process where it had been interrupted. Other visits followed and among the issues under discussion were the minutiae of the friendship treaty.

As in the past, and indeed in the future, the keenness to engage purposefully is demonstrated by the capacity to ignore or pass over acts which would otherwise have been deemed highly provocative. Between September 1981 and August 1982 there were three hijackings of Indian aircraft. In September 1981, an Indian Airlines aircraft on a Srinagar–Delhi flight was forcibly taken to Lahore by Sikh extremists. Pakistan security successfully terminated the hijacking, arresting the hijackers and securing the safe release of the passengers, crew and aircraft. The Indian cabinet commended the action and thanked the Government of Pakistan for the steps it took. The fly in the ointment, not ignored but not also made a big issue of at the time, was the five hijackers themselves. They were not handed over for trial in India; Pakistan's position being that they would be tried under its law. The question of extradition, much as in the case of Dakoo Bhupat as far back as the early 1950s, would remain too problematic an issue to be addressed.

Two of the hijackers were finally sentenced to life by a Pakistani court. Two others were, after serving their sentence, deported to India in 2000 to face judicial action again. The main ringleader was, however, not deported. On the whole, this was a repeat of the September 1976 hijacking, notwithstanding the fact that the first was by Kashmiri extremists and the latest by Sikh extremists. In August 1982, there were two more hijacking attempts but in both these cases the Pakistani authorities refused to let the aircraft land in Lahore. The Government of India was to thank Pakistan for its action in preventing the landing and thus pre-empting what would have otherwise become another security nightmare involving safety of passengers.

The high point of the engagement with Pakistan during Indira Gandhi's second term was a four-hour stopover by President Zia in Delhi en route to Indonesia in November 1982. This was the first visit by a head of state from Pakistan since the 1972 Simla Agreement. The Indian foreign secretary M.K. Rasgotra recollects that it produced 'much goodwill'. Shortly thereafter, a senior Pakistani minister attended the closing ceremony of the Asian Games in Delhi. The Asian Games also witnessed an India–Pakistan hockey final in which, Rasgotra recollects, 'the Indian hockey team was roundly thrashed by the Pakistan team. We were making progress!' [13]

If President Zia's brief stopover in Delhi was generally welcomed in India, there were some critical voices too. P.N. Haksar, some would say the key architect of Simla Agreement but now no longer in Prime Minister Gandhi's favour, was one of them. According to Rasgotra again, he wrote to Indira Gandhi an 'extraordinary letter criticizing her decision to shake hands with Bhutto's murderer'. Indira Gandhi herself was dismissive of this view: 'He is living in the past.'[14]

Zia was to visit Delhi again some four months later for the NAM summit. In his address to the gathering, Zia made only a single reference to Kashmir—that of seeking 'a just settlement to the problem of J&K'. There was a perfunctory response from India later that 'the question was of the return of Kashmir territory under Pakistan's occupation' and that the Simla Agreement precluded raising bilateral matters in international forums.

If things then appeared to be on course, this was a chimera and in a few months things began to unravel. Three separate sets of issues overlapped and this convergence was too much of a burden for bilateral diplomacy alone to bear. These were: the 'Movement for the Restoration of Democracy in Pakistan'; the growing interest of both armies in the Siachen glacier; and the continued militancy and terrorism in Punjab in India with evidence of Pakistani support and instigation too overwhelming to be ignored. The ongoing discussion on the draft treaty of friendship and non-aggression or the joint commission was far too narrow a base to limit the fallout, which resulted from these three factors.

By mid-1983, President Zia-ul-Haq had been in power for almost six years. The Pakistani political class led by Benazir Bhutto and the Pakistan Peoples Party was restive. The 'Movement for the Restoration of Democracy' (MRD) was launched on 14 August 1983 and this became a platform for agitation against President Zia and the military government. Concentrated mainly in Sindh, it nevertheless did get support from the aged 'Frontier Gandhi' Badshah Khan. Alongside the PPP-led political movement against Zia's military dictatorship were other streams, such as Sindh demands for greater autonomy and recognition of their cultural and linguistic identity. There was also restiveness in Balochistan and many protagonists of Baloch nationalism found refuge in Afghanistan, whose government, dominated by the Soviet Union, had its own scores to settle with the Pakistan authorities.

From mid-1983 onwards, the front pages of prominent Indian newspapers were extensively covering the anti-Zia agitation in Sindh.[15] To many, history appeared to be repeating itself, 'a rerun of the film made during the 1968-69 turmoil that brought down Field Marshal Ayub Khan'.[16] Rumours of repressive measures used by the Pakistan Army, widespread arrests and fatalities were regularly reported and commented on. The India factor in Sindh acquired an unusual prominence when in late August 1983 both Foreign Minister Narasimha Rao and Prime Minister Indira Gandhi commented in detail on the Sindh situation.[17] The foreign minister spoke in parliament with reference to the concern expressed by the members of parliament about the detention of Badshah Khan. The prime minister spoke in a meeting of the ruling Congress party. Both sets of remarks were enveloped in denials of interfering in Pakistan's internal affairs but the purport was clear enough.

There are two versions of what Indira Gandhi said in an All India Congress Committee meeting in August 1983.[18] A sanitized version is: 'The people of Pakistan had long been demanding democracy and struggling for it. While we were sad at the total situation in that country and could not close our eyes at what happened (there) we had no desire to interfere.' This sanitized version was adequate for the purpose intended, but what she had actually said had been headlined in Indian newspapers and included references to the hanging of Zulfikar Ali Bhutto, the 'torture of Begum Nusrat Bhutto', the treatment of Badshah Khan, etc. Inevitably, strong Pakistani protests followed. Indira Gandhi followed up with a letter to President Zia about Badshah Khan: the parliament of India, she wrote, 'is greatly concerned at his detention' and hoped for his release. President Zia's reply was terse and referred to her 'distinct lack of regard for the principle of non-interference'.[19]

Indira Gandhi's comments acted, of course, as a signal to her own party. Demonstrations by Congress workers outside the Pakistan high commission and a 'Vishwa Sindhi Sammelan' seminar in October 1983 at whose inauguration both the president and the prime minister were present and in which Congress MPs participated, all contributed to the atmospherics of this time.[20]

Also Indira Gandhi's interest in the Sindh agitation was much talked about within India, analysed and even disputed. Former prime minister Charan Singh and former foreign minister Vajpayee strongly criticized this approach even as the Pakistan government protested that 'a new doctrine of interference' was being enunciated.[21] Certainly, many in India also saw a new approach. Girilal Jain, editor of *The Times of India* commented sarcastically that the 'Government of India must possess an extraordinary capacity for being surprised, if it is indeed surprised, over the Government of Pakistan's protests.'[22]

So, what led to this course of action? First, evidence was growing that Pakistani intelligence agencies were deeply involved in assisting Khalistani terrorists and extremists in Punjab. India repeatedly complained to the Pakistan government only to be met with predictable but strenuous denials. The Punjab situation had come to occupy an increasingly large political space in India. To many, it was almost axiomatic that Pakistan would fan the flames in Punjab, if for no other reason than to avenge the loss of East Pakistan. Apart from the Punjab militancy, it was the US entry into the subcontinent through the Afghanistan situation that also concerned India. Keeping great powers out of the subcontinent was an Indian priority and its centrality is in no way diminished by the fact that this was rarely articulated bluntly as a policy objective. Indira Gandhi's motives for her remarks about democracy in Pakistan were analysed in media at that time and many suggested that this was the primary motive: 'In his pronouncements General Zia has been quite friendly. But he has brought back the United States as an active force in the region and secured highly sophisticated weapons from it which have made it obligatory for us to modernize our armed forces in a big way at the cost of straining our resources.'[23]

President Zia's personal diplomatic skills of trying to convince important Indians of his genuine desire to promote friendly relations could often disarm many. 'As president, he would address every visitor as "sir" and at the end of the meeting, would not only escort the visitor to the car, but also hold the door open for him'. This 'display of humility and courteousness' could disarm many. During a visit to Islamabad, George Fernandes, formerly a cabinet minister in Morarji Desai's government and a prominent trade unionist, had been saying that when he meets the president he would insist on a meeting with Benazir Bhutto, then under detention. 'However, on return, he was instead full of praise for the president who had addressed him as "sir" and sought his views on handling trade unions, and we got the distinct impression that he had not pressed for a meeting with Benazir.'[24] Others were less easy to please. During the NAM summit in March 1983 in Delhi, President Zia called on the then president of India, Zail Singh, and expressed his desire for peace with India. Zail Singh replied in Punjabi 'that a woman cannot do two things at the same time—*Akh bhi maare, taay gunghat bhi kaddae.*' (She cannot wink provocatively and cover her face at the same time).[25] While laughter all round accompanied this comment, both the Indians and the Pakistanis present knew precisely what was implied.

We get an unusual dissident Pakistani perspective of this time through a husband and wife from Sindh who chose exile in India to escape possible imprisonment in Pakistan. The noted Urdu poetess and novelist Fahmida Riaz and her husband Zafar Ali Ujjan with their two small children lived in exile in India from March 1981 till the end of 1987. Leaving Pakistan became necessary on account of sedition charges being pressed on them for advocacy through their writings of support of the executed Zulfikar Ali Bhutto and his daughter Benazir and in general against Zia's martial law. An invitation to Fahmida Riaz to participate in an Urdu mushaira in Delhi became the means by which this exile began. In India, the famous poetess Amrita Pritam acquainted Indira

Gandhi directly of the plight of the couple. Fahmida Riaz was thereafter appointed as 'poet in residence' in the Jamia Millia University and the family was to stay in a guest house of the university. Ali Ujjan was also given a research appointment.[26]

Zafar Ali Ujjan has written about his stay in India and the considerable acquaintance he developed with the country's political leadership. Apart from occasional meetings with Indira Gandhi, others he met included Giani Zail Singh, the Union home minister in the early years of his stay in India, P.N. Haksar, Indira Gandhi's former principal adviser, K. Subrahmanyam, the leading strategic analyst, G. Parthasarathy, then chairman of the Policy Planning Division in the MEA, communist leaders such as Harkishen Singh Surjeet and E.M.S. Namboodiripad apart from numerous journalists, political leaders, poets and writers. Despite their exile status and existence, Ali Ujjan and Fahmida Riaz were thus well connected with political and literary circles in India. They travelled extensively across India with Ali Ujjan delivering lectures in different cities on the need for India to support the people of Pakistan against martial rule. He encountered enthusiastic audiences and possibly this had much to do with the fact that Pakistanis in exile in India and on a lecture circuit were relatively rare.

The response he received was, however, somewhat disappointing to him. Writing about an audience in Ulhasnagar, a concentration near Bombay of 1947 Sindhi refugees from Pakistan, Ali Ujjan observed: 'I was convinced that among Sindhis, I was welcome as a Sindhi not as a democrat from Pakistan.'[27] Similarly invited to speak to the Institute of Defence Studies and Analysis—an important government think tank—by its director K. Subrahmanyam in 1981 Ali Ujjan was equally disappointed: 'All listened with rapt attention but when they asked questions, no question was about democracy. Everyone wanted to know about the Islamic Bomb, a phenomenon beyond my comprehension.' Ali Ujjan has given an account of the questions he and Fahmida Riaz often encountered during their travels and lectures through India: from Sindhi and Punjabi migrants nostalgic queries about the villages and towns they or their parents had come from; in Calcutta about the break-up of Pakistan and the creation of Bangladesh; the condition of Hindus in rural Sindh, etc. The lack of interest in democracy in Pakistan did not, however, entirely surprise Ali Ujjan. During an earlier visit to India in

1979 he had met an out of power Indira Gandhi at her house and found she had 'reservations about the potential and unity of democratic forces confronted with brutal military dictatorship'.[28]

For many in Pakistan, the Indian response to the MRD movement had many shades of the East Pakistan experience only thirteen years earlier. General K.M. Arif, Zia's chief of staff, recollected his own version and analysis of these events: 'India fished in Pakistan's troubled waters. The Sindhi dissidents found a safe haven across the India–Pakistan border. The Indian support, initially covert, soon became overt. Mrs Indira Gandhi threatened that India could not remain indifferent to the cause of the people of Sindh.'[29]

General Arif goes on to describe a meeting between the Indian Army chief General K. Sundarji and a Pakistani officer, Major General Nishat Ahmad, in late 1986. The two knew each other having attended a course in the United States some time ago: 'Sundarji told Nishat that if Pakistan could help the Sikhs in the Indian Punjab, India too possessed a "Sindh card".'[30] Such perspectives and views, whether real or based solely on hearsay, added to the mental state of siege in Pakistan: A US–USSR stand-off over Afghanistan leading to the re-emergence of the old alliance of the Soviet Union and India against Pakistan.

Many in Pakistan were equally convinced that in the Indian scheme of things, action against Pakistan was a way out of the Punjab crisis. 'Some visiting Indian opposition leaders warned Pakistan that a cornered Mrs Indira Gandhi was looking for an excuse to teach Pakistan a lesson ... she planned to externalize her internal failures.'[31] In this assessment, it was Zia who saved the day as 'he declined to be provoked and made conciliating statements ... he had no intention of involving Pakistan in a multidirectional threat. While playing it cool with India, he wanted to fully concentrate on the Afghanistan problem.'[32]

The speeches of the Indian prime minister and foreign minister, occasional demonstrations and protests as also the stay of stray dissidents were carefully tracked and categorized in Pakistan as the surface manifestations of a deeper and more malignant Indian involvement in dissident political activity in Sindh and in Pakistan generally. What gave the responses in India a larger-than-life profile with the Government of Pakistan was the bitter animosity Bhutto's execution had raised in many in Sindh as well as the activities of Zulfikar Ali Bhutto's two sons—Murtaza and Shahnawaz. Soon after his father's execution, Murtaza left Pakistan and set up the 'Al Zulfikar Organization', a 'guerrilla resistance group' headquartered in Kabul but with assistance from Libya, Syria and—Pakistani intelligence believed—India.[33]

Al Zulfikar's most spectacular act was to hijack a Pakistani aircraft to Kabul and then to Damascus in March 1981. The passengers were held hostage and freed only when Zia-ul-Haq agreed to the release of fifty PPP activists from jail. This happened after a Pakistan official on board was killed and six Americans threatened with a similar fate.[34] Thereafter in early 1982, Al Zulfikar also attempted the assassination of President Zia—one attempt was almost successful.[35] Press coverage given to Murtaza Bhutto in India was often sufficient cause to many in Pakistan to suspect an Indian hand behind and support for Al Zulfikar and amplify concerns about Indian and Afghan intelligence acting together. How much this preyed on minds of the Pakistani authorities is suggested by Zia's response when the Indian high commissioner Natwar Singh raised the question of handing over the Sikh extremists responsible for the September 1981 hijacking of an Indian aircraft to Pakistan. The President said that 'the men would be given to us once enquiries were completed' and that he 'hoped that the goodwill shown by Pakistan with regard to return of the hijackers would be reciprocated when any member of the Al Zulfikar group used Indian soil to attack him and his regime'.[36]

Political and diplomatic moves in the early 1980s, intense as they were, faded in the face of another looming confrontation. This was in the most inhospitable part of the western Himalayas, which became the intersection point of Chinese, Pakistani and Indian strategies to dominate these heights. Point NJ 9842 of the ceasefire line of April 1949 suddenly acquired a new resonance as Pakistan and India sought to outguess each other in a chess game to reach and command the Siachen glacier. In the 1962 India–China conflict, the Chinese had forcibly occupied the 'right ear' of J&K—the Aksai Chin. In the border settlement between China and Pakistan in March 1963—announced as the Swaran Singh–Z.A. Bhutto talks commenced—Pakistan conceded an area of 2,700 square miles (6,993 sq.km) of territory to China. This was an area to the west of Aksai Chin—the Shaksgam Valley. India, of course, did not recognize this agreement: What was Pakistan's locus standi, it felt, to cede territory in J&K?

The significance of the area beyond point NJ 9842 lay in the phrase used in the 1949 ceasefire line delineation—thence north to the glacier. What was 'thence north'? To India, normal cartographic principles meant that the line must follow the topography of the area—the watersheds and the mountain ranges. From the late 1970s, Pakistani maps had, however, started to show the Line of Control beyond NJ 9842 as a straight line extending to the Aksai Chin, in effect bringing the Siachen glacier into Pakistan's side of the line. This meant that the Chinese-controlled Aksai Chin and Shaksgam Valley would now be separated only by Pakistan-controlled territory. For Indian military strategists and thinkers, the motive was straightforward—Pakistan was claiming the glacier in concert with China and this continuous stretch of territory controlled by Pakistan and China would pose a threat in the future to Ladakh and Kargil.

These maps acquired an even greater importance as reports came in of Pakistan sponsoring mountaineering expeditions into this area. Amidst intelligence of a possible sudden Pakistan military move to control the glacier, the Government of India decided in early 1984 that the Indian Army should pre-empt this by establishing its own posts and defensive positions. When this was done, it was through a relatively small but logistically difficult and dangerous operation. Its success led inevitably to the Pakistan Army's attempts to dislodge the Indian troops. These attempts failed but to secure existing positions Indian deployments grew even in the face of an inhospitable terrain and climate. Then, as a military officer has explained:

> Militaries the world over are particular about securing the next height and the Indian Army is no exception to that visceral military compulsion. The belief that if one does not take the next higher ground, the enemy will, creates that unending urge. It leads to the occupation of ground which would otherwise have been left unoccupied. The Pakistan Army, driven by the same logic, probed and prodded.[37]

With India dominating the heights, the Pakistan Army was kept at some distance from the glacier. Meanwhile, the politics of the relationship superimposed its own logic on this military push and back push. The terrorist attacks and unrest in Punjab meant that any loss of territory, howsoever notional, to Pakistan was politically not acceptable. A strong line had also to be taken particularly given the China angle. In Pakistan, the failure of the army first to prevent the Indians from dominating the glacier and then to dislodge them was an embarrassment to President Zia and as exhaustion grew with his regime it became a point of criticism of the army.

In this new struggle for heights, the narratives of both India and Pakistan were naturally opposed to each other. For Pakistan, this was India dishonouring the Line of Control to occupy what was so far a no-man's-land. For India, it was a necessary step, given Pakistan's depictions of the Siachen area in its maps and the military moves being planned to cement this cartographic aggression and achieve a fait accompli. The one point that both would agree on was that this was a clash in the most inhospitable area in the world for armies to engage and that far more casualties were because of the terrain and the weather than on account of military action.[38]

Amidst the 1983–84 anti-Zia agitations led by the MRD in Sindh and the increasingly violent turn that extremism in Punjab was taking in India, in May 1984 a new Pakistan ambassador, Humayun Khan, arrived in Delhi. A Pathan himself, he had many old friends and acquaintances as he and his brothers had been at school in India before 1947. He arrived at what he thought was a relatively better time of the relationship, and in his words, relations 'were showing a rare upward trend'. Humayun Khan gathered this impression from the meetings between the Indian and Pakistani foreign secretaries on a friendship and non-aggression treaty in 1984. While Humayun Khan was conscious of the trouble areas—Punjab terrorism and militancy, as also the growing clashes in Siachen—these appeared to be then only 'faint clouds visible on the horizon'. In brief, Humayun Khan was hopeful that the diplomatic process would bear fruit.[39] Within a few days, however, reality intruded with the hijacking of an Indian Airlines aircraft to Lahore by Sikh militants. The passengers, after a harrowing 16–18 hours of being confined in the aircraft, were flown back on a Pakistan aircraft and the hijackers taken into custody. The aircraft also was safely returned to India. The hijackers were not handed back, consistent with earlier cases.

Within a few days of this incident, Humayun Khan's introductory courtesy call on Prime Minister Indira Gandhi was fixed. Humayun Khan later recalled that he expected some expression of relief at the peaceful end of the hijacking and perhaps even some appreciation of the role of the Government of Pakistan. The prime minister spoke little during the meeting but what she felt was fully conveyed at the beginning itself.

> She received me, not with a handshake or the normal Indian namaste, but with the traditional Muslim greeting of aadab arz, somewhat raising my expectations. Her first sentence, however, took me back. With a wry smile, she said, '*Aap ke aatey hee hadsa ho gaya*,' meaning, 'As soon as you have arrived a mishap has taken place.' Quite nonplussed I made an effort to highlight the positive aspects of the episode like the rescue of the passengers, the arrest of the culprits and the cooperation between officials of both countries at Lahore airport. She cut me short to say, 'But you did not allow our people to meet the hijackers or search their luggage.' Naturally, I was thrown a bit off balance by the Prime Minister's directness and even more by the long silences that followed her opening remarks. I managed to say a few words about my determination to work for better relations and the clear instructions of my Government to that effect. She spoke only one more sentence. 'We have never been against good relations.' The interview lasted seven minutes.[40]

But even the hijacking was a sideshow to the main event unfolding, which was the storming of the Golden Temple in Amritsar in June 1984 by the Indian Army to flush out terrorists holed up inside who were using the shrine as a defensive complex. Casualties were heavy as was the damage to the shrine. 'Operation Blue Star' became a milestone and a marker in the modern history of India. The army commander at Amritsar said that the militants bore arms and ammunition with Pakistani markings and this was added evidence that the militants in the shrine had Pakistan's covert support.

In India, regardless of what view one had of the roots of militancy in Punjab, no one doubted that Pakistan would do whatever it could to abet it. In Pakistan, denials were vehement including from the president himself. But often the manner of the denial itself convinced many in India both of his complicity as also that the predominant mood in Pakistan was one of schadenfreude: India was facing what Pakistan had in East Pakistan. In a speech in July 1984, President Zia spoke at great length on relations with India while denying any Pakistani involvement in terrorist events in Punjab:

> Thirteen years ago, when India committed a naked aggression against East Pakistan, the state of affairs in Pakistan was such that our own misdeeds had recoiled on us. East Pakistan was separated and it became Bangladesh. I have always said that we have no grudge against them and we always pray that may almighty Allah shower his blessing upon Bangladesh. ... But you should know that certain facts cannot be erased from the memory just because 13 years have passed. The people who trained the Mukti Bahini at that time have now joined the Sikhs in their agitation. One of them is Brig. (Retd) Shah Baig Singh. He is one of those who instigated the people in East Pakistan against the Government of Pakistan, trained them, attacked Pakistani territory in collaboration with them and when the Indian forces entered into East Pakistan, guided them towards the targets.[41]

President Zia's point also was that the arms found in the Golden Temple could well have been those which the Pakistan troops had surrendered in 1971! But the specifics apart, the larger comparison being drawn was not lost on audiences in either country. Zia's choice of words clearly conveyed to many in India the similarities in Pakistani eyes of East Pakistan in 1971 and East Punjab in 1984. His reference in the speech to 'Brigadier Shah Baig Singh' was to Shabeg Singh, a decorated Indian Army officer involved in the Bangladesh war in 1971. He was subsequently dismissed from the Indian Army on charges of corruption and drifted thereafter to Sikh extremism. He was one of those holed up in the Golden Temple in June 1984 and was killed there. The fact that a Bangladesh war hero led the terrorists inside the Golden Temple is seen in Pakistan to this day as India getting a dose of poetic justice.

In the last week of August 1984, there was another hijacking to Lahore. This time the Pakistan authorities refused to let the aircraft stay but refuelled the aircraft before it was flown to Dubai. In Dubai, the passengers were rescued, the hijackers arrested and handed over to India. This was in obvious contrast to the standard Pakistani position of not handing over militants who had hijacked aircraft from India. To Humayun Khan in New Delhi: '... this showed up Pakistan in a bad light and it was alleged that our Government had tried to persuade the UAE not to hand them over.'[42]

More serious was the fact that a pistol was handed over to the hijackers during the refuelling in Lahore. This was revealed by K. Subrahmanyam—the noted strategic expert and civil servant—one of the passengers on the hijacked aircraft. On Pakistan's denial, the origins of the pistol were traced back from the manufactures in Germany who confirmed that the weapon was sold to a government agency in Pakistan. According to Humayun Khan, 'Zia showed great displeasure when the evidence finally proved our involvement'. [43] Most, if not all, Indians held, then and now, a less benign interpretation.

But as each such event was overtaken by another, many had a deepening sense of foreboding that a major crisis in India–Pakistan relations was imminent. Certainly, this was the assessment in Pakistan: '... by September 1984, there was open talk of Mrs Gandhi taking retaliatory action against Pakistan'.[44] One possibility, much speculated about, was an air strike against Pakistan's principal nuclear installation at Kahuta, near Rawalpindi. In June 1981, the Israeli air force had destroyed an under-construction reactor in Iraq and since then there was an ever-present apprehension in Pakistani thinking about a possible Indian strike using the Israeli action as a template.

As the crisis in Indian Punjab continued, Zia himself mentioned a possible attack as press reports from the US speculated and added credibility to this possibility. He hoped, Zia said, India would not take any step that could be a 'prelude to war'. Variants of the Indian air strike theory were a joint India–Israel and even a joint India–Soviet Union operation using Afghanistan as a base. In Pakistan, the folklore is that as apprehension increased about possible Indian airstrikes on Kahuta, the chairman of the Pakistan Atomic Energy Commission quietly told his Indian counterpart, during a conference in Vienna, of the retaliation that would follow on Indian nuclear facilities.[45] Whether true or not, most Pakistanis implicitly believed that such an attack was imminent and only Pakistan's firm position that such a step would lead to a war averted it.

This swift downward trend in bilateral relations took place amidst other events that appear incongruous. During 'Operation Blue Star' at the Golden Temple, the information ministers of India and Pakistan were meeting in Islamabad to see how cooperation in media-related issues could create a positive atmosphere. In October 1984, when the possible Kahuta attack theory was very much alive, the Indian cricket team was in Pakistan for a Test series. This was a desultory series—bad umpiring, hostile crowds and a tense political atmosphere were not conducive for a good tournament. With the two-Test series drawn, worse was to follow.

In the middle of a One-Day cricket match between India and Pakistan on 31 October 1984, came the news of Indira Gandhi's assassination. The match was abandoned. The enormity of this development put the sharpening of India–Pakistan tensions temporarily aside, but an editorial in *The Times of India* on the morning of her assassination does convey the mood in New Delhi at that time.

> Mrs Gandhi has quite understandably been concerned over the US supply of sophisticated weapons to Pakistan and Islamabad's alleged involvement with the Akali extremists in Punjab. Each development is disturbing in itself; together they must be a source of deepest anxiety. ... Denials cannot dispose of the reality that the recent upheaval in Punjab has given Pakistan a harmful leverage in its dealings with India and the US arms supplies can give it the necessary confidence to use this leverage ... For all we know, India–Pakistan relations may have entered, and for this country, a far more dangerous phase.[46]

Pakistan's condemnation of the assassination was unambiguous; a three-day state morning was observed and President Zia attended the funeral in Delhi. Did this represent the full spectrum of Pakistani sentiment at the passing of the person, who more than anyone else, had broken the country in two? We get a hint of the thinking at that time in Pakistan in the recollections of Sartaz Aziz, then a member of President Zia's cabinet and subsequently foreign minister in the 1990s and later:

> By October 1984, tensions with India suddenly grew while the Russian offensive in Afghanistan was threatening our western borders.

> Many ministers including myself, argued for a change of course in Afghanistan because the Russians could work through India by raising the ultimate cost of our Afghan policy. The President while agreeing with the logic of these arguments said something very unusual: 'I know it will not be easy to defeat a superpower and I am also aware of the problem and obstacles but I also believe in miracles.' The first 'miracle' happened on 31st October, 1984 when Indira Gandhi was assassinated, leading to a sudden reduction of tensions between India and Pakistan.[47]

Attitudes to and memories of Indira Gandhi thus have an enigmatic quality in Pakistan. Disliked, even feared, she was also genuinely admired in some quarters; a figure whose qualities and attributes were for many in Pakistan an implied critique of Pakistan's own leadership.

Zia and Rajiv Gandhi had a meeting soon after the funeral. They met alone without any officials present. According to Humayun Khan, Zia dictated an account of the conversation and '... it clearly indicated that the prospects for putting bilateral relations back on track held some promise'. President Zia and Prime Minister Rajiv Gandhi met at least four times thereafter in other countries as both attended international or regional events. Humayun Khan also gives a flavour of that early period of Rajiv Gandhi as prime minister:

> More important than the official exchanges were those at the people's level. I had the pleasure of hosting hundreds of Indian friends at musicals by renowned Pakistan vocalists like Mehdi Hassan, Ghulam Ali, Farida Khanum, Reshma and Abida Parveen. These events generated enormous goodwill and positive interest in Pakistan. I was besieged with requests for videotapes of Urdu dramas aired by Pakistan television.[48]

The Doon School held its golden jubilee celebrations at this time and a large contingent of Pakistani old boys attended. Rajiv Gandhi, an alumnus himself, was among the prominent attendees and in his address at the opening ceremony 'every reference to the visitors from Pakistan was loudly cheered'.[49]

Amongst all this bonhomie, nevertheless, there were those who were more discerning. Humayun Khan again recounts:

An unusual visit (was) by a group led by the Governor of West Punjab, Makhdoom Sajjad Hussain Quereshi. A gifted conversationalist with an unmatchable sense of humour, the Makhdoom had a hilarious session with Giani Zail Singh, the Indian President. They both spoke in Punjabi ... the conversation included a number of witty asides about a shy young man accompanying the governor whose name was Nawaz Sharif and who had obviously come along for fun. Speaking of the improvement in India–Pakistan relations Gianiji with uncanny accuracy observed, '*khambey te lug gaey, par bijli hali nayeen chali*'. (The poles are up but the electricity has not yet started to flow).[50]

To many Pakistanis, or at least those who were keen to move forward, Rajiv Gandhi spelt huge promise. To Humayun Khan it appeared: 'In his own unassuming way, he soon let it be known that a generational change had taken place and that he was not burdened with the baggage of the past. Unlike his mother he held no ingrained animosity towards the military regime in Pakistan.'[51] President Zia made a brief visit to Delhi in December 1985 in response to Rajiv Gandhi's suggestion that he stop over while returning from Sri Lanka. The visit capped a year in which things looked better than at any time since the end of the Janata Party government in 1979.

The Rajiv–Zia meeting of December 1985 had a specific outcome related to the rumours that had circulated in Pakistan about a possible Indian attack on Kahuta. Humayun Khan recollects:

The most important outcome of President Zia's visit was a totally unexpected one. When the two leaders emerged from their private session in the evening to join their delegations for refreshments, Rajiv casually asked the President if it would be a good idea for the two countries to enter into an agreement not to attack each other's nuclear facilities. For a moment Zia was taken aback, but he quickly recovered his composure and enthusiastically welcomed the proposal. The Indians had played this very close to their chest and at no stage during the preparations for the summit had the subject been raised.[52]

The final agreement took some three years to come but it is one of the few that has been annually reiterated on 1 January every year, no matter how deep a crisis the relationship has plummeted to.

But if both sides frequently expressed a desire to move ahead and move on, the portfolio of problems was accumulating. Pakistan's assistance to terrorism and militancy in Punjab topped the list, but other points were no less difficult. Pakistan's position on J&K, increased clashes in Siachen and Pakistan's fears and anxieties regarding India's support to extremist groups in Sindh, such as the Al Zulfikar Organization. Indian anxieties about Pakistan's nuclear programme and Pakistani apprehensions about a possible Indian strike at them were factors which also were not to fade away.

But the Zia visit kick-started a process of ministerial and official interaction. By their very nature, these enabled some practical measures to be agreed upon. So, as in the past—as would be the case in the future—even high-level exchanges would find themselves engrossed with the mundane. Thus, V.P. Singh visiting Pakistan as finance minister a few days after President Zia's visit to India, agreed with his counterpart, the well-known economist Mahbubul Haq, that direct dialling facilities (instead of booking trunk calls) should be started and that telex facilities be upgraded. Some limited liberalization of Pakistani restrictions on trade with India was also initiated.[53]

If all this appeared to suggest a situation of thaw, discordant notes were also frequent and intense. For instance, in early February 1986 the Pakistan minister of state of foreign affairs made a statement in the Senate condemning a local court judgment in India to remove the locks on the Babri Masjid to enable people to worship the idols inside. In India, this was seen as blatant interference and the response was swift. External Affairs Minister Bali Ram Bhagat said in the Lok Sabha that such statements were against the Simla Agreement and promotion of good neighbourly relations. He further added: 'On our part, we have refrained from commenting on reports of sectarian riots, denial of democratic rights and restriction on freedom of religious worship to minority communities including the Ahmadiyas in Pakistan ...'[54]

It was, however, militancy and terrorism in Punjab that cast the longest shadow. Pakistan's denials of involvement or complicity of the ISI were vehement and consistent, and it tried hard to appear sincere. On one occasion in early 1986, the Pakistan foreign minister Sahibzada Yaqub Khan explained at some length to the Indian ambassador S.K. Singh:

> Discussing the Sikh issue, which he called the most important factor between us, we must not leave any stone unturned to assure you we are not involved. He kept asking what is the help Pakistan can give to the Sikhs. What is Pakistan's capability. What can be the ramifications of the problem. ... I pricked the balloon by reminding him of the handing over of the pistol to the hijackers by a senior Pakistani official. He did not contradict me. He merely said that the problem is behind us. He then said that he has noticed whenever the Sikh problem is close to solution, Indo-Pak relations improve; whenever the Sikh problem deteriorates, so do Indo-Pakistan relations. ... He then went on to give me a long story of how both the DIB (Director of Intelligence Bureau) and the Chief of Inter-Services Intelligence are senior army officers who have earlier served under (him). They have given their personal and solemn assurances on the basis of a lifetime honour that they are making no intelligence efforts in the direction of Indian Sikhs.[55]

These protestations appeared less than sincere to the Indians who felt that Pakistani disclaimers were invariably general in character and rarely addressed the increasingly voluminous and detailed evidence against the ISI. Nevertheless, regular contacts and meetings at the official level seemed to reflect a steady upward trend in bilateral relations.

But how deceptive a surface calm can be soon became evident. In November 1986 at a SAARC summit in Bangalore, the Pakistani delegation was led by Prime Minister Mohammed Khan Junejo, who was appointed in March 1985 as a civilian front for Zia. No one had any doubts, however, where real power lay in Pakistan. In fact, much to Junejo's consternation, the posters welcoming SAARC leaders had Zia's picture instead of his! One of the points raised by Junejo with Rajiv Gandhi was that the Pakistan Army was worried about a large-scale military exercise by India called Operation Brasstacks close to the Rajasthan–Sindh border. Rajiv Gandhi assured the Pakistan PM that the exercise was routine but he would have it scaled down to address Pakistan's concerns. In India, some held the view that Pakistan was deliberately exaggerating the annual military exercises in India to create a sense of crisis and draw in the United States.[56]

The matter seemingly ended there; but in the second half of January 1987 it blew up into a full-fledged crisis. However, this occurred amidst other developments in India which blurred the entire picture. For one, the Indian foreign secretary received in effect a dismissal order from Rajiv Gandhi in the midst of a press conference on 19 January. A reporter from Pakistan had sought an elaboration from the prime minister of the foreign secretary's recent statement in Islamabad that Rajiv Gandhi had agreed to visit Pakistan in 1987. The prime minister's response was that 'you will soon be talking to a new foreign secretary'[57] about this. This was only days after the Indian defence ministry had briefed journalists about a massive Pakistani troop build-up and that Pakistan had mobilized virtually its entire reserve. Soon thereafter, Indian Army deployments at the border or close to it were also reported. In Pakistan, the large exercise about which Prime Minister Junejo had expressed concern was viewed as having the potential for a sudden armoured thrust into Sindh. As a result, its own reserve formations were moved closer to the border.

Foreign Secretary A.P. Venkateswaran's unceremonious removal was unrelated to troop movements but the coincidence added to the sense of crisis in both countries. It also illustrated that what appears seemingly innocuous from one point of view has great importance from another. Foreign Secretary A.P. Venkateswaran had visited Pakistan in end-December 1986, where he was continuously queried and pressed, including by President Zia, about Rajiv Gandhi visiting Pakistan in 1987 in his capacity as chairperson of SAARC as was the established convention. Venkateswaran had responded positively, which was the reason for the question put to Rajiv Gandhi at his press conference on 19 January. While there may have been reasons unconnected to Pakistan and of a more interpersonal nature in the foreign secretary's removal, nevertheless the Pakistan factor could not be wished away. In India, the next day, in the front pages of newspapers, the foreign secretary's very public dismissal competed with descriptions of India's concern at Pakistan's troop deployments.[58] If a major situation was brewing, not all were fully conscious of it. Humayun Khan got a sense of the magnitude only when he was asked to see Minister of State for External Affairs Natwar Singh very early one morning. Humayun Khan describes the encounter:

> Whenever we met, he was informal and friendly. On that morning, however, he had a stern expression and my initial attempts at

> bonhomie fell absolutely flat. He sat me down and said he had a most important and urgent message to be conveyed to my Government. He then took out a piece of paper and read slowly from it so that I could write it down verbatim. It was a sombre message which stated that the Pakistan Army had moved two divisions, including an armoured division, from their peacetime locations in the Multan and Gujranwala areas to the Punjab border. India regarded this as an offensive move and unless these troops went back to their peacetime locations within 24 hours, India would be compelled to move its own forces to the border 'for purposes of defence'.[59]

Humayun Khan was 'astounded' at the ultimatum and possibly doubly so because he had no reason to presume that such a crisis was brewing over Operation Brasstacks. He conveyed to Islamabad that it would be a tragedy if a conflict was to erupt merely because of suspicion and lack of communication. In Delhi, and for the Indian public at large, the sense of crisis was further exacerbated by the US and Soviet ambassadors being briefed about Pakistan's aggressive deployments. Natwar Singh had, however, been equally surprised at the turn of events and he describes how he was suddenly asked by Rajiv Gandhi to accompany him to the airport to receive a dignitary coming to India as the chief guest for the Republic Day parade. 'On the way to Palam, to my utter surprise, Rajiv said, "Natwar, are we about to go to war with Pakistan?" Natwar Singh told Rajiv Gandhi that he knew nothing about this and goes on to relate: 'The Prime Minister said that neither did he.' Natwar Singh recalls, 'I was appalled.'[60]

By early February the Brasstacks crisis had receded with a visit by the Pakistan foreign secretary to New Delhi and an agreement on mutual redeployment. One result—which took some years to translate into a written agreement—was that both sides would in future notify the other in advance of military exercises being carried out to preclude a similar situation arising. There is, however, one further sideshow to this chain of events. At the height of the Brasstacks crisis, journalist Kuldip Nayar was in Islamabad for the wedding of a prominent Pakistani journalist and editor Mushahid Hussain. The latter informed him on his arrival that the scientist in charge of Pakistan's nuclear programme, A.Q. Khan had agreed to meet him and give an interview. 'I was flabbergasted', writes

Kuldip Nayar.[61] During the interview itself Nayar's aim 'was directed towards learning whether or not Pakistan had a nuclear bomb'. Khan in the interview was initially evasive and Nayar says he decided to provoke him since '(e)goist as he was, he might fall for the bait'. In Kuldip Nayar's description of what happened:

> I concocted a story and told him that when I was coming to Pakistan, I ran into Dr Homi Sethna, father of India's nuclear bomb, who asked me why I was wasting my time because Pakistan had neither the men nor the material to make such a weapon. Khan was furious and began pounding his hand on the table: 'Tell them we have it; we have it.' Mushahid was taken aback and looked distraught.[62]

A.Q. Khan went on to say that the bomb had been tested in their laboratory and 'we are satisfied with the results'. Finally he warned Nayar, 'If you ever drive us to the wall, as you did in East Pakistan, we will use the bomb.'

This interview was sometime in the last week of January 1987, just before the visit of the Pakistan foreign secretary from 30 January. It was not, however, published by the *Observer* in London till end-February and appeared on 1 March. It did attract considerable attention although the specific India–Pakistan crisis had passed by then. Clearly, the interview was arranged for Nayar to highlight Pakistan's nuclear capabilities in the crisis period of end-January although equally plausibly it may not have been the intention that A.Q. Khan should say all that he did. Obviously, it was not anticipated that the news would not break immediately. The story was denied immediately with A.Q. Khan claiming that a private meeting at Mushahid Hussain's behest was reported as an interview. The delay in publication in fact turned out to be an embarrassment to Pakistan. When the story finally appeared, the US Congress was to pass a bill for aid to Pakistan in turn requiring a presidential certification that Pakistan did not possess a nuclear weapon. In the event neither the certification nor the bill was held up, although the issue received a far greater amount of attention than it would have otherwise. What is also interesting is how much attention and analysis in India and Pakistan at the time went into the timing of the interview, the delay in its publication and its coincidence with the Operation Brasstacks crisis. In Pakistan itself, there were those who saw an Indian conspiracy in the interview being published just when the US Congress was to take up the Pakistan aid bill. Prime Minister Rajiv Gandhi was asked if this was so and his reply was in itself a classic: 'We can conspire with anyone', he said, 'but not Kuldip Nayar.'[63]

In memories of that period what is generally believed to have eased the situation was an announcement by President Zia-ul-Haq that he would visit India to witness an India–Pakistan cricket match. The crisis had, in fact, eased by then but the image of cricket diplomacy resolving tensions has endured. This was President Zia's fifth visit to India. It stood in obvious contrast to the reluctance of Rajiv Gandhi to even confirm a visit to Pakistan and his dismissing his foreign secretary for having done so.

But Zia's visit and meeting with Rajiv Gandhi did also have a considerable impact on the overall atmospherics and added greatly, including in India, to his image as an adept diplomatic player. On his return to Pakistan, he was asked in a press conference whether 'in his cricket diplomacy he had been engaged in defensive batting while the other side hurled only bouncers'. His reply was: 'But you have completely ignored Zia-ul-Haq's sixer.'[64] If the majority would have seen the 'sixer' as a propaganda coup he had secured, this was by no means the only explanation given of what appears to be an innocuous enough statement. In one view, influential at the time, the entire furore over Brasstacks was designed only to send the message of Pakistan's nuclear capability. Zia's reference to the sixer he had hit was therefore probably a reference 'to the communication on Pakistan's nuclear capability'.[65]

In any event the crisis emerged and eased out of nowhere. That the foreign secretary's dismissal and the military build-up were somehow linked was a source of speculation in both countries and some effort was put in to decipher the signal being sent. But most of all, it left everyone, as one newspaper editorial put it, 'baffled' and perhaps more than anything else it was a graphic illustration of how deep mistrust was.[66]

After the crisis, as official and occasionally ministerial exchanges continued, both countries reverted to their respective preoccupations. For India, Sri Lanka dominated the neighborhood radar. For Pakistan, it was the new situation emerging in Afghanistan as the Soviet Union's intention to withdraw became clear. There were major domestic preoccupations too. President Zia was faced with an increasingly assertive prime minister Junejo, whom he had appointed as a safe and compliant civilian head of government. For Rajiv Gandhi, it was the toll that the Bofors corruption case was taking on him politically. He did visit Pakistan in January 1988—but this was a brief two-hour-long condolence visit to Peshawar on the death of Badshah Khan. No meeting with President Zia took place—perhaps it was not even thought of.

In any event, his presence at Badshah Khan's funeral was viewed by many in Pakistan negatively and hardly as a reaching out. After a foreign secretary's summary public dressing-down and dismissal, a 'real' visit by Rajiv Gandhi was too delicate an issue to be broached—and the Pakistanis also generally refrained from pushing that envelope too much. That a foreign secretary would be so summarily dealt with because he was forthcoming about Rajiv Gandhi visiting Pakistan sent a message too obvious to be misunderstood and too direct to pretend that the episode had not occurred.

Why was Rajiv Gandhi so reluctant to visit Pakistan? That he visited almost as soon as Benazir Bhutto became prime minister suggests that it had much to do with Zia's military dictatorship. Then there were concerns about Pakistani complicity with militancy in Punjab—too fundamental an issue then to be papered over. But Zia's five visits to India since Indira Gandhi's re-election in 1980 without a return visit from India does stand out to this day as an important, if unusual, feature of this period. Why did he do this? Those close to Zia give us a sense of his thinking. He was playing a dangerous game in Afghanistan with an increasingly embattled Soviet Union. It made sense to make sure that tensions on his eastern front never spilled into something more serious.

This was, as Zia's tenure progressed, no easy task. Siachen, for instance, was a major embarrassment since the Pakistan Army had clearly been worsted by its counterpart in the race to occupy the heights controlling access to the glacier. 'For evident reasons,' wrote Iqbal Akhund, 'Zia-ul-Haq had not allowed the Siachen events to be publicized.' However, once Benazir returned to Pakistan in 1986 she criticized the military regime and Zia for losing Pakistani territory because of negligence and timidity. The 'loss' of Siachen was becoming a major political issue. Both armies bore the brunt of the casualties inflicted by the terrain and the weather but the Indian troops had the more difficult time since they had to hold the heights and their supply lines were much longer. Though efforts were made to find a way out, from 1987 onwards, this proved a difficult knot to untie.

In the post-Brasstacks period, two special India–Pakistan initiatives stand out as examples of how even relatively benign moves can be misunderstood. In mid-1987, a dying Badshah Khan was in India for medical treatment and on 10 August that year it was announced that he would receive India's highest award—the Bharat Ratna. This was the first time that a foreign national was being so honoured and, in fact, the only other foreign recipient to date is Nelson Mandela. Badshah Kahn's son Wali Khan received the award at a special investiture ceremony on 15 August at Rashtrapati Bhavan, New Delhi.

It was a deeply symbolic moment for many in India, for Badshah Khan was one of the last of Mahatma Gandhi's close associates. After Partition, he was under house arrest or in jail or in a self-imposed exile in Jalalabad in Afghanistan for prolonged periods. Seen in Pakistan, with some justification, as one who never reconciled himself to the Partition of the subcontinent, the prolonged periods of military rule also meant that he was viewed as one whose basic loyalties to the country were suspect. India giving him its highest award was perceived differently in different parts of Pakistan. For his followers and admirers in the Frontier, it was no more than the acknowledgement of his close historic ties to India. Humayun Khan, a Pathan himself and the Pakistan ambassador in India during Badshah Khan's last visit, was to comment, 'I have not seen any man command as much respect and affection in India as Badshah Khan.'[67] Others, in Punjab or in the government, took a less benign view. This was India interfering in Pakistan's internal affairs as also consolidating its political constituency amongst Badshah Khan's followers. The fact that the latter included many amongst the Pashtuns in southern Afghanistan made it easy to cast the step in a more sinister light.

The following year, on 14 August 1988, the Government of Pakistan conferred the Nishan-e-Pakistan on former Indian prime minister Morarji Desai. This is generally described as Pakistan's highest civilian award. It is, in fact, usually awarded to foreign leaders and to that extent differs from the Bharat Ratna. The award, whatever may have been President

Zia's motives, was read in multiple ways in India. The ruling Congress party criticized it strongly, demanding that Desai 'reject the award with the contempt it deserves'; that it 'was also a part of General's Zia's design of interference in the internal affairs of India', and that the Pakistan president was abetting terrorists in Punjab.[68] The then home minister Buta Singh also voiced the widespread feeling that the award was a reaction to the Bharat Ratna conferred on Badshah Khan: it was, he said, 'calculated mischief' to belittle the great honour conferred on Badshah Khan.[69] Others saw this as one more example of President Zia's 'formidable skills at public relations to manipulate Indian opinion' and that he 'could not have found a subtler way to convince the Indian people that the Rajiv Gandhi government is wholly to blame for the dismal state of Indo-Pakistani relations'.[70]

The aged Morarji Desai's decision to accept the award was, however, also to be strongly defended—including from unexpected quarters. K.R. Malkani, the former editor of the *Organiser* and a senior leader of the Bharatiya Janata Party and the RSS wrote to *The Times of India* amid the award controversy that 'Pakistan has honoured itself in honouring' Morarji Desai and in doing so 'Pakistan has expressed trust and confidence in an Indian statesman, which is all to the good.' Desai's government executed a foreign policy that was a great success and 'we should hope we both trust more and more leaders on the other side of the Radcliffe Line'.[71] In any case, Morarji Desai had mounted his own defence: 'It's the duty of the biggest country to keep good relations with all its neighbours. That's the way I thought and that's what I did.' At the award ceremony, almost three years later, the Government of India was represented by Subramanian Swamy, then a cabinet minister in India's second non-congress government.

The reason for the long delay in the actual conferment of the award was that fate had intervened in between. The death of Zia-ul-Haq on 17 August 1988 in a mysterious plane crash meant that all scenarios were changing. In the elections that followed, the Pakistan Peoples Party, with Benazir Bhutto as its leader, emerged as the single largest party. Her victory was not an outright one and her government was to be based on 'a sharing of power between the PPP and the Zia establishment'.[72] As part of the legacy of Zia's Pakistan, the award was put on the back burner and was to be conferred only after she, in turn, had made way for the next incumbent.

Benazir's return was that of an exiled princess reclaiming her birthright. She was a charismatic leader, akin to Rajiv Gandhi in India. The first exchange of letters between them went beyond the customary felicitations between two heads of government. Both referred to their respective parent signing the Simla Agreement; Rajiv Gandhi spoke of himself and Benazir being 'both children of an era which followed the creation of Pakistan' and of the need 'for removing the irritants which have needlessly vitiated relations between our countries in the past'.[73] Fortuitously, the annual summit of SAARC was to be held within less than a month of Benazir Bhutto's swearing in on 2 December 1988. In contrast to his studied reticence to visiting Pakistan throughout the Zia period, Rajiv Gandhi was now keen to visit, and a bilateral visit was combined with the SAARC summit. Things appeared to be just right to make a fresh start. GenNext was taking over. Mani Shankar Aiyar, then in the Prime Minister's Office (PMO), while admitting that Benazir Bhutto's government lacked political strength, being a minority government, and that 'the limits of her manoeuvrability were set by the armed forces', still felt '... the air seemed pregnant with possibilities'. [74]

In contrast to this upbeat perception, Iqbal Akhund, recently appointed as Benazir Bhutto's national security adviser, recollects otherwise. Despite a 'personal sympathy between the two young leaders' the 'chicken or egg conundrum of the India–Pakistan relationship—good relations first or a Kashmir settlement first—asserted itself. There were other strains, which the discerning could and did notice. The summit took place against the backdrop of an attempted overthrow of the Government of the Maldives by mercenaries. This was forestalled only by Indian troops being hurriedly airlifted to the island in response to desperate pleas from the Maldivian government. Many Pakistanis saw this 'as a drama staged by the Indian intelligence agency RAW to gain for India a military foothold on the Island'.[75]

There were other discordant notes. President J.R. Jayewardene of Sri Lanka and President General H.M. Ershad of Bangladesh went out of their way to praise Zia-ul-Haq. Benazir was 'put out of countenance, for there was no diplomatic or proper way in which she could react and she had to sit through these adulatory references to the man who had taken her father's life ... and hounded and persecuted her family and herself'. She, however, bided her time and kept her cool till her closing address when 'she tried to even the score by paying tributes to Sheikh Mujibur Rahman and Sirimavo Bandaranaike'.[76]

Apart from these nuances, things on India and Pakistan appeared positive. This was the first visit by an Indian prime minister after Jawaharlal Nehru's visit in 1960 to sign the Indus Waters Treaty—discounting a brief airport stopover by Lal Bahadur Shastri in 1964 and Rajiv Gandhi's flying condolence visit to Peshawar for Badshah Khan's funeral. *The Times of India* editorialized:

> The psychological backdrop of the visit was truly unprecedented. No Pakistani leader has won so much sympathy and even admiration in India as has Benazir Bhutto on account of her charisma and strength of character. Her triumph that followed an unremitting struggle against a theocratic dictatorship was widely hailed in this country as a happy augury for a swift normalization of ties between two democratic and non-aligned nations.[77]

While there could be 'no room for gushing enthusiasm' since she had yet to consolidate her position, the very fact that she repeatedly reiterated 'her reference to the Simla accord as the framework for the future of India–Pakistan relations is a matter of satisfaction'. During the visit, an agreement reached and finalized earlier with President Zia, on non-attack on each other's nuclear facilities, was formally signed. There was also a consensus that the earlier discussions of the defence secretaries on Siachen, to reach a mutually satisfactory pullback of forces, should be continued. The unstated premise was that a Siachen agreement could jump-start a larger process of normalization.

The headline and the image that endured was of two young leaders who, endowed with the charisma of their parents and therefore equipped to untangle the past, would forge ahead. A second visit by Rajiv Gandhi to Pakistan was thereafter quickly confirmed—this would be the first real stand-alone bilateral visit (the earlier visit was clubbed to the SAARC summit) by an Indian prime minister since 1960. Thereafter Rajiv Gandhi in his speech in Islamabad in July 1989 spoke of the 'lapse of over ten thousand days between the last visit of a Prime Minister of India to Pakistan and my visit here last December' and that within 'two hundred days I have come back to Islamabad'. It is, he said, 'given to all of us to be creatures of history. Let us ...try to create history.'[78]

Siachen appeared one way of making real progress. But here the issues were difficult. If both agreed that troop withdrawals plus status quo ante was the best feasible outcome, the question was how to make it a real status quo whose permanence would be respected on the ground. For India, the solution was straightforward: redeploy *after* marking existing troop positions of each side on a map and on the ground and both then undertake to honour these positions by way of written agreement. For Pakistan, this meant legitimizing India's occupation by stealth of the heights. Its preferred option was withdrawal and each side marking positions they had withdrawn to. This was unacceptable to India—what would stop Pakistan from occupying the heights once they had been vacated? These issues have dogged every discussion of Siachen since.

In most Pakistani accounts, India, after first agreeing to a Siachen pull-out in June 1989 in a meeting between the two defence secretaries, went back on its word as public criticism and resistance to the move made Rajiv Gandhi lose his nerve.[79] Certainly, immediately after the June 1989 meeting, the Pakistani media interpreted the joint statement issued as a breakthrough and a major gain for Pakistan. Some Indian newspapers too reported the conclusion as being an Indian pullback. To correct such interpretations, the Government of India denied that any agreement on withdrawal had been reached since what was being discussed was the present and future positions on the glacier. In Pakistan, this interpretation led to the charge of backtracking.[80]

A variant to these accounts was given by Benazir Bhutto herself in an interview to the Indian magazine *Outlook* shortly before her own tragic assassination in December 2007. This was in response to criticism in India that she could not be relied upon to clamp down on terrorists acting against India at Pakistan's behest:

> Does anyone remember those times or is public memory so short that no one recalls the extremely difficult conditions India faced during the Sikh insurgency 20 years ago? India was in a complete mess.

> Does anyone remember that it was I who kept my promise to Prime Minister Rajiv Gandhi when we met and he appealed to me for help in tackling the Sikhs? ... Have they forgotten the results of that meeting and how I helped curb the Sikh militancy?
>
> If anyone kept their word, it was me. Not Rajiv. He went back to India and then called me on his way to the Commonwealth to say that he could not keep his promise to withdraw from Siachen and that he would do it only after the elections. Now, if I haven't raised the subject or complained all these many years, why is it being raised now?[81]

But the Rajiv Gandhi–Benazir Bhutto initiative had more fundamental odds stacked against it than just differences over how and where to redeploy forces in Siachen. Firstly, it overlooked the mood of triumphalism in the Pakistan Army as the Soviets withdrew from Afghanistan: Pakistan was the front-line state that had led, first to the defeat of a superpower and then to its collapse. On this count, Pakistan's stock—and especially of its army and the ISI—was high. The mood of that time is captured by a memento preserved in a Pakistan Army mess at the Khyber Pass—a gift from a visiting army chief of West Germany, presented to the Khyber Rifles, the regiment that traditionally guards the pass connecting Afghanistan and Pakistan. It is a small piece of rubble from the Berlin wall mounted on a plaque which reads: 'To the Officers and Troops of the Pakistan Army—For Striking the First Blow'.

The end of the cold war, the fall of the Berlin wall and maps—frozen since the late 1940s—being redrawn in Europe, suggested to many in Pakistan that the moment when geopolitical and cartographical realities could be altered had come. This was a mood not easily amenable to compromise. Secondly, Rajiv Gandhi's term was coming to an end and entangled in corruption charges and scandals, his government had lost not just the political initiative but also its moral authority. And finally, after a long, peaceful interlude of a quarter-century, the Kashmir Valley was astir again. For many in Pakistan, it appeared that the time to settle Kashmir had come. India was buffeted by economic crisis, political and social demoralization and rising communal polarization over the Babri Masjid. Punjab in India was still gripped by militancy and terrorism. Most of all, Pakistani security and intelligence agencies had gained experience from the decade-long Afghan jihad on how to direct militants to a successful finish in a covert war.

As the hope that the Afghan experience could be applied against India in Kashmir gained ground in Pakistan, and the election results heralding Rajiv Gandhi's defeat in end-1989 came in, India–Pakistan relations were poised for a nosedive again. This time around, it was to be under a non-Congress government—India's second since 1947.

The crisis which the new government in Delhi faced within days of taking over was of a character that would throw any government—new or old—off balance. Rubaiya Sayeed, the newly appointed home minister's twenty-three-year-old daughter was kidnapped in Srinagar and the release of several militants in custody was demanded for her safe return. For any government, anywhere in the world, this was a nightmare situation. The kidnapping sent multiple messages. Mufti Mohammad Sayeed was a prominent politician of Kashmir. He was the first Muslim to be appointed home minister of India. For Prime Minister V.P. Singh's coalition, the crisis was a setback in its earliest days that it could never recover from. For the next two years, it lurched from one crisis—external and internal—to the next. It meant, moreover, an ominous start for its Pakistan policy.

I.K. Gujral, foreign minister in India's second non-Congress government, was a veteran foreign policy hand with lots of ideas about how to improve India–Pakistan relations. But the kidnapping meant that relations with Pakistan began on the worst possible note. The V.P. Singh government was sworn in on 2 December 1989 and the kidnapping happened on 8 December. Its resolution a few days later, with the release of the militants from custody, as demanded by the kidnappers, coloured all future perceptions of the government as weak and incapable of standing up to pressure.

At one stage in desperation the Government of India also appealed to the Government of Pakistan to ensure the girl's safety. Gujral was later to recollect bitterly the proforma and minimal statement issued from Pakistan's foreign ministry in Islamabad in response: that such acts 'are contrary to Islamic precepts' and hope that the matter will be resolved 'through negotiations'.[82] The Pakistan statement also explicitly clarified that it had issued its appeal 'on humanitarian grounds' and specifically at the 'request' of India. In India, this statement could be read in only one way—Pakistan delighting in India's discomfiture over this fresh crisis in Kashmir.

All in all, it was an ominous start. It left a residue of bitterness amongst those in the new government in India who may have hoped to forge a new relationship much as Morarji Desai and A.B. Vajpayee had attempted during 1978–80. Even more serious was the situation in Kashmir itself. 'Rubaiya Sayeed's kidnapping opened the floodgates of insurgency' is one recollection of the time.[83] A quarter-century later, Mufti Mohammad Sayeed was to say to a journalist with regard to the kidnapping saga: 'That is a guilt I will carry to my grave.'[84] In Kashmir Valley, the writ of the state and government authority seemed to be crumbling in the face of terrorist attacks and large demonstrations ignoring curfew orders leading finally to police and military action with consequent fatalities.

In Pakistan, according to some accounts, this posed a real dilemma for Benazir Bhutto. After all, both she and her party had made improvement of relations with India a priority and a major plank of her foreign policy. On the other hand, she was a Pakistani and Kashmir was Kashmir. In an internal meeting in January 1990, she is quoted as having said: 'It is difficult to keep up the momentum for normalization while the situation in Kashmir is daily going from bad to worse.' At the same time the options before her were clear: 'We are not going to be defensive about our position. We support self-determination for Kashmir, to be exercised through a plebiscite, and no one must be left in any doubt about that.'[85]

In India, it seemed obvious that there was a strong Pakistani hand in the troubles—guiding, funding and arming a militant separatist movement and exercising control over political figures in Kashmir through acts of intimidation, including assassinations on the ground. Some had doubts whether this was Benazir Bhutto's policy and pointed to the controlling hand of the army and the ISI on key foreign policy issues, especially anything related to India. For most, this debate over the responsibility or otherwise of the civilian government was time wasted in esoteric hairsplitting while Kashmir burnt, the writ of the state shrank and casualties increased. There was sufficient evidence—arms, infiltration and money—of the Pakistani footprint.

During the kidnapping crisis, Amanullah Khan, self-declared head of the Jammu Kashmir Liberation Front (JKLF), addressed a press he former Union Education Minister Nurul Hasan, who was my friend when we were together in the Indira Gandhi Government. fter the partition of India Yakub had moved over to Pakistan. g a leading member of the Soviet Academy of Sciences, he [Nurul an] would stay with us during his frequent visits to Moscow. s, he was a useful link between the missions of India and Pakistan. re was never an occasion when relations between our missions re tense, not even when our respective home governments were at ggers drawn'. Yaqoob and I had even gone to the extent of hosting oint dinner to bid farewell to N.G. Sudarikov, who was in charge the South Asia desk in the Soviet Foreign Ministry.[86]

he Gujral–Yaqub Khan meeting of January 1990 is significant only for what transpired in it but also for how two interlocutors knew each other reasonably well could walk away from it with cally different accounts of what happened. The visit coincided with articularly bad time in the Valley. The Rubaiya Sayeed kidnapping s fresh in everyone's mind. On 17 January, a few days before Yaqub an's arrival, Chief Minister Farooq Abdullah had resigned protesting appointment of a new governor, Jagmohan, regarded as a tough ministrator who could restore law and order and put down militancy. e government had possibly chosen Jagmohan to erase the impression eated by the Rubaiya kidnapping of being too 'soft'. Within a few hours f his being sworn in, governor's rule—which meant that the Central overnment would administer the state through the governor—was mposed on Jammu and Kashmir. Many Delhi newspapers of 22 January 1990, the day the Pakistan foreign minister arrived in Delhi, had carried the banner headline that thirty-five persons had been killed in Kashmir by police and paramilitary firings the day before.[87] This was largely the result of firing at the Gowkadal bridge, in the heart of downtown Srinagar, and the death toll was, in fact, it was to emerge, much higher.

There was, however, a larger, if at the time silent, tragedy under way in the Valley. Its small but culturally and intellectually significant Hindu minority found itself facing a concentrated and venomous campaign from extremist groups led by the Hizb-ul-Mujahideen and the Jammu Kashmir Liberation Front. Beginning with selected assassinations, this campaign by 18 January had reached a fever pitch with many mosques blaring threats against the Hindus amidst calls for jihad. From the night

conference in Rawalpindi listing out the kidnappers
confirmation for anyone who read a newspaper in
complicity. It is a different matter that many in P
especially in the ISI, had a jaundiced view of the JKL
Kashmir becoming a province of Pakistan but for its i
Amanullah Khan himself had served time in Pakistani
the average Pakistani, charged up by the rhetorical at
streets, if the JKLF was leading the charge in 'Indian He
be it since the whole point was to support the Kashmiri
'Indian tyranny'.

It was in this context that a meeting took place in earl
in hindsight must rank as a classic India–Pakistan exchang
minister of Pakistan, Sahibzada Yaqub Khan, was in Delhi
January as part of a SAARC tour—Pakistan then was still
SAARC having hosted the last summit. His Indian counterpar
had been one of the key cabinet ministers dealing with the Rub
kidnapping just about a month earlier. He was also at the he
in India wanting normalization of relations with Pakistan.
from Lahore, Gujral had made no secret of his views in this
far and would not do so in future too. He had around him
of like-minded intellectuals, journalists and public figures wh
consistently to advocate better relations between India and P

Gujral, having served as ambassador to the Soviet Union earli
highly regarded nationally and internationally as a senior political
in India with first-hand knowledge and experience of practical diplo
Sahibzada Yaqub Khan was similarly a greatly respected figu
Pakistan and internationally. In 1971, he had recommended a poli
approach to the East Pakistan crisis rather than a military crackdo
When his view was not accepted, he asked to be transferred out of E
Pakistan and emerged as perhaps the only Pakistani general who survive
the 1971 crisis with his reputation not just intact but enhanced. Both
ministers, moreover, knew each other well—they were ambassadors of their respective countries in Moscow in the late 1970s. There were also other connections and in Gujral's account:

> He [Yaqub Khan] was a scion of the princely state of Rampur and was related to the former President of India Fakhruddin Ali Ahmed

of the 19 January, a panic-stricken exodus of the Hindus to the safety of Jammu and elsewhere began. Estimates of the numbers who fled that night itself are unclear but that day heralded what would take the rest of the year to finish—an effective and comprehensive ethnic cleansing of the Valley as about 300,000 persons left their home. The ancient community of Kashmiri Pandits were now refugees in their own country. Since then, they observe 19 January as 'Exodus Day'.

The Yaqub Khan–I.K. Gujral meeting was, therefore, a high-level India–Pakistan meeting in the worst of circumstances. In Gujral's account, Yaqub Khan delivered a war ultimatum during their meeting. Although they knew each other well, Gujral describes how Yaqub Khan in the meeting 'avoided looking into my eyes', 'his tone was shrill', while delivering a message 'approved at the highest level' that 'he was instructed to say that the situation in Kashmir was risky and could lead to perilous consequences'. His main point was that 'Pakistan had never accepted that Kashmir was a settled issue. It remains a disputed territory and our claims to it are very much there.' While Yaqub Khan did not use words such as 'ultimatum' or 'war', for Gujral 'the tone of his hard message was clearly to that effect'. Yakub Khan also told Gujral that 'the joshwallas (meaning the hawks) on our side were now centre stage' and that they 'sometimes talk of the 1965 war and sometimes of the war of 1971'.[88]

Some accounts of this conversation say that Yaqub Khan used the phrase 'the clouds are roaring with thunder' and 'there is lightning in the skies' and these were, in fact, a veiled nuclear threat.[89] J.N. Dixit, then the Indian high commissioner in Pakistan, who was present in Delhi for Yaqub Khan's visit also writes about the meetings in a similar vein: Yaqub Khan's visit was to 'pressurize, perhaps even intimidate India' and that he was 'stern and admonitory in his pronouncements'. Gujral was cautioned that 'war clouds would hover over the subcontinent if timely action was not taken'.[90] Much the same message, and in Gujral's recollection, with the same tone was delivered later to Prime Minister V.P. Singh who maintained a 'dignified silence'.

The next day Gujral describes his response in a meeting, alone with Yaqub Khan, in the Pakistan high commissioner's residence:

> I told him in a firm tone that we had had a high-level meeting to discuss what we believe was a war ultimatum to me and I had been

instructed to tell you in no uncertain terms that you would be well advised to appreciate the strength and resilience of the Indian State.[91]

In Gujral's recollection, this firm position made Yaqub Khan deny that he had conveyed an ultimatum for a war or a 1965-like operation. At this point Gujral says he told Yaqub Khan 'that he must know that the Indian psyche shaped by a history of thousands of years would go through anything, even genocide, but it would not permit secession'.[92]

Pakistani accounts of these meetings, however, paint a different picture. Iqbal Akhund, Benazir Bhutto's national security and foreign affairs adviser, says that on hearing Yaqub Khan's account of the Delhi talks, many in the cabinet felt that he (Yaqub Khan) 'had not been clear and forceful enough in expressing Pakistan's position on Kashmir'.[93] According to Akhund, Yaqub Khan came back with nothing new on the Indian position except 'a quotable phrase' by Gujral: 'Don't forget, Minister, that every Indian carries on his shoulders the burden of a thousand years of history.' In Yaqub Khan's telling of the story, at least to Iqbal Akhund, Gujral and the Indians saw the Kashmir situation in terms of Hinduism's epochal struggle against Islam. Gujral's own version is of reference to the spiritual unity of India for thousands of years which nothing could shatter. Akhund also writes that years later when Gujral told him of Yaqub Khan's 'war ultimatum' he was surprised because the latter was 'a man of smooth and circuitous phrases, not to lay about him with ultimatums'. Gujral, however, also mentioned Yaqub Khan's ultimatum to Benazir Bhutto a year and a half later, when she visited India for Rajiv Gandhi's funeral. Her response was, 'God is my witness. I never knew about it till I saw your public statement. I had asked Yakub about it. He denied that there was any such exchange.'[94] What Gujral clearly felt, indeed was convinced about, was that Yaqub Khan was delivering a message directly from the Pakistan Army, unknown to Benazir Bhutto. He was, after all a former general himself, not in Benazir Bhutto's party and ultimately 'such was the oddity of Pakistan's polity'.

In these divergent accounts, the underlying theme is the wide difference of position and aspiration in both countries about Jammu and Kashmir. After a quietude of a quarter-century, it would be Kashmir's turn again to dominate India–Pakistan relations in the coming years.

7

Hopes for the Future in a Troubled Decade

HOW TWO SUCH PRACTISED hands as Yaqub Khan and I.K. Gujral could leave different accounts of the same conversation has been much analysed and discussed up to this day.[1] Different explanations, apart from what either side believed, have been offered. Some in Pakistan believe that Gujral—disappointed at the line Yaqub Khan was taking and seeing a setback to his cherished idea of India–Pakistan reconciliation—ended up misunderstanding the message his Pakistan counterpart was delivering. Another explanation is that Yaqub Khan, personally upset and angry at recent developments in Jammu and Kashmir, especially at the shootings in the Valley reported on the day of his arrival, went beyond what he may have intended and ended up taking a much harder line than he wanted. Whatever may be the real explanation, the situation on the ground continued to deteriorate and rhetoric on both sides further ratchetted up. That Yaqub Khan on his return to Pakistan was to deliver a speech on TV and Radio on the situation in Kashmir confirmed both that there was serious tension brewing between India and Pakistan as also that his visit to India had not gone well.

The overall climate was thus one of tension and suspicion. Routine troop movements were frequently misinterpreted, leading to further spikes in tension and there were many localized situations of self-fulfilling prophecies. There were other aggravating factors. JKLF leader Amanullah Khan, sitting in Rawalpindi, issued a steady stream of statements of marching with thousands of supporters across the LOC from Pakistan into the Kashmir Valley in India. An opposition politician in Pakistan,

Sheikh Rashid, set up a training camp in Rawalpindi for volunteers who would be trained to fight for Kashmir.[2] In India, intelligence and media reports both pointed to the many training camps and launch pads that had come up in Pakistan-occupied Kashmir manned by veterans of the Afghan jihad and some young men from the Kashmir Valley who had crossed the LOC to get arms and assistance from Pakistan.

On 5 February 1990, amidst a Pakistan-wide 'Kashmir Strike', Nawaz Sharif, the then chief minister of Punjab, and Prime Minister Benazir Bhutto competed to not let the other appear more committed to the liberation of Kashmir. A large crowd, some say thousands strong, tried to cross the LOC into Jammu and Kashmir. After repeated warnings, the Indian border guards fired at the mob crossing over, leading to several casualties. A few days later, another such attempted crossing was again fired upon.[3] Incidentally, since 1990, 5 February has become a permanent fixture of Pakistan's political calendar as 'Kashmir Solidarity Day' or *Yaum-i-Yakjehti*.

To many in India, it seemed clear enough that Pakistan was attempting a repeat of a less covert Operation Gibraltar of 1965 or at the very least trying to add to the intensity of domestic turbulence in J&K. The Bharatiya Janata Party in the opposition demanded hot pursuit and strikes across the LOC on staging camps. Benazir Bhutto, addressing a rally in Muzaffarabad on 13 March 1990 spoke of a '1000-year war' for Kashmir. A few weeks later, addressing parliament, Prime Minister V.P. Singh said if a war was forced on India, 'we are not going to stop till we have achieved our objectives' and that Pakistan had to see if 'it could fight for even a thousand hours'.[4]

Amidst this charged rhetoric, infiltration across the LOC increased as did incidents of terrorism and violence in J&K. Inevitably, troop movements on both sides were analysed as indicative of offensive plans in the making. That this was the conventional exercise time for both armies in the plains of Punjab and on the Sindh–Rajasthan border made for a situation where normal could be read as abnormal, or a real military threat. The chief of the army staff of Pakistan, General Aslam Beg, was regarded as someone who saw current events in the broad sweep of Islamic history: Pakistan could, in this view, ride the crests created by the Islamic revolution in Iran and the Soviet defeat in Afghanistan. A large military exercise General Aslam Beg had executed at this time—

the Zarb-e-Momin—raised in India the same concerns that Brasstacks had in Pakistan earlier.[5] Worst-case scenarios anticipated in India was that a Pakistani armoured thrust would seek to take advantage of unsettled conditions in Punjab and Kashmir. Indian counter-deployments in turn triggered Pakistani anxieties.[6] In Pakistan, apart from other apprehensions, there was the fear of an Afghan–Indian concert—the danger that 'India might seek [the then President of Afghanistan] Najibullah's collaboration and take out Kahuta [Pakistan's principal nuclear facility] with an Afghan scud missile'.[7]

A close associate of Benazir Bhutto suggests that an intense debate was under way in early 1990 in the Pakistan military and intelligence set-up on the Kashmir situation: '... the reaction to the movement was highly emotional and the instinct was to give it full and unreserved support. There were those who saw the spontaneous uprising of the Kashmiris as a 'historic turning point, a now or never opportunity to settle the Kashmir dispute'.[8] The US ambassador in Islamabad recalled being told by policymakers in Pakistan that 'the combination of Islamic zeal and Afghan nationalism had defeated the powerful Soviet Union, and the same should be true when Islam was systematically injected into Kashmir.'[9] There was also, quite apart from the Kashmir-related sentiment, the desire for a tit for tat for Bangladesh.

If there were saner voices and counsel—and these finally prevailed—nevertheless, Pakistani actions, and more important, the way they were being anticipated in India, meant that tensions remained high. It was certainly the case that external powers—in particular the US—was half convinced that more serious clashes were imminent or even that another subcontinental war was in the offing. In fact, the tension level had peaked in February and an April 1990 meeting in New York between Gujral and Yaqub Khan had somewhat eased the situation.[10]

But the high-tension levels of the past few months had left a deep impression on many. The US felt that tensions were still too high for a time when governments in both countries were tottering. Benazir Bhutto's government would be dismissed in August 1990. In India, the V.P. Singh government stumbled on till November, but it was continuously wracked by crises created by conflicting demands of the alliance partners. India–Pakistan tensions, arms build-ups on the borders, agitation in the Kashmir Valley alongside widespread terrorist violence and infiltration from Pakistan—led many analysts to believe that all the components of a major war were falling in place.

Receiving increasingly alarmist reports from its ambassadors in India and Pakistan, the US president dispatched his deputy national security advisor Robert Gates to India and Pakistan in May 1990. Some three years later, the Gates mission was to be described in the *New Yorker* as a last-ditch effort by President Bush, 'convinced that the world was on the edge of a nuclear exchange between India and Pakistan'.[11] This was an alarmist account by the journalist Seymour Hersh based on a one-sided reading of the facts but it has, nonetheless, left a deep imprint in public memory. The Gates mission did, however, succeed in starting a regular dialogue process between India and Pakistan. Between July 1990 and October 1991, there were five rounds of discussions between the foreign secretaries. In the words of a Pakistani insider, these talks '... even more quickly than expected, started going around in small circles'.[12] These five meetings generated a large amount of paper but nothing of great substance or of interest to those outside the relatively small foreign policy and strategic communities in both countries. Nevertheless, these were helpful in keeping up a veneer of normalcy in an otherwise bad situation. Clearly, while the crisis had eased even before the Gates visit, both governments also quietly used the opening it provided to de-escalate the tension and rhetoric from the high levels reached in early 1990.[13]

Even in this fraught environment, the mood in these talks often fluctuated—depending on the interlocuters—between acrimony and polemics on the hand and a more positive attitude on the other to see what could be done in practical terms to improve or at least manage a bad situation. The Indian high commissioner and later foreign secretary J.N. Dixit describes how the mood could alter with personalities, as for instance when Shaharyar Khan became foreign secretary of Pakistan. While he stated Pakistan's position on Kashmir firmly enough, '... the flights of abuse and peroration that one of his predecessors, Tanvir Ahmed Khan, used to employ were completely absent'.[14]

These rounds of talks also produced two agreements, reached earlier but formally concluded now. The first was an agreement on 'Prevention of Air Space Violations', to ensure that military aircraft kept a certain distance from the other country's airspace. The second was that each side would share details in advance of military exercises and troop movements being carried out on or near the international border or the Line of Control. Both agreements were steps to prevent recurrence of misreading of intentions as had happened during the Operation Brasstacks exercise of 1986 or the more recent spike in tension in early 1990 following the Pakistani Zarb-i-Momin. These agreements, signed in April 1991, were evidence, at least to those who were on the inside, that small steps forward are possible even in generally adverse circumstances. For others, it suggested that while the peak of the 1990 crisis was a thing of the past, the overall situation was far from stable. There were, in fact, other developments in motion and, as in the past, these were of a magnitude that diplomacy alone could not cope with.

The crisis of 1990 has been with some merit described as a 'compound' crisis since four different arcs intersected in early 1990.[15] Firstly, it was the 'first post cold war crisis'. It occurred amidst the onset of the collapse of the Soviet Union and unlike in the past it was the United States as the sole superpower which involved itself in the India–Pakistan interface. Secondly, it was believed to have the potential of a nuclear confrontation. An exaggerated notion of this was portrayed by the Seymour Hersh article referred to earlier but that such concerns did exist in the United States and elsewhere at the time is nevertheless true. Thirdly, it was a regional crisis with the situation in Jammu and Kashmir itself deteriorating and coming to occupy centre stage. Fourthly and finally, it was an internal political crisis in both countries with an unstable coalition government in India and a weak civilian government in Pakistan for the first time after over a decade of military rule.

The crisis itself passed relatively quickly although the structural factors underpinning it remained. From mid-1990 other international events had major implications for both India and Pakistan—in particular the Iraqi invasion of Kuwait (August 1990) and the Gulf War of 1991 thereafter. In May 1991, Rajiv Gandhi was tragically assassinated. For his supporters, the fresh political impulse he had bought to bear on relations with Pakistan died with him. Nawaz Sharif, as prime minister of Pakistan, attended the funeral—as did his predecessor Benazir Bhutto—

perhaps the first of his many future symbolic steps to underline the need for improving India–Pakistan relations. A few weeks later, he sent a message through a special envoy to the new prime minister of India, P.V. Narasimha Rao, that Pakistan desired normalization of relations. There was, however, other crisis situations developing—partly because of Kashmir but also from a totally unexpected direction.

In India, the Babri Masjid agitation led by the Bharatiya Janata Party was gaining momentum. On 31 October 1991, a supercharged mob stormed the disputed structure and planted saffron flags on its domes. Some damage to the structure and surrounding walls also took place, adding a new dimension to the tensions resulting from the Kashmir situation and the polemic emerging from Pakistan. A week or so earlier, Shiv Sena activists dug up the cricket pitch at the Wankhede stadium in Bombay. This was soon after its leader Bal Thackeray said he would call for a Bombay bandh in case a scheduled One-Day International (ODI) between the Indian and Pakistani cricket teams took place. A few days later, Pakistan called off the planned five-match tour of India. Cricket was, in fact, a good barometer of the political atmospherics prevailing and matches between India and Pakistan entered a long hiatus of almost a decade and a half.

All this was only setting the stage for 1992. Through that year, continuing tensions in Kashmir along with the Babri Masjid agitation proved to be an explosive combination. In February 1992, another march by the JKLF to cross the LOC was stopped, this time by Pakistani forces. In the police firing and clashes at least seventeen people were killed. Nawaz Sharif said that the Government of Pakistan would not allow such a crossing as '... we did not want a fourth war with India'.[16] To many, it did seem that India and Pakistan had stepped back from the brink again. Another attempt was made by the JKLF to cross the LOC in end-March 1992 only to be stopped by Pakistani forces, but in a more controlled fashion, without loss of life.

An increase in the baiting and ill-treatment, including on occasion physical violence, of each other's diplomats—something that happened between India and Pakistan with a far greater frequency than elsewhere in the world—was a reflection of these growing tensions. Amidst all this, the Pakistan team won the Cricket World Cup in March 1992. President R. Venkataraman sent a congratulatory message to his counterpart in

Islamabad. It was left to Foreign Secretary J.N. Dixit to ruefully recall, some years later, that such exchanges '... only serve to increase the scepticism of public opinion in both countries about the incongruity of it all'.[17]

As the Babri Masjid agitation rolled on in India, it seemed to push all other aspects of India–Pakistan relations into the background. The final act, the demolition of the structure in December 1992, led to a wave of revulsion in Pakistan against the treatment of Muslims in India. For the religious right, it provided a ready-made platform to consolidate its cadres. Revenge attacks against the minorities of Pakistan were the means to even the score. In the immediate aftermath of the demolition in Ayodhya, over 120 temples were destroyed in Pakistan. Some churches and Gurdwaras too were attacked. The Indian consul general's house in Karachi was attacked and ransacked.

The Ayodhya demolition and the revenge attacks in Pakistan saw both governments weigh into each other. For the Government of Pakistan, the demolition was 'a despicable act of the extremists', an 'abhorrent act of extreme fanaticism', presenting 'before the world the true and ugly face of Indian secularism'.[18] In India, these Pakistan reactions came on top of its own sense of dismay and shock that a court-protected structure could be destroyed by a supercharged mob in broad daylight as the state stood aside and the whole world watched. Events in Pakistan were, thus, seized on with energy. The violence there was described as 'state terrorism unleashed on the minority communities', and comments by Pakistan on the Babri Masjid as 'gross interference'. Remarks made by President Ghulam Ishaq Khan in the national assembly were described as his 'habitual ... vituperative rhetoric over India', 'highly provocative, malicious and intended to inflame public opinion.'[19]

Amidst this mutual bashing, some other scores were settled. The Government of Pakistan decided to reduce to a minuscule number the size of the Indian consulate in Karachi, long described as a nest of spies. The fact is that the outreach it commanded in Karachi and Sindh because of 'visa power' was something many in Pakistan found difficult to stomach. The Government of India, on its part, formally communicated that it had decided that Pakistan's request for Jinnah's old house in Bombay for use as its consulate could not be agreed to. This was no more than the formal communication of a decision taken a decade earlier but the point is that this was a season of mutual bashing. There was no question, of course, of a dialogue in this atmosphere. A further fallout of the Babri Masjid demolition was the postponement of the SAARC summit, originally scheduled to be held in Dhaka in December 1992. Incidentally, there had been a similar pattern of attacks on Hindu minorities and temples in Bangladesh following the Babri Masjid demolition.

But worse was to follow and this was a series of bomb blasts in Bombay with heavy loss of life in March 1993. The leaders of the underworld gang who had carried this out were found to have received sanctuary in Karachi and the explosions themselves were guided and masterminded by Pakistan's Inter-Services Intelligence. This was revenge, pure and simple. Dawood Ibrahim, the leader of the underworld family responsible for this attack has continued to evade Indian and international law and has been for a quarter of a century now and remains still a principal bone of contention between India and Pakistan. In the face of evidence that Dawood Ibrahim is in Pakistan, the bland denials, for the past quarter-century, to the contrary have become almost a textbook illustration of the deception and bad faith that forms the core of India–Pakistan relations.

As it happens, Prime Ministers Nawaz Sharif and Narasimha Rao did meet in Dhaka when the postponed SAARC summit was held in April 1993. But it was a formalistic meeting, made doubly so by the fact that soon after his return to Islamabad, Nawaz Sharif was dismissed by President Ishaq Khan. In the fracas that followed, fresh elections were held and Benazir Bhutto returned as prime minister in October 1993—a little over three years after her own dismissal.

Benazir Bhutto's return to power led to a brief attempt to resume some engagement and, surprisingly given the overall adverse situation, the foreign secretaries did meet in early January 1994. But the meeting was doomed to failure even before it took place. It was foregrounded by events in the Kashmir Valley, which suggested a government in India paralysed by conflicting compulsions and almost powerless to enforce its writ. In mid-October 1993, a group of militants holed themselves up in the Hazratbal shrine holding some 150 pilgrims, including women and children, as hostages. They demanded safe passage, threatening otherwise to blow up the mosque along with the sacred relic of the holy Prophet.

After a gap of three decades, the Hazratbal Mosque in Srinagar was again on the front page of every newspaper in India and drawing also huge coverage internationally. The general perception was of a government paralysed by past images—the first Hazratbal crisis of 1963, of Operation Blue Star in the Golden Temple in 1984 and, most of all, of the more recent destruction of the Babri Masjid. The bulk of the political leadership, appalled and distressed at this situation, was unanimous on one point—not the slightest risk of damage to the shrine could be taken. For the security forces, keen on a swift flushing out operation, this left no real choice except a protracted siege. A complex negotiation process began both with the militants inside and their dispersed and diffuse leadership outside. The terrorists inside made the most of the publicity they were getting and daily blow-by-blow accounts of the siege and Pakistan's role dominated the Indian media.[20] For many in Pakistan, the struggle for Kashmir seemed now realistically to be in the final stages. At some early stage, as in all negotiations, a softening in some of the militants was noticed—leading to food and supplies being sent to the militants and the hostages. 'Hot biryani' being given to terrorists entered India's political vocabulary then and has remained in that lexicon—a representation or a metaphor of state softness towards Pakistan in general and terrorists in particular.

As the siege ended in mid-November 1993, it left a residue of bitterness that would endure. What was regarded locally by many in Kashmir Valley as a successful conclusion—surrender of the militants, no damage to the shrine and not a shot fired—was for most of India a humiliation. For most in Pakistan, it was another step towards victory and Kashmir's impending integration with Pakistan.

Against this backdrop, J.N. Dixit, the Indian foreign secretary, travelled to Pakistan on 1 January 1994. Prime Minister Benazir Bhutto was not in Islamabad. Somewhat to everyone's surprise a call on her was arranged in Karachi and a special aircraft was provided for the foreign secretary to reach there. But all this was trying to put a veneer of normality, even cordiality, on a situation which was, for the time being at least, beyond what diplomacy could patch up. Soon after the departure of Dixit, the Government of Pakistan announced that further talks were meaningless unless India was prepared to discuss the status of Kashmir and remove security forces from the Hazratbal shrine. Formal talks between India and Pakistan now entered a long pause. Pakistan then made two 'semi-formal' proposals—semi-formal because they were made through the medium of 'non-papers'. One of these listed the 'Modalities for the holding of a Plebiscite in Jammu and Kashmir'. The other was no less provocative for India: measures required to create a propitious climate for peaceful resolution of the Jammu and Kashmir dispute and other issues. Not surprisingly, both were seen as polemical and grandstanding exercises. India responded with proposals of its own—peace and tranquility on the LOC; Siachen; India–Pakistan joint commission; confidence-building measures. For the Pakistan foreign office, the absence of Kashmir in this list meant that this was not a serious initiative.[21]

With bilateral diplomacy suspended the stage was being set for a different kind of contest. The view in Pakistan was that developments in India and in J&K—the Rubaiya kidnapping, the Babri Masjid demolition, the Hazratbal siege, etc.—pointed to a situation and atmosphere conducive to gain traction for J&K internationally. International condemnation of India would act to further strengthen the Kashmir 'freedom struggle'. What fuelled this assessment was the spread of militancy in the Valley and the confidence in the Pakistan Army that the Afghanistan template was yielding results for Kashmir. The US position too seemed to be more impatient with India and sympathetic to Pakistan regarding the situation in the Kashmir Valley.

An assistant secretary of state, Robin Raphel, long regarded by Indians as being firmly in Pakistan's camp (her former husband had been US ambassador in Pakistan and, in fact, had been killed along with President Zia in the air crash), had made comments that verged on questioning the accession of J&K to India. Speaking to journalists in October 1993, she had said that the United States viewed the 'whole of Kashmir as a disputed territory the status of which needs to be resolved' and that this meant 'we do not recognize the instrument of accession as meaning that Kashmir is forever an integral part of India'.[22] These remarks coincided also with the ongoing siege at the Hazratbal Mosque in Srinagar.[23] The uproar in India over this statement drowned out the analysis that in substance this was not so much a change of US policy as an upfront, if undiplomatic and crude, assertion of it. In the background of all these factors considered conducive to its position, Pakistan, soon after suspending the dialogue with India, tabled a resolution in the UN Human Rights Commission in Geneva in February 1994 on the human rights situation in Jammu and Kashmir.

Kashmir was ostensibly back in the United Nations after a long gap. The Human Rights Commission (HRC) was, however, an institution which gave a considerable role for non-governmental organizations and human rights activists in its deliberations. Media and popular attention are encouraged as means of debating issues. Diplomacy here moves out of closed rooms into open platforms. In effect, then, the deliberations in the commission became an India–Pakistan contestation in a Western capital. Public opinion in both countries seized on the confrontation with energy. This was a prestige clash occurring amidst real tensions, plus the usual recriminations and distrust. In India, there was some visible nervousness and the then foreign secretary K. Srinivasan recalls Prime Minister Narasimha Rao's apprehension: 'In the final week or so before the time for a vote, Narasimha Rao became very shaky. Was there some other way out, he asked me anxiously ... I assured him that the numbers were on our side. He looked very dubious.'[24]

The tabling of the resolution led to an NGO war in Geneva with both countries marshalling their resources. India found only two accredited NGOs (under the HRC rules only these could speak, apart from member countries of the commission)—the venerable All India Women's Conference and a trade related research institution—Research and Information Systems. The Pakistanis were similarly stretched relying on the World Society of Victimology, although some in India felt that the Pakistanis had marshalled other NGOs earlier. For India, the stakes were high—the adoption of the resolution would mean a public loss of face and loss of morale in India. To the scaremongers, defeat would mean a shot in the arm for the Pakistan-sponsored militancy in the Valley. In Pakistan too there were similar pressures—defeat would mean a setback to the Kashmir cause. In public perception, it would also be a defeat for the government's diplomacy: with Pakistan, a member of the UN Security Council (as it was then) and the Valley on fire, how could the government not convince the international community about the repressive tactics being used by India in Kashmir?

In the end, both did a lot of heavy lifting. Both governments fielded high-powered delegations and deployed high-level envoys to lobby foreign capitals. To many in India, this investment of diplomatic and political capital was itself objectionable even if necessary. Foreign Secretary Srinivasan recalls:

> We felt indignant that we were obliged to descend to the level of the Pakistanis and playing into their hands, since one of their prime objectives has invariably been that they should cut India down to the same size as themselves and establish a bogus parity. When you stoop to bandy words with someone lesser than you, the whole world sees you both as equal.[25]

But there were two instruments employed by the Government of India which transformed a high-voltage diplomatic exercise into a national endeavour. Firstly, both Houses of parliament adopted a common resolution on 24 February 1994 declaring the whole of Jammu and Kashmir an integral part of India and demanding that Pakistan must vacate the part of Jammu and Kashmir it had forcibly occupied through aggression in 1947–48. This parliamentary articulation of a position hitherto implicit or left understated was, in fact, a bigger change than many at that time saw. Secondly, the leader of the opposition in parliament was asked to lead the Indian delegation to the Human Rights Commission. This was none other than former foreign minister Atal Bihari Vajpayee. The Kashmir leader and former chief minister Farooq Abdullah and minister of state in the Ministry of External Affair (MEA) Salman Khurshid were the other notables in the Indian delegation. This was a show of symbolic and real bipartisanship. It was a politically astute move by Prime Minister Narasimha Rao but also showed how high the stakes were. Prime Minister Benazir Bhutto made a brief visit to Geneva to bolster support for Pakistan to counter which the then Indian finance minister Manmohan Singh also visited Geneva.

As rhetoric and counter-rhetoric bounced off each other, both sides counted the line-up in their favour. Finally, Pakistan withdrew the resolution to spare itself a defeat if the matter was voted upon. For the Indian camp this was a resounding victory and when A.B. Vajpayee and Salman Khurshid flew back to Delhi, they received 'a euphoric welcome usually given to victorious cricket teams', as a journalist commented.[26] K. Srinivasan was to remember his 'surprise by the national jubilation' with which Vajpayee and Khurshid were received.[27]

But despite the victory, the cognoscenti in India realized how bruising this bout had been. Srinivasan summarized the position, which led to Pakistan withdrawing the draft resolution. 'The number of votes in favour of Pakistan's draft resolution was always going to be small; our reckoning was that ours would be somewhat higher—something like 7 for us and 4 for Pakistan, with all the rest, constituting the vast majority of members, abstaining.'[28]

On his return, A.B. Vajpayee commented: 'For a great nation like us, there was a certain humiliation involved in having to go around begging for votes on a human rights issue. Let us now use this reprieve to clean up our act in Kashmir or there will be a Geneva every few months.'[29]

The failure to have the resolution adopted meant enormous domestic criticism for Benazir Bhutto's government. The line adopted by the government that Pakistan had succeeded in internationalizing Kashmir had few takers. To appease public opinion, the effort had to be continued with. Therefore, the next session of the UN General Assembly saw a replay of the Geneva contest. Jamsheed Marker, then the Pakistan ambassador to the UN, recalls: 'Foreign Minister Sardar Asef Ahmed Ali's statement to the General Assembly was amongst the longest on record, with elaborate references to Kashmir, and I am not sure whether the modest applause that it evoked at the end was motivated by appreciation or relief.'[30]

A UN resolution of some kind had become a domestic political issue and requirement in Pakistan. Nawabzada Nasrullah Khan, a prominent opposition leader, headed the Pakistan delegation to the United Nations. In Marker's recollection, the Nawabzada 'started from Pakistan with the fiery endorsement of his supporters ringing in his ears, and visited a couple of European capitals where his meetings with the local Pakistani communities convinced him of the support from the Governments where they resided as immigrants'. Marker soon found that his professional advice not to press the issue was being disregarded. The danger was: 'A heavily defeated resolution would wipe out our claims under the previous Security Council Resolutions which had been the bedrock of our position on Kashmir over the past three decades.' As Marker persisted with his advice his arguments 'were angrily brushed aside' and he realized 'that once again we were dealing with the damaging issue of national self-denial'.[31] In the event, it was plain speaking by fellow Islamic countries such as Morocco and Indonesia that made Pakistan desist from tabling a resolution that would not find support. Foreign Secretary Srinivasan recalls:

> On my reckoning, we would have won a vote in the UN with plenty to spare. Few countries, other than Pakistan's most fervid backers, wanted to get on the wrong side of India. Most countries were sick and tired of the repeated raising of Kashmir by Pakistan and wanted to find a way to rebuff them. And the intricacies and passions connected with the Kashmir question deterred any but the most hardy or thin skinned countries from getting too deeply involved.[32]

If this was a second defeat for Pakistan, and seen as such, India had also to show flexibility. Foreign Secretary Srinivasan thus found: 'While Kashmir was an internal domestic problem it was clear that we could not keep the international wolf from the door and more particularly the NGO interest, unless some major steps were taken domestically to address international concerns.' All this meant pushing in precisely those areas where there was considerable resistance to change. While these steps helped consolidate India's position internationally and gave to the situation in J&K greater transparency, nevertheless building a consensus around them was a difficult and tense process. During this time, K. Srinivasan recalls a particularly fraught meeting in which practically everybody concerned with J&K in the government was present. At the start, Srinivasan outlined '... the fragile international position that India would find itself in, if we did not show any forward political movement in the state'. At this point, Prime Minister Narasimha Rao '... suddenly and unexpectedly flew into a furious temper, declaiming almost hysterically that he would never surrender the gains made by Nehru and Indira Gandhi.... The meeting was rocked to its heels by Narasimha Rao's angry outburst.'[33]

At this stage, Rajesh Pilot (MOS in the home ministry and a kind of point man for J&K matters in the government)

> broke the mounting tension by interrupting the Prime Minister in his tirade, and shouting him down with a screaming outburst of his own, to the effect that he was being marginalized and sabotaged in his efforts in the State ... and that the present status quo in Kashmir served no purpose. As dramatic theatre, it was grand opera.[34]

Decisions taken then and through this process included allowing the International Committee of the Red Cross access to prisoners, releasing leading dissidents and agreeing to fresh elections to end the stint of governor's rule since 1990. The elections were eventually held in 1996 after over six-and-a-half years of governor's rule.

Through this period, a steady deterioration in India–Pakistan relations continued. In December 1994, soon after its UN General Assembly (UNGA) bid on Kashmir fell through, Pakistan decided to close the Indian consulate in Karachi accusing it of terrorist activities. The Pakistan consulate in Bombay had been voluntarily closed earlier by the Pakistan government on the grounds of the continuous difficulties in normal functioning. In any case, the closure in Karachi was predictable and anticipated for some time. The formal announcement, after the Babri Masjid demolition, by the Government of India that Jinnah's old house would not be given to the Government of Pakistan for use as its consulate, no doubt, hastened the process.

At the diplomatic level, the pieces that comprise the veneer of even a halfway normal relationship were thus falling apart. Each fresh episode seemed to make earlier variants pale in comparison. In early 1995, the situation in Kashmir appeared to be stabilizing and the catchphrase in use then was that a political process would further cement this. A big setback was, however, in the offing. Militants holed up in a shrine—this time the Charar-i-Sharief, one of Kashmir's oldest and most sacred religious sites—had been dominating the news since early 1995. After a long siege, the shrine and a large part of the surrounding town were burnt to the ground in a firefight with security forces on 11 May 1995.

The leader of the terrorists—a 'Major' Mast Gul, a veteran of the Afghan jihad—acquired through the siege a larger-than-life image, especially in Pakistan. As the shrine burnt to a cinder, Mast Gul escaped and reappeared in Pakistan to a hero's welcome, particularly from the religious parties. Portrayed as a war hero by the local media and the right wing, the public gathering he addressed in the Liaqat Bagh in Rawalpindi drew a crowd of some 4,000–5,000.[35] In it, Mast Gul called for 5,000 martyrs from Rawalpindi and even in a pre-live-TV age such words could not help but resonate strongly across the border. For India, this confirmed not just Pakistan's complicity but the extent to which it could go in J&K.

The burning of the Charar-i-Sharief shrine, therefore, added another layer of bitterness and mistrust. The story, however, does not end there. About a decade and a half later, Mast Gul re-emerged publicly in Pakistan in early 2014 from a long hibernation. He was now in a different camp, having joined the Tehrik-i-Taliban Pakistan (TTP), the organization responsible for carrying out numerous attacks against Pakistani targets—civil and military. Naturally, there were many in India who saw this as poetic justice and hoped for further retribution on Pakistan.

As the free fall in India–Pakistan relations continued and hastened in the mid-1990s, two other enduring legacies of this time are worth pausing over. During the visit of the US deputy national security advisor Robert Gates in 1990, one idea which generated much enthusiasm amongst the Americans was of promoting an unofficial or non-official dialogue between India and Pakistan, drawing in former policymakers, journalists and public figures. From this idea emerged the Neemrana Dialogue, so named because its first meeting was held in a heritage resort—the Neemrana Fort hotel—on the outskirts of Delhi. Former diplomats with experience of India–Pakistan issues, retired military officers, journalists, civil society activists and public intellectuals from both sides were carefully identified and chosen for participation. The Neemrana process became, henceforth, a catchphrase for India–Pakistan discussions in which opinion makers and experts outside either government would try and find common ground to break the existing logjam. Till the late 1990s, this dialogue was funded by the United States Information Service (USIS). Gradually, the US state department started losing interest as it 'became increasingly obvious that the participants were failing to influence their governments to accept ideas that they had themselves rejected when they were in power'.[36] The dialogue, however, continued for another decade as both the governments, of India and Pakistan, agreed to fund participation after the US withdrew—perhaps more because of the status of the participants but also because stoppage would have added to the accumulating portfolio of bilateral negativity.

Regardless of the value the Neemrana conversations added to India–Pakistan discussions, it did become a template for the future. The idea of mixing up former policymakers and policy influencers in both countries for candid discussions caught on and, over the years, such dialogues have multiplied and acquired the overall description as 'Track II'. A common feature to many of these was that they were sponsored and funded by one or the other Western capital concerned at India–Pakistan tensions. The Neemrana process was thus replicated by others. The Belusa Group[37] brought together Indians and Pakistanis with experience of diplomacy and military affairs in another US initiative. The Germans, Canadians, Australians and others were among the countries who sponsored such meetings, many of which continue till date. Some have copied the Neemrana participation—a mix of different professions and interests from both countries. Others have sought to be more specialized—limiting participation to retired military or intelligence officers. From the late 1990s, the Norwegians sponsored the regular meeting of journalists as a means of reducing the intensity of the media wars that periodically erupted.

The impulse behind each of these attempts was clear enough—a sense of frustration that relations had remained frozen for so long combined with the apprehension of escalation with the de facto and then de jure nuclear weapon status of both. How successful these have been, is a different matter. Often, older roles and positions transfer seamlessly from the official to the non-official dialogue. There is thus a non-official engagement conducted almost on official lines. Occasionally, there is some fresh, even lateral, thinking, seeking to contribute something new to the India–Pakistan intergovernmental agenda. The difficulty then arises of selling these new ideas to either government and facing the expected cynicism about a 'change of heart'. For those attending such conferences, reactions varied. For the former diplomats, especially those who have served in or dealt with the other country, it is generally a smooth transition from official to non-official positions on India–Pakistan issues—there being little difference between the two. For the academics and journalists too, the experience though novel is still familiar as many of them had opportunities to interact with their opposite numbers. The most interesting are the responses of former intelligence and military officers—for many coming face-to-face with the adversary for the first time. An initial bewilderment at the opposite position encountered sometimes also mutates into a 'can do' spirit as if the entire portfolio of problems can be resolved by their respective fraternities. For all the participants, it remains a moot point whether their older certainties become a little weaker.

There was a second and separate trajectory in this non-official interface. While it shared in part the same impulse as 'Track II', it was nevertheless also powered by other sentiments, and possibly could trace older roots. In September 1994, around the same time as the Indian and Pakistani delegations at the UNGA were exchanging barbs over Kashmir, a group of Indians and Pakistanis were meeting in Lahore. Consisting of human rights activists, retired civil servants, politicians and academics, this meeting concluded with the decision to establish a 'Peoples Forum for Peace and Democracy' (PFPD). Prominent signatories to the joint statement included, from India, Nirmal Mukherjee, the last of the ICS officers to remain in service and a former cabinet secretary, and Rajni Kothari, a prominent political scientist; from Pakistan, the journalist-cum-human rights activist I.A. Rahman and Mubashir Hasan, finance minister in Zulfikar Ali Bhutto's first cabinet. This meeting in Lahore took place at a time of fraught relations between the two countries and the joint statement issued spoke of the 'urgent need for saner voices to prevail'. It also recommended that 'war and attempts to create war hysteria should be outlawed', 'a process of denuclearization and reversal of the arms race should be started', 'religious intolerance must be curbed', and for Kashmir, 'a peaceful democratic solution of it involving the peoples of Jammu and Kashmir is the only way out'.[38]

A larger meeting took place subsequently in New Delhi in February 1995 where the India–Pakistan Peoples Forum for Peace and Democracy was formally launched. (Incidentally, when Indians use the name they put India before Pakistan and the Pakistanis when they do so put India later!) This was the first major civil society joint grouping to emerge from the India–Pakistan imbroglio and it has continued to function and meet since then. Some of the drama associated with this first meeting was later recapitulated by Mubashir Hasan, one of its main protagonists.

> The big question mark was whether the Government of India would issue visas. Never had such a delegation of independent minded persons ever sought visas in such a large number. With breath held we waited for the word from the High Commission in Islamabad. Hardly anyone believed that the permission would come. But come it did, barely two days before the date of departure. Next morning, in a section of the Pakistani press a news item appeared that Government of India was paying the fare and they would be the guests of the Indian government and they would pass resolutions in the convention which would favour India. Next day editorials full of vitriolics appeared against the Pakistani participants as also statements of some national leaders condemning them and demanding the government stop the visit. Regardless, nearly one hundred reached Delhi to meet an equal number from India.[39]

The original impulse for this grouping goes back to the period of high tension in early 1990 when foreign minister Yaqub Khan's visit to Delhi set alarm bells ringing. In April 1990, two groups of prominent Indians issued public appeals to arrest a downward slide to war. The signatories to one of these included Badr-ud-Din Tyabji, Rajeshwar Dayal, Swaran Singh, Kewal Singh, P.N. Haksar, General J.S. Aurora, amongst others. The names cited are incidentally a cross section of Indian policymakers on Pakistan since the 1950s. Similar statements and appeals came from across the border and from this emerged the idea of small groups of concerned citizens meeting whenever possible. In India, the Centre for Policy Research (CPR) and the India International Centre (IIC), both in New Delhi, were the two institutions most frequently hosting such meetings. As these meetings gathered momentum, the idea of a permanent grouping emerged, leading to the Lahore meeting of September 1994 and the first convention.

The PFPD's annual conventions thereafter continued but in the memories of its old-time supporters two of the early ones stand out. One of these was in Calcutta in December 1996—the fourth convention—where about 300 delegates attended, roughly an equal number from each side. The high point of this was a large public march from College Street to the Esplanade. The next convention was in Pakistan, and was, for these peace activists, also a milestone. It was held in Peshawar in November 1998—full of resonance for the Indians because of the city's many associations, not least Badshah Khan and his Red Shirts movement. Yet, there were also many fears and doubts about the choice of the city—with the Taliban in power in Afghanistan, Peshawar posed many risks, it was felt, for a large Indian contingent. The doubts and fears, it turned out, were needless, and for those who attended it has remained an enduring memory.

For I.A. Rahman in Lahore, this impulse of reaching across the border had older roots than the crisis situation of the early 1990s.[40] He writes, describing the two-decade-long process, of how he came to be associated with the PFPD: 'It was in the 1970s that we started discussing peace seriously. When a few friends decided to form an India–Pakistan Friendship Society, I had no hesitation in joining them.' But in those early years this was an 'audacious venture' and 'the intelligence agencies had instructions to chase anyone who entertained ideas of peace between India and Pakistan'. It was, therefore, 'impossible to sustain the initiative launched by the friendship society'. Nevertheless, the idea grew through quiet and secret meetings. But the secrecy meant that the dialogue process was 'empty' and of no use 'because it neither helped the evolution of a pro-peace outlook, nor did it lead to a better dissemination of the essential message'. The next step was when the then director of the Centre For Policy Research, V.A. Pai Panandiker suggested a South Asian normalization effort—this was a semi-academic enterprise with papers presented and published thereafter as books. The South Asian canvas was useful because it meant a more structured discussion and was also fruitful because in a bilateral dialogue, 'More often than not, Indian and Pakistani delegates would come with a predetermined mind to quarrel with each other, but in broader-based South Asian dialogues they had to behave themselves and refrain from indulging in emotional outbursts.'[41]

'But', I.A. Rahman recollects, 'we were still far removed from the people'. There were other obvious difficulties:

> We met many people who were keen to advocate peace, but they deserted us subsequently when we explained that peace meant conflict resolution, ending disputes and building consensus through negotiations. They would talk of peace in an abstract sense. Their ardour cooled when it was realized that peace would often collide with their vested interests.[42]

For I.A. Rahman, the Peoples Forum for Peace and Democracy meant that the incipient peace process had 'finally acquired a definite rhythm' as it created a platform from which thinkers and the masses could together push their establishments forward and against what he called the transformation of 'their differences into quasi-religious ideologies'.

If such 'positives' about the future emerged from an incipient peace movement, there were strong cross-currents and disputing voices from the opposite direction too. The rise of 'peace activism' was often to be greeted by a measure of derision and the charge of woolly-headedness against former policymakers. Often the view also was that these individuals including senior journalists were sometimes vulnerable to manipulation by the Pakistan government. J.N. Dixit was, for instance, to write that 'at the risk of provoking objections and criticism I must mention Pakistan has made this attempt with senior and thoughtful journalists like George Verghese, Pran Chopra, the late Dilip Mukherjee, Ajit Bhattacharjea, Bhabani Sengupta' but that this effort failed.[43]

There were, however, more powerful critiques of Pakistan developing in the public sphere simultaneously with the traction peace activism seemed to generate. Indian cinema, in particular, Bollywood, was from the early 1990s looking seriously at Pakistan. As a 'bad' neighbour Pakistan had been a presence in Indian cinema from the beginning—but it was a very subtle and consciously understated one. The Partition prism informed many films and in these too references to Pakistan were often cast in metaphors—the evil younger brother or the malevolent outsider disrupting a happy family, etc. Even in the war film *Upkar*, set during the 1965 war, Pakistan as a term, or as identification of the enemy, was not used in the film's script. After the 1971 conflict, some films on the struggle for Bangladesh were made but here the focus was on the events leading to the 1971 war and the situation in East Pakistan.

The 1990s were to see a big change as Bollywood ended its long silence on Pakistan and a large number of film-makers engaged with the experience of terrorist attacks in Punjab, Jammu and Kashmir and finally in Bombay itself as in March 1993.[44] In a film such as *Border* (1997) Pakistan is a central theme as the enemy country and the film was about a famous battle of the 1971 war in Rajasthan. If this has Pakistan as the overt enemy, there were others in which it is a malevolent force stoking terrorism in India. *Roja* (1992), *Sarfarosh* (1999), *Fiza* (2000), amongst others, make this decade stand out as the one that began Bollywood's interface with Pakistan. In *Roja* a young south Indian is kidnapped by Pakistani terrorists while on a visit to Kashmir and his young wife has to struggle to ensure that he is released. The travails of the young south Indian couple underline the pan-Indian threat that Pakistan poses. *Sarfarosh* focuses on a young police officer's effort to combat Pakistan-sponsored terrorism. *Fiza* is about the inroads Pakistan has made into India in terms of sponsoring terrorist activities. Films such as these both followed and led the public mood of anger and frustration and marked the beginning of a certain set of depictions of Pakistan that have also endured even as peace activism sought to create a softer more benign image. In the future, public debate in India on Pakistan would inevitably also include Bollywood in it.

The early meetings of the PFPD and of the Neemrana Group had in the mid-1990s an additional cachet as they took place when talks between the two governments remained suspended and polemics over terrorism and Kashmir continued. Nevertheless, there were wider changes afoot in both countries. As India headed for its eleventh general elections in 1996, its internal politics had an obvious interest for Pakistan—particularly in terms of how the BJP would perform. The election results were inconclusive—the BJP emerged as the single largest party but could not gather enough allies to form the government. After a thirteen-day interregnum with A.B. Vajpayee as prime minister, a coalition government under H.D. Deve Gowda took office on 1 June 1996 and I.K. Gujral found himself as foreign minister again.

For many in the Peoples Forum for Peace and Democracy, both in India and in Pakistan, this was propitious—Gujral was, for all practical purposes, one of them. Many of those in what was being called the 'Peace Movement' were his old friends and associates. As foreign minister, albeit in a weak coalition, he was generally regarded as having a key role to play on all foreign policy issues and especially Pakistan because of his special interest and background. Soon after assuming office, Prime Minister Deve Gowda wrote to Prime Minister Benazir Bhutto in June 1996 that the foreign-secretary-level dialogue be resumed. A similar offer was made by Gujral to his counterpart. No reply was received and Gujral said as much in press interviews some six months later.

There, however, seemed to have been no real expectation of any substantive engagement with Pakistan at this stage. Alongside the change in India, Pakistan too was undergoing a transition but a far more traumatic one, especially so for Benazir Bhutto herself. Allegations of corruption concerning her husband and a deteriorating relationship with President Farooq Leghari were part of her problem. At the same time, Karachi and large parts of Sindh were in the grip of extreme sectarian violence and Shia and Sunni groups had it out with each other on a daily basis. In September 1996, Benazir's brother and Zulfikar Ali Bhutto's sole surviving son was gunned down in a firefight with the police. Murtaza's differences with Benazir and especially with her husband Asif Zardari and even more so the Pakistan Army's suspicion of his older links with Indian intelligence agencies made his killing a mystery then, as it remains now. President Leghari's growing proximity to the army was the final link in the chain and Benazir Bhutto's second dismissal followed in November 1996. In the elections that followed the PPP was decimated and Nawaz Sharif was back in power for the second time—but this time with a clear majority of his own.

Many in Pakistan noticed that there were two unusual features in this election. The first was that India was not a campaign or political issue—the principal combatants, the PPP of Benazir Bhutto and the Pakistan Muslim League (PML) of Nawaz Sharif kept election rhetoric about India at a low level. Second, and even more unusual, was the fact that Nawaz Sharif made improvement of relations with India one of his campaign planks. A politician from Punjab—long and still considered the centre of anti-India sentiment and action—aiming to be prime minister, taking this position when tensions with India remained high was certainly novel. This repositioning of Pakistan's principal political parties—the PPP and especially the PML—was such a contrast from the Kashmir-centric debates of the early and mid-1990s that even informed opinion in India was to take time in registering it. Continued infiltrations, cross-border violence and terrorist attacks in India obviously also worked to both obscure and diminish the value of this change further.

Nawaz Sharif's victory and his stated view on the necessity of improvement in relations with India put all the pieces in place for ending the long impasse since January 1994. This had been a state of no dialogue, generally tense relations punctuated by sharp and polemical public exchanges and regular clashes along the LOC and terrorist violence in J &K. The US, now the world's sole superpower, was leaning on both India and Pakistan to resume dialogue and take some steps to reduce tensions. This was prompted both by concerns about sudden escalation of tensions as also by the larger consideration that some normalization of relations may enable both countries to sign the Comprehensive Test Ban Treaty (CTBT). The latter was, however, a forlorn hope.

In the event, Prime Minister Nawaz Sharif was quick to respond to the Indian offer of talks. The Pakistan foreign secretary was in Delhi by end-March 1997. This was the first formal, bilateral meeting after a gap of over three years. Both governments sought to convey a positive approach by announcing some optical-friendly steps before the meeting. Pakistan released several Indian children in its custody after the fishing vessels they were in had been apprehended inside Pakistani waters. Gujral publicly thanked the Government of Pakistan for this step as also the Pakistani philanthropist Abdul Sattar Edhi whose charitable trust had looked after the children. Gujral also announced several visa relaxations for Pakistani nationals to visit India. Some of these had, in fact, been recommended by his friends in the PFPD for the past 2–3 years. If these steps look so small to be insignificant now, the attention and acclaim they drew at the time underlines the atmosphere of hostility that had prevailed till then.

The foreign secretaries' meeting, however, coincided with one of the United Front government's many recurring crises. The Congress announced withdrawal of support to the Deve Gowda government even as the talks were taking place in Delhi. It was too fraught a time domestically to bring Pakistan into the equation, particularly because many in the political spectrum strongly felt Gujral's policy towards neighbours, especially towards Pakistan, was one of appeasement. Gujral was, therefore, extra cautious and in his recollection:

> The Congress was also being held responsible for damaging the prospects of any improvements in Indo-Pakistan relations that might have emerged from the Foreign Secretary level talks.
>
> With the Indo-Pak talks going off track, I asked the Foreign Secretary not to issue any joint statement. I also instructed him not to say anything about Kashmir.[45]

The Pakistan foreign secretary returned without any steps being decided upon. The ice had, however, been broken and the understanding was that another round of talks would be held soon. To that extent, the political crisis in Delhi was also convenient as it could be held responsible for no specific outcomes. Unspoken also was the obvious—much would depend on what happened to the government. In the event, the United Front government survived but had to change the prime minister. I.K. Gujral suddenly found himself catapulted to that position in April 1997.

Amongst Gujral's friends and advisers were those at the forefront of efforts to improve relations with Pakistan, as indeed he was himself. Most prominent amongst these was Bhabani Sengupta, an analyst and journalist covering regional and international affairs as also a gifted author in Bengali under the name 'Chanakya Sen'. A public intellectual before the term was as commonly or frequently used as now, Bhabani Sengupta was only the more prominent of many like him who were in Gujral's circle. Their interactions in the India International Centre and the Centre for Policy Research in New Delhi reinforced Gujral's own world view that given a history of poor relations with China and Pakistan and the dangers this posed to its northern and western borders, India needed to have good relations with all its other neighbours. To achieve this, India should be prepared to act unilaterally and non-reciprocally, i.e., give or make concessions without expecting anything in return because of its immense size and population. This was what used to be termed flatteringly as the 'Gujral doctrine'.

There were many critics of this policy. Some rejected it as appeasement while others said that Gujral had only repackaged and attached his name to a set of policies already followed by India since Independence. Nevertheless, the Gujral doctrine had a currency from the time he was foreign minister under Prime Minister Deve Gowda and acquired an even greater vogue when he became prime minister himself. On becoming prime minister, Gujral appointed Bhabani Sengupta as his 'Officer on Special Duty'. This was still a time when lateral inputs into policymaking was looked askance and the critics found a ready target in Bhabani Sengupta. To them in Gujral's thinking, and with the ballast being provided by Sengupta and others, a radical change in Indian foreign policy was being made: 'The Gujral doctrine is a marked departure from the existing assumptions in South Block ... Indian foreign policy has centred on national self-interest; the Gujral doctrine operates on other assumptions.'[46]

Bhabani Sengupta's appointment as an adviser to Gujral ran into difficulties almost immediately. He was also less than adept himself—claiming that he had considerable influence on Gujral and that the 'Gujral doctrine' was his idea. Former prime ministers Chandra Shekhar and A.B. Vajpayee criticized in parliament a letter Sengupta had written in 1974 criticizing India's peaceful nuclear explosion. This criticism was joined in by other parties leading Gujral, politically weak as he was, to announce that he had accepted Sengupta's resignation.

The criticism in parliament had many strands—that Sengupta was pro-American; that he was the father of the Gujral doctrine; that he was pro-Pakistani and was for handing over Siachen to Pakistan. Some of Gujral's and Sengupta's detractors had a more general problem with Pakistan-related peace activism and these two were easy targets. Pakistan thus had a lot to do with the whole controversy, although it was never meant to be one of the neighbours the Gujral doctrine was meant to apply to. While many of Sengupta's contrarian views—easily found in print—made him particularly vulnerable, he was important also because he seemed representative of Gujral's inner circle. One Delhi journalist described this inner circle as 'FOGs or Friends of Gujral (in short Fogies)' concentrated largely in Delhi and having attributes as follows: 'With a few notable exceptions like Sengupta, many fogies are united by a common language—Punjabi—and wistful nostalgia for a lost tongue, Urdu. Which is why they are most with the one cause that binds these two strands of inheritance: Indo-Pakistan Friendship.'[47]

Sengupta himself seemed conscious of the fact that the attack on Gujral through him from A.B. Vajpayee was possibly less to do with Pakistan than with the politics surrounding weak coalitions after an electoral process which did not give a clear verdict. In an interview, shortly after his resignation, he commented, combining asperity with insight: 'Mr Vajpayee probably believes there should be no improvement of ties with Pakistan except under his leadership.'[48]

For many others, however, the Centre for Policy Research (CPR) and the India International Centre (IIC) stood out for the intellectual ballast they provided to the seemingly contrarian thinking of I.K. Gujral and his circle: The IIC saw, through the 1980s and 1990s, regular and intense discussions in the so-called 'Saturday Club'—an informal weekly gathering of retired civil servants, journalists and out of work politicians. The CPR—a serious think tank and one of the earliest in India not dependent entirely on government funding—was for years the intellectual lair of Gujral, Sengupta and others. There were many in its faculty who firmly believed that Track II dialogue (or Track II diplomacy as it was increasingly being called) of the kind initiated through the Neemrana Dialogue was the way forward to break the India–Pakistan logjam by injecting fresh ideas into it. Others gave primacy to greater people-to-people contact and public advocacy as by the Pakistan–India Peoples Forum for Peace and Democracy. Two of the initiators of the PFPD from India, Rajni Kothari and Nirmal Mukherjee, were both long-standing faculty in the Centre for Policy Research.

Despite the criticism heaped on this strand of thinking, it did acquire a certain currency. It is by no means the case, as its critics often alleged, that participation in the PFPD was exclusively or even largely from Delhi or Punjab. Even in its early meetings, we find fairly representative participation from the southern states and from Bengal—both distant from Pakistan and Partition-induced nostalgia. It was, in fact, a broad umbrella in which participation came from trade unionists, environmentalists, human rights activists, students, academics and journalists apart from a fair number who was just interested or saw participation as the best way of critiquing the status quo. But there was also a wider context to this activity and it drew on a larger constituency than just contrarian intellectuals, retired civil servants, foreign policy thinkers, peace activists or old 'Lahore-nostalgics'. The larger point was that the Neemrana-type Track II activity funded largely by Western sponsors, an incipient and largely spontaneous 'peace movement' represented by the PFPD, the coincidence of Nawaz Sharif and I.K. Gujral at the helm of their respective countries were all independent factors that seemed to be coalescing together. What gave this convergence importance was an approaching anniversary of great symbolic significance.

The fiftieth anniversary of the separate and independent existence of India and Pakistan infused at that time a larger meaning to the future of India–Pakistan relations. 'Breaking an old mould', 'reconciliation', 'normalization', 'peaceful coexistence', 'durable peace' were catchwords in circulation. The twenty-fifth anniversary of Independence in 1972 had not had the same resonance, largely because the then recent break-up of Pakistan was a much larger event. Possibly also, 1947 was then still far too contemporary an event. But 1997 was different with two new generations in place to reflect on the past. The fiftieth anniversary was thus approached from multiple directions—a celebration of democracy in India, concerns about internal stability in Pakistan, an exploration of what Partition meant after the creation of Bangladesh, a good measure of Raj nostalgia in the English-speaking world, etc. But there was in this heady cocktail also the underlying concern about the future of India–Pakistan relations after fifty years of a largely adversarial relationship.

India now had a new prime minister—a weak one, no doubt, but someone who had decided views on India's relations in its neighbourhood. For many, the omens could not be better. Gujral was born in 1919 in Jhelum in Punjab. He received, in his words, his 'political communion' in Lahore and memories of the city remained with him of nostalgia and mystery 'like peeling off the seemingly unending layers of an onion'. Nawaz Sharif had fought and won an election in which he made improving relations with India one of his electoral planks. He was best known as a pragmatic and forward-looking businessman.

For protagonists of better relations between the two countries, there could thus be no better combination than Nawaz Sharif and I.K. Gujral at the helm of their respective governments. Their first meeting as prime ministers was in Male in May 1997 during a SAARC summit. Some days before he travelled for the meeting, Gujral telephoned Nawaz Sharif. 'We did not discuss anything substantial but it was a pleasant conversation.' The following week in Male, Gujral recalls, '... the personal chemistry between the two of us was excellent and we felt at home with each other. Our wives became reasonably friendly within a short period of time.'[49] This was evidently a meeting of two Punjabis from the same city—Lahore.

It was decided to move ahead and the foreign secretaries were tasked to continue to meet and draw up a framework on how to proceed further.

In brief, the process that had stopped in January 1994 and been revived in March 1997 was being continued with, for whatever it was worth. The foreign secretaries, thereafter, met in Islamabad in June 1997 and then again in New Delhi in September 1997. Gujral and Sharif too kept meeting—in September 1997 in New York and in October 1997 in Edinburgh for the Commonwealth summit. Each of these meetings had its own element of drama and suspicions in the delegations accompanying the respective prime ministers—both about the other side and about their principals!

What was, however, being finalized was an eight-element dialogue process covering a gamut of India–Pakistan relations: J&K, the nuclear issue, terrorism, Sir Creek, Siachen, trade, the Tulbul Navigation Project, and cultural ties and visa-related issues. There was not much disagreement on the identification of the issues—each had been discussed since at least the 1980s. The Tulbul project in J&K was more technical in nature—a means of reducing silting in the Jhelum and a navigation lock, by building a structure at the Wular Lake through which the river passes. For India, this was a useful way to increase navigability of the Jhelum up to Baramula. For Pakistan, this was a dam being built on the Jhelum—a western river of the Indus Water Treaty. Work on the project was suspended in the late 1980s and has not been resumed since. The project was discussed innumerable times by the Indus commissioners of both India and Pakistan and its inclusion in the eight-point dialogue process was to have a full portfolio of all India–Pakistan issues.

So what was novel in this dialogue agenda was not each issue in itself but that they were being packaged together. The problem arose over how much primacy to give to terrorism and J&K—for Pakistan, Kashmir could not just be another element in the package and for India, the approach required more even-handedness. In Pakistan, the view also was that India was trying to withdraw from any discussion on Kashmir. There were opposite suspicions in India about Pakistan's Kashmir-centric approach and Gujral recalls a conversation with Nawaz Sharif in Edinburgh when both were there for the Commonwealth summit in October 1997:

> The Pakistani Prime Minister started the conversation by offering to sell us surplus electricity. I responded positively but soon his offer

> was shot down by Shamshad Ahmad and Gohar Ayub Khan (Foreign Secretary and Foreign Minister respectively) on the plea that since 'other issues' were pending, selling surplus electricity may not be practicable. I left the matter at that ... What was surprising was that the prime minister's own colleagues could, in a brazen style, defy him in our presence.[50]

News of this spread quickly enough reinforcing doubts in India about Pakistan's interest or intentions about anything other than Kashmir. Kuldip Nayar's view was that in his conversations with Nawaz Sharif, Gujral was able to get a measure of agreement that some steps forward on trade should not be linked to Kashmir:

> Sadly, the mindsets of the bureaucrats from Pakistan ruined the deal. One of them said during the meeting; 'Mian Sahib, what about Kashmir?' Nawaz Sharif remained silent and then went on to discuss trade with Gujral. Trade was, however, never resumed, and it became apparent that the bureaucrat's remark proved to be the last word.[51]

Nevertheless, despite all the posturing, suspicion and doubt, progress was made in that it was agreed that all the eight subjects identified would be discussed as part of a comprehensive package known thereafter as the Composite Dialogue. Jammu and Kashmir and peace and security would be discussed by the foreign secretaries. The other subjects by the respective secretaries of the departments concerned. To many in Pakistan, this was an agreement on minimals but still better than nothing and in any case, better than the long-past Simla stalemate on Kashmir. Conversely, many in India felt that at Gujral's pushing a major concession had been made to Pakistan but it was still an acceptable one since progress on other issues—trade, terrorism, culture, people-to-people contacts—was not contingent on Kashmir.

However, time had run out for I.K. Gujral's crisis-ridden government as it ran out of allies. Fresh general elections were to be held in February–March 1998. That I.K. Gujral and Nawaz Sharif could have restarted a dialogue process halted since 1993 was not a small achievement, especially given the overall poor atmospherics, the frequent clashes on the LOC and, most of all, the continued infiltration and terrorist attacks in the Kashmir Valley. Did the personality and personal inclination of the two prime ministers constitute the full explanation for this small success, or were there other factors also pushing both countries forward? Certainly, at the time much was made of the difference that Nawaz Sharif and I.K. Gujral had brought to bear on a process to improve relations. But more than personalities and personal inclination, there were other factors at work, exemplified by events to follow as a new government and a new prime minister took charge in India.

Victory in the election and consequent assumption of power by the BJP-led National Democratic Alliance (NDA) in April 1998 was followed by the carrying out of five nuclear tests on 11 and 13 May. The domestic triumphalism accompanying the announcement by India of its new status as a nuclear weapon power convinced many in Pakistan that a nightmare was upon them: A 'Hindu revivalist' party, unreconciled to the creation of Pakistan was going to steer Indian policy. Pakistan carried out its reciprocal nuclear tests on 28 May, domestically accompanied by similar euphoria and triumphalism, amidst an India–Pakistan war of words. The rest of the world looked on appalled and no amount of pressure or threat of consequences had, in fact, deterred either country.

A 'frenzy of critical rhetoric' descended first on India and then on Pakistan. Both, more so India, faced what has been termed correctly as the 'Charge of the Invective Brigade'.[52] Each had, in fact, good and internally consistent reasons—both with respect to each other as also the rest of the world—to carry out the tests. But as rhetoric and counter-rhetoric bounced off each other, May 1998 seemed to encapsulate a half-century of India–Pakistan history.

At times the tensions appeared more real than just rhetoric. On the night of 28–29 May, the Indian high commissioner in Islamabad was woken up for a post-midnight summons to the foreign office. He was informed there of 'credible' information of an impending attack by India on Pakistan's nuclear installations. Any such move, the high commissioner was informed, would lead to a 'swift and massive retaliation with unforeseen consequences'.[53]

For many in India, Pakistan and the rest of the world, this old-style duelling now appeared more dangerous and irresponsible than ever before. For pessimists the world over, the end of the millennium appeared to be on a note confirming that the old fears of a nuclear Armageddon were not exaggerated. But here again, anyone who predicted a linear movement in India–Pakistan relations were to be proven wrong.

In a few weeks' time, Prime Ministers Nawaz Sharif and A.B. Vajpayee agreed that a forthcoming SAARC summit in Colombo would provide the venue for a meeting and both evidently had made up their minds to prove the doomsayers wrong. In Colombo, Prime Minister Vajpayee agreed to resume what Nawaz Sharif and I.K. Gujral had agreed to earlier—the Composite Dialogue so that terrorism and Kashmir could be discussed alongside less contentious issues. The 'composite' structure implied that lack of progress on one issue need not hold up others but also that all issues would be discussed. Statements issued by both foreign offices spoke of the changed context of both being nuclear powers and the corresponding need to build trust, reduce conflict and set aside the bitter legacy of the past.

Optically, both governments sought to convey this message through an India–Pakistan cricket series. This was the first after a ten-year gap and took place in January 1999 barely six months after the nuclear tests. Shaharyar Khan, the former Pakistan foreign secretary found himself appointed as the manager of the Pakistan cricket team, obviously 'because of my diplomatic experience', as he put it, since the 'tour aimed at establishing equable relations between the two countries against the backdrop of acute tension'.[54] Notwithstanding the intentions and hopes of the governments, there were many opposed to the whole enterprise. Shaharyar Khan recollects the Shiv Sena in Mumbai announcing a boycott of the tour and its leader Bal Thackeray 'pouring out threatening invective against the visit of the Pakistan team'. As the pitch in Delhi was dug up in protest, Shaharyar Khan found he was given a dual responsibility: 'achieving optimum public relations benefit' but also the authority 'to abort the tour if necessary'. The game, however, was on and Shaharyar Khan was surprised to discover the attitudes he encountered. In Gwalior, after a warm-up game, he found the road from the stadium to the airport 'lined four rows deep on both sides ... to wave farewell to the visiting Pakistan team'. 'After forty years in government,' Khan recollects, 'I had come to recognize a sponsored crowd ... from a genuine, spontaneous gathering.' The people in Gwalior were 'totally spontaneous'. He tried to explain to a bemused Pakistani team why he found this so significant: 'Gwalior had traditionally been the bastion of extremist political forces. It was from Gwalior that Nathuram Godse had hatched his conspiracy to assassinate Mahatma Gandhi.'[55]

Similarly, in Chennai and Mohali, the venue of a Test match and an ODI respectively, Shaharyar Khan felt that something 'had changed in crowd attitudes'. In the latter, 10,000 Pakistani fans came to a tremendous reception and in his recollection 'the hospitality shown to the Pakistani fans was tremendous'. In Chennai, the victorious Pakistani team received a standing ovation from the spectators—an unbelievable scene being beamed live to Pakistan audiences and something which was recalled as a milestone even a decade later. In Calcutta, the venue of the final Test, on the other hand the experience was different. An impending Indian loss and a controversial run out of India's star player Sachin Tendulkar led to the crowd rioting and the stadium had to be cleared for play to resume. A report in *Wisden* reads: 'Spectators started burning newspapers in the stands and hurled stones, fruit and plastic bottles on to the field. The match was held up for over three hours as about 65,000 people were removed by police and security men. The crowd's anger was still concentrated on Tendulkar's run-out, but there was little viciousness in the riot; it was born of disappointment rather than anti-Pakistan feeling.'[56] Shaharyar Khan concurs that the crowd trouble was a show of frustration not aimed at the Pakistan team. Nevertheless, as the most popular spectator sport in India was played without spectators, the incident was a reminder that linear progress in India–Pakistan matters, howsoever desirable, could also be very elusive and, furthermore, there was no unanimity in India where Pakistan was concerned.

Prime Minister Vajpayee was prepared to go beyond cricket or the use of right expression by the two foreign offices to indicate that both governments were trying to make progress. He did so by employing political symbolism in a way never attempted so far in the India–Pakistan diplomatic terrain. In February 1999, he made an official visit to Lahore travelling on a newly established bus service between Delhi and Lahore. This act of a short ride (the prime minister's journey was from the

Indian border check-post of Attari to the opposite post in Pakistan of Wagah) to cross the border on a bus introduced political theatre and sentiment into the existing mould of distrust and suspicion. It was new since it meant speaking by symbolic action rather than through official statement or communique. Vajpayee brought with him in the bus film stars, former cricket greats, artists and peace activists. It was almost as if he was inviting into mainstream diplomacy all those persons and all the activities that sought to push India–Pakistan relations into a less fraught track. Diplomacy, it appeared to many in both countries, was changing from how to structure and sustain a diplomatic dialogue process to constructing a peace process.

The sheer symbolism consciously and unambiguously attached to the visit makes it stand apart from past initiatives—Rajiv Gandhi in 1989 or Jawaharlal Nehru in 1960. In the background of the fiftieth anniversary of Independence of India and Pakistan in August 1997, the nuclear tests of May 1998 and the approaching new millennium, the 'Bus Yatra' as it was called seemed to herald that an inflection point had been reached in South Asia. The naysayers were temporarily silenced as the world applauded and India and Pakistan celebrated. Among the highlights of Vajpayee's visit to Lahore was his going to the Minar-i-Pakistan, a monument that symbolized the creation of Pakistan as a separate country. This was a reiteration—if one was needed—that India accepted the reality of Pakistan.

The Lahore summit was not without, in the language of diplomacy, substantive content. A declaration signed by Vajpayee and Nawaz Sharif committed both governments to improving relations, to 'intensify' the composite dialogue process and efforts to resolve 'all issues, including the issue of Jammu and Kashmir'. In terms of agreements signed at the head of government level, it ranked with other seminal landmarks so far of India–Pakistan diplomacy: the Indus Waters Treaty and the Tashkent and Simla Agreements. Other outcomes included an agreement to have consultations on each other's nuclear postures and doctrines—at the least, reassuring to the rest of the world about both being responsible nuclear weapon states, to notify each other in advance of ballistic missile tests and of nuclear 'accidents', prevent incidents at sea between their respective naval vessels and aircraft, upgrade communication links between military commanders, etc. Less publicized was another decision of the two prime ministers—that each would appoint a trusted representative to meet quietly to discuss what could be the way forward for Jammu and Kashmir. Prime Minister Nawaz Sharif's representative was Niaz Naik—a former Pakistan foreign secretary and high commissioner to India. Prime Minister Vajpayee appointed R.K. Mishra, a journalist and editor. The object itself was clear—discussions held in private would be constructive and reduce possibilities of media and public pressures influencing each side's approach. This was the beginning of the concept of the India–Pakistan backchannel that gained much traction a few years later. For the moment, however, it remained little more than an idea on account of what was to take place in the immediate future.

Vajpayee's Lahore visit and the summit with Nawaz Sharif was thus the triumph of symbolism and on this rode what appeared to be the great fiftieth anniversary breakthrough. It was, however, not to be. One Pakistani account called it 'a grand if ephemeral success'.[57] There were also discordant signs, during the visit itself—for the naysayers on both sides to later argue, and they did with some force—that publicity stunts were not going to advance India–Pakistan relations. Even as Vajpayee began his journey to Pakistan, news was coming in of fresh terrorist attacks in J&K; the chief of the army staff of Pakistan—General Pervez Musharraf—was not present at the ceremonial line-up on Vajpayee's arrival; there were hostile demonstrations by religious parties during Vajpayee's stay in Lahore, and although these were firmly put down, the muddying of waters in the ongoing bonhomie was evident.[58] If all this could be set aside during the euphoria of Lahore, these were to provide, only a few months later, powerful arguments against grand gestures.

Soon after Vajpayee's return his government fell—losing a parliamentary vote of confidence by a single vote in April 1999. As India's politicians geared up for national elections—the third in as many years—intelligence started accumulating from early May 1999 of unusual infiltrations across the Line of Control from Pakistan in the snowy heights of Kargil in Jammu and Kashmir. Pakistani denials of their involvement and references to mujahideen activity by alienated and insurgent Kashmiris were too familiar to carry credibility. Jaswant Singh summed up the mood of incredulity in the government:

> What on earth is happening? What was Pakistan attempting to do by this forced aggression in the Kargil sector, particularly so soon after the Lahore bus journey? I could not fathom why those hopes, generated by Lahore, had to be abandoned, why should the promise of peace be choked so soon after.[59]

The surprise Pakistani intrusion ensured that the twentieth century in India and Pakistan would not end on the positive note of the Lahore bus initiative and the Lahore Declaration. How the Lahore process would have developed and matured, left to itself, thus has to remain one of the great counterfactuals or 'what ifs' of recent South Asian history.

With the intrusions detected, it was clear that they would have to be repelled by force. From Pakistan, denials continued and as the Indian Army battled its way from peak to peak, diplomacy also continued. A telephone conversation between Vajpayee and Nawaz Sharif led to a visit to Delhi by the Pakistan foreign minister Sartaz Aziz on 12 June 1999 to meet Jaswant Singh to see if a way out could be found. Both the visit and the meetings in New Delhi stand out amongst India–Pakistan diplomatic encounters at a time when tensions could not be higher or sentiments more aroused. The drama associated with that visit remains alive to this day. General Pervez Musharraf had visited China a few days earlier, in the last week of May. During his stay there, he had two long telephone conversations with the deputy army chief of Pakistan about the progress of the Kargil operations. These conversations were intercepted and recorded by Indian intelligence and played to the domestic and international media the evening before Sartaz Aziz arrived in Delhi. Aziz recalled that as soon as his aircraft landed, the Pakistani high commissioner 'showed me a stack of newspapers, each carrying the taped conversation' and that his 'heart literally began to sink'. This was obviously because:

> Our entire plank that certain Kargil heights were occupied by the Kashmiri mujahideen during winter months and that the LOC in that sector was not fully demarcated, so we needed to take steps to

demarcate them and that in the meantime India should not raise the tempo of hostilities, stood fully exposed.[60]

Sartaz Aziz, a trained economist and civil servant–turned politician had a weak hand to play but he tried nonetheless to play it manfully. His affable and mild personality and manners conceal a firm and committed disposition towards arguing Pakistan's case on Kashmir and he sought to do so. Jaswant Singh, a former cavalry officer who carried his military bearing wherever he went, was in no mood for a long discussion. He was, moreover, doubly outraged—a little earlier the Pakistan Army had handed over the bodies of six Indian soldiers: 'taken prisoners earlier and killed in captivity ... These bodies had been mutilated and disfigured, an outrage that I could scarcely countenance'.[61] In the meeting, there was nothing to discuss. Sartaz Aziz's proposal to have a ceasefire and discuss the entire issue of clarifying the LOC was to Jaswant Singh, and to his colleagues in the government, so 'totally irrelevant that I could scarcely hide my impatience'. The sense of the meetings and the atmosphere surrounding it was summarized by a senior Pakistan diplomat: 'Sartaz Aziz was accorded a frigid and hostile reception. India took a rigid no negotiation stance, insisting on Pakistani withdrawal of personnel from Kargil before discussion on any other issue. Briefing the press after the meeting, the Indian foreign minister used the word 'demand' three times in one minute.'[62]

For India, the position was clear—there was nothing to discuss unless Pakistan first withdrew its forces from across the LOC. It was a position that none could disagree within the international community too, and as the scale of the Pakistani provocation became clear, Pakistan's isolation grew as indeed did international pressure on it. The military situation had in any case by now turned in India's favour and on 13 June an attack on a key peak—Tooling—had begun and it successfully ended on 17 June. The political decision taken was that India would not widen the war by crossing the LOC and limit its operations to clearing its territory of all intrusion. This meant that the military operation was constrained in numerous tactical ways. But this self-imposed limitation meant that international pressure would focus solely on Pakistan.

International pressure on Pakistan, and equally exasperation with it, was now immense and many in its government realized that that the army chief had landed them in an impossible position. Sartaz Aziz, in fact, recalls Nawaz Sharif telling him 'Musharraf has landed us in a terrible mess' and he had to 'find some honourable exit strategy'. The way out found was a rushed summit with President Clinton in Washington on 4 July in which Pakistan upheld the sanctity of the Line of Control—in effect a code that it would withdraw whatever intrusion by its troops that remained. Sartaz Aziz recalls the very tense atmosphere on their return from the United States: 'The whole Nation wanted to know the truth. Why did we undertake this operation if we could not sustain it?'[63] India celebrated victory as Vijay Divas on 26 July but there was a more sombre mood in Pakistan as it deliberated over this question. For many, this was a double betrayal—the failure to make progress in Kashmir as well as the failure to gain a victory against India. Shades of Tashkent were reappearing.

The Kargil 'war' from May to June 1999 has been the subject of numerous analyses from different points of view. It retains an enigmatic quality both in India and in Pakistan. In India, the central issue is how were Pakistani intentions not deciphered? It soon became clear that the intrusion had been planned even before the Lahore visit of Vajpayee took place and were possibly even taking place as the visit was in progress. There was, in the thinking of most Indians, much more involved here than a failure of military or tactical intelligence. Much more was at stake than the initial gains the Pakistan Army made in the Kargil heights because of the advantage of surprise being with them.

The central issue for most Indians was of trust. In Jaswant Singh's usual evocative turn of phrase, 'It is not just the Line of Control that has been violated, it is the territory of trust that has been transgressed.'[64] Even more fundamental was the question of Indian capacity to assess and gauge Pakistani intentions *at all*. Nawaz Sharif had appeared to be the strongest prime minister to have emerged in Pakistan since Zulfikar Ali Bhutto's early years a quarter-century ago. He had in this current tenure, and within a year and a half of his election in February 1997, secured the resignation of the president, the chief justice and the chief of the army staff. No political threat to him was visible and he had been seemingly sincere in reaching out to India and welcoming Vajpayee. So, how could such a major intrusion take place leading to India and Pakistan having their third undeclared war? The Kargil battles were covered live by India's latest technology leap—twenty-four-hour live television. But apart from the scenes of battle and bravery, what received full-time attention was this central issue: How do we read and evaluate Pakistan? That question continues to reverberate in India still.

In Pakistan too, questions of trust are integral to discussions about Kargil. It is, in one account, a kind of Rashomon effect—with a General Pervez Musharraf story and a Prime Minister Nawaz Sharif story diametrically opposed to each other. In the Musharraf telling, Kargil was a limited military operation intended to retain focus on Kashmir and by bringing about relatively small realignments in the Line of Control to improve Pakistan's negotiating position with India. In this telling, Prime Minister Nawaz Sharif knew about the operation from the beginning and had sanctioned it. In Nawaz Sharif's account, on the other hand, General Musharraf acted without political approval from the prime minister and recklessly created a war-like situation bringing international opprobrium on Pakistan for disrupting the peace process initiated in the Lahore summit.[65]

If in India the issue arising from Kargil was of trusting Pakistan, the trust question in Pakistan was generated by the nature of the civil–military equation and of the India factor in moulding the overall state of civil–military ties. But amidst the acrimony, the blame game and the self-flagellation in Pakistan, there was also a deeper understanding of the 'agonizing dilemmas Pakistan faced in regard to the Kashmir issue'. The dilemma for Pakistan was summed up as: 'If it did not act, India claimed to have achieved a final solution; if it did, it incurred the risk of war.'[66]

The Kargil intrusion ended with the military eviction of Pakistani troops as the Indian Army stormed peak after peak eliminating or forcing the withdrawal of the intruders. At its end if the world was more aware of Kashmir's role in India–Pakistan tensions, the idea of internationalizing Pakistan's concerns had barely succeeded: exasperation with Pakistan's military adventurism and recklessness was the principal sentiment. There was also a grudging respect for India for securing its military and political aims without expanding the conflict and risking a nuclear confrontation. By the time the Kargil operation ended, the most effective talking point deployed by India against

Pakistan was thus also the most obvious one. As it became clearer that Pakistani intrusions had begun while the rest of the world was still applauding the Lahore summit, all that India needed to say about Pakistan was: nuclear powers do not behave like this.

In the mid-term elections held in September–October 1999, Prime Minister Vajpayee's National Democratic Alliance (NDA) was re-elected. On 13 October, as he and his new cabinet were sworn in, the main topic of discussion, however, was not the new government in India but Pakistan. The final act in the Kargil drama played out in the midst of another of those bizarre India–Pakistan coincidences. On 12 October, Pakistan had undergone another military coup with General Pervez Musharraf toppling the government and imprisoning Nawaz Sharif. For Sartaz Aziz, Kargil was thus only a link in the longer chain of Pakistan history.

> No one knows the real story of the assassination of Prime Minister Liaqat Ali Khan in Rawalpindi on 16 October 1951. The lessons from the 1965 war, especially the responsibility for the September's ill-planned attack near Jammu have never been fully recalled. The story of the 1971 war, in which we lost half the country, was documented by the Hamood-ur-Rahman Commission but its report was suppressed ... and finally the Kargil fiasco has produced more questions than answers.[67]

If the coup silenced discussions in Pakistan about its Kargil misadventure this was only temporary. As President Musharraf's regime entered its last phase, the publication of his autobiography, *In the Line of Fire*, in 2006, ignited a debate which continues to this day. The debate is reminiscent of Operations Gibraltar and Grand Slam which led to the 1965 India–Pakistan war. Shamshad Ahmad, the Pakistan foreign secretary during the Lahore visit of Prime Minister Vajpayee and who had reached agreement on the setting up of the Composite Dialogue in 1997 during Prime Minister Gujral's tenure was to comment about Kargil: 'The operation also misjudged the Indian ability and the will to fight back and had assumed that India would never retaliate with an all-out offensive against Pakistan. In other words, it was not prepared for what Musharraf describes "the unreasonably escalated Indian response."'[68]

The similarity thus stands with Ayub Khan's own acknowledgement that his mistake in 1965 was the failure to establish a 'counter syndicate' before embarking on Operation Gibraltar. Many in India and elsewhere in the world would, nevertheless, also point to Pakistan's predisposition to self-blame rather than introspection as being part of the problem. However, almost before the victory celebrations over Kargil and the NDA electoral victory had ended, another India–Pakistan crisis was to provide the final act to close the year 1999 and the twentieth century. This was through the eighth hijacking of an Indian aircraft to Pakistan, and it was to be the most traumatic of them all.

On 24 December 1999, an Indian Airlines aircraft flying from Kathmandu to Delhi was hijacked and first taken to Amritsar. IC-814, the caller name of the aircraft, flew then to Lahore, to Dubai and finally to Kandahar in Taliban-ruled Afghanistan. The hijackers demanded the release of a large number of terrorists and infiltrators from Pakistan in Indian jails in exchange for the 160-odd passengers and crew. One passenger—a newly-wed returning from his honeymoon—was killed and as the hours stretched into days, India and the world were riveted to the drama being enacted in the airfield in Kandahar where the aircraft landed on 25 December. An Indian negotiating team arrived in Kandahar and using the Taliban as intermediaries brought down the number of terrorists to be released from over thirty to three—Masood Azhar, Mushtaq Zargar and Omar Sheikh. Mushtaq Zargar has been described as 'a particularly brutish low life Kashmiri terrorist' responsible for forty murders including many Kashmiri Hindus which had forced the exodus of Kashmiri Pandits from the Valley from 1990 onwards.[69] Omar Sheikh, a British national and a former London School of Economics student, was responsible for the kidnapping and killing of Western tourists holidaying near Srinagar. Masood Azhar, a Pakistani, had been in Indian custody since 1994 when he was captured in India while trying to consolidate the ranks of the militant group he led and managed at the behest of the ISI. All three had been in the forefront of the jihad in Kashmir and nobody in India had any illusions about their close links with the ISI.

As the agony of the passengers continued, India was engrossed with this hijacking drama and negotiation to an extent beyond description. Forced to negotiate and rely on the Taliban whose government they did not recognize, aware of the numerous links between the Taliban and the Pakistan government and ISI now in the control of a dictator responsible for Kargil, this was a nightmarish scenario. If most saw a revenge being exacted by Pervez Musharraf for the Kargil fiasco and defeat, they can hardly be blamed or faulted. The final act of the drama was Jaswant Singh, the Indian foreign minister, taking the three terrorists to Kandahar, and their release in exchange for the exhausted and traumatized passengers and crew. It was, in Jaswant Singh's words, 'a searing experience' as he battled 'between two moral rights: saving the lives of the innocents and a fight against terrorism'.[70] As his aircraft flew with the three terrorists to Kandahar, he wondered 'what to term his mission—a rescue mission, an appeasement exercise, a flight to compromise or a flight to the future?'.[71]

For many Indians, the whole event was a national humiliation and a volley of questions faced the government then and these continue to resurface to this day during any discussion on terrorism: the mishandling of the initial hours of the hijacking that allowed the aircraft to take off from Amritsar and leave Indian territory; should the foreign minister have gone personally to Kandahar as if to crown India's hour of humiliation, etc. There were more fundamental issues involved and the more discerning pointed to them. All three of the terrorists released in Kandahar had been in custody in India for at least 4–5 years. Had they faced expedited trials and been convicted, would not have India's diplomatic position been stronger? But most of all the questions concerned Jaswant Singh—his going to Kandahar became the symbol of India's humiliation at the hands of terrorists supported by Pakistan. In one insider account 'when the time came for Kandahar, Jaswant Singh raised his hand and said, "I'll go."'[72] In doing so, and to his everlasting credit, he took the bullet on behalf of the government. Why did he go? In his words 'somebody had to go' and he felt that as foreign minister the responsibility was his.[73] These were possibly reasons impossible to explain publicly but derived from deeply ingrained notions of what constitutes responsibility and leadership.

What were the reactions in Pakistan? Many there felt that the release of the terrorists was 'the ultimate humiliation for the hardline Hindu nationalist government of Atal Bihari Vajpayee'. There were numerous others who saw 'the hijacking as an Indian conspiracy to malign Pakistan'. The hijacking of the Indian Airlines aircraft Ganga in 1971 which formed part of the break-up of East Pakistan story in Pakistan got a fresh lease of life. The media war was intense—but louder in India because Pakistan had yet to witness the technology leap into 24/7 news reporting. For some in Pakistan, the connection of their country with the hijacking was a troubling experience. In the account of a senior journalist:

> In the first week of January 2000, Masood Azhar resurfaced in a Karachi mosque and addressed thousands of people who had gathered there. ... He triumphantly declared that he would not rest until he had destroyed America and India. Watching that spectacle, I remembered calling a senior official in Islamabad expressing my concern over his public appearance and his inflammatory speech. A few minutes later the official called back with a message from the then ISI chief that 'I was hallucinating' and that it must be a recorded speech. One is not sure if the country's top spymaster could be so clueless.[74]

Nevertheless, many in Pakistan also felt it natural to savour a moment of triumph at the humbling of their foe:

> While the ordeal may be over for the hostages, the hijackers, the Kashmiri prisoners and the authorities in Kabul and Islamabad, the Indian government continues to reel in its aftermath. The badly battered authorities in New Delhi are trying to cover up India's humiliation by making public promises of revenge. However, regardless of when and how this promised revenge is exacted, many analysts believe that the hijacking has dealt a major blow to the Indian government which had, until now, been claiming that it had crushed the uprising in Kashmir. Many fear that the release of the three fighters may have set a bad precedent and could end up inspiring other separatists, not just in Kashmir but in many other parts of India where insurgencies have been under way for years. Pakistan, on the other hand, has been lucky to have come out relatively unscathed.[75]

The final word on IC-814 had, however, not been written and two of the three terrorists released by India continued to make news thereafter. Masood Azhar was later believed to have been involved in attempts to kill Musharraf. This may not, in fact, be true. The protective cloak of Pakistani intelligence agencies continues to be wrapped around him even as Indian demands for justice have become an international issue. In 2016 China vetoed, at Pakistan's request, an Indian move to have him listed as a terrorist by the United Nations. The Chinese defence of Masood Azhar has continued since and is perceived in India as a third power using Pakistan to check India. Omar Sheikh similarly acquired an amplified profile after he was held responsible for the killing of Daniel Pearl. Sentenced to death by a Pakistan court he remains in prison. The fact that the sentence has not been carried out reveals much about the deep links between such individuals and Pakistan intelligence and military authorities. Both cases have contributed greatly to Pakistan's poor reputation today, so it is debatable whether it escaped 'unscathed' from the IC-814 drama.

The twentieth century thus ended with relations between India and Pakistan perhaps worse than they had ever been—the violence, wars and the acrimony of the past all included. The trauma the hijacked passengers underwent, the humiliation of compromising with terrorists, the triumphalism in many circles in Pakistan are experiences that cannot easily be erased from public memory. But the surprising thing is that they were put aside in a relatively short period. Prime Minister Vajpayee addressing the nation as the new millennium dawned did so as the aircraft bringing the besieged passengers from Kandahar was landing in Delhi.[76] He spoke, therefore, of the need to combat terrorism as being the first resolution the country had to make and that the 'battle against terrorism can be won'. But those listening to the prime minister that new millennium eve were interested also to hear him say that 'Terrorism is only one of the challenges we will have to overcome.' He went on to speak about the need to make India a developed country and reminded citizens that 26 January 2000 would mark India's golden jubilee as a republic.

Such thoughts were not limited to Vajpayee—how to look beyond Pakistan was a question rapidly acquiring a larger relevance in India—all this even as the India–Pakistan trajectory that led from the Lahore bus journey to Kargil to the coup d'état and finally to Kandahar was being dissected minutely. The rise of China and its astonishing growth over the past two decades had begun to focus minds in India on the future. Vajpayee's final resolution for India in the new century seemed to sum this up when he said, 'Let us make the new century an Indian century.' How would Pakistan figure in this new age was the obvious enough quandary and dilemma for India.

8
A New Century but an Old Terrain

AS A NEW CENTURY and millennium dawned, just two-and-a-half years after both India and Pakistan completed half a century of their existence as sovereign entities, naturally much reflection devolved on their mutual contestations but also on their divergent evolution. Seen from a fifty-year perspective, the obvious point of divergence was in the contrasting polities in both countries. Democracy in India had flourished and the one area where Pakistan had failed was most evidently in evolving democratic institutions.[1] That Pakistan's latest coup in October 1999, expeditiously upheld by its Supreme Court, coincided with a new government being sworn in India after a smooth electoral process, exemplified that failure. Dramatic contrasts such as these, however, obscured another fundamental transformation at work. The more discerning in both countries reflected over and drew policy conclusions from this change, for it was as much a contrast as that between the evolution of democratic institutions in both countries.

In economic indicators, Pakistan had consistently outperformed India through the 1960s, '70s and '80s. In the period 1980–89, Pakistan's economic performance, in terms of industrial and agricultural growth, was far better than India's. In the 1990s, this position started reversing as Indian growth rates became significantly higher. From near-identical per capita income in 1990, India's GDP per capita in 2012 was US $1,520 as compared to Pakistan at US $1,260. A more striking contrast comes out when an indicator called the purchasing power parity (PPP) is used. In 1990, Pakistan and India had near-identical per capita PPP income—$1,360 and $1,380 respectively. In 2001, the Pakistan figure was $1,860—a 37 per cent increase. India's PPP per capita, on the other hand, in this decade more than doubled to US $2,820. Over the next decade, while Pakistan's PPP per capita income rose to $2,891 in 2012, the Indian figure had risen even higher to $3,876.[2] Other economic criteria also bring out this divergence. Export growth through the 1990s in India was double that of Pakistan; gross capital formation growth four times as much.[3]

Clearly, the two political economies were on different paths. A compelling, if indirect, illustration of this growing economic and social divergence between India and Pakistan comes in the field of popular culture—that of the film industry. The changing fortunes of cinema in India and Pakistan encapsulated a half-century of divergent history in a manner no statistic can. What is striking in Pakistan is how dramatically the economic slowdown reflected itself in an area not directly related. The withering of cinema in Pakistan had, of course, many causes. The most cited is the wave of conservatism ushered in by Gen. Zia-ul-Haq's military regime from 1979, intent on fighting the United States' war in Afghanistan through the instrument of a religious war. But there were additional reasons and one observer has pointed to the 'social and cultural introversion' of the Pakistani middle class from the late 1970s.

This, combined with the proliferating video cassette player, 'kept many Pakistanis, including regular cinemagoers, comfortably stationed in their homes, enjoying smuggled Indian films on video tape away from the cultural, social and political fallouts of Zia-ul-Haq's rampaging 'Islamization project' impacting life outside their homes'.[4] As cinema theatres closed across the country, the great Urdu film industry of Lahore, which had hoped not so long ago to compete and best Bollywood, was dying. At the end of the century, an industry which had produced 80–100 films annually, was now in its death throes with barely two to three films coming out every year.[5] Cinema was and remains the most obvious and evident symptom of the pulling away of India in the growth curve. But there were other evident manifestations even more difficult to digest for an elite and populace wedded to the idea of parity with India and, over the 1970s and '80s, to besting it in economic terms.

The late 1990s and the early part of the twenty-first century, in fact, encapsulate the downturn in Pakistan in more than economic terms. Identified with the medieval excesses of Taliban regime in Afghanistan, the reckless misadventure in Kargil and General Musharraf's old-fashioned coup d'état further dented Pakistan's image. Public confidence and self-esteem, notwithstanding the euphoria of the nuclear tests, were shaken. After the nuclear tests, sanctions were imposed on both India and Pakistan but India, with its larger and still self-contained economy, was less vulnerable. In Pakistan, a run on foreign exchange assets was feared and withdrawal from foreign currency accounts were frozen. People could not withdraw their money, causing what has been termed 'Pakistan's greatest crisis of confidence'.[6] The impact was, of course, most on the moneyed and upper middle classes. But these were the most articulate and connected with the larger investment fraternity.

This contrasting economic picture provides background to a great deal of what happens between India and Pakistan from 2000 and up to today. For one, it led to diverging indices in the social sector—in terms of literacy, access to health care, etc. More than the actual statistical record, however, the contrast lay in self-perceptions—and especially elite self-perceptions—in the two countries. India was increasingly being spoken about as the new growth story, attractive to foreign investors as a base for manufacturing and as a huge market. The opening up of its economy since the early 1990s had created a sense of confidence in a large and growing middle class. The exuberance of this strata was driving not just external perceptions of India but increasingly its own perceptions of the world.

There would not have been too many in India overly impressed by the reversal of Indian and Pakistani growth patterns since the early 1990s. Their attention was riveted to a far greater extent on another equally dramatic emerging contrast—that between China and India. In 1990, the GDP of India and China was roughly equal in nominal and PPP terms. By the beginning of the new century or thereabouts the Chinese economy was double that of India using the same index. This was the result of earlier and deeper economic reforms. Indian anxiety on this comparison was growing to the extent that it had started to define all external perspectives—whether economic or strategic. What this meant for most Indians was a benchmarking of itself not with South Asia but with the wider region and internationally as the central issue for the new century.

Pakistan by contrast seemed trapped in the past century—in Afghanistan, in its internal civil–military morass and in confrontation with India. India seemed to want to graduate out of its neighbourhood, indeed, at times seemed impatient with it. Pakistan, on the other hand, was evidently heading in the opposite direction—more and more self-absorbed and almost compulsively addicted to India and Afghanistan. Strategic and diplomatic support to the Taliban regime in Afghanistan meant that much of its medieval image rubbed off on Pakistan too. The sanctuary provided to the al Qaeda in Afghanistan and in its own territory and the continuous use of terrorists in Kashmir—of which the Kandahar hijacking was the latest manifestation—meant that the perception of Pakistan as a vital part of the international terrorism hub gained even greater traction. Pakistan, long used to the Western alliance behind it, found the going tough.

A dramatic illustration of this divergence was provided during the US president Bill Clinton's visit to South Asia in March 2000. His visit covered India, Pakistan and Bangladesh. The visit was the first to South Asia by a US president in over two decades. The visit to Bangladesh, the first ever by a US president, stood apart. But it was the India leg which attracted the most attention as he spent five days over several cities and conducted an exercise in public diplomacy seldom seen before or since. After an address to the Indian parliament, he was mobbed by cheering members of parliament from the extreme left to the right of the political spectrum. As these images circulated the world, it was clear that all the old acrimony of the India–US interface was now part of an older, closed chapter. In Jaswant Singh's summation:

> The popular mood was ripe for a quantum jump and President Clinton's visit effected just that. He came when India's mood towards the United States was fully attuned and accommodating. He said and did all the right things, sure in the knowledge that he would find a receptive audience, by touching the right chords, by comparing 'Indo-US relations as having the elasticity of Indian classical music because it required improvisation by the players'.[7]

The visit to Pakistan, on the other hand, could not have been a greater contrast. Limited to six hours, it was shrouded in secrecy and security the likes of which are seldom encountered in state visits. The Pakistani historian Ayesha Jalal wrote, for instance, that in 'sharp contrast to the adoring crowds that had greeted Clinton everywhere in India, the streets of Islamabad were empty'. She cites Robert Fisk, the well-known UK journalist that Islamabad was turned into 'a city without a people in a country without a voice'.[8] For most Pakistanis, what was more galling was an almost admonitory televised address to the people in which he handed out advice such as 'The answer to flawed democracy is not to end democracy, but to improve it.' If a more pointed reference to General Musharraf's military coup could not have been made, that this was being said by a foreigner made it even more difficult to swallow. His reference to Kashmir was equally disappointing: 'We cannot and will not mediate or resolve the dispute in Kashmir,' and 'It is wrong to support attacks against civilians across the line of control.' The UK magazine the *Economist* noted after the visit was over that it would take time to diagnose whether Mr Clinton has sobered Pakistan or enraged it.[9]

In fact, the answer was quite clear early enough. The contrast between the character of his visits to India and Pakistan was so obvious that most Pakistanis felt an even greater sense of isolation. Many felt betrayed—after all many of Pakistan's present ills were acquired during the period of the 1980s when US–Pakistan relations were the closest ever and the use of jihad as a political and military instrument was forged to strengthen the US–Pakistan alliance against the Soviets in Afghanistan. But it was also evident to all that the factor that had changed the most was the perception the external world had of India and this changed perception was now driving events in South Asia.

Prime Minister Vajpayee possibly understood these changes better than his usually taciturn personality (except while speaking extempore on a public platform) revealed. As the year 2000 dragged on in a no-war-no peace state between India and Pakistan, many wondered what the next steps would be, if any. The Kargil conflict and the IC-814 trauma had left a deep imprint on the Indian polity. Yet, as India's profile in the world went up, so did the expectation that it will act in its own neighbourhood. Kuldip Nayar has put it negatively and somewhat uncharitably but he is spot on in diagnosing Vajpayee's approach: 'Anti-Pakistan feeling was strong in the BJP. Vajpayee was an exception because he realized that without an equation with Islamabad he would not receive the attention he sought from world leaders.'[10] He could have put it otherwise: Vajpayee, and possibly India as a whole, wanted to engage with the world on a whole host of issues apart from Pakistan. But a state of high tension with Pakistan meant that world attention would remain riveted on this relationship rather than on what was possible with and in India itself.

We get a sense of all this from a 'message' at the end of 2000, then termed as his 'Musings from Kumarakom', a resort in Kerala where Prime Minister Vajpayee was ending the year:

> Our country is facing many problems that are a legacy of our history. I wish to share my views on two of them. One is the long-standing problem with Pakistan over Jammu & Kashmir and the other is the Ram Janmabhoomi–Babri Masjid dispute at Ayodhya.
>
> A self-confident and resilient nation does not postpone the inconvenient issues of yesterday to a distant tomorrow. Rather, it strives to decisively overcome the problems of the past so that it can pursue its developmental agenda for the future with single-minded determination. I have heard many of my countrymen tell me that, now that we have entered a new century and a new millennium, it is time we found lasting solutions to these two problems, one of which is a legacy of the last century and the other a legacy of the last millennium. I agree with them.[11]

Both Pakistan and Jammu and Kashmir had, in fact, been in the government's focus for some time. L.K. Advani, the deputy prime minister recalls:

> Between October 1999 and early 2001, our Government adopted a three-pronged approach. We intensified the fight against cross border terrorism in Jammu and Kashmir and elsewhere in India. In fact, we declared that India would not resume talks with Pakistan unless it stopped aiding and abetting cross border terrorism. ... And we broadened and strengthened our diplomatic offensive to make the world community understand both the reality of the Kargil War and Pakistan's continued sponsorship of terrorism in India.[12]

In November 2000, Vajpayee had announced a month-long 'ceasefire'—more accurately a 'Non-initiation of Ceasefire Operations' against militant groups by Indian security forces. This was at the beginning of Ramzan—the Islamic month of prayer and fasting. It was thereafter extended and went on for some six months in all. The aim, of course, was to restore a greater sense of calm in the Kashmir Valley and create a reprieve for civilians caught between the pressure of the militant groups and the counter-insurgency efforts of the security forces. That this would also provide a respite to the militants who were to use it to regroup and consolidate was the conscious risk taken, since the objective was to strengthen the forces of moderation and bring about a semblance of calm. As the ceasefire period ended, Vajpayee was keen to follow up with something else. The question was what would that 'something' be? The answer that emerged surprised all and enraged many. In L.K. Advani's account:

> [O]ne day in May 2001, when the Prime Minister had called me and Jaswant Singh for lunch at his house to discuss the next course of action, I suggested to him, 'Atalji, why don't you invite the General to come to India for talks? It does not matter if your Lahore initiative failed. It was highly appreciated both at home and abroad. Similarly, your invitation to him will be welcomed as an act of statesmanship, both within India and internationally.'[13]

External Affairs Minister Jaswant Singh and, more importantly, Prime Minister Vajpayee himself agreed. The invitation to President Musharraf to come to India for a summit meeting and the announcement about the end of the ceasefire came simultaneously on 23 May from the Ministry of External Affairs. It was, in effect, a public acknowledgement that the position of 'no talks without cessation of support to terrorists', constantly articulated by the big three in the government—A.B. Vajpayee, L.K. Advani and Jaswant Singh—was not meant to be taken literally. This reversal infuriated many and the naysayers were numerous. The coincidence of the summit invitation and the ending of the 'ceasefire' was also noted and much commented upon. Was the former to cover up the failure of the six-month ceasefire? One comment at the time was that the ceasefire was 'an idea whose time had gone'.[14] Others criticized the BJP not so much for the two decisions taken as for a more fundamental misstep—combining the invitation to Pakistan with the internal matter of Kashmir. Yet others objected to talking to Pakistan at all.

This debate has by no means ended. Whatever may have been the reason or the mix of reasons, one important factor was that revealed by Advani—it is better to be taking and retaining the initiative rather than being reactive. It was to subsequently emerge that Deputy Prime Minister Advani had secretly been in touch for some time with the Pakistani high commissioner in New Delhi through a journalist. The high commissioner conveyed the impression too of Pakistan's exhaustion with its isolation and Musharraf's keenness for opening of a dialogue. Vajpayee himself did not, obviously, see a status quo without high-level contacts, clashes on the LOC and an overall tense atmosphere as something that was sustainable. Certainly, there was the sense in India that Pakistan stood isolated, its army had received a bloody nose in Kargil, and General Musharraf was in the doghouse following his coup. Pakistan's economy was in a downturn following sanctions and its own constraints, and its people and elite felt an acute sense of isolation. For those in favour of engagement, this was a good time to talk to Pakistan when its leadership would be more realistic.

In India, the government's explanations emphasized the broad vision and statesmanship that underlay the invitation. This was the threads of Lahore being picked up again. In Pakistan, analysis of what could have led to the Indian change of heart varied. Some felt that the situation in Kashmir was getting more and more untenable for an India now increasingly conscious of its larger international role and image and it was, moreover, exhausted by the drain caused on its political capital by tensions over Kashmir. This was a view not unmixed with triumphalism and when inevitably picked up in India, made the Vajpayee decision to invite Musharraf even more unpalatable to many. Others in Pakistan were conscious of the opportunity General Musharraf had been provided to do some damage control post-Kargil, which would be a big step forward in the ending of its international isolation.

The summit itself took place in Agra on 15 and 16 July but began in Delhi with the attendant ceremonial of a visit by a head of state. In this hangs a tale too. General Musharraf had, after the October 1999 coup, styled himself chief executive. The incumbent president, in the form of a Nawaz Sharif acolyte, Muhammad Rafiq Tarar, continued till 20 June 2001 when he was packed off and Musharraf was sworn in as president. This sudden change was related to the forthcoming Delhi visit and India found that the protocol required for a presidential visit would now necessarily have to form part of the programme.

As is well known the summit itself ended in failure and the mutual accusations and recriminations about it continue to this day. The drama associated with the summit, in fact, overshadows its ultimate failure. It is useful to see parallels with the Ayub–Nehru talks of 1960, which had similarly ended without success and perhaps both sets of interactions shared the same subjective reasons for the failure to proceed ahead. Moreover, just as Kargil was the first conflict covered live on television, Agra was the first 'live' summit. With large media contingents from both countries descending on Agra each minutiae of the interactions were covered threadbare and inevitably there is an India story and a Pakistan story.

A peripheral issue vitiated the start somewhat—Musharraf had an interaction with Indian editors which was telecast on the same day. In this, according to the Pakistani foreign minister Abdul Sattar, Musharraf projected 'his persuasive views on the need to resolve the Kashmir dispute to a spellbound audience in both countries'.[15] His counterpart Jaswant Singh noted that Musharraf came across as 'belligerent' and that a 'grandstanding fever had induced General Musharraf into a great deal of unrestrained comment'. Matters went downhill thereafter and a draft statement being negotiated between Jaswant Singh and the Pakistan foreign minister Abdul Sattar did not make progress on the predictable issues of Kashmir and terrorism. For President Musharraf, a resumption from where things had been left at Lahore was not enough; for the Indians, a greater primacy to Kashmir, which was what was being demanded, was just not on the cards post-Kargil, and with the threat terrorism posed.

Curiously, in Pakistan, this failure to make progress is blamed on hardliners in the Indian cabinet and amongst the civil servants present. In fact, the divergence in the respective positions made any squaring of the circle difficult because perceptions of the summit itself were fundamentally different. For many Pakistanis and perhaps for Musharraf himself, the Agra invitation came because the situation in J&K had become untenable for India, and Vajpayee was looking for a way out. In India, the invitation was a lifeline being large-heartedly extended to an isolated Pakistan. During the summit both set of interlocuters, despite wanting to make progress, found themselves confronting the basic fallacy of their fundamental assumption—that the other was in a position of weakness! From this followed all the drama and some amount of confusion, which seemed to encapsulate this India–Pakistan summit.

A long meeting with Vajpayee, held to see if matters could still be retrieved, resulted in a monologue—with Musharraf talking and Vajpayee not saying anything. In Musharraf's account, 'I told him bluntly that there seemed to be someone above the two of us who had the power to overrule us. I also said that today both of us had been humiliated. He just sat there, speechless.'[16] He was fifty-eight, a Pakistani general who was also head of state, master of all he surveyed, convinced of the logical and positive nature of his approach and sure of achieving what his compatriot civilian politicians were incapable of. Vajpayee was almost two decades older and someone who had spent the last fifty years dealing with the ups and downs of a career in democratic politics. The ghosts of the failed Ayub–Nehru summit of 1960 not so imperceptibly hovered in the background.

The reverberations of the failure were loud. Yet that the summit took place at all meant that Kargil and the hijacking had receded and other meetings were possible. Jaswant Singh after the summit had said, 'we will pick up the threads' suggesting that other meetings would follow. The Pakistan foreign minister similarly said that the summit was 'natamam, not nakam' (inconclusive, not a failure).[17] That this was not to be was because of the global narrative on terrorism changing with the 9/11 attack in New York and in its wake two audacious terrorist attacks in India—the first on the Jammu and Kashmir Legislative Assembly in Srinagar on 1 October and the second on 13 December in New Delhi on, no less, the Indian parliament itself. It was clear that whatever balance was going to be found between India and Pakistan on the issues of terrorism and Kashmir would have to be a new one and in an environment in which equations were rapidly changing.

The US declared war on terror centred on Afghanistan, and Pakistan catapulted itself into the position of a favoured and valuable ally, a position it understood well and was comfortable in. This meant a public reversal of its existing policy of support to the Taliban regime—for some, a difficult choice to make and even more difficult policy to implement. Very few, among the Pakistani elite or among its strategic community, had doubts that General Musharraf was doing the right thing in supporting the United States. For, as one account stated:

> (T)he horizon was dark with dangers. Pakistan might be bracketed with the Taliban, declared a 'terrorist' state and its territory subjected to attacks to neutralize resistance. Pakistan's vital interests would be in jeopardy if India was given a free hand against Pakistan. The Kashmiri freedom struggle might be labelled as a terrorist insurgency; Azad Kashmir and Pakistan territory could be attacked under the pretext of eliminating terrorist bases.[18]

The sudden change in policy towards the Taliban and Afghanistan was, in this view, an act of 'clairvoyance'.[19] It meant the end of its international isolation and the resumption of generous aid flows, and the financial inflows were very large. Most of all, the change was from being a pariah to becoming a close ally. There was, of course, a heavy price to pay and the cost was to become clearer to many Pakistanis as years passed. The US aligned with the Tajik-dominated Northern Alliance—not just bitter enemies of the Taliban but close to India and supported by it for years and hence enemies of Pakistan. Overnight, Pakistan became virtually part of a military alliance against its former ally and in effect contributing to bring friends of India to power in Afghanistan. With the passage of time, the critique of Musharraf's turnaround has become stronger, not least because of the space conceded to India in Afghanistan. Nevertheless, at the time the decision was taken there was little resistance, barring from the religious right, and that too was for record rather than to be taken at face value.

All this happened as tensions with India reached a new high over the attack on the J&K Legislative Assembly in Srinagar and then the attack on the Indian parliament. The latter, notwithstanding Pakistan's denials of its involvement and condemnation of the attack, led to a wave of indignation and rage in India surpassing even the emotions generated by the Kargil conflict. The attack took place when the parliament complex was teeming with members and ministers. Mercifully, none of them was injured but seven security and other staff were killed as were all the attackers. As terrorist strikes go, it was a failed attempt but the fact was that the Indian parliament had been targeted and attacked. Speaking in parliament a week later, Deputy Prime Minister and Home Minister L.K. Advani said:

> Last week's attack on Parliament is undoubtedly the most audacious, and also the most alarming, act of terrorism in the nearly two-decades-long history of Pakistan-sponsored terrorism in India. This time the terrorists and their mentors across the border had the temerity to try to wipe out the entire political leadership of India, as represented in our multi-party Parliament. Naturally, it is time for all of us in this august House, and all of us in the country, to ponder why the terrorists and their backers tried to raise the stakes so high, particularly at a time when Pakistan is claiming to be a part of the international coalition against terrorism.[20]

In the public mind, there was not the slightest doubt about Pakistan being involved in this latest and greatest outrage. Alongside Pakistani denials of involvement was also the charge that the attack was staged by Indian intelligence agencies to add to the existing pressure on Pakistan. These insinuations, coming from authoritative spokespersons, aggravated the mood of anger in India. That the government had to do something was clear but would it go to war was the question asked not just in India and Pakistan but across the world. The US action in Afghanistan as the Taliban regime was bombed out of existence in response to the 9/11 attack had become, without it perhaps being intended as such, a benchmark to measure responses to major terrorist attacks. India's response after the parliament attack, therefore, remains debated and disputed, in terms of its adequacy, up to this day.

In the second half of December 2001, the government announced several measures—reducing the size of Pakistan's diplomatic mission in India, a ban on Pakistani overflights over Indian airspace, stoppage of services of the Samjhauta Express and the Delhi–Lahore bus service. In effect, India was being insulated from Pakistan by all links being shut off. Since the 1971 war, this was the most drastic set of measures instituted against Pakistan except that diplomatic relations were not broken. This was a comprehensive act of distancing from Pakistan which one journalist called 'the interstate version of Gandhi's non-cooperation movement'.[21]

What attracted most attention, however, were the military steps taken, which had all the features of a full-scale mobilization of the Indian Army. Leave was cancelled, training establishments closed and soldiers were recalled to their units. Trains brought reserve stocks of ammunition to forward positions. This was 'Operation Parakram' and it was a gigantic exercise involving not just the strike formations which remain in some state of readiness but reserve forces. Combatants, fighting vehicles, guns, ammunition, fuel and all manner of supplies had to be moved to the J&K, Punjab, Rajasthan and Gujarat borders. By the first week of January the pieces were in place to undertake major offensive action. In the words of one seasoned military observer, at this stage 'expectation had reached fever pitch, morale was at an all-time high, and the officers and troops eagerly awaited orders to be allowed to cross the IB [international border]'.[22] Pakistan mobilized too and simultaneously built up the narrative that India was being faced down. To an extent its smaller size helped—Indian Army mobilization, given its large land mass, was slower and gave the Pakistan Army the time to strengthen its defensive positions. For the public in both countries it did look for some time, from early January, when mobilization was complete, that some military action was imminent: armies do not mobilize for nothing.

For the rest of the world, the India–Pakistan stand-off appeared to be a sideshow to the main events in Afghanistan. The Taliban regime in Afghanistan was toppled and Hamid Karzai was sworn in as the new president. Nevertheless, the US and its allies in Afghanistan saw the dangers a possible India–Pakistan confrontation had for the 'global war against terror'. Pressure on Pakistan to act against the homegrown terrorists targeting India using its territory was therefore huge. India was advised to show restraint—a failed attack on the Indian parliament should not become the basis for undermining the larger global concert against terrorism which was surely in India's interest. However, the plus point for India was that there was now greater international and US support and understanding with regard to terrorist groups based in Pakistan. The downside was that Pakistan had a greater relevance for the US and its allies in Afghanistan, and beyond a point it was not in their interest to push Pakistan on an India-related issue.

Operation Parakram was, in Jaswant Singh's description, 'coercive diplomacy'. To what extent it worked as an exercise in coercion depends on whether you talk to an Indian or a Pakistani, excluding of course the contrary opinions that will come from the dissidents in both directions. Tension levels came down when President General Musharraf in an address to his country on 12 January committed that Pakistani territory would not be allowed to carry out terrorist attacks against India. Those arguing that Musharraf had blinked referred to his statement in the speech that 'No organization will be allowed to indulge in terrorism in the name of Kashmir'. Some manner of a crackdown on terrorist groups identified by India as being responsible for the parliament and other attacks was also carried out. Clearly, the mobilization and the international pressure on Pakistan had yielded some result. This was enough to declare a small victory for 'coercive diplomacy' but not more than that. Scepticism was the predominant sentiment in India about the steps Pakistan had taken. Thus, while tensions receded somewhat, troops remained mobilized on the border and the other restrictions announced including the ban on overflights, suspension of travel and transport links and downsizing of diplomatic missions remained in place.

Foreign Minister Jaswant Singh, who has an army background, was the acknowledged strategic thinker in Vajpayee's cabinet. He found himself at the centre of the different, conflicting stresses comprising Pakistan policy at that time. Others were similarly placed including Brajesh Mishra, the national security adviser and also the prime minister's principal secretary and confidant. Yet, Jaswant Singh was the public face of the government, and to see the crisis through his eyes is, therefore, instructive. What were India's aims in resorting to the massive mobilization that dwarfed the diplomatic steps of cutting of cross-border links and downgrading diplomatic representation? For Jaswant Singh, the answer was threefold: 'to defeat cross border infiltration without conflict; to contain the national mood of "teach Pakistan a lesson"; and in the event of war, to destroy and degrade Pakistan's war fighting capabilities'.[23] These aims were not publicly disclosed then in this form but variants were in the public domain. At the time, the contradiction between the first and the third aims was seized on as an illustration of the government's policy being impulsive, and not thought through. The fact that the contradiction was understood and consciously accepted as a part of policy was nevertheless the key to such limited success as it had. In Jaswant Singh's words '... these aims, if not fully, were substantially realized'.

While opinions have varied on this judgement, what is equally of interest is Jaswant Singh's analysis of the challenges he faced in implementing this policy—the most taxing that sapped his resolve were the internal issues including carrying 'conviction with colleagues'. He was, in fact, encountering a conundrum which all previous Indian governments had also faced and would do so in the future: How was the government 'to carry the nation's mood, to contain its belligerence, its desire for revenge and retaliation, but give it a sense of achievement, of having diplomatically defeated the enemy'? In parallel was the task—devolving on him more than anybody else as foreign minister—of carrying conviction with the international community. This meant conveying the extent of India's outrage and seriousness in securing its aims, while at the same time reassuring them of its intent in not letting matters escalate beyond a point. Managing these contradictory postures was at the heart of a foreign minister's responsibilities in dealing with Pakistan in the wake of a major terrorist attack. His successors would also undergo similar experiences in the future.

From mid-January, although tensions did ease slightly, the face-off continued. In India, the stand-off on the border was even temporarily pushed into the background by an unconnected development. Large-scale Hindu–Muslim communal rioting in Gujarat in late February and early March 2002 led to both official criticism and even stronger public comment in Pakistan. Criticism and condemnation of these events were strong also in other foreign capitals. For many in Pakistan, this was obviously an opportunity to focus the spotlight on India and amongst President Musharraf's statements was one calling on the international community 'not to be complacent or take a biased view in its response to combat this evil in whichever form it manifested and wherever it existed'.[24] If Pakistan's tactics were on expected lines and were brushed aside as par for the course, there was nevertheless one novel feature in the reactions in that country to the communal rioting and loss of life in Gujarat. Unlike in the past, and most notably in the aftermath of the Babri Masjid demolition in 1992, there was no retaliatory violence against minorities or minority shrines in Pakistan in 2002. In contrast to his negative image in India as also in Pakistan amongst many democrats, General Musharraf's tenure was evaluated positively by the beleaguered Hindus of Pakistan—both in the aftermath of the Gujarat riots of 2002 and subsequently. In Pakistan, this was also an occasion to project itself as a moderate and tolerant Islamic society.

Nevertheless, Pakistan was having to battle hard against international censure at this time as episode after episode demonstrated the deep roots of terrorism and militancy there. The US journalist Daniel Pearl was kidnapped and killed in February 2002—the killer was Omar Sheikh, the British national released by India in Kandahar to secure release of passengers of the hijacked IC-814. It subsequently also emerged that after his release he lived in relative freedom in Lahore and possibly was one of the many involved in the planning to execute the 9/11 attack in New York and elsewhere in the United States. Then in March 2002 a church in Islamabad's diplomatic enclave was targeted in a terrorist attack and several US and foreign nationals killed. The immediate result was a further depletion in the size of Islamabad's diplomatic community—in turn enhancing Pakistan's sense of crisis and isolation. For a large majority in India, Pakistan's chickens were coming home to roost and increasingly more and more people outside India too shared its assessments of Pakistan as the epicentre of terrorism.

A greater crisis on the India–Pakistan front was in the offing. On 14 May 2002, terrorists attacked families of Indian army personnel in Kaluchak in Jammu and Kashmir. The attack on the army camp led to over thirty fatalities, most of whom were army wives and children. For the Indian Army, mobilized already, this was 'almost the last straw' and the attack on the families was 'a slur on their honour'.[25] An additional military measure announced at this time was the forward deployment of Indian naval vessels in the Arabian Sea—the signal being of course that the navy, far superior to Pakistan's, could bottle up Karachi port—Pakistan's lifeline in many ways. To show that this was serious, warships from the eastern coast were redeployed to the Arabian Sea. The drums of war were beating louder than even after the parliament attack.

Jaswant Singh found himself in a minority that counselled restraint and did so to avoid falling into 'a classical trap: deliberate provocation launched for inviting a predictable retaliation, thus both time and place being of the adversary's choice'.[26] The threat of major combat and the risk of its escalating to the nuclear level was real enough to invite visible and active involvement of the United States in trying to bring down tensions. This meant counselling restraint to India and putting pressure on Pakistan to wind down on cross-border infiltration, thus addressing India's core concerns. The US interest in the India–Pakistan face-off was immense and obvious. It wanted the focus to remain on Afghanistan and for this a larger Pakistani Army presence on the Pakistan–Afghanistan border areas was essential to bottle up the Taliban and al Qaeda elements. For many in India this advice—not to get provoked, not to compromise the American effort on Afghanistan, not to push Pakistan too much—was irksome in the face of nationwide public anger at continued attacks from Pakistan.

To make sure these pressures worked, many countries led by the USA and the UK advised their nationals in India to leave immediately and evacuated staff from their diplomatic missions. Amongst other things this led to the curtailment of the issue of visas in India and foreign investors in the stock market started expressing concern about a possible war. Often measures such as these have a more immediate impact than back-room counsel by diplomats, and curtailment of visa issue has been described as an instance of the United States' own brand of coercive diplomacy![27]

The crisis eased as evidence came in of the closing down of terrorist launch pads near the LOC in Pakistan and consequently infiltration started coming down. This was presented to India through the United States which received in addition—its officials told the Government of India—strong assurances from Pakistan, meaning General Musharraf personally, that no further cross-border activity would take place. For many in the government in India this result, howsoever unsatisfactory to others, was a good enough outcome of the pressure put on Pakistan and the leverage exercised through external powers—especially the US. A victory of sorts, howsoever partial, could again be declared. The easing of tensions was publicly signalled by calling back the Indian Navy from its forward positions and a lifting the ban on Pakistani overflights announced after the parliament attack. At the same time, the army mobilization on the borders was not touched. For Jaswant Singh the takeaway was:

> [O]f central importance here is patience, a finely tuned sense of 'strategic restraint' as a tool of military diplomacy, and even though

> coercive diplomacy has the appearance of being passive, particularly in the India–Pakistan context, it is a very difficult policy to employ, and unquestionably it is the correct approach.[28]

What explains this emphasis on restraint, the policy that finally prevailed? In retrospect three elements are decipherable. Firstly, the reluctance of the political leadership to rely on military means to attain desired objectives unless they were virtually guaranteed success. India's political class had no patience with notions of the 'fog of war'. Answerable to a demanding public opinion, they were uncomfortable to leave matters entirely in military hands since they knew that the India–Pakistan military balance was relatively evenly poised and made even more so with nuclear weapons in Pakistan's hands. If guaranteed success was not assured, this option was not a desirable one and less preferable to limited use of the military as a part of a larger exercise of coercive diplomacy. This was itself quite a gamble given the significant human and material costs of Operation Parakram.

Secondly, Prime Minister Vajpayee, his national security adviser Brajesh Mishra and others in his cabinet had a certain faith in India's growth story since the early 1990s and, in the contest with Pakistan, were convinced that in a fundamental and long-term sense India was forging ahead. This view, although rarely stated, underpinned a great deal of government policy at the time and instinctively was shared by large sections of an otherwise belligerent middle class that had gained the most in the past decade and a half. Since India was 'winning' by simply doing well, and not just doing better than Pakistan, why risk that progress with a larger conflict and escalation that may be difficult to control?

Thirdly and finally were the possibilities of using the long stand-off with Pakistan to advantage in Jammu and Kashmir by strengthening its internal political process. For Jaswant Singh, this was one of the 'undeclared aims' of the stand-off and it is, in fact, the area where the most significant outcomes were visible.

Assembly elections were held in J&K in September–October 2002 and the results showed a voter turnout of around 44 per cent across the state and 31 per cent in the Kashmir Valley—not ideal but given the history of the state since 1989 a considerable step forward.[29] In the

1996 election, the voting percentage was 54 per cent and regarded as less credible by many but in that year even holding the election was an achievement. The 2002 election was, thus, widely judged as possibly the best in the state's recent history in terms of being fair. Although it saw a high level of violence, including some infiltration from across the LOC, nevertheless the stand-off of the past months and the fact that a large number of troops stood mobilized ensured that violence and infiltration would not destabilize the election. The presence of international observers and media gave to the electoral process greater legitimacy. The changed international environment on terrorism post 9/11 also helped.

The result in terms of who won—the outcome was a coalition government of the Congress and Mufti Mohammad Sayeed's party, the Peoples Democratic Party (PDP)—was less important than a successful election with a reasonable voter turnout. In fact, that the ruling BJP–National Conference alliance lost added even more credibility to the process. It was a considerable success for the government and Jaswant Singh, savouring it after the months of tension since the December 2001 attack on parliament and the longer roller coaster since Kargil writes: 'Though this was a domestic process, the election was for me, a very satisfying Foreign Office success too.'[30] In this perspective, diplomacy and strategic restraint had worked in a changed international environment in which Pakistan found itself on the defensive as far as a key element of its policy—supporting terrorists in J&K to bring about a change in its status—was concerned.

Incidentally, the J&K elections coincided with one of Pakistan's more flawed elections—providing one more example of the different trajectories of both countries. In early April 2002, a referendum was held in Pakistan on General Musharraf continuing as president for a further five years. The whole of Pakistan was declared a single constituency with voters having to vote yes or no to the following question:

> For the survival of the local government system, establishment of democracy, continuity of reforms, end to sectarianism and extremism, and to fulfil the vision of Qaid-i-Azam, would you like to elect President General Pervez Musharraf as President of Pakistan for five years?

The referendum in which 97.5 per cent of votes were declared to have answered yes was to be described as a 'transparent scam' accompanied by large-scale rigging of virtually every conceivable kind.[31]

A few months later, in October 2002, Pakistan's general elections were held in which again there was comprehensive pre-poll and other kinds of rigging. Amongst the improvisations resorted to ensure defeat of the mainstream opposition were numerous changes to the election laws. For instance, only those who had graduate degrees could contest. Simultaneously, certain certificates awarded by madrasas were treated as graduate degrees. Such measures ensured that a breakaway faction of Nawaz Sharif's Pakistan Muslim League, which was in the Musharraf camp, could come to power supported by a combination of religious parties—known as the Muttahida Majlis-e-Amal (United Council of Action). The acronym—MMA—also conveniently stood for the 'Mullah Military Alliance' believed to be a central feature of Zia's Pakistan was now resurrecting itself under Musharraf.

The election, despite the rigging, was important to Musharraf by giving him a civilian government as a front. It also brought the religious parties into the government—important because Pakistan was now a front-line state in a West-led war against a fellow Islamic country, and the religious parties Musharraf now bound to his side were themselves supporters of the Taliban. Giving these religious groups a stake in Musharraf's new scheme of things reduced, somewhat at least, the intensity of their cadres' opposition to the policy of joining the US against the Taliban. The point, however, is that the rigged April referendum and flawed October general election provided the inevitable contrast with the J&K election; in fact, the results of the latter two came out almost at the same time. While many in the West were relieved at the civilian veneer Musharraf had acquired, the contrasting picture with the more successful J&K elections served as an additional point of pressure on Pakistan to move against terrorists targeting India.

In Pakistan, the claim of General Musharraf that Pakistan had successfully faced down India over the course of 2002, and especially in May–June 2002, also enjoyed wide currency. The calling back of the Indian naval ships was described, in authoritative Pakistani statements, as inevitable since the ships could not stay out for too long with the onset of the monsoons. General Pervez Musharraf writes in his autobiography that after a ten-month stand-off—'a hair trigger eye ball to eye ball confrontation'—'the Indians blinked and quite ignominiously agreed to a mutual withdrawal of forces'.[32] The response to the announcement of the end of the overflight ban was also cool. In Pakistani calculations, India had resorted to the ban impulsively based on the historical memory of 1965 and 1971 but Pakistan no longer was vulnerable since it did not have an eastern wing any more. In 2002, the ban of overflights, which Pakistan had reciprocally applied to Indian aircraft also now hurt India more simply because of the higher density of Indian air traffic going west. There was also the view that ending the ban at this stage would only serve to enhance Indian access to Afghanistan and it was in Pakistan's interest that it remained. So, the respective ban on overflights continued for some more months and India would, in fact, later be pressing for its removal.

But the Indian pressure had taken its toll. Most Pakistanis realized this was also because it overlapped and converged so much with Pakistan's very negative image rapidly crystallizing in many countries including those which invested heavily in it in political and diplomatic terms. What Pakistan went through in 2002 was not diplomatic isolation—on the contrary, the Afghanistan situation made it a sought-after interlocuter, and political leaders, ministers and chiefs of military from all over the world periodically descended on Islamabad. Substantial aid flows were also coming in. But in 2002, it was a demoralized populace and cynical intellectual community that observed Pakistan's power play, largely because of the association the country evoked with terrorism and terrorists the world over. For the more perceptive in Pakistan, the J&K election also demonstrated that neither in a tactical or in a strategic sense, had Pakistani efforts in Kashmir since Kargil been of any great utility.

The blowback in Pakistan itself of promoting terrorism and extremism in Afghanistan and India had taken a heavy toll. On 8 May 2002, just a few days before the terrorist attack on Kaluchak, an attack on an upmarket hotel in Karachi targeted French naval engineers and killed eleven of them. About a month later, just as the crisis with India was easing, the US consulate in Karachi was attacked with several fatal casualties. By end-2002 Pakistan was frequently being called 'the most dangerous place in the world'. Prime Minister Vajpayee's intuitive grasp of this informed his Pakistan policy even as the policy appeared to lurch from having to deal with one provocation after the other.

In the aftermath of the J&K election, the question that drew a great deal of attention was whether it was time to end the ten-month-long mobilization of the Indian Army. The costs had been considerable. Till March 2002, 'the army had lost 176 men in the operation due to mishaps in minefields, mishandling ammunition and explosives and traffic accidents'.[33] The financial cost was estimated at ₹800 million. A larger question was of what next with Pakistan, if anything. K. Subrahmanyam, India's most prominent and influential defence analyst and strategic thinker in a newspaper article recommended continuing with the status quo of full army mobilization *and* having a dialogue with Pakistan *before* beginning de-escalation.[34] Similar advice came in from other quarters too although many from the armed forces pointed to the problems arising from a large-scale and inactive comprehensive mobilization of troops for such a long period. But the government, or at least the prime minister, had made up its mind and the demobilization order was issued on 16 October—in fact, a day after Subrahmanyam's article recommending otherwise was published. Many were unhappy at the decision and there were many dark mutters about US pressures leading to this decision: the gains from Operation Parakram seemed intangible and the threat of terror attacks had not receded. But Prime Minister Vajpayee and NSA Brajesh Mishra seemed clear that enough had been extracted and that a new phase had to be embarked upon.

It would nevertheless take some months more before the outlines of this policy became clear, even to those in the government or close to Vajpayee. After the announcement of the demobilization of troops in mid-October, official statements from both sides remained bellicose, shelling and firing on the Line of Control continued as also did intimidation and harassment of Indian diplomats in Pakistan and vice versa. The official mood in India also was seemingly against any further initiatives with Pakistan without a winding up of what was now increasingly called the 'infrastructure of terror'.

Change was, however, brewing and this was demonstrated dramatically in Kashmir and by the prime minister himself where he addressed simultaneously a domestic constituency and Pakistan. On 18 April 2003, in a public meeting in Srinagar, Vajpayee spoke movingly about sharing the pain of Kashmiris and that 'the doors of our heart will also remain open for you'; Insaniyat (Humanism), Jamhooriyat (Democracy) and Kashmiriyat (Kashmir's tradition of Hindu–Muslim unity) would be his guiding principles in resolving Kashmir's problems—internal and external. He then went on to offer friendship to Pakistan, in words that have since become famous: 'We are again extending a hand of friendship but hands should be extended from both the sides. Both sides should decide to live together' and, 'Not guns but brotherhood alone can resolve issues.'[35]

Evidently, Vajpayee was looking beyond just a thaw. Possibly, what was happening elsewhere in the wider region also weighed on him—Saddam Hussain's Iraq had crumbled falling to the American forces on 9 April. With the US in Afghanistan, regional stability, as Vajpayee understood it, was in a flux. But he also perhaps felt that standing still vis-à-vis Pakistan, after the October 2002 demobilization, as many then advised, would inevitably lead to a regression. Violence in J&K may have come down statistically and in a comparative sense but the situation remained tenuous. On 23 March, 2003, twenty-four Hindus had been targeted and killed by terrorists in Nandimarg, an isolated hamlet in Kashmir. On the same day, Abdul Majeed Dar, a prominent former militant commander who had turned against violence and now stood for dialogue, was assassinated—possibly by his former comrades at a nod from Pakistan's ISI. Early in April, both the foreign and defence ministers of India, Yashwant Sinha and George Fernandes respectively, had spoken, in the context of the ongoing US military action in Iraq, about the appropriateness of pre-emptive strikes against Pakistan in the face of continuing terrorist attacks. Clearly, left to itself, as the year advanced, another 'hot' summer was inevitable and if this happened the gains since mid-2002 would be threatened.

As it happened, the 'hand of friendship' speech of 18 April 2003 was reciprocated by Pakistan and things moved quickly thereafter. On 2 May, Prime Minister Vajpayee announced that a new high commissioner would be stationed in Islamabad—diplomatic ties, in other words, were being restored to ambassadorial level. Pakistan's prime minister—in place since the October 2002 election—Mir Zafarullah Jamali wrote and invited Prime Minister Vajpayee to visit Pakistan. Vajpayee responded the same day—he looked forward to visiting Pakistan and discussions should take place at the official level on all issues to prepare the ground. More than the language used in the correspondence, it was the fact that it was taking place that mattered. It was clear enough in any case that a discussion once begun at any level would have enough on the plate to keep it going.

But apart from the officialese exchanged, there was now a larger public enthusiasm on both sides to strengthen the thaw further. Within days, delegations of members of parliament were visiting across the borders in both directions and there was already talk of an India–Pakistan Test series. In August, meeting with a group of Indian members of parliament, General Musharraf suggested a ceasefire by both militaries across the Line of Control. It would take some weeks for this idea to be put into effect but India–Pakistan peace had, in the course of 3–4 months, suddenly become the flavour of the season in both countries. This was in total contrast to the past four years since Kargil and, in fact, with the tense 1990s that public enthusiasm itself appeared to be driving things forward.

Both governments now competed in announcing packages of confidence-building measures (CBMs): release of prisoners, announcement of free medical treatment, scholarships, easier visa processes were accompanied by more innovative suggestions being shared. Even before existing travel links by air and on the surface route were restored new ideas and suggestions were being talked and speculated about. Among them were restoring the Khokhrapar–Munabao rail link across the Sindh–Rajasthan border, which remained snapped since the 1965 war, restarting a Karachi–Mumbai steamer service and establishing a bus link between Srinagar and Muzaffarabad. There were also numerous low-hanging fruits available—from restoration of road, rail and air links to trade, sporting and cultural contacts, quite apart from the larger issues of Jammu and Kashmir and terrorism.

The ceasefire on the LOC came into effect on 26 November 2003 and the resumption of overflights on 30 November. The ceasefire came on an Eid—greeted wholeheartedly by villagers on both sides. It also enabled India to complete the fencing of the LOC—long regarded as an indispensable instrument to stem further infiltration from Pakistan. As the ceasefire was extended to Siachen, guns fell totally silent, after at least twenty years, across the entire India–Pakistan interface. From October 2003 infiltration levels started coming down dramatically as did reports that the terrorist groups and extremist leaders in Pakistan were being more tightly muzzled than ever before.

This cluster of agreements and confidence-building steps accompanied by a sea change in public atmospherics was, in fact, focused on the big-ticket item—a visit by Prime Minister Vajpayee to Pakistan. A postponed SAARC summit now scheduled for January 2004 provided the platform and Prime Minister Vajpayee was in Pakistan for a second time since his visit to Lahore a little over five years ago.

Notwithstanding the popular acclaim that accompanied these moves and countermoves in both countries, there were many naysayers and doubters. In Pakistan, the initial reaction to Vajpayee's 'hand of friendship' amongst the India watchers in its strategic community was one of slight bewilderment. The initiative had challenged a firmly held assumption that the tensions of 2002 would be maintained by the 'Hindu nationalist' BJP till the next general election as animosity with Pakistan was a vote winner in India. With Vajpayee traversing a path in a diametrically opposite direction, there were also wider conspiracy theories—that Pakistan was being outwitted by the wily Indians in a complicated chess game over Kashmir; that the ceasefire on the LOC was a ploy which Musharraf had swallowed and the Indians were using it to complete the fencing of the LOC and further cement the status quo in J&K, etc. There was also disapproval of the grand plans of wide-ranging cultural contacts and economic links now being spoken about—not just by peace activists but also by senior figures in government. More than anything else was the apprehension that the engagement was taking place when the odds favoured India because of its booming economy, stronger international profile and, most of all, because it was able to corner Pakistan using terrorism and a conducive international environment as additional leverage. In India too, there was inevitably a large doubters' camp. Was there hard evidence that any of the demands on Pakistan regarding the terrorist groups and their 'infrastructure' had been met? Others pointed to pressures from the US as being the central driver in the government's policy initiatives. Inevitably, there was also the view that Vajpayee was setting himself up for another, a third disappointment.

Dramatic events in Pakistan in December 2003 did lead to some change in such thinking. General Pervez Musharraf narrowly escaped with his life following two assassination attempts on 14 and 25 December

2003 by vehicle-borne suicide bombers. The attacks were executed almost to perfection. After the second attack Musharraf appeared on national television to quell rumours that he had been killed. He looked so visibly shaken that it was evident that the escape had been a narrow one. More than anything else this convinced many in India—both in the government and public opinion generally—that Pakistan's options on using terrorists had narrowed considerably since 9/11. No longer could it direct militant groups to carry out attacks outside Pakistan and expect to be spared the blowback, which was obviously reaching unacceptable levels. Engagement with Pakistan, as Prime Minister Vajpayee had embarked upon again, appeared now both sensible and essential.

For the time being at least, all doubters were quiet as Vajpayee attended the SAARC summit in Islamabad on 4–6 January 2004. The summit provided a convenient platform to highlight an India–Pakistan rapprochement—this would demonstrably be to the benefit of the whole region. For the Indian delegation, the central takeaway was set as Pakistan, recognizing the changed world since 9/11, committed itself to renouncing the use of terrorists and proxies. Without this no meaningful engagement was possible. For Pakistan, the key was to start a dialogue on Kashmir and simultaneously end the high state of tension with India. The outcome pleased both although the Indian side was happier. Pakistan's expectations were met by an agreement to restart the Composite Dialogue, which included Jammu and Kashmir, that had been interrupted by Kargil. For India, the joint statement issued on 4 January at the end of the Vajpayee–Musharraf meeting contained a key sentence: 'President Musharraf reassured Prime Minister Vajpayee that he would not permit any territory under Pakistan's control to be used to support terrorism in any manner'. This sentence more than anything else illustrated the new environment that Pakistan faced and was as explicit an acknowledgement as possible that many ground realities had changed. Vajpayee had, in short, secured in Islamabad what he could not get at the Agra summit in 2001 but in the process also created a platform for future India–Pakistan engagement that would enable him to satisfy the doubters back home.

The politics of the summit apart, what was striking about it was the infectious and heady atmosphere of goodwill it created. To report on it possibly the largest ever congregation of Indian and foreign journalists ever assembled in Pakistan—perhaps even in South Asia—was present in Islamabad. Their reports added to the sense of exhilaration that the Islamabad summit represented a tipping point in India–Pakistan history, and the future would be different from the past. As contrarian and discordant voices in both countries fell silent, at least temporarily, it was Vajpayee himself who obliquely hinted at the difficulties that may still lie ahead. His last engagement in Islamabad was laying the foundation stone of a new Indian high commission complex. Speaking to a largely Indian audience, principally the high commission staff and families and the Indian media contingent visiting Pakistan for the summit, Vajpayee hoped that the foundation stone he had laid would lead to a building strong enough to face the storms that lay ahead and keep its inhabitants secure.[36] In the heady atmosphere of that time this reference was overlooked by most but clearly there was an implied, if concealed, note of caution in his speech as he concluded his third major tryst with Pakistan in five years.

On his return, Vajpayee moved towards an early general election. The Lok Sabha was dissolved in February 2004, nine months before its scheduled term expired. The Pakistan card was only the final one that the government had played before going for a mid-term election—strong economic growth created the confidence that this was the time to go to the people and come back with a stronger mandate. From February to May as India engrossed itself in the campaign to elect the thirteenth Lok Sabha, part of its attention, as also in Pakistan, was riveted on an Indian cricket team touring Pakistan after a gap of a decade and a half.

The Indian team spent a leisurely five weeks in Pakistan playing five One-Day Internationals and three Tests. Optically, it was possibly the most powerful way of demonstrating that something new was stirring in the subcontinent. Crowded as the narrative has been in the past few years, this is therefore a good moment to freeze the frame and look at longer trends and forces operating in the subcontinent and how these impacted on the India–Pakistan story.

The 1990s saw the initiation of another trend—barely discernible then, but very evident in hindsight. Globalization had its own profound impact in Indian and Pakistani societies and showed up in curious ways in their interface. Both Indians and Pakistanis were now travelling as also living outside their countries in larger numbers than ever before. For many, if not most, Indians or Pakistanis meeting—as a student, traveller or a business executive working in a foreign or multinational firm—someone from the other country in a more neutral environment could be a curiously unsettling experience. In this situation, the contestations of the subcontinent were not forgotten but usually set aside. Friendships flourished as both learned to navigate around no-go areas likely to cause friction in interpersonal relationships

Within India and Pakistan, proximity was growing even as relations remained tense. The technology of the Internet meant that Indians and Pakistanis were now directly in touch with each other and the traditional filters of government policy were no longer that effective. Newspapers and magazines could be read now at virtually the same time and communications over email meant an intensity of contact that was new. As television and the Internet fundamentally changed news gathering, reporting and entertainment, it was evident that life would not be the same in the specific context of bilateral relations.

Globalization and technology transformations had other impacts also and curiously enough it was in the terrain of cricket that these were most evident. Through the contested 1990s India and Pakistan played against each other in only one series with three Test matches in India in 1999. In the earlier decade, troubled too but less so, between 1978 and 1989 India and Pakistan played some twenty-nine Tests. But the 1990s was not a desert for India–Pakistan cricket as globalization transformed a traditional game of South Asian elites beyond all recognition. In the 1990s, there were as many as forty-five One-Day International contests between India and Pakistan, of which over 80 per cent were in neutral venues—Singapore, Toronto, Sharjah, etc.[37]

In March 1996, with no bilateral dialogue in place and tensions at a high, India, Pakistan and Sri Lanka jointly hosted the 1996 Cricket World Cup and in the words of one journalist 'India's glitterati' went to Lahore for one of the matches.[38] This is not to say that the crowds in either country had put aside the past, for in the India–Pakistan contest the match was described for the viewers as 'waging war, even a Jihad or Dharmyudh'.[39] Yet the Wills Trophy—as the 1996 World Cup was known—meant that even if the two were doing nothing else together they could still co-host an international sporting tournament. They could also do so with some panache. When some teams refused to play on grounds of security in Sri Lanka, which was a co-host, a joint India–Pakistan team played a solidarity match in that country against its national team.[40] Then, even in the midst of the Kargil conflict, India and Pakistan played against each other in the next Cricket World Cup in the supercharged June of 1999 and that too in England with its large Indian and Pakistani diaspora.

Clearly the world was changing and with it, the assumption was, so would India and Pakistan. But it was India which was embracing this new globalized environment with greater fervour as its diaspora expanded and its economy opened up to foreign companies and investment. As the gap between it and Pakistan increased, foreign investment became a new buzzword in India and brought its own set of expectations on the future of the subcontinent to the table. The India tour of Pakistan in March–April 2004 was appropriately enough sponsored by and called the 'Samsung' series. That globalization, multinational trade and investment would open new avenues in India–Pakistan relations clearly was the assumption.

If India appeared to be the crucible of these huge economic changes, the reception that the Indian team got in Pakistan suggested to many that in that country too things had changed, perhaps irrevocably. The first contest in the series was an ODI in Karachi. That the Indian team could play in this city, given its reputation as a hotbed of criminals and terrorists seemed by itself a leap of faith. Karachi had been out of the international cricket circuit since the terrorist attack in May 2002 on the hotel where the visiting New Zealand cricket team was staying. Both the match and the tour had been abandoned. For many Indians, this was the city that had provided Dawood Ibrahim sanctuary and where Omar Sheikh, of IC-814 fame, had killed Daniel Pearl.

Former foreign secretary Shaharyar Khan was now chairman of the Pakistan Cricket Board (PCB). Persuading the Board of Control for Cricket in India (the BCCI) and then the players and their families and finally the Government of India to agree to a match in Karachi was for him an uphill but essential task. The final compromise reached with the BCCI and the Indian security agencies was that a one-day match would be played in Karachi. It was, in fact, an outstanding success—although India won, the spectators cheered as if it was a home side victory. The Karachi match set the tone for the rest of the series as the team toured

Lahore, Multan, Rawalpindi and, significantly, Peshawar. The 'whiff of grapeshot' that accompanied many India–Pakistan matches was not just absent but as Shaharyar Khan recollects:

> The Karachi ODI had set an unparalleled high-water mark in crowd conduct so that the Indian team appeared totally relaxed in the Qissa Khwani bazaar of Peshawar, the shops of Anarkali and visits to historic sites. The atmosphere for the tour was festive, like a carnival. Again, shopkeepers, restaurant owners, taxi and rickshaw drivers would charge reduced or no fares from Indian supporters.[41]

The matches in Lahore saw a virtual deluge of Indian visitors including Bollywood stars, socialites, politicians and others; it appeared as if 'a veritable cross-border invasion of Indian supporters had taken place' and 'they came by train, bus and air, the industrial moguls in their private jets'.[42] The first match at Karachi also had some Indians—principally the distributers of Samsung products in India. But there were two more unusual sets of visitors. The first was the current generation of the Nehru family—Priyanka and Rahul Gandhi. The second was more poignant for many Pakistanis—Dina Wadia, the Quaid-i-Azam's only child, and Nusli Wadia, her son. This was Dina Wadia's first visit to Pakistan since her father's death in 1948. The visit was private and consciously kept as such at her request. However, as Shaharyar Khan recalls, it 'had a deep impact on the people of Pakistan. The India–Pakistan series had led to Jinnah's family visiting Pakistan for the first time in over fifty years.'

Overall the reaction to the cricket tour was a 'political statement that the people of Pakistan had made'. Hitherto Pakistan had been dominated by military dictators who had determined 'the state of relations between Pakistan and India'. For Shaharyar Khan, the public reaction to the tour by the Indian team was 'the spontaneous reflection of the people's voice'. Certainly, around the world there were many who saw the cricket series of 2004 as heralding a more fundamental change, and the UN Secretary General announced a special award to the two teams for bringing about peace through sport.

There were more subtle factors at play also in this vast and spontaneous goodwill that greeted the Indian team and Indians in general at this time—not least of which was Pakistan's external image. Through the years, regardless of what was happening on the India–Pakistan front or despite its new-found relevance in the global war against terror, Pakistan's profile had continued to deteriorate. For many Pakistanis, the burden of living in a country regarded as a sanctuary and operational base for terrorists and being the crucible of extremism was heavy enough. To this burden was added that of being a proliferator of nuclear weapon technology. In February 2004, A.Q. Khan, the 'father of the Pakistani bomb' was seen and heard by a shocked populace apologizing for the proliferation network he had set up. In late 2003, the United States had presented Musharraf with evidence of the technology being secretly sold by A.Q. Khan to Iran, North Korea and Libya. He was arrested and asked to apologize in public and disclose all in return for being spared further punishment. It was a deeply traumatizing moment for most Pakistanis as they watched a great national icon destroyed by his own greed and in the process 'tarnished Pakistan's image indelibly'.[43] That this latest dent on Pakistan's image coincided with an upswing in relations with India seemed intangibly to make this relationship suddenly more valuable.

As this India–Pakistan engagement grew at the popular level the results of the Indian general election came in. The BJP-led NDA was convincingly defeated and a Congress-led coalition, the United Progressive Alliance (UPA), formed the government. Dr Manmohan Singh was the new prime minister of India. If he was best known as an economist and the finance minister who had launched market-friendly reforms in India, he was also a child of the Partition of India. About fifteen years old in 1947, he was originally from the Chakwal district of Punjab—one of the areas which had seen total ethnic cleansing with all the Sikhs and Hindus of the area moving to India. His family had undergone all the traumas of Partition and possibly this implanted in him the conviction that there was no choice but to move on.

In Pakistan, the reaction to the election result had different strands. The peaceful political transition, taken for granted in India, was in itself an implied comment on military rule in Pakistan. Yet curiously and ironically, there was some measure of apprehension at the return of the Congress—seen now as the custodian of the values that had created all the problems of the past, and was responsible for the break-up of Pakistan in 1971. The new foreign minister, K. Natwar Singh, was well known from the time he was India's high commissioner during the early 1980s. He had, it was believed, many of Indira Gandhi's prejudices against Pakistan. 'Sir, Kashmir is in my bone marrow,' he had once responded to President Zia-ul-Haq telling him 'Kunwar Sahib, Kashmir is in my blood.' For Natwar Singh this was 'a mutually fruitless play of words' and exemplified how President Zia and he 'frequently assaulted each other with good manners'.[44] For many Pakistanis of a generation later, memories and stories of such exchanges, however, did not bode well for the future. There were other reasons cited for concern in Pakistan and one columnist confidently wrote on 15 May 2004 that 'Under the new dispensation, the India–Pakistan peace process is likely to suffer a setback' and went on to explain why:

> Keeping in view the hard realities of India's political scene, no non-BJP government, least of all a government led by Sonia Gandhi, can afford to initiate a meaningful dialogue with Pakistan to solve the Kashmir issue because even a small concession on this matter will be dubbed a sell-out. Only Vajpayee, with his unquestionable Hindu nationalist credentials, had the stature and the standing to quieten the chauvinists and hard-liners and push through the peace process with Pakistan to its logical conclusion.[45]

In the event, these assessments were wrong as in fact they had been wrong after the NDA led by the BJP had come to power in 1998 or when the Janata Party with the Bharatiya Jana Sangh as a vital component had assumed office in 1977. The change in government in India saw, if anything, a stronger push to build on the momentum left by Prime Minister Vajpayee and the NDA government. From late 2004, the dialogue process started showing results. Easiest were the steps to restore the status quo as existed before the attack on parliament: Delhi–Lahore travel by rail and road, the restoration of full-strength diplomatic missions, issuing more visas, etc. More substantive progress was evident to the public in both countries as agreement was reached on restarting the Khokhrapar–Munabao rail link, which resumed finally in February 2006. If this was a tangible takeaway, it was also with some symbolic value, restarting something which had not functioned since 1965. Similarly, in the other areas of the Composite Dialogue such as trade, cultural cooperation and tackling drug trafficking, progress, even if limited, was relatively easy given the general upswing in the relationship.

Those issues where a territorial implication existed, progress was slower; for instance, in the case of Sir Creek. Similarly, where deep-rooted prejudices or irrational fears existed, such as to do with sharing of river waters, progress was minuscule and the discussions on the Tulbul Navigation Project (or the Wullar Barrage as Pakistan termed it) were largely formulaic. Even more complicated was anything to do with Jammu and Kashmir, either conceptually or on a specific issue such as Siachen and whether it could be demilitarized. Here, ground covered almost two decades earlier at the time of Rajiv Gandhi and Benazir Bhutto was traversed again—an agreement that India would withdraw from the glacier and the surrounding heights. The sticking point now, as then, was demarcating positions on the ground—something unacceptable to Pakistan as it would make the positions held by India acquire a de jure status.

But if these old positions had not changed, certain ground realities had. Firstly, Indian positions in Siachen now were well entrenched with supply lines established. There was no pressing reason for the Indian Army to think of withdrawing; the high casualty rates because of altitude and climate were largely a thing of the past. Secondly, and more significantly, given the recent history of the Pakistani intrusion in Kargil, the question posed in India was that even if Pakistan agreed to a demarcation of the positions India would withdraw from, what was the guarantee that Pakistan Army would not occupy those heights after our troops had withdrawn? If the LOC, whose demarcation had been mutually agreed upon decades earlier, on maps and on the ground, could be infringed at Kargil, what would stop a similar action at Siachen in the future? The Pakistani response to this was invariably that a new step forward had to be taken to build trust. That this failed to carry conviction is not surprising as many of the principal interlocutors in India, both on the military side as well as among the civil servants had experienced Kargil first-hand and been witness to the high casualty rate when positions at heights had to be retaken.

Even more difficult was the question of where to make a start in discussions on Jammu and Kashmir, where positions were further apart than any other issue under discussion in the Composite Dialogue. The big plus here was that the ceasefire, in place since November 2003, was holding, infiltration in J&K was down and finally terrorist groups in Pakistan seemed to be under some sort of a leash. This, combined with the dramatic upswing in relations, created an environment where new possibilities could be discussed and older ideas, long dormant, could be revisited.

The oldest of these was on softening the Line of Control—permitting travel from Jammu and Kashmir to Pakistan-Occupied Kashmir and vice versa across the LOC. As far back as 1960, just before the signing of the Indus Waters Treaty, the Indian high commissioner to Pakistan, Rajeshwar Dayal, had spoken to Prime Minister Nehru about the 'Free Territory' of Trieste, contested by Italy and Yugoslavia. Dayal had been ambassador to Yugoslavia before moving to Pakistan and knew this curious case well. Trieste city was largely Italian-speaking; the outlying regions were Slovenian and Croatian (then part of the unified Yugoslavia). The Free Territory of Trieste was created by the UN in 1947 but as contestations continued, the US–UK forces occupied the city and Yugoslavia the rest of the Free Territory. Rajeshwar Dayal was later to write that 'timely international intervention' settled the issue and 'the agreement, though provisional, has been more durable than many definitive treaties. It meets the felt needs of both sides, while sidestepping the contentious question of sovereignty.' Dayal also recalled that the prime minister 'seemed particularly interested in the analogy of the Trieste agreement'.[46]

The idea of 'sidestepping sovereignty' came independently to others too. John Kenneth Galbraith, John F. Kennedy's ambassador to India, used to speak of 'bypassing the territorial issue by some arrangement by which the Pakistanis have access to the valley of Kashmir'.[47] In journalist Kuldip Nayar's recollection, 'Galbraith had undertaken what he called a Harvard Exercise. ... He suggested the reopening of the road between Rawalpindi and Srinagar through Baramulla, Uri and Muree and the resumption of trade and tourist traffic, while India's military rights in the Kashmir Valley were to remain intact.'[48] Similarly, George Verghese, then an emerging bright star of Indian journalism, had in the aftermath of the Kutch conflict spoken about a possible way forward by taking the Kashmir problem out of its 'emotional communal context'. In part, this could be achieved by 'facilities for free movement by Pakistanis to and from the Vale across a "soft" frontier, special trade protocols, etc.'[49] The 1965 war buried this idea but in 1969 Sheikh Abdullah, in Kuldip Nayar's recollection, told him, 'the border should be "soft" so that Pakistanis had easy access to the Valley'.[50] We find it resurfacing after the 1971 war when the astute D.P. Dhar, one of Prime Minister Indira Gandhi's closest advisers, had visited Pakistan in April 1972 preparatory to the Simla summit. What was to be the future of the ceasefire line of 1948 was the obvious question. In March, just before this meeting, Bhutto had told Kuldip Nayar: 'We can make the ceasefire line as the basis of initial peace. Let the people of Kashmir move between the two countries freely. One thing can lead to another.'[51] In the meeting Dhar, according to one of the Pakistanis present, had spoken in similar terms: 'The people on both sides could start by crossing the line freely, separated relatives and friends could get together and then greater accommodation could be achieved.'[52] These ideas were not in the agreed outcomes of Simla and were not even discussed there—possibly then in the aftermath of the break-up of Pakistan such ideas could not be tossed around as there were other, more pressing issues that dominated the agenda. In the contested 1990s, as the so-called Track II and non-official exchanges made a beginning, many in India and in the United States were dusting off these older ideas and different variants of Galbraith's and Verghese's loud thinking surfaced. The Kargil intrusion and subsequent developments again pushed such thinking aside. Softening of the LOC by 'sidestepping sovereignty', remained dormant as a concept, but still not entirely forgotten.

The idea re-emerged during and in the immediate aftermath of the Vajpayee–Musharraf summit in Islamabad in 2004. The new government, taking over from the NDA dispensation, not just adopted but made it its own as it embarked on the far from easy negotiation to put it into effect. The logic behind this was clear enough: if there had to be progress in easing the Jammu and Kashmir tangle, both internally and vis-à-vis Pakistan, disaggregating it was the best way forward. A bus from Srinagar to Muzaffarabad for the first time since October 1947 appeared more doable as a first step than any other. There were, however, innumerable issues of disputed sovereignty to resolve, which made the modalities of implementing a bus service difficult. Would travel be on passports and based on visas? If so, this meant recognizing the legal status of the other country in its respective part of J&K. There were also deep suspicions on the Pakistani side. Would confidence-building measures such as a bus service detract from the political issues of self-determination for Kashmiris, etc?

The idea was, however, popular enough, especially in J&K and POK, not to allow these doubts to gather traction. The question of travel modalities was handled by a permit system rather than passport and visas. The permits would be provided by 'designated authorities' on both sides, sidestepping thereby the issue of either government being named in the piece of paper and thus its sovereignty being recognized. The bus service when it finally began in April 2005 was likened by the more enthusiastic as ranking with the fall of the Berlin Wall. The massive earthquake in October 2005, which caused huge devastation in Pakistan-Occupied Kashmir was a factor which further focused the political and bureaucratic mind on cross-LOC linkages. There were thereafter other high points resulting from the India–Pakistan dialogue—the train services between Khokhrapar and Munabao earlier referred to, another bus service across the LOC from Poonch to Rawala Kot, an agreement to start trade across the LOC which was to happen finally in October 2008, among others.

Certainly, by the end of 2005 the traditional acrimony seemed to have largely been overshadowed by a general sense that progress was inevitably going to be made. That change was in the air was suggested also by the visit by L.K. Advani, the former deputy prime minister of India, to Pakistan in May–June 2005. He had long been regarded in Pakistan as the man behind those who brought down the Babri Masjid and the foil in the BJP to Vajpayee's outreach for peace. The visit was, however, conducted on lines to prove these critics wrong. It was filled with nostalgia as he visited his old house and school in Karachi. Included in the itinerary was a visit to the mausoleum of Muhammad Ali Jinnah where he wrote some complimentary words about Pakistan's founder. Advani's praise for Jinnah and an oblique reference to him as 'an ambassador of Hindu–Muslim unity' was incomprehensible to many in India. The outrage was such that he was forced to offer to resign as president of the Bharatiya Janata Party; the resignation was later withdrawn but the clamour in the party over his remarks did not die down. Why he did so was analysed threadbare at the time. Was it because people of his generation who had witnessed the trauma and the long after-effects of Partition now felt that if a chance existed to break the mould, it should be supported. Or was it a tactical and political ploy by a seasoned politician to move to the mainstream and discard his older hard-line image? Nevertheless, this position on Jinnah and the strong negative reaction to it from his party back in India, was curiously, for many in both countries but more especially in Pakistan, almost a confirmation that change was in the air and only the diehards were resisting it.

New precedents were, in fact, being set in more than one direction. Since the early 1990s, India had planned the construction of a 450-MW hydroelectric project on the Chenab, one of the western rivers of the Indus allotted to Pakistan under the treaty with limited 'non-consumptive' rights of use for India. Predictably, Pakistan had objected to the Baglihar Hydroelectric Project as being against the Indus Waters Treaty. For the next decade, it remained under discussion between the two Indus Commissioners and then the governments without any real progress. As the stalemate continued, Pakistan's approach was that the treaty provided for international arbitration in the event of a major disagreement. Somewhat to its surprise, and to that of many of their opposite numbers, India agreed that a World Bank–appointed neutral expert be allowed to decide what should be done. This was a break with its traditional approach of keeping outsiders out of India–Pakistan disputes—most notably in the Salal agreement of 1977 India had compromised on design features to reach a bilateral agreement. For water engineers and diplomats alike, the Baglihar case was thus the breaking of the 'Salal mindset'. The award of the neutral expert, permitting the project with some new design features, was accepted by both, if more grudgingly by Pakistan, and it also set the precedent for other projects on the western rivers.

It was the new post-2004 environment in the India–Pakistan equation that allowed the arbitration award to be claimed as a victory by both sides. There were, of course, discordant voices too. For some in Pakistan, the success of the Baglihar arbitration was a cause for anxiety that remains to this day—a path was being trodden by which India would build more upstream projects and cumulatively acquire greater control over the western rivers. For the time being, however, for majority opinion in both countries, rational thinking seemed to be trumping historical baggage. Engineers rather than diplomats or politicians were finally evaluating hydroelectric projects on the western rivers as the Indus Waters Treaty had originally envisaged in 1960.

This environment was also aided by President Musharraf regularly punctuating the India–Pakistan political chronology by statements expressing the need for flexibility on stated positions on Jammu and Kashmir. In October 2004, he mentioned the need for identifying separate regions within J&K as it had existed before 1947, demilitarizing them and then 'changing their status'. Sometime later, he said that while the LOC cannot be made permanent it can be made irrelevant and started speaking of self-governance. A serious dialogue on Kashmir with flexibility, he said in speeches and televised addresses, meant that solutions unacceptable to both be put aside and thereafter solutions looked for from the other options remaining. All this cumulatively became known as Musharraf's four-point proposal. In his words:

> Firstly, identify the geographic regions of Kashmir that need resolution. At present the Pakistan part is divided into two regions: Northern Areas and Azad Kashmir. The Indian region is divided into three regions: Jammu, Srinagar [sic] and Ladakh. ... Second, demilitarize the identified region or regions and curb all militant aspects of the struggle for freedom. ... Third, introduce self-governance or self-rule in the identified region or regions. ... Fourth, and most important, have a joint management mechanism with a membership consisting of Pakistanis, Indians and Kashmiris overseeing self-governance.[53]

Whatever he may have said or meant, this was a language neither India nor Pakistan was used to hearing. In India, the initial reactions were largely that these were trial balloons to apply pressure and best left alone till such time that a formal proposal was received. The reaction in Pakistan, if less articulate, was of greater anxiety and concern since long-cherished positions of self-determination through a plebiscite based on the UN Security Council resolutions and the claim that Kashmir, as an unfinished agenda of Partition, rightly belonged to Pakistan were consciously being diluted.

That the two governments were on a common track to reach some understanding was the view of many as Prime Minister Manmohan Singh echoed similar sentiments: There could be no redrawing of borders but they could be reduced to 'just lines on a map'; travel and trade across the LOC should take place effortlessly; J&K and POK could work out mechanisms for cooperation between themselves, etc. That some of the major separatist representatives in Jammu and Kashmir were meeting senior officials and being allowed to travel to Pakistan added to the sense of expectation that some manner of change in the status quo was under discussion. Finally, that there were discussions taking place on Jammu and Kashmir between designated representatives of both countries—which came to termed as the 'backchannel'—was well known, even if their substance was not. Carried out between the representatives of Prime Minister Singh and President Musharraf, it was the most intensive discussion that had taken place on Kashmir to date between India and Pakistan. That the substance of it was entirely out of the public domain also possibly meant that it was pragmatic and focused on deliverables.[54]

In April 2005, President Musharraf visited India after the launch of the Srinagar–Muzaffarabad bus and the visit coincided with the return visit of the Pakistan cricket team to India. Some of the discussions took place as both delegations, including President Musharraf and Prime Minister Singh, watched a match in Delhi. The statement issued at the end of the visit spoke of the peace process now being 'irreversible'. It would have seemed so, as terrorist attacks abated and the LOC ceasefire held. These were heady days made even more so with the realization that only 3–4 years ago there were regular and intense shelling and firing across the very frontiers that buses, goods and people were now regularly traversing.

In this environment, the realms of possibility seemed to be endless—trade and investment offered new opportunities as did the scope for cultural contacts. If economic growth, foreign investment and globalization were the new buzz words in India, to many it was self-evident that these were precisely the engines to lift India and Pakistan out of their six-decade-deep morass. Optically powerful gestures and steps seemed to suggest to many that the inflexion point had been crossed. During President Musharraf's visit to Delhi in April 2005 both governments agreed to reopen the Karachi and Mumbai consulates, which had been closed for over a decade. Even more powerful was President Musharraf's decision in early 2006 to permit the commercial screening of Bollywood films—banned since the 1965 war—in Pakistan. Many thought this was the ultimate litmus test even if it was implemented slowly beginning with a colour version of a classic of the 1960s *Mughal-e-Azam*. In Pakistan, the assessment was that what little remained of its cinema industry would disappear unless theatres were revived. The only means this could be done was to allow the screening of Indian films.

Bollywood too was entering a new phase of its engagement with Pakistan. The end of the last century and the early years of the twenty-first saw a number of films dominated by the recent past of Kargil and terrorist attacks. *Gadar* (2001), *Lakshya* (2004), *LOC Kargil* (2003) following on similar ones of the 1990s were amongst the films that reflected public anger and disenchantment with Pakistan. But the easing of relations and the upbeat expectations for the future meant that films portraying Pakistan and Pakistanis in a softer and more positive light started being made and were doing well commercially. *Main Hoon Na* and *Veer Zara* were unsurprisingly released in 2004 and were the heralds of this trend. Their commercial success in Pakistan encouraged others and focused the minds of distributors and producers to the potential of Pakistan as a market for Bollywood. For those advocating change in the India–Pakistan interface, if the Pakistan market could influence Indian film-makers to temper the hostility of the past decade, what better example could there be of globalization, trade and investment fostering change.

If change of an elemental kind seemed to be in the air, apart from cinema and cricket, there are other instances that appeared to illustrate this. From early 2004, and gathering momentum as the year progressed, there was an explosion in what was officially called people-to-people contacts or civil-society interactions.

One such trajectory is of Pakistan's first rock band 'Junoon' led by its charismatic guitarist Salman Ahmad. In India to stage the group's concert tour in May 1998, Salman Ahmad found himself in the midst of the polemics surrounding the nuclear tests. His remarks to the BBC—'we want cultural fusion, not nuclear fusion'—meant official ostracization in Pakistan and being termed a 'traitor', part of 'India's subversive propaganda', and finally someone who had 'blasphemed against the two-nation theory'.[55] He and his band were also charged with 'disagreement with the national opinion over the nuclear tests' and banned from official state media. Salman Ahmad, however, persisted. The fact that he was a US national meant relatively easier travel into India and one of his trips took him to Patiala where his mother originally came from. Her ancestor had been a notable in the Patiala princely court and visiting his old properties gave Salman the idea of a music video—*Ghoom Tana*—on the theme of India–Pakistan peace.[56]

Ghoom Tana was unusual in that Salman Ahmad persuaded the renowned Indian classical singer Shubha Mudgal to sing the background song with him. The well-known actress Nandita Das acted alongside him with Naseeruddin Shah providing some of the voice-overs.[57] The short, seven-minute film has a simple storyline. A young man (Salman Ahmad) promises his dying mother that he would go to India and return a precious piece of jewellery their Hindu neighbour had left with them as he fled a riot-stricken Lahore in August 1947. So, five decades later Salman Ahmad journeys to Patiala, where the neighbour now is, and after returning the jewellery stays with him and his daughter-in-law and grandson. The daughter-in-law (Nandita Das) is a war widow—her husband was killed in an India–Pakistan war, possibly Kargil. The video and the song end with Salman Ahmad returning to Lahore, leaving his guitar behind for Nandita Das's son. The music video was thus presenting a different way of reading the past and the future of the subcontinent—almost as if a new generation was seeking to rewrite the legacy it was born with. Shot in Salman Ahmad's ancestor's old house, situated on Namdar Khan Road (named after him), *Ghoom Tana* remains a popular piece of music, but in the heady years 2004–06, it captured the atmosphere of the time.

That the past and the present seemed to be colliding was the thought which struck others too. One such occasion was when the sisters Uzra Butt and Zohra Sehgal acted together after a gap of some forty years. The play was *Aik Thee Nani* (Once there was a Grandmother) and is the story of two sisters separated by Partition. Written in 1993, it had been staged in many places but a special performance was in Mumbai in 2004 with Uzra Butt and Zohra Sehgal acting together at the Prithvi theatre where they had performed in the 1940s. For some in the audience who remembered earlier performances of the two, this was an electrifying moment as if something new was emerging.[58]

Instances of this kind can be multiplied. Kuldip Nayar had started with a small group of friends in 1996—the year before the fiftieth anniversary—the practice of lighting candles at the Wagah–Attari border crossing point. Ten years later, Nayar found a gathering of tens of thousands and in his words the small ritual had become a 'people's movement' and a 'catharsis of two nations who had lost a million lives during the Partition and many thousands in the three wars ... since then'.[59] But the fact is that no matter how spontaneous and widespread such sentiment and interaction was, it was enabled by the supportive atmosphere created by the intergovernmental dialogue process.

The heady atmosphere with the Composite Dialogue showing results, regular high-level political interactions and a mushrooming people-to-people interface was for many, and especially those who had been activists in the peace process since the 1990s, intoxicating. Nevertheless, certain lines had to be respected and those getting carried away reminded of ground realities of the India–Pakistan interface. The veteran journalist Balraj Puri writes about the 'failure of many Indians to reconcile themselves to the reality of Pakistan' and that 'some wanted to undo it through love'. In one India–Pakistan peace meeting in Delhi, he recollects, several old Gandhians spoke of Hindu–Muslim harmony in the past and British policies leading to the Partition which 'would be undone one day and the wall between the brothers would be demolished like the Berlin Wall'.[60] Puri describes what happened next:

> I was extremely embarrassed as were my Pakistani friends. I intervened to sternly assert that two topics were completely banned in the conference: Hindu–Muslim relations as the subject of the conference referred to the relations between the two countries and not the two communities. Also banned was any talk of undoing partition as the minimum condition of normal relations—not to speak of friendship. We had to respect the distinct identity of the other. As the final draft of the outcome of the conference was prepared by me, I could assuage the feelings of the Pakistani guests.[61]

Sovereignty and respecting the Partition, therefore, placed limits on what could and could not be said in these India–Pakistan meetings. To question its fundamentals was, however, in some cases a deliberate and conscious decision. The acknowledged sole leader of the Mohajirs of Pakistan, Altaf Hussain, visited Delhi in November 2004. He had been living in exile in London since 1991 when the movement he led faced a military crackdown. The accompanying violence and counter-violence since had defined the Mohajir landscape in urban Sindh and Altaf Hussain has been at the centre of all debates around it—a hero for his followers and a long-distance extortioner and criminal for others. The Mohajirs themselves—refugees from UP and Bihar who made their way to Pakistan in 1947—remain the Partition story's greatest enigma. At the forefront of the demand for a separate Muslim homeland, their life in Pakistan was an increasingly embittering experience from the 1980s onwards. Even so, many Mohajirs would have baulked at the language Altaf Hussain used in India that November: Partition was a blunder, the greatest tragedy in the history of mankind, it was not a division of the land but a 'division of blood', and India should give asylum to those Mohajirs in Pakistan who faced repression from its establishment.[62]

For most Pakistanis who were not Mohajirs or Altaf's supporters, this was treason and the speaker a traitor. The speech is telecast to this day whenever a point has to be scored against Altaf Hussain or his party the Mutahid Quami Movement (MQM). If outrage against it was huge, open criticism, nevertheless, was comparatively muted since the MQM then was a coalition partner in Musharraf's civilian government. But the fact that President Musharraf himself was a Mohajir gave to Altaf's speech many other subtexts and underlined also the numerous sub-currents of the India–Pakistan peace process. In India, Altaf Hussain's comments were a sign of changing public opinion. In Pakistan, a less sanguine view was taken by many: Altaf Hussain was scoring points and embarrassing mainstream Pakistani opinion.

But overall, public opinion and governments seemed to be working in tandem and suddenly visiting the other country was the trendy and right thing to do, cutting across generations. Poets and writers, musicians and artists, politicians and businessmen, all ranges of professionals from chartered accountants to dentists, teachers and students found themselves describing their interactions with counterparts across the border as contributing to the 'peace process' between India and Pakistan. These multiple streams often also had other common threads. One, certainly, was the Punjab–Punjab interactions taking place between India and Pakistan. It was as if an East and West Punjab grand reconciliation was emerging out of the India–Pakistan engagement. That part of the subcontinent which had seen total and unabashedly brutal ethnic cleansing in 1947, been the principal site of the battles of the 1965 and 1971 wars, seemed to be putting the past behind it.

This regional dimension to the India–Pakistan engagement was something new. Perhaps it was related to wider political changes in both countries. In India, federalism or the rights of states had enormously strengthened through the coalition governments of the 1990s. In each of these, regional parties had played important roles altering in the process the older balance between Centre and states. It required former diplomat Badr-ud-Din Tyabji, a veteran observer of the India–Pakistan relationship, to take note of this development in foreign policy terms. Reflecting on the missed opportunity of what he had called the 'golden period' of India–Pakistan relations (after Jawaharlal Nehru's Karachi visit in September 1960), Tyabji said:

> I think that at that time, the Punjabi sentiment should have been played much more by us. East Punjab had a role to play which we ignored. The Punjabi sentiment as a unifying force should have been utilized for promoting Indo-Pakistan friendship and understanding. ... We did not favour this then, because at that time in the early 1950s we were inclined to frown on regional sentiments. We wanted a strong Centre; and regionalism of any kind looked sinister.[63]

From the 1990s all this changed rapidly and the change was evident in the India–Pakistan interface with both halves of Punjab celebrating the progress being made. In Pakistan, the rise of this sense of Punjabi identity had, on the other hand, much to do with the ideological straitjacket fostered by long years of authoritarian military rule. An incipient Punjabi literary movement from the 1990s found it useful to forge cross-border links with the Indian Punjab. Writing in Punjabi rather than only in Urdu became an implied comment against linguistic homogeneity which military regimes encouraged and desired.

The Punjab–Punjab interactions had, therefore, a different quality to them as a celebration of Punjabi and a common culture would assert themselves in gatherings as varied as trade fairs, literary seminars, sporting contests, music concerts or youth and student gatherings. The underlying theme for many was of nostalgia, loss, reconciliation and finally a sense of hope. A set of verses by the great Punjabi poet Ustad Daman became almost a leitmotif of many such gatherings, whether taking place in India or in Pakistan, the only requirement being that there were Punjabis present:

Barbad ihna azadian ton
Hoye tusi vi ho hoye assee vi haan
Lutan wale ne raj ke lutea hai
Soye tusi vi ho soye assee vi haan
Laali akhiyan di payi dasadi hai
Roye tusi vi ho roye asee vi haan.

It is popularly believed that Ustad Daman (died 1984) had first recited the poem in which these verses are, at an early Indo-Pak mushaira in Delhi which Prime Minister Nehru had also attended. Half a century later, to many Punjabis on both sides of the Radcliffe Line, these verses seemed to encapsulate the tragedy of the division of Punjab as well as a beacon of hope and reconciliation. A free translation is:

We were ruined in the name of freedom
as were you,
We were looted as we slept
as were you
The redness in our eyes reveals that we have wept
as have you.

Epilogue

AS WE MOVE FROM the past into the present, this story can be concluded with even broader strokes.

If 2006 appeared to be pregnant with possibilities, it was also the year when the unwinding began. Why it did so is till today a matter of speculation but the milestones of the reversal are clear enough. The pause in major terrorist attacks in India ended with multiple bomb explosions in Mumbai suburban trains in July 2006—as many as seven and all within a ten-minute period. Over 200 people were killed. A Pakistan connection was immediately suspected and many foresaw that a huge burden had now been placed on the dialogue process.

It would be salvaged following a summit meeting between President Musharraf and Prime Minister Manmohan Singh in Havana in September through the creation of a joint anti-terror mechanism. Thereafter, in January 2007 Prime Minister Manmohan Singh in a speech spoke eloquently of a dream that one day 'while retaining our respective national identities, one can have breakfast in Amritsar, lunch in Lahore and dinner in Kabul. That is how my forefathers lived. That is how I want my grandchildren to live.'[1] To many who worked for a better India–Pakistan relationship, in both countries, such sentiments encapsulated the thrust of their efforts to overcome the setback caused by the terrorist attack of July 2006. But the damage that had been done was considerable; the question that now hovered over the public and policymakers alike in India was whether there was a design behind this very major terrorist attack and what would India do if there was another. Were the factors that had led to two-and-a-half years of adherence to the January 2004 commitment on terrorism by General Musharraf being undermined by some new forces in Pakistan? For a public fearful of more attacks, the prime minister's speech and an earlier one in Amritsar when he spoke about the destinies of India and Pakistan being interlinked seemed out of touch with reality.

There were other pressures building up from mid-2006 indicating that the Musharraf era was not going to last forever. In August 2006, Nawab Akbar Khan Bugti, former ruler of one of the constituent princely states of Balochistan, was killed in a shoot-out with the Pakistan Army following a long stand-off. His demands and the movement he led are less significant than the fact of his killing for he was no ordinary tribal chieftain. He was a former chief minister and governor of Balochistan and had also served as a minister in the federal government. Well known as a senior, if eccentric, political figure, his killing and then a shabby funeral caused a wave of revulsion against President Musharraf and to an extent the army. Was the president and chief of the army staff going too far in what he was doing? Naturally, this question encompassed also his initiatives with India on Kashmir.

The India–Pakistan dialogue was now entangled with President Musharraf's personal standing in Pakistan. As his popularity plummeted, the portfolio of errors expanded. If the signs of this was emerging in 2006, in 2007 they were unmistakable. The dismissal and arrest of the chief justice in March 2007 unleashed a popular agitation by lawyers. Heavy-handed tactics to deal with it consolidated opposition from diverse sides—the political class, the religious parties, the media, etc. Soon thereafter followed a military operation in July 2007 against a religious seminary—the Lal Masjid—in the heart of Islamabad, believed to be providing sanctuary to militants carrying out attacks against government and military targets. The death toll and the consequent revenge terrorist attacks further accentuated the sense of crisis in Pakistan. The diminishing of Musharraf's personal stature led to hitherto silenced opponents of his India policy surfacing, and here all the doubts about his approach to Kashmir consolidated and, it is widely believed, were strongest now in the army—his core constituency.

The debate in Pakistan—if it can be called that since it was hardly an open discussion—revolved around departing from the traditional Pakistani positions on the UNSC resolutions, self-determination for the Kashmiri people and plebiscite. For most, the central issue was Musharraf's failure to commit himself to radically change the status quo in Kashmir in favour of Pakistan. Others worried that this was hardly an opportune time for substantive negotiations on an issue such as Kashmir when the gulf between India and Pakistan had widened so much and Pakistan's international standing and image was at its lowest point in its sixty-year history. For a third strand, the difficulty began with the commitment given by President Musharraf in January 2004 that Pakistan would not permit territories in its control to be used for acts of terrorism against India. This was, in this view, a one-sided commitment as well as an implied acceptance that Pakistani territory was being used in this manner. If this had underpinned the India–Pakistan dialogue process, it was, in one assessment, 'a responsibility ... almost impossible to honour'.[2] How could Pakistan possibly guarantee that there would be no terrorist attacks on India from its soil? Through 2007 in Pakistan not many could disagree with this critique of Musharraf's assurance as terrorist attacks spread across the length and breadth of the country.

The sum and substance of all this amounted to a deep anxiety about and contempt for 'Musharraf's defeatism'.[3] This was the damning phrase to be employed by Abdul Sattar, Musharraf's own former foreign minister and a Pakistani veteran of most India–Pakistan negotiations since Simla in 1972 to Agra in 2001. One casualty also was the backchannel. In the changed environment of President Musharraf's growing isolation, it was now just as untenable as after the Kargil intrusion the first such attempt had been.

The year 2007 saw more than just the unravelling of Musharraf's rule and the consequent erosion of the dialogue process with India. The spectre of instability itself was now hovering over Pakistan. That Musharraf's rule was ending was heralded most by the calling of a general election in which exiled leaders Nawaz Sharif and Benazir Bhutto would also participate. The elections scheduled for January 2008, however, had to be postponed—Benazir Bhutto was assassinated on 27 December. This marked the end of a year in which the very furies of hell appear to have been unleashed on Pakistan as terrorist attacks increased and targeted not just Pakistanis of all walks of life but all the institutions of state including the military. That Pakistan was at war with itself was exemplified by Benazir Bhutto naming three individuals who were to be held responsible in case something was to happen to her: former ISI director general Hamid Gul, Intelligence Bureau chief, Brigadier Ejaz Shah, who had in the past also been in the ISI, and the then Punjab province chief minister Arbab Pervaiz Elahi.[4] The known links of the first two with different extremist groups and the fact that they were former army officers was sufficient, to many, to suggest a link between the assassination and a beleaguered army having to cope with civic unrest and terrorist violence alike.

The truth behind Benazir Bhutto's assassination will probably remain a mystery for many years to come. Or as in the case of Liaqat Ali Khan's assassination or Zia-ul-Haq's death in an air crash, it may never be revealed. But the assassination did have one important, possibly unintended, consequence. The response to it in India, and especially in the Indian political leadership, was one of unadulterated dismay. Benazir was a figure they knew—this was true across the political spectrum from the BJP to the Congress—since the Simla summit in 1972 where she had accompanied her father Zulfikar Ali Bhutto as a young woman. Her elimination in this manner shook out of the schadenfreude many in India had felt at Pakistan's descent into chaos over 2007. If Pakistan was imploding, this posed potential dangers too serious to be ignored. As Pakistan, mired in grief, finally voted the PPP back to power to head a coalition government, in India there was the growing realization amongst many who mattered that doing serious business with the post-Musharraf dispensation was the only means available to help stabilize the situation in Pakistan.

By August 2008 Musharraf himself was on the trek he had forced Benazir Bhutto and Nawaz Sharif to undertake—exile in London. While he had continued in office real power had flown away from him once he stepped down as chief of the army staff in November 2007. His successor as president was Benazir Bhutto's husband and now the guardian of the Bhutto charisma—Asif Ali Zardari. He had been in custody from 1996 to 2004, was viewed with dislike and suspicion by many in the Pakistan Army not least because they fundamentally distrusted his political inclinations and instincts—including on India. He was both a popular and unpopular figure in Pakistan—the former because he was now the custodian of the Bhutto legacy and the latter because of the numerous corruption allegations surrounding him.

With the winding down of the Musharraf era, the Pakistan Army was left bearing the burden of his unpopularity as also the odium of being unable to prevent the continued onslaught of terrorist attacks. Also with his departure, the discomfort many had felt with the initiatives on Kashmir and the equanimity with which he apparently had permitted an Indian consolidation in Afghanistan now crystallized and was transformed into something akin to paranoia at the prospect of Asif Ali Zardari implementing and taking forward a similar agenda. That India, shaken by Benazir Bhutto's assassination, may show greater expedition in moving forward added to this anxiety and imparted to it a sense of urgency. These concerns converged with older and more elemental sentiments of hostility and jealousy as an elusive parity seemed now to be slipping away forever. That was certainly the view amongst many in Pakistan as the Indo-US Civil Nuclear Agreement was followed by an unconditional India-specific Nuclear Supply Group waiver in September 2008. Almost unnoticed the storm clouds were building up.

Notwithstanding the internal security meltdown Pakistan was going through, represented by Benazir Bhutto's assassination and the spread of terrorist attacks, optimists could see some positive signs. The media, civil society and finally the judiciary all seemed to have strengthened themselves in the last phase of Musharraf's tenure and in opposition to his regime. A new government led by the PPP came to power through an electoral process that was credible. The political class appeared to have been tempered and moderated by this latest round of military rule that had endured for eight years. There seemed to be a willingness of the different political parties to work the system rather than look to the army for support against political rivals. The change in the presidency, from Pervez Musharraf to Asif Ali Zardari, itself was, remarkably for Pakistan given the history of this institution, carried through with dignity and with constitutional proprieties and protocol maintained. As far as relations with India were concerned many in the new cabinet had been supporters of a normalized India–Pakistan relationship for decades. The PPP itself was regarded as the most committed to improving ties with India at the national level. In the 2008 election campaign, India was not a factor.

Yet terrorist attacks across India showed no signs of abating alongside evidence that the curbs placed on the groups in Pakistan believed to be responsible were increasingly being diluted. That this was more than an internal change in Pakistan had appeared self-evident to many in India as the period overlapped with a dramatic rise in terrorist attacks across north and south India. These were perceived as indicative of the old order striking back as Musharraf's hold weakened. On 26 January 2007 as the Indian high commission in Islamabad prepared for its Republic Day reception, the hotel where it was to be hosted was attacked by terrorists. The attempt was unsuccessful in that none of the high commission personnel were injured. Even if no direct link could be established, the impression certainly was that terrorist groups dormant since early 2004 were now resurfacing. In February 2007, the Samjhauta Express, on its journey from Delhi to Lahore, was the target of a terrorist attack with sixty-eight fatal casualties, most of whom were Pakistani nationals. At the time, the Pakistan-based terrorist group Lashkar-e-Taiba (LeT) was suspected of carrying out the attack, with the obvious motive being to disrupt a weakening India–Pakistan engagement. But it was to be alleged later that the attack may have been the work of an Indian right-wing extremist group but having the same motive. If true, this was proof in fact that terrorism knows no borders.

The most dramatic and with direct linkages to Pakistan was a terrorist attack on India but outside India with the Indian embassy in Kabul being targeted in July 2008. A number of personnel—security and diplomatic—were killed. This was, in fact, a new low even for India–Pakistan relations—each other's diplomatic missions had not been targeted in this manner even in the worst of times in the past. The evidence pointed strongly to a Pakistani hand and was to many a reminder that internal change in Pakistan was going to determine the future trajectory of India–Pakistan relations. Clearly, those opposed to the Indian presence and its high profile in Afghanistan were behind the attack. The new civilian dispensation in Islamabad could, however, also make a convincing enough case that the attacks were as much to throw the dialogue process off track as to harm India and that the new Government of Pakistan must be given more time to attend to the revanchists, whether in its army, or elsewhere. If things could still limp along in terms of official meetings and interactions, it was largely because of the hope in India that perhaps the late Benazir Bhutto's party in government would be able to somehow put things together and reverse the negative emerging trends.

Asif Ali Zardari as president of Pakistan certainly tried to strengthen those hopes. Addressing a conference in New Delhi on 22 November 2008 through a video link, he quoted Benazir Bhutto saying that every Pakistani had a 'little bit of India' within as every Indian had a little bit of Pakistan. If such symbolism was appealing to some, it also raised troublesome questions for others and especially so in Pakistan. But Zardari's interaction this time went beyond employing such symbolism when he also made references to Pakistan committing itself to a 'no first use' of nuclear weapons.[5] In India, this was confirmation that the ills that plagued India–Pakistan relations would rapidly disappear if civilian authority could consolidate and grow in strength. In Pakistan, there were many to whom such thinking on nuclear policy was heresy—for not only was nuclearization forced on Pakistan by India but also nuclear weapons were what stood between Pakistan and India's massive conventional military force. If anything, such statements further reinforced doubts about President Zardari and the PPP amongst many in Pakistan.

Within days, this debate was itself history as on 26 November 2008 the terrorist attack on Mumbai cast aside earlier precedents. With civilians specifically targeted in India's financial capital and a terrorist captured alive to reveal the meticulous military-type planning and execution of the operation, it was clear that things could not go on as before. Pakistan acknowledged that the terrorists had indeed mounted the attack from Pakistan and the one in Indian custody was also a Pakistani national. This admission, while by no means voluntary, was still novel and for some in India a change from the blanket denials of the past. Nevertheless, the scale of the attack placed question marks over the future of India–Pakistan relations that have remained unanswered. That the attackers were from the LeT was clear enough. That the wider conspiracy and planning behind it involved more than just the group's top leadership also became evident during the duration of the attack itself.[6]

In the aftermath of the Mumbai attack, the debate that had taken place after the attack on the Indian parliament in December 2001 recurred—what kind of action should be taken? The conclusion was that diplomacy would work better than any other means used.[7] That this was an attack carried out with military precision on civilians, at a time when both the Indian and Pakistani governments were groping to reassemble the process disabled since early 2007, meant that the needle of suspicion was on the Pakistan Army and the ISI, more pointedly than ever before. That such an assessment was also shared widely across the world created a more supportive environment to put pressure on Pakistan. Even more so, possibly such an assessment was shared by many in Pakistan itself, including many in President Zardari's government. The Pakistan foreign minister was, in fact, in Delhi when the terrorist attack began in Mumbai. To some, this was the clearest possible evidence that the civilian government was not culpable. Further evidence came when it suggested in the aftermath of the attack that the director general of the ISI visit India immediately. This offer, formally communicated by the Pakistan Foreign Office, remained stillborn as it was possibly made with the approval of President Zardari but without the approval of the army. For most people in India, therefore, all this meant not so much the innocence as the irrelevance of the civilian government.

In an atmosphere of international outrage at the quality and the scale of the attack, some of the LeT leadership was placed on a UNSC list of terrorists under sanctions, which in turn led the Pakistani authorities to impose some restrictions on the outfit's functioning and cadres. Most countries realized that action of this kind would help in reassuring public opinion in India that the perpetrators of the attack were going to be brought to justice, no matter where they maybe. Yet, diplomacy, as a means to induce Pakistani action against the planners of the attack had its limits, and these were revealed in the aftermath of 26/11 as older anxieties and paranoia about India asserted themselves in Pakistan. The terrorist attack became the cause for a virulently defensive reaction in Pakistan. Criticism from the media and public opinion in India, whose outrage and anger was difficult to contain, could be projected as aggression. Accusations that the Mumbai attack was, in fact, an Indian intelligence operation soon surfaced. From this it was a short step to resisting action against the attack's mentors, planners and financiers. Defending terrorists became a defence of Pakistan's sovereignty.

The Mumbai attack was a fatal blow to the India–Pakistan dialogue process for no larger hole could have been made in the 6 January 2004 assurance. An equal casualty was obviously the 'peace process' which had shown such vigour during 2004–06. Its protagonists and participants in India were appalled not only at the Mumbai carnage but equally at the assertion of an old-fashioned, stand-up-against-India patriotism that surfaced in Pakistan and enveloped in its protective cloak the Jamaat-ud-Dawa—the new name for the Lashkar-e-Taiba—leadership that had masterminded the attack. As in the past, the Pakistan Army found that when it wrapped the flag around itself and took a stand against India, people of Pakistan would rally around it. In this situation, to project the deep outrage in India as 'aggression' was a relatively straightforward step. The question often discussed in India was the extent of culpability of the Pakistan Army and ISI or in a more general sense the 'Pakistani establishment' in the attack itself. This was not an inaccurate line of analysis but missed one central point: the establishment in Pakistan is not so much a bundle of institutions but also is 'a tendency, a certain outlook'.[8] It was an assertion of this mindset that ensured that the ringleaders of the attack were then and have remained so protected.

The fact that the Lashkar-e-Taiba leadership and the planners of the attack could mount a successful legal defence, despite the clear evidence that existed implicating them, confirmed both official complicity and support and ruled out the possibility of it being a rogue operation. So, what was the logic behind the attack? The answer must lie in the chain of events beginning with disillusionment with Musharraf at his 'compromising' on key Pakistani concerns with India, and continuing to the assassination of Benazir Bhutto and the election of Zardari as president.

That there was no complete breakdown in India–Pakistan relations after the Mumbai terror attacks was largely the result of the efforts of Prime Minister Manmohan Singh and his commitment to the process initiated by Prime Minister Vajpayee that he had inherited in 2004. In March–April 2009, his party and its coalition successfully fought the general election to a second term of government. His efforts to rebuild what was lost, however, faltered in the face of public disapproval. July 2009 saw a valiant attempt to resurrect the suspended dialogue process in Egypt, in Sharm el-Sheikh at the margins of a NAM summit. In a meeting with Pakistan's prime minster Yusuf Raza Gilani, agreement was reached that contacts would continue to address outstanding issues and improve atmospherics. The statement issued had also a reference to Pakistan's concerns about terrorist incidents in Balochistan. This acted as a lightning conductor for public opinion in India. It implied, or so it seemed to many, a moral equivalence in the concerns of both countries regarding terrorism and was seized upon as an example of Prime Minister Manmohan Singh's sentiment-driven approach to Pakistan.

The chorus of public disapproval was not just an opposition move to embarrass the government but represented real outrage at this attempt at 'moving on' barely nine months after Mumbai incident without any purposeful action against the ringleaders of the terror attack. Efforts to explain the intricacies of the civil–military equation or the opportunity provided by a new civilian government in Pakistan could not but flounder in the face of this public anger. Some months later, the dialogue process did resume but that its overall environment had changed was illustrated by its name being changed from 'composite' to 'resumed'. Clearly, the Mumbai attack had meant the end of a particular phase of India–Pakistan engagement. Even the most ardent of its defenders had to concede that no matter how promising it had been, there was simply no going back to business as usual. It is not as if specific attempts at normalization in different areas did not continue. They did, and for this the initiative was often by Manmohan Singh's government. A more liberal visa agreement was signed in September 2012. The Pakistan cricket team even toured India for a short series in December 2012–January 2013. But each such effort, and there were others, to show normalcy were always limited by the question looming over government and the public alike: is there a major terrorist attack in the offing? Tensions with Pakistan with serious clashes on the LOC also reached a peak from end-2012, sinking in the process an agreement being negotiated to normalize India–Pakistan trade. That many saw the brooding presence of the Pakistan Army in this latest setback was not surprising. The LOC clashes from 2013 onwards effectively meant that even a formulaic official dialogue was not a political doable for Prime Minister Manmohan Singh's government, which was entering the final years of its second term.

In any event, Pakistan itself was enveloped in crisis from other directions. As terrorist attacks on population centres, airports, military installations and other targets—hard or soft—continued and increased in intensity and dramatic impact, relations with Afghanistan and then with the United States also plummeted. Cricket again provides a good example of Pakistan's growing isolation and internal disarray. A terrorist attack on the visiting Sri Lanka cricket team in 2009 had meant that Pakistan could no longer be a venue for international cricket as no country was now prepared to take the risk of touring Pakistan. The 2011 Cricket World Cup further drove this point home. Meant originally to have been played across South Asia, Pakistan found that it was the odd country out when the matches were played in Bangladesh, Sri Lanka and India.

The morphology of terrorist attacks in Pakistan from 2007 onwards suggested to many in India and elsewhere a structural retreat of the Pakistan state with some chunk of internal sovereignty ceded to extremists and terrorists. The cession appeared to be in part geographical in the tribal areas of Pakistan abutting the Durand Line that divided the Pashtun tribes. But there appeared to be an external cession of sovereignty too as coinciding with the beginnings of US president Obama's tenure, CIA and US military drone strikes in Pakistan territory increased exponentially.

However, 2011 held even greater shocks when Osama bin Laden was located and killed by US special forces. That he had been living in relative comfort near Pakistan's military academy in Abbottabad raised questions about the country's complicity with terrorists even more pointedly than before. For most Indians, this was no more than a vindication of all that they had been saying about the Pakistani state for years.

Not unexpectedly, the bin Laden raid meant that the Pakistan military faced an extent of public odium unusual for Pakistan. Three questions were posed frequently at that time: how was bin Laden able to live undetected in Pakistan and in a developed suburb of Abbottabad; how could US forces make such a deep incursion into Pakistan for the raid and not be challenged; and, finally, who was responsible for the fiasco and the damage this caused to Pakistan's image. None of these questions has been satisfactorily settled to date and bin Laden's end is one more mystery in Pakistan's list of unnatural exits—Liaqat Ali Khan, Zia-ul-Haq and Benazir Bhutto. That the Pakistan military took a beating was inevitable but the bin Laden raid was not the only factor. The continuous terrorist attacks demoralized public opinion as much, and repeatedly showed that the security institutions of the state were powerless to stem the tide of these strikes. No more damning indictment of the Pakistan

Army was possible than that it was failing to protect its people. Not unexpectedly, the period after mid-2011 sees a veritable see-saw in civil–military tensions and contests adding to further public demoralization.

The years 2012 and 2013 saw an unusual situation in Pakistan with both the Pakistan Army under its chief General Ashfaq Kayani and the Pakistan Peoples Party led by the president of Pakistan, Asif Ali Zardari, competing for public unpopularity and odium, even as their core constituencies remained intact. The army because of the continued terrorist attacks, the Osama bin Laden humiliation and for the spectre of instability ruling the country; President Zardari for the country's manifold problems, corruption charges and his eccentric style of functioning. Nevertheless, Pakistan had achieved an important milestone by mid-2013. For the first time in its existence an elected government in a civilian dispensation had completed its term. Clearly, howsoever slowly and incrementally, something in Pakistan was also changing. The general elections in Pakistan in May 2013 saw Nawaz Sharif return to power as prime minister about a decade and a half after he was ousted in the post-Kargil coup. In public, he reiterated his 1997 election campaign promise—that improving relations with India would be a priority and that it was in Pakistan's interests to strive for this goal. Nawaz Sharif's third time as prime minister began as Prime Minister Manmohan Singh's second was entering its last year. The next steps would have to await a new government in India.

The installation of the BJP-led NDA government with Prime Minister Narendra Modi began unusually. SAARC heads of state and government were invited to the swearing in and even more unusually Prime Minister Nawaz Sharif also accepted the invitation. It was a moment to rank with Vajpayee's Lahore visit of 1999 or Rajiv Gandhi's visits of 1988 and 1989. This was the Indian prime minister's own initiative and even more unusual for that. A tipping point again seemed to be approaching and within grasp. A scheduled meeting between the foreign secretaries in August 2014, agreed as a first step by Prime Ministers Modi and Nawaz Sharif, was however cancelled when the Pakistan high commissioner held a meeting with Kashmiri separatists. The step was akin to Prime Minister

Indira Gandhi's decision in 1981 to postpone a meeting of foreign secretaries because of references made to Kashmir in a UN meeting and was powered by the same impulse. But, as in 1981, the freeze was only temporary as the Indian foreign secretary was in Islamabad in March 2015 in another effort by the Indian prime minister to move forward. This was, however, not to be a breakthrough as within days, one of the prime accused in the Mumbai attack conspiracy and against whom a desultory trial had been in process was released on bail. No government could have gone against the wave of public outrage that engulfed India then and the initiative ended there. Amidst all this the Line of Control saw frequent ceasefire violations and this provided a barometer reading for the state of the relationship.

Another reading was provided by the contestations over the Kishanganga Hydroelectric Project on a tributary of the Jhelum. Pakistan, claiming that the project violated the Indus Waters Treaty, had taken the matter to the permanent court of arbitration. The court partially upheld some of its contentions but on the crucial point of the project coming up at all gave India the go ahead. But even acceptance of an arbitration award requires the minimums of a positive relationship as the Baglihar case had demonstrated and the issue remained unresolved. There were other even more serious tensions brewing. For many in Pakistan, the coming to power in December 2014 of a coalition government in Jammu and Kashmir, in which the BJP was an equal partner with the Peoples Democratic Party led by Mufti Mohammad Sayeed after another successful assembly election was a strategic setback: it appeared that while Pakistan was stuck in its domestic morass, India was running away with the ball in Kashmir. Again, from this assessment flowed consequences that were predictable as infiltration increased amidst growing clashes on the LOC, and groups such as the Lashkar-e-Taiba asserted a new-found relevance. In India, all this was seen as no more than the dust being removed from an existing field manual of the Pakistan Army.

As 2014 progressed, Pakistan's domestic turbulence acquired an added intensity with political agitation led by the opposition leader Imran Khan on the one hand combining with terrorist strikes on all manner of civilian targets as also attacks on the army, navy and air force itself. Pakistan seemed to be defenceless against all except India, and there were more serious clashes on the LOC between the two than ever seen since the November 2003 ceasefire. In Pakistan itself, accusations against India for taking advantage of its domestic turbulence grew shriller as did the conviction that Pakistan's problems with its domestic terrorists was the consequence of coordination between Afghan and Indian intelligence agencies. Yet, alongside all this and somewhat to everyone's surprise, the Pakistan Army suddenly seemed to be more conscious of the burden of popular expectations where terrorism was concerned. A terrorist attack on a school in Peshawar in which a large number of children were brutally slaughtered appears as a turning point. The army began operations against militant and extremist groups that had been carrying out attacks in Pakistan with a sense of purpose and vengeance not expected either in Pakistan or outside. This was operation Zarb-i-Azb and it continued over 2015 with an unabated intensity.

The duration of the operation as also such success as it achieved had major consequences for Pakistan. Firstly, it damaged the sanctuaries and bases in the tribal areas of the north-west where many anti-Pakistan elements had congregated under the loose rubric of the Tehrik-i-Taliban Pakistan (TTP). It did not or could not eliminate or fatally damage the TTP but it did roll them back to a great extent. Secondly, and more importantly, it restored public confidence and morale in Pakistani cities as people suddenly found that the tables were being turned on the terrorist groups, which had operated with such impunity in Pakistan. These two positives, in turn, had other consequences. Most prominent of these was a rise in public esteem and popularity of the Pakistan Army which Musharraf's closing years, the Osama bin Laden raid and the terrorist onslaught inside Pakistan had so badly dented. The restoration of the army's image was not just domestic but also external. For close allies such as China, it was both a reminder of where power was returning to in Pakistan as also of the country's innate potential. A closer alliance between Pakistan and China seemed natural in the circumstances but it is powered as much by China's appreciation of Pakistan's potential as by its concerns about its downward slide for a decade or more. For Pakistan, Western and especially US impatience and cynicism can now be more effectively dealt with given a Chinese bulwark.

For India and Afghanistan military strikes against the TTP confirmed further that the Pakistan Army did have the capacity to act against terrorists but it was selective in doing so and clearly excluding from its action groups which targeted India and Afghanistan. More ominous was the fact that the army's new-found confidence also acted as a boost for those within it advocating the conventional approach of using militant proxies against these two immediate neighbours.

The other negative fallout of the Pakistan Army's rise in public esteem was on the civilian dispensation, and the see-saw of the civil–military equation resembled a chessboard of moves and countermoves. Inevitably, relations with India loomed large in this contest. An effort made in a summit meeting between Prime Ministers Narendra Modi and Nawaz Sharif at Ufa, Russia, in August 2015, somewhat unsurprisingly could not secure domestic approval in Pakistan. The cognoscenti in both countries would have noted, however, that while the initiative for the move had once again come from India, the response from Prime Minister Nawaz Sharif had also, notwithstanding his domestic difficulties, been positive. But clearly, it had been for India as the larger and more stable power to take the initiative.

That the year would not end on a negative note but rather on one of hope was because of an unscheduled stopover in Lahore by Prime Minister Modi on Christmas Day 2015. To the outside world, this was as intuitive an initiative as Vajpayee's 'hand of friendship' speech of April 2003. Clearly, India's prime minister was not one to give up easily in his search for answers and a way forward. The sheer power of its symbolism—an Indian prime minister putting his own political capital behind India–Pakistan peace—evoked the sense of strong continuities of decades of policy—from Rajiv Gandhi to I.K. Gujral to A.B. Vajpayee and Manmohan Singh. That it did not work this time around too is a different matter. But evidently, it is not the last word on the subject for that phase of this history is yet to be completed.

'The future,' in India–Pakistan relations, 'lies in the past,' High Commissioner Natwar Singh cryptically wrote as he reflected on the beginning of his tenure in Islamabad in 1980.[9]

So, does the past hold any secrets, and are there any central threads to this tangled history? There are in fact many, and different readings will reveal even more. Those which are obvious stand out. Very clearly the overhang of the past is real. This is both the true weight of history and also how the present affects and changes the past: older issues and disputes transform and mutate themselves to acquire new characteristics and often an even sharper intensity. There are, therefore, no 'pure' legacy issues. What appears seemingly old is, in fact, also quite new. The entire India–Pakistan portfolio would fall in this category—from Kashmir to river waters, from terrorism to trade. Kashmir posed a different set of issues after 1979 and 1990 than it did before the Islamic revolution in Iran, the Soviet invasion of Afghanistan, its defeat there, and the consolidation of military rule again in Pakistan. The river waters question is also fundamentally different now than at the time when the Indus Waters Treaty was signed, as water scarcity, climate change and the demands of hydroelectric power in Jammu and Kashmir raise issues beyond water sharing. Terrorism as an instrument of state policy, even if still used extensively and often with effect, is nevertheless now a double-edged sword to a far greater extent than earlier. The logic of trade and economic cooperation is too compelling to be resisted by government policy on nationalist grounds. But implementing a policy of trade and economic normalization for a government in Pakistan is even more difficult now than ever before as the economic gulf between India and Pakistan continues to widen.

Internal change and conflict have always had a major impact on external policy. If this is true of both countries, the domestic turmoil in Pakistan in the new millennium has been of an order which raises fundamental questions about its capacities. On this count alone the Pakistan of this phase is different from that in the past as domestic and external travails now coexist not just, as in the past, with anxiety, paranoia, a sense of victimhood and historical injustice but also with growing state weaknesses and incapacities. But in each of these and other issues enough of the old remains to create the impression that nothing has changed in India—Pakistan relations. But clearly, enough has changed to make sure that the older solutions will not work.

Secondly, however specific and peculiar to India and Pakistan each of these issues may appear to be, the global environment has always profoundly affected the India–Pakistan interface and will do so in the future too. Too parochial a perspective, no matter how zealously held, will ultimately have to face up to this reality. The United States, the Soviet Union/Russia and China have been and are a presence in South Asia not just in terms of military and political influence but as an economic and intellectual force.

Thirdly, neither the extent of goodwill nor the extent of hostility in each country for the other can be underestimated. As even this sketchy and subjective history has shown in every decade numerous individuals saw the immediate future of India–Pakistan ties with a great deal of realistic optimism. Events proved them wrong on each occasion. But by the same token, efforts to bring about some positive change have never been deterred by past failures or by the prophets of pessimism. 'After such knowledge, what forgiveness' is a principle discarded long ago by practitioners of policy and perhaps never held at all except briefly for tactical purposes.

But is the repetitive pattern itself impervious to change? Many think so and one sober assessment recently was of India and Pakistan 'Shooting for a Century' up to 1947 and perhaps beyond.[10] Others would disagree and point to new benchmarks that are scoring over traditional rivalries and revanchist ideology: the mantra of economic growth and the transformative powers of technology for the peoples of India and Pakistan who are younger now than ever before. But have the past twenty years been that different from the previous fifty? Some changes are evident. Unlike the long period of gestation required for even a minimal normalcy to be restored after the 1965 and 1971 conflicts, recovery after Kargil and the parliament attack or even a partial recovery post-26/11 Mumbai was relatively quicker. Does this suggest a change? If the question naturally arises from a historical survey, the answer is not one for a history to provide as those who may live in an era of great change also have the most difficulty in recognizing it.

Finally, given the cyclical patterns that dominate this chronology and narrative, the traditional divides of hawks and doves fade in importance—at some stage and for some period of time each camp will be proven right before it is again proven wrong. That is what, more than anything else, makes for such a curious history.

Notes

1: The Setting of the Mould

1. For details on Europe see, for instance, R.M. Douglas, *Orderly and Humane: The Expulsion of the Germans after the Second World War*, New Haven: Yale University Press, 2012. The total mortality, on account of this expulsion and displacement, is mentioned by Douglas as 0.5 million to 1.5 million, which is of the same order of magnitude as mortality on account of the Partition of India.
2. Tai Yong Tan and Gyanesh Kudaisya, *The Aftermath of Partition in South Asia*, London: Routledge, 2000, p. 237.
3. Mewat District Census 2011 data, http://www.census2011.co.in/census/district/226-mewat.html (accessed on 21 March 2017).
4. See, for instance, Abdul Sattar, *Pakistan's Foreign Policy 1947-2012: A Concise History*, Karachi: OUP, 2013, 3rd edition, p. 21.
5. B.L. Sharma, *The Kashmir Story*, New Delhi: Asia Publishing House, 1967, pp. 47–48.
6. Yaqoob Khan Bangash, *A Princely Affair: The Accession and Integration of the Princely States of Pakistan, 1947-1955,* Karachi: OUP, 2015, pp. 143–44.
7. Pyarelal, *Mahatma Gandhi: The Last Phase*, Vol. II, Ahmedabad: Navajivan Publishing House, 1958, p. 700; S. Gopal, *Jawaharlal Nehru: A Biography*, Vol. II, Delhi: OUP, 1979, p. 24.
8. Sisir Gupta, *Kashmir: A Study in India Pakistan Relations*, New Delhi: Indian Council of World Affairs, 1966, p. 175.
9. Srinath Raghavan, *War and Peace in Modern India*, Ranikhet: Permanent Black, 2010, p. 142. For an analysis of how the British

worked to contain the war and in the process thwarted Indian plans for offensive operations, see, C. Dasgupta, *War and Diplomacy in Kashmir, 1947-48*, New Delhi: Sage, 2002, pp. 197–98.

10. Lt Gen. V.R. Raghavan, *Siachen: Conflict Without End*, New Delhi: Viking, 2002, p. 23.
11. David Haines, *Indus Divided: India, Pakistan and the River Basin Dispute*, Gurgaon: Penguin-Viking, 2017, p. 42.
12. Jawaharlal Nehru to G.C. Bhargava, 28 April 1948, in S. Gopal (ed.), *Selected Works of Jawaharlal Nehru*, Vol. 6, (Second Series), Delhi: Oxford University Press, 1987, pp. 61–62.
13. Wali Khan, *Facts Are Facts: The Untold Story of India's Partition*, Peshawar: Bacha Khan Trust, 2006 reprint, p. 181.
14. *The Times of India*, 12 August 1947, cited in A.G. Noorani, *The Destruction of Hyderabad*, New Delhi: Tulika Books, 2013, p. 165.
15. Yaqoob Khan Bangash, *A Princely Affair: The Accession and Integration of the Princely States of Pakistan, 1947-1955*, p. 167.
16. *Bombay Chronicle*, 28 March 1948, cited in A.G. Noorani, *The Destruction of Hyderabad*, p. 165.
17. Reply to question by Balkrishna Sharma on 30 March 1948, *Constituent Assembly of India (Legislative) Debates, Official Report*, Vol. IV, 1948, pp. 2744–45, cited in S. Gopal (ed.), *Selected Works of Jawaharlal Nehru*, Volume 5, (Second Series), Delhi: OUP, 1987, pp. 299–300.
18. Sri Prakasa, *Pakistan: Birth and Early Days*, Meerut: Meenakshi Prakashan, 1965, p. 122.
19. Inder Malhotra, 'Jostling for Junagadh', *The Indian Express*, 14 June 2010.
20. K.K. Aziz, *Rahmat Ali: A Biography*, Lahore: Vanguard, 1987, pp. 50–73.
21. Ibid., p. 296.
22. Ibid., p. 300.
23. Ibid., pp. 228–29.
24. Ibid., p. 300.
25. Ibid., p. 481.
26. Ibid., p. 320.
27. Tanvir Ahmad Khan, 'The Rahmat Ali Controversy', *Daily Times*, Lahore, 9 September 2005. The author is a former foreign secretary of Pakistan.
28. O.H.K. Spate, 'The Partition of the Punjab and Bengal', *The*

Geographical Journal, Vol. 110, No. 4/6, October–December 1947, pp. 201–18.

29. Penderel Moon (ed.), *Wavell: The Viceroy's Journal, London*: OUP, 1973, p. 245; Dr Ishtiaq Ahmed, 'Splitting India, Part VII', *Friday Times*, Lahore, 1–7 November 2013.
30. Tahir Kamran, 'Past Recast: Partition of Punjab', *The News*, 30 August 2015.
31. I am grateful to Ashish Ray and Laila Sumpton, granddaughter of Mian Azim Husain, for some of these details.
32. E.N. Mangat Rai, *Commitment My Style*, New Delhi: Vikas Publishing House, 1973, p. 114.
33. Arun Bhatnagar, 'It was the Indian Civil Service that kept Pak going in the early years', *Sunday Guardian*, 8 August, 2015. http://www.sundayguardianlive.com/opinion/2590-it-was-indian-civil-service-kept-pak-going-early-years (accessed on 1 May 2017).
34. 'Special Political Reports from the High Commission of India in Pakistan, Karachi', F. No. F.4-1/57-Pak I-Part II, 1957, Archives and Record Management Division, Ministry of External Affairs, New Delhi. Afzal Husain was the brother of Sir Fazl-i-Husain and then the vice chancellor of the Punjab University in Lahore.
35. https://www.findagrave.com/cgi-bin/fg.cgi?page=pv&GRid=43429702&PIpi=22671028 (accessed on 21 March 2017).
36. Mohammad Yunus, *Persons, Passions & Politics*, New Delhi: Vikas Publishing House, 1980, p. 82.
37. Ibid., p. 136.
38. Ibid.
39. In the foregoing, I have relied for details, unless otherwise stated, on K.L. Gauba's autobiography *Friends and Foes* (1974) and his long interview preserved in the Oral History Transcripts in the Nehru Memorial Museum and Library (NMML), New Delhi, Accession No. 76.
40. 'K.L. Gauba', in Rohini Singh (ed.), *Sex, Scotch & Scholarship: Khushwant Singh Selected Writings*, New Delhi: UBS Publishers, 1992, p. 79.
41. *Uncle Sham* reviewed by William L. Langer, *Foreign Affairs*, Vol. VIII, No. 1, October 1929. https://www.foreignaffairs.com/reviews/capsule-review/1929-10-01/uncle-sham (accessed on 23 March 2017).
42. K.L. Gauba, *Friends and Foes*, New Delhi: Indian Book Company, 1974, p. 84.
43. K.L. Gauba, *Sir Douglas Young's Magna Carta*. A copy is preserved in the Nehru Memorial Museum and Library, New Delhi.

44. K.L. Gauba, *Friends and Foes*, p. 236.
45. K.L. Gauba, *The Consequences of Pakistan*, Lahore: Lion Press, 1946.
46. Ibid., p. 27.
47. K.L. Gauba, *Passive Voices: A Penetrating Study of Muslims in India*, New Delhi: Sterling Publishers, 1973.
48. K.L. Gauba, *Pakistan Today*, Introduction by Khushwant Singh, Bombay: Thackers, n.d.
49. 'K.L. Gauba', in Rohini Singh (ed.), *Sex, Scotch & Scholarship*, p. 81.
50. M.J. Akbar, *Blood Brothers: A Family Saga*, New Delhi: Roli Books, 2006, p. 235.

2: Working Together?

1. In this discussion, I have drawn heavily on Pallavi Raghavan, 'The Making of South Asia's Minorities', *Economic and Political Weekly*, Vol. 51, No. 21, 21 May 2016, pp. 45–52.
2. Agreement reached at the Inter-Dominion Conference on the Treatment of Minorities, Calcutta, 15–18 April 1948, in Avatar Singh Bhasin (ed.), *India Pakistan Relations, 1947-2007: A Documentary Study*, Vol. IX, New Delhi: Geetika Publishers, 2012, pp. 7176–79.
3. Ibid., p. 7177.
4. P.N. Chopra (ed.), *Collected Works of Sardar Patel*, Vol XIII, (1 January 1948–31 December 1948), Delhi: Konark Publishers, 1998, p. 265. See also 'India Prepared for All Eventualities', *The Times of India*, 5 November 1948, p. 1.
5. Telegram from Jawaharlal Nehru to B.C. Roy, 23 November 1948, in S. Gopal (ed.), *Selected Works of Jawaharlal Nehru* (Second Series), Vol. 8, Delhi: Oxford University Press, 1989, p. 347.
6. Jawaharlal Nehru to B.C. Roy, 5 June 1949, S Gopal (ed.), in *Selected Works of Jawaharlal Nehru*, (Second Series), Vol. 11, Delhi: Oxford University Press, 1991, p. 366.
7. 'India Pakistan Relations', MEA F. No 20/38/50, 1950, Archives and Record Management Division, Ministry of External Affairs, New Delhi. This information was given in a detailed reply given by Prime Minister Nehru to a question in parliament by H.V. Kamath on 1 August 1950.
8. 'Annual Political Appreciation Report for the year ending 31 December 1950 from the Deputy High Commissioner for India in Pakistan', Dacca, F. No. 2-13/51 Pak I, 1951, Archives and Record Management Division, Ministry of External Affairs, New Delhi.

9. Ibid.
10. Nurul Amin to B.C. Roy, 18 February 1950, 'Correspondence between the Prime Ministers of India and Pakistan', MEA F. No. 1-BL/50, 1950, Archives and Record Management Division, Ministry of External Affairs, New Delhi, p. 20.
11. Ibid., p. 17.
12. Liaqat Ali Khan to Jawaharlal Nehru, 6 March 1950, 'Correspondence between the Prime Ministers of India and Pakistan', F. No 1(10)-BL/50, 1950, Archives and Record Management Division, Ministry of External Affairs, New Delhi, p. 107.
13. Avatar Singh Bhasin (ed.), *India–Pakistan Relations, 1947-2007: A Documentary Study*, Vol. IX, p. 7261.
14. 'Annual Political Appreciation Report for the year ending 31 December 1950 from the Deputy High Commissioner for India in Pakistan', Dacca. MEA F. No. F2-13/51 Pak I, 1951, Archives and Record Management Division, Ministry of External Affairs, New Delhi.
15. Srinath Raghavan, *War and Peace in Modern India – A Strategic History of the Nehru Years*, Ranikhet: Permanent Black, 2010, pp. 149–87.
16. V. Shankar, *My Reminiscences of Sardar Patel*, Vol. II, Delhi: MacMillan, 2015, pp. 92–94.
17. Oral History Transcripts, B.K. Acharya, Nehru Memorial Museum and Library (NMML), Accession No. 894, p. 53.
18. 'India Pakistan Relations', MEA F. No.20/38/50, 1950, Archives and Record Management Division, Ministry of External Affairs, New Delhi, pp. 5–6.
19. 'Annual Political Appreciation Report for the year ending 31 December 1950 from the Deputy High Commissioner for India in Pakistan', Dacca, MEA F. No. F2-13/51 Pak I, 1951, Archives and Record Management Division, Ministry of External Affairs, New Delhi.
20. I have been guided by the approach and conclusions in Pallavi Raghavan, 'The Making of the India Pakistan Dynamic: Nehru, Liaqat and the No War Pact Correspondence of 1950', *Modern Asian Studies*, Vol. 50, No. 5, September 2016, pp. 1645–78.
21. Pallavi Raghavan, 'India-Pakistan's 1950s Code on Media Portrayal of Each Other Is Relevant Even Today', *The Wire*, 15 January 2017, https://thewire.in/98761/india-pakistan-press-code-media-portrayal/ (accessed on 15 March 2017).

22. Supreme Court of India, *Brij Bhushan and Another vs The State of Delhi*, 26 May 1950, Indian Kanoon, http://Indiankanoon.org/doc/43043 (accessed on 1 May 2017).
23. Arurdra Burra, 'What self-styled nationalists could learn from the Hindu Right's own past record on free speech', Scroll.in, 27 January 2016. https://scroll.in/article/802327/what-self-styled-nationalists-could-learn-from-the-hindu-rights-own-past-record-on-free-speech (accessed on 1 May 2017).
24. 'Propaganda: Anti Pakistan in India: Publication of alleged objectionable item in Daily *Pratap* dated 10th October, 1953, protest from the High Commission of Pakistan in New Delhi', MEA F. No. PIII/53/55524/1, Archives and Record Management Division, Ministry of External Affairs, New Delhi.
25. 'Anti-India Propaganda in Pakistan - An editorial in *Dawn* dated 21/1/1954- Protest to the Govt of Pakistan', MEA F. No. PIII/54/55615/2, Archives and Record Management Division, Ministry of External Affairs New Delhi.
26. 'Propaganda - An article entitled "Conspiracy is out": protest from the Pakistan High Commission', MEA F. No. PIII/54/55517/1 of 1954, Archives and Record Management Division, Ministry of External Affairs, New Delhi.
27. 'Propaganda – Anti-Indian in Pakistan: Protest to the Government of Pakistan', MEA F. No. PIII/53/55627/2 of 1953, Archives and Record Management Division, Ministry of External Affairs, New Delhi.
28. The details about Bhupat and his stay in Pakistan have been described in the file, 'Extradition of Bhupat from Pakistan', MEA F. No. P1/52/1853/201 of 1952, Archives and Record Management Division, Ministry of External Affairs, New Delhi.
29. Ibid., p. 20.
30. *Blitz, Bombay*, 10 April 1951.
31. Ibid., p. 75.
32. S. Gopal, *Jawaharlal Nehru: A Biography*, Vol. II: 1947–56, Delhi: Oxford University Press, 1979, p.128.
33. Ibid., p. 132.
34. Oral History Transcripts, B.F.H.B. Tyabji, Accession No. 312, NMML, New Delhi. p. 56.
35. Ibid., p. 57.
36. S. Gopal, *Jawaharlal Nehru: A Biography*, Vol. II, p. 182.
37. Oral History Transcripts, B.F.H.B. Tyabji, p. 57.

38. Letter to Mohammad Ali Bogra, 10 November 1953, in S. Gopal (ed.), *The Selected Works of Jawaharlal Nehru*, (Second Series), New Delhi: Jawaharlal Nehru Memorial Fund, distributed by Oxford University Press, 1999, Vol. 24, p. 416. See also S. Gopal, *Jawaharlal Nehru: A Biography*, Vol. II, pp. 184–85.
39. Badr-ud-Din Tyabji, *Memoirs of an Egoist*, Vol. I, 1907 to 1956, New Delhi: Roli Books, 1988, p. 276.
40. Dr Afzal Iqbal, *Diary of a Diplomat*, Karachi: Hamdard Foundation Press, 1988, p. 76.
41. Ibid., p. 82.
42. Ayesha Jalal, *The State of Martial Rule: The Origin of Pakistan's Political Economy of Defence*, Cambridge, UK: Cambridge University Press (CUP), 1990, pp. 180–86.
43. Oral History Transcripts, B.F.H.B. Tyabji, p. 60.
44. Ayesha Jalal, *The Struggle for Pakistan: A Muslim Homeland and Global Politics*, Cambridge, Massachusetts: Harvard University Press, 2014, pp. 91–93.
45. Afzal Iqbal, *Diary of a Diplomat,* pp. 84–85. Mushtaq Ahmed Gurmani was then the governor of Punjab
46. Ramachandra Guha, 'Passages through India', *The Hindu*, 20 June 2004, citing a report in the *Dawn* of the last week of January 1955.
47. These details are in F. No. 2-30/55- Pak I, Fortnightly Report- Lahore- for the first half of April, 1955, and F. No. 2-33/55 Pak I, Fortnightly Report- Lahore for the second half of April, 1955. Archives and Record Management Division, Ministry of External Affairs, New Delhi.
48. Afzal Iqbal, *Diary of a Diplomat*, p. 83.
49. Ibid. p. 84.
50. Jawaharlal Nehru to C.C. Desai, 27 February 1955, in S. Gopal (ed.), *Selected Works of Jawaharlal Nehru*, (Second Series), Vol. 28, New Delhi: Oxford University Press, 2001, p. 235.
51. Jawaharlal Nehru to Ghulam Muhammad, 27 February 1955, ibid., p. 232.
52. Ibid., p. 287.
53. Ibid., p. 259.
54. Ibid.
55. Ibid., p. 257.

3: Highs and Lows

1. High Commissioner to Commonwealth Secretary, 26 March 1956, in 'Special Reports - Indian Mission in Pakistan, Karachi' F. No. 4-1/56 - Pak I, Part I, 1956, Archives and Record Management Division, Ministry of External Affairs, New Delhi.
2 Ayesha Jalal, *The State of Martial Rule: The Origins of Pakistan's Political Economy of Defence*, Cambridge, UK: Cambridge University Press, 1990, p. 206.
3. Rajeshwar Dayal, *A Life in Our Times*, New Delhi: Orient Longman, 1998, p. 282.
4. Note of High Commission of India, 17 January 1959, in Avatar Singh Bhasin (ed.), *India Pakistan Relations 1947-2007: A Documentary Study*, New Delhi: Geetika Publishers, 2012, Vol. II, p. 632.
5. Rajeshwar Dayal, *A Life in Our Times,* p. 283.
6. High Commissioner to Commonwealth Secretary, 29 June 1960. Avatar Singh Bhasin (ed.), *India Pakistan Relations, 1947-2007, A Documentary Study*, Vol. II, Geetika Publishers, 2012, p. 800.
7. Ibid.
8. Ibid., pp. 801–02.
9. Rajeshwar Dayal, *A Life in Our Times*, p. 269.
10. Ibid., p. 552.
11. Ibid., p. 287.
12. Y.K. Gundevia, *Outside the Archives*, Hyderabad: Sangam Books, 1984, p. 229.
13 Ibid.
14. 'Storm over Berubari', *Economic and Political Weekly*, 10 December 1960, p. 1785.
15. Y.K. Gundevia, *Outside the Archives*, p. 229.
16. Ibid.
17. I have relied for these figures on N.D. Gulhati, *Development of Inter-State Rivers: Law and Practice in India,* Delhi: Allied Publishers, 1972. Other sources cite varying figures. S. Gopal gives a figure of ₹83 crore. See *Jawaharlal Nehru: A Biography*, Vol. III, Delhi: Oxford University Press, 1984, p 143.
18. Daniel Haines, *Indus Divided: India, Pakistan and the River Basin Dispute*, Gurugram, Haryana: Penguin Random House India, 2017, p. 157.
19. Ibid.

20. B.K. Nehru, *Nice Guys Finish Second*, New Delhi: Penguin, 1997, p. 256.
21. Kuldip Nayar, *Distant Neighbours: A Tale of the Subcontinent*, New Delhi: Vikas Publishing House, 1972, p. 94.
22. *The Times of India*, 11 November 1965.
23. Rajeshwar Dayal, *A Life in Our Times*, p. 294.
24. Ibid., pp. 300–01.
25. Ibid., p. 318.
26. Ibid. Kuldip Nayar met Manzur Qadir in 1972 and gives a similar account of the Nehru–Ayub Khan meetings. Kuldip Nayar, *Distant Neighbours*, p. 95.
27. Rajeshwar Dayal, *A Life in Our Times*, p. 318. See also Altaf Gauhar, *Ayub Khan: Pakistan's First Military Ruler*, Lahore: Sang-e-Meel, 1993, p. 198. Ayub Khan's account is also of interest and can be seen in Mohammad Ayub Khan, *Friends Not Masters: A Political Autobiography*, London: Oxford University Press, 1967, pp. 116–23.
28. Jawaharlal Nehru's note on meeting with President Ayub Khan, 21 September 1960, in Madhavan K. Palat (ed,), *Selected Works of Jawaharlal Nehru*, (Second Series), Vol. 63, Delhi: OUP, 2016, p. 527.
29. Rajeshwar Dayal, *A Life in Our Times*, p. 290.
30. See for instance, Aitzaz Ahsan, 'Why Pakistan Is Not a Democracy', in Meghnad Desai and Aitzaz Ahsan (eds), *Divided by Democracy*, New Delhi: Roli Books, 2005, p. 109.
31. Kuldip Nayar, *Distant Neighbours,* p. 102.
32. General K.M. Arif, *Khaki Shadows: Pakistan 1947-1997*, Karachi: Oxford University Press, 2001, p. 39.
33. See Srinath Raghavan, *War and Peace in Modern India*, New Delhi: Permanent Black, 2010, p. 268.
34. Rajeshwar Dayal, *A Life in Our Times*, p. 312. Gundevia mentions this episode as occurring in October. Dayal's account would place it in end August which is more likely as he also relates going back to Pakistan and reporting that there were no Pakistani troop movements towards the ceasefire line in September 1962.
35. Y.K. Gundevia, *Outside the Archives*, p. 216.
36. S. Gopal, *Jawaharlal Nehru: A Biography*, Vol. III, New Delhi: OUP, 1984, p. 217.
37. K.M. Arif, *Khaki Shadows*, p. 39.
38. Gohar Ayub Khan, *Glimpses into the Corridors of Power*, Karachi: OUP, 2007, p. 50.

39. Srinath Raghavan, *War and Peace in Modern India*, pp. 309–10.
40. Cited in Howard B. Schaffer, *The Limits of Influence: America's Role in Kashmir*, New Delhi: Penguin, 2009, p. 81.
41. Y.K. Gundevia, cited in S. Gopal, *Jawaharlal Nehru: A Biography*, Vol. III, p. 257.
42. Y.K. Gundevia, *Outside the Archives*, p. 261.
43. Ibid., p. 280.
44. Abdul Sattar, *Pakistan's Foreign Policy 1947-2012: A Concise History*, Karachi: OUP, 2013, p. 88.
45. Avatar Singh Bhasin (ed.), *India Pakistan Relations 1947-2007: A Documentary Study*, Vol. II, p. 880.
46. Y.K. Gundevia, *Outside the Archives*, pp. 306–07.
47. Salman Taseer, *Bhutto: A Political Biography*, New Delhi: Vikas Publishing House, 1980, pp. 59–60.
48. Cited in ibid., p. 60.
49. Farooq Bajwa, *From Kutch to Tashkent: The Indo Pakistan War of 1965*, Delhi: Pentagon Press, 2014, pp. 92–93.
50. Ibid.
51. Lt General Mahmud Ahmed, *Illusion of Victory: A Military History of the Indo-Pak War-1965*, Karachi: Lexicon Publishers, 2002, p. 24.
52. Abdul Sattar, *Pakistan Foreign Policy*, p. 105.
53. E.N. Mangat Rai, *Commitment My Style: Career in the Indian Civil Service*, New Delhi: Vikas Publishing House, 1973, pp.231, 233.
54. Lt Gen. Gul Hasan Khan, *Memoirs*, Karachi: Oxford University Press, 1993, p. 229.
55. J.N. Dixit, *India-Pakistan: In War & Peace*, New Delhi: Books Today, 2002, p. 168.
56. Ibid.
57. C.P. Srivastava, *Lal Bahadur Shastri, Prime Minister of India: A Life of Truth in Politics*, Delhi: Oxford University Press, 1995, p. 367.
58. 'Mehta's Plane Believed Shot Down by Enemy', *The Times of India*, 21 September 1965, p. 1.
59. Manu Pubby, 'After 46 yrs, the healing touch: Pak pilot says sorry for mistake', *The Indian Express*, 10 August 2011.
60. E.N. Mangat Rai, *Commitment My Style*, p. 239.
61. Kewal Singh, *Partition and Aftermath: Memoirs of an Ambassador*, New Delhi: Vikas Publishing House, 1992 reprint, p.154.
62. Ibid., p. 155.

63. Iqbal Akhund, *Memoirs of a Bystander: A Life in Diplomacy*, Karachi: OUP, 1997, p. 90.
64. Kewal Singh, *Partition and Aftermath*, p. 162.
65. Kewal Singh, *Partition and Aftermath*, p. 171.
66. Ibid., pp. 172–73.
67. Ibid., pp. 191–92.
68. Avatar Singh Bhasin (ed.) *India Pakistan Relations 1947-2007: A Documentary Study*, Vol. II, pp. 1238, 1241.
69. C.P. Srivastava, *Lal Bahadur Shastri, Prime Minister of India*, p. 229.
70. E.N. Mangat Rai, *Commitment My Style*, p. 229.
71. T.C.A. Srinivasa Varadan, *Federal Concept: The Indian Experience*, edited by Chandra Chari,New Delhi: Centre for Policy Research and Allied Publishers, 1992, p. 17.
72. Ibid., p. 230.
73. Afzal Iqbal, *Diary of a Diplomat*, Karachi: Hamdard Foundation Press, 1988, 2nd ed., p. 120.
74. *The Times of India*, 6–7 October 1965.
75. The full line is; *Ai vatan ke sajeelay jawano, Mere naghme tumhare liye hain* (O splendid soldiers of my land, My songs are for you!). Shuja Nawaz, *Crossed Swords: Pakistan, Its Army, and the Wars Within*, Karachi: Oxford University Press, 2008, p. 209.
76. C.M. Naim, 'The Consequences of Indo-Pakistani War for Urdu Language and Literature: A Parting of the Ways?' *The Journal of Asian Studies*, Vol. 28, No. 2, 1969, pp. 269–83.
77. I have relied for these details on C.M. Naim, 'The Consequences of Indo-Pakistani War for Urdu Language and Literature'.

4: From One War to Another

1. Piloo Mody, *Zulfi My Friend*, Delhi: Publications Division, 1973, p. 83.
2. Aitzaz Ahsan, 'Why Pakistan is not a Democracy', in Meghnad Desai and Aitzaz Ahsan (eds), *Divided by Democracy*, New Delhi: Roli Books, 2005, pp. 108–09.
3. S. Nihal Singh, *From the Jhelum to the Volga*, Bombay: Nachiketa Publications Limited, 1972, p. 21.
4. Fahmida Riaz, *Pakistan: Literature and Society*, New Delhi: Patriot Publishers, 1986, pp. 82, 84.

5. Rikhi Jaipal, *Memories of a Half Life and Flowers of Grass*, New Delhi: Allied Publishers, 1991, pp. 108–09.
6. Arjun Subramaniam, *India's Wars- A Military History 1947-1971*, Noida: HarperCollins, 2016, p. 326. Needless to say, there are different accounts of territories captured during the war by either side.
7. C.P. Srivastava, *Lal Bahadur Shastri, Prime Minister of India: A Life of Truth in Politics*, Delhi: Oxford University Press, 1995, p. 240.
8. Iqbal Akhund, *Memoirs of a Bystander: A Life in Diplomacy*, Karachi: OUP, 1997, p. 103.
9. Ibid., p. 123.
10. Salman Taseer, *Bhutto: A Political Biography*, New Delhi: Vikas Publishing House, 1980, p. 63.
11. Iqbal Akhund, *Memoirs of a Bystander: A Life in Diplomacy*, p. 123.
12. Salman Taseer, *Bhutto: A Political Biography*, p. 62.
13. Ibid., p. 69.
14. S. Nihal Singh, *From the Jhelum to the Volga*, p. 120.
15. Fahmida Riaz, *Pakistan: Literature and Society*, p 84.
16. Rikhi Jaipal, *Memories of a Half Life...*, pp. 102–03.
17. B.K. Nehru, *Nice Guys Finish Second*, New Delhi: Penguin, 1997, p. 430.
18. Iqbal Akhund, *Memoirs of a Bystander*, pp. 128–29.
19. Jamsheed Marker, *Cover Point: Impressions of Leadership in Pakistan*, Karachi: Oxford University Press, 2016, p. 67.
20. Farooq Bajwa, *From Kutch to Tashkent: The Indo-Pakistani War of 1965*, London: Hurst, 2014, p. 344.
21. Letter from the Ministry of External Affairs to Indian Heads of Mission regarding progress of normalization of relations with Pakistan, 8 February 1967. Avatar Singh Bhasin (ed.) *India Pakistan Relations 1947-2007: A Documentary Study*, New Delhi: Geetika Publishers, 2012, Vol. II, p. 1208.
22. Kewal Singh, *Partition and Aftermath: Memoirs of an Ambassador*, New Delhi: Vikas Publishing House, 1992 reprint, p. 236.
23. Iqbal Akhund, *Memoirs of a Bystander*, p. 130.
24. Lieutenant General Mahmud Ahmed, *Illusion of Victory: A Military History of the Indo-Pak War-1965*, Karachi: Lexicon Publishers, 2002, pp. 533–34.
25. Kewal Singh, *Partition and Aftermath*, p. 182.
26. Muhammad Reza Kazimi, *Z.A. Bhutto and the Historiography of 1971*, Karachi: Literma Publishers, 2014, p. 21.

27. Khadim Hussain Raja, *A Stranger in My Own Country*, Karachi: OUP, 2012, p. 108.
28. Kewal Singh, *Memoirs of an Ambassador*, p. 243.
29. Ibid., p. 358.
30. The full details of the entire meeting were graphically described by the Indian ambassador in Morocco later. Gurbachan Singh, 'India at the Rabat Islamic Summit (1969)', *Indian Foreign Affairs Journal*, Vol. 1, No. 2, April–June, 2006, pp. 105–20.
31. Abdul Sattar, *Pakistan's Foreign Policy 1947-2012: A Concise History*, Karachi: OUP, 2013, p.124.
32. Iqbal Akhund, *Memoirs of a Bystander*, p. 183.
33. *The Times of India*,27 September 1969.
34. M. Asghar Khan, *We've Learnt Nothing from History: Pakistan: Politics and Military Power*, Karachi: Oxford University Press, 2005, p. 238.
35. Ibid., p. 49.
36. Jamsheed Marker, *Quiet Diplomacy – Memoirs of an Ambassador of Pakistan*, Karachi: OUP, 2010, p. 130.
37. Ibid., p. 131.
38. Muhammad Reza Kazimi in the Introduction to Major General (Retd) Khadim Hussain Raja, *A Stranger in My Own Country*, p. xiii.
39. Iqbal Akhund, *Memoirs of a Bystander*, p. 204.
40. Hamoodur Rahman Commission Report, http://img.dunyanews.tv/images/docss/hamoodur_rahman_commission_report.pdf (accessed on 15 March 2017).
41. Iqbal Akhund, *Memoirs of a Bystander*, p. 205.
42. J.N. Dixit, *India-Pakistan: In War & Peace*, New Delhi: Books Today, 2002, pp. 216–17.
43. Rafi Raza, *Zulfikar Ali Bhutto and Pakistan 1967-1977*, Karachi: Oxford University Press, 1997, pp. 203, 205.
44. Lawerence Ziring, *Pakistan: The Enigma of Political Development*, Folkestone, Kent: Dawson Publishers, 1980, p. 231.
45. Sarmila Bose, *Dead Reckoning: Memories of the 1971 Bangladesh War*, New Delhi: Hachette, 2011.
46. Ibid., p. 271.
47. Ibid., pp. 176–77.
48. Raja Tridiv Roy, *The Departed Melody: Memoirs*, Islamabad: PPA Publications, 2010, 2nd reprint, p. 218.
49. Ibid., p. 230–31.

5: Picking Up the Pieces

1. Javid Iqbal, *Encounters with Destiny: Autobiographical Reflections*, a translation of *Apna Garebaan Chaak*, Karachi: Oxford University Press, 2006, p. 177.
2. Shahid M. Amin, *Reminiscences of a Pakistani Diplomat*, Karachi: Karachi Council of Foreign Relations, 2009, p. 102.
3. P.N. Dhar, *Indira Gandhi: The Emergency and Indian Democracy*, New Delhi: Oxford University Press, 2000, p. 197.
4. Ibid., p. 200.
5. Ibid., p. 205.
6. Abdul Sattar, *Pakistan's Foreign Policy 1947-2002*, Karachi: Oxford University Press, 2013, 3rd edition, pp. 156–57.
7. Ibid., pp. 140–41.
8. K.N. Bakshi, 'Simla Agreement (1972): From Military Victory to a Diplomatic Defeat?' *Indian Foreign Affairs Journal*, Vol. 2, No. 3, July–September, 2007, pp. 105–19.
9. Ibid.
10 Humayun Khan and G. Parthasarathy, *Diplomatic Divide*, New Delhi: Roli Books, 2004, p. 43.
11. Mohammad Yunus, *Persons, Passions and Politics*, New Delhi: Vikas Publishing House, 1980, pp. 193–97.
12. Ibid., p. 195.
13. Ibid., p. 197.
14. Iqbal Akhund, *Memoirs of a Bystander: A Life in Diplomacy*, Karachi: OUP, 1997, p. 196.
15. Srinath Raghavan, *1971: A Global History of the Creation of Bangladesh*, Ranikhet: Permanent Black, 2013, pp. 254–55.
16. Rafi Raza, *Zulfikar Ali Bhutto and Pakistan 1967-1977*, Karachi: Oxford University Press, 1997, p. 214.
17. Kewal Singh, *Partition and Aftermath: Memoirs of an Ambassador*, New Delhi: Vikas Publishing House, 1992 reprint, p. 331.
18. Robert Alden, 'China's first veto bars Bangladesh', *The New York Times*, 26 August 1972. http://www.nytimes.com/1972/08/26/archives/chinas-first-un-veto-bars-bangladesh-soviet-union-and-india-are.html (accessed on 21 March 2017).
19. This is the view presented by Abdul Sattar amongst many others. See Abdul Sattar, *Pakistan's Foreign Policy 1947-2012: A Concise History*, Karachi: OUP, 2013, 3rd edition, pp. 127–28.

20. Khalid Hassan in *Friday Times*, April 2003. Cited in an article by Nadeem F. Paracha in *Dawn,* 16 April 2017. Khalid Hassan was with Bhutto at that time.
21. Abdul Sattar, *Pakistan's Foreign Policy*, pp. 127–28.
22. Lieutenant General Depinder Singh, *Field Marshal Sam Manekshaw: Soldiering with Dignity*, Dehradun: Natraj Publishers, 2002, pp. 7, 196, 200–03.
23. Rafi Raza, *Zulfikar Ali Bhutto and Pakistan,* p. 219.
24. Ibid., p. 220.
25. Kewal Singh, *Partition and Aftermath*, p. 337.
26. Ibid., p. 338.
27. Rafi Raza, *Zulfikar Ali Bhutto and Pakistan*, p. 221.
28. Feroz Hassan Khan, *Eating Grass: The Making of the Pakistani Bomb*, New Delhi, Cambridge University Press, 2013, p. 119.
29. Kewal Singh, *Partition and its Aftermath,* p. 345.
30. Abdul Sattar, *Pakistan's Foreign Policy*, p. 160.
31. K.L. Gauba, *Pakistan Today*, Bombay: Thackers, n.d., p. 13.
32. Kewal Singh, *Partition and Aftermath*, p. 370.
33. Ibid., p. 350.
34. Kewal Singh, *Partition and Aftermath*, p. 357.
35. Rikhi Jaipal, *Memories of a Half Life and Flowers of Grass*, New Delhi: Allied Publishers, 1991, p. 171.
36. U.N. General Assembly, 30th session, Official Record of the Two Thousand Three Hundred and Eighty-sixth Meeting, held at Headquarters, New York, on Tuesday, 21 October 1975. (A/PV.2386) 21 October 1975, p. 610. http://www.un.org/ga/search/view_doc.asp?symbol=A/PV.2386 (accessed on 15 March 2017).
37. Iqbal Akhund, *Memoirs of a Bystander*, pp. 233, 235.
38. Nadeem Farooq Paracha, *End of the Past: Eyewitness Pakistan*, Lahore: Vanguard Books, 2016, pp. 173–93; and by the same author 'Pakistan's Contrary Years (1971-77): A Cultural History of the Bhutto Era', *Dawn*, 4 December 2015. https://www.dawn.com/news/1223761 (accessed on 1 March 2016).
39. Iqbal Akhund, *Memoirs of a Bystander*, p. 225.
40. Rafi Raza, *Zulfikar Ali Bhutto and Pakistan*, p. 222.
41. K.L. Gauba, *Pakistan Today*, p.16.
42. Rafi Raza, *Zulfikar Ali Bhutto and Pakistan,* p. 214.
43. Rikhi Jaipal, *Memories of a Half Life*, p. 172.
44. Iqbal Akhund, *Memoirs of a Bystander*, p. 217.

45. Jagat S. Mehta, *Negotiating for India: Resolving Problems Through Diplomacy*, New Delhi: Manohar, 2007, p. 161.
46. Jagat S. Mehta, *The Tryst Betrayed: Reflections on Diplomacy and Development*, New Delhi: Penguin Books, 2010, pp 217–18.
47. Shahid Amin, *Reminiscences of a Pakistani Diplomat*, Karachi: Karachi Council of Foreign Relations, 2009, pp. 91–92. Fida Hussain's diary entry about his call on Indira Gandhi is more cryptic. 'She said she had seen statements of our Prime Minister which were likely to cause misgivings in the public mind. She said that this was not what was stipulated in the Simla Agreement.' Syed Fida Hussain, *Pakistan: The Promise of the Early Years: A Memoir (1908-1977)*, Lahore: Zeenat Publications, 2016, p. 255.
48. Shahid Amin, *Reminiscences of a Pakistani Diplomat*, p. 255.
49. Avatar Singh Bhasin (ed.), *India Pakistan Relations 1947-2007: A Documentary Study*, New Delhi: Geetika Publishers, 2012, Vol. IV, pp. 2330–31.
50. Syed Fida Hussain, *Pakistan: The Promise of the Early Years*, p. 245.
51. Avatar Singh Bhasin (ed.), *India Pakistan Relations 1947-2007: A Documentary Study*, Vol. IV, p. 2336; Syed Fida Hussain, *Pakistan: The Promise of the Early Years*, p. 251.
52. Shahid Amin, *Reminiscences of a Pakistani Diplomat*, p. 93.
53. Salman Taseer, *Bhutto: A Political Biography*, New Delhi: Vikas Publishing House, 1980, p. 171.
54. Ibid.
55. Shahid M. Amin, *Reminiscences of a Pakistani Diplomat*, p. 95.
56. Ibid.
57. Ibid., p. 96.
58. Ibid., p. 97.
59. Javid Iqbal, *Encounters with Destiny: Autobiographical Reflections*, p. 176; 'Iqbal's grandson hopes for "Saare Jahan Se Achha ties"', *The Times of India*, 22 May 2015.
60. A.N.D. Haksar, 'The Secret Summit', *The Times of India*, 14 July 2001. The article was written just before and in the context of President General Parvez Musharraf's visit to India for the Agra summit in 2001.
61. Jagat S. Mehta, *Negotiating for India*, p. 181.
62. Ibid., pp. 211–12.
63. Shahid M. Amin's *Reminiscences of a Pakistani Diplomat* has these details. See pp. 99–100.

64. Shashi Tharoor and Shaharyar Khan, *Shadows Across the Playing Field: 60 Years of India–Pakistan Cricket*, New Delhi: Roli Books, 2009, Kindle location 622, 629, 657, 671 and 1710.
65. Ibid., Kindle location 2291.
66. Avatar Singh Bhasin (ed.), *India Pakistan Relations 1947-2007*, Vol. IV, p. 2453.
67. Jagat S. Mehta, *Negotiating for India*, pp. 204–05.
68. Ibid., p. 206.
69. Ibid., pp. 213–14.
70. For details of this episode see Jagat S. Mehta, *The Tyrst Betrayed: Reflections on Diplomacy and Development*, pp.300–01.
71. Cited in Abdul Sattar, *Pakistan's Foreign Policy 1947-2012*, p. 213.
72. Jagat S. Mehta, *Negotiating for India*, p.171.
73. Mani Shankar Aiyar, 'The (Hi)story of One Lakh Visas', *Indian Foreign Affairs Journal*, Vol. V, No. 4, Octobet–December 2010, pp. 480–504.
74. Abdul Sattar, *Pakistan's Foreign Policy*, p. 213.
75. Khushwant Singh, *Truth, Love & a Little Malice: An Autobiography*, New Delhi: Viking–Ravi Dayal, 2002, pp. 330–31; 'Pak plea for lease of Jinnah House rejected', *The Times of India*, 3 December 1983.
76. Sri Prakasa, *Pakistan: Birth and Early Days*, Delhi: Meenakshi Prakashan, 1965, p. 83.
77. Abida Sultan, *Memoirs of a Rebel Princess*, Karachi: Oxford University Press, 2004, pp. 211–12.
78. Avatar Singh Bhasin (ed.), *India Pakistan Relations 1947-2007*, Vol. IV, p. 2472.
79. J.N. Dixit, *India–Pakistan: In War & Peace*, New Delhi: Books Today, 2002, p. 245.
80. Jagat Mehta reviewed J.N. Dixit's *India–Pakistan: In War & Peace* and contested Dixit's view therein. Jagat S. Mehta, *Rescuing the Future: Bequeathed Misperceptions in International Affairs*, New Delhi: Manohar, 2008, pp. 268–85.
81. Pran Chopra (ed.), *Contemporary Pakistan: New Aim and Images*, New Delhi: Vikas Publishing House, 1983, pp. 2–3. These views are in his introductory essay, 'Unheard Voices'.
82. Bashiruddin Ahmed, 'A Quest for Validation', in Pran Chopra (ed.), *Contemporary Pakistan*, pp. 11–42.
83. Bimal Prasad, 'A Quest for Understanding', in Pran Chopra (ed.), *Contemporary Pakistan*, pp. 43–51.

84. Ajit Bhattacharjea, 'Gut Changes', in Pran Chopra (ed.), *Contemporary Pakistan*, pp. 109–17.
85. Ibid.
86. Mani Shankar Aiyar, *Pakistan Papers*, New Delhi: UBS Publishers Distributers Ltd, 1994, pp. 10–11.

6: Dissidents and Crisis

1. Abdul Sattar, *Pakistan's Foreign Policy 1947-2012: A Concise History*, Karachi: OUP, 2013, p. 173.
2. Human Rights Watch, 'The Mass Forced Return of Afghan Refugees: Pakistan Coercion, UN Complicity', 2017, https://www.hrw.org/sites/default/files/report_pdf/pakistan0217_web.pdf (accessed 20 February 2017).
3. Record of talks between President Zia-ul-Haq and Special Envoy of Prime Minister, Sardar Swaran Singh, Islamabad, 2 April 1980, in Avatar Singh Bhasin (ed.), *India Pakistan Relations, 1947-2007: A Documentary Study*, Vol. IV, New Delhi: Geetika Publishers, 2012, p. 2521.
4. Ibid., p. 2522.
5. Cited in Pranay Gupte, *Mother India: A Political Biography of Indira Gandhi*, New Delhi: Penguin Books, 2012, p. 418; Inder Malhotra, *Indira Gandhi: A Personal and Political Biography*, London: Hodder & Stoughton, 1989, p. 268.
6. Ibid., p. 269.
7. 'Record of meeting of Indian Ambassador K. Natwar Singh with the President of Pakistan General Mohammad Zia-ul-Haq, 10 January 1981', in Avatar Singh Bhasin (ed.), *India Pakistan Relations, 1947-2007: A Documentary Study*, Vol. IV, p. 2556; Natwar Singh, *One Life Is Not Enough*, New Delhi: Rupa & Co., 2014, pp. 201–02.
8. Interview to Inderjit, March 1981, published as 'The General's Turn' in Pran Chopra (ed.), *Contemporary Pakistan: New Aim and Images*, New Delhi: Vikas Publishing House, 1983, p. 154.
9. Avatar Singh Bhasin (ed.), *India Pakistan Relations, 1947-2007: A Documentary Study*, Vol. IV, p. 2545.
10. 'Kabul issue must not hit ties: PM', *The Times of India*, 20 July 1980, p. 9.
11. J. N. Dixit, *India-Pakistan: In War & Peace*, New Delhi: Books Today, 2002, pp. 242–43; Verinder Grover and Ranjana Arora (eds), *50 Years of Indo-Pak Relations*, New Delhi: Deep and Deep Publications, 1998, pp. 510–13.

12. *The Times of India*, 17 September 1981, p. 1.
13. Maharaja Krishna Rasgotra, *A Life in Diplomacy*, New Delhi: Penguin Books, 2016, p. 333.
14. Ibid.
15. In the second half of August 1983 front page articles in *The Times of India* include '6 more die in Sindh riots', 19 August; 'Sindh Railway track damaged', 20 August; 'Police firing on Sindh mob', 21 August; 'Students join anti-Zia stir', 22 August; 'Mob violence in Sindh town', and 'Pak events belie sceptics', 23 August; 'Airforce used in show of might', 24 August, etc. See also an article by Bhabani Sengupta on Pakistan titled 'On the Boil' in *India Today*, 15 September 1983.
16. Inder Malhotra, 'Is History Repeating Itself?', *The Times of India*, 25 August 1983, p. 8.
17. 'India voices concern', *The Times of India*, 26 August 1983; 'PM justifies Pak stir for democracy', *The Times of India*, 27 August 1983.
18. On two versions, see Girilal Jain, 'Turmoil in Pakistan', *The Times of India*, 30 August 1983.
19. *India Today*, 15 October 1983. This magazine devoted a cover story to India's troubled relations with its South Asian neighbours. The peg in this were the statements by India on the MRD agitation and the exchange of letters between the Indian prime minister and President Zia. The text of President Zia's reply to Mrs Gandhi was shared by the Pakistan embassy in Delhi with journalists.
20. *The Times of India*, 19 October 1983.
21. *The Times of India*, 30 August 1983.
22. Ibid.
23. Girilal Jain, 'Turmoil in Pakistan'.
24. Nilima Lambah, *Recollections of a Diplomat's Wife*, New Delhi: Roli Books, 2008, p. 72. Mrs Nilima Lambah was the wife of the then deputy high commissioner of India in Islamabad.
25. Ibid., p. 75.
26. Zafar Ali Ujjan, *Exile in the Land of Raam and Raawan*, Islamabad: Kabir Publications, 2009, pp. 20–21 and 24.
27. Ibid., p. 66.
28. Ibid., p. 25.
29. General K.M. Arif, *Working with Zia: Pakistan's Power Politics, 1977–1988*, Karachi: Oxford University Press, 1995, p. 221.
30. Ibid.
31. Ibid.

32. Ibid.
33. Hein G. Kiessling, *Faith, Unity, Discipline: The ISI of Pakistan*, Noida: HarperCollins, 2016, pp. 129–30.
34. Nadeem F. Paracha, 'Al Zulfikar: The Unsaid History', *Dawn*, 9 April 2010, https://www.dawn.com/news/813223/al-zulfikar-the-unsaid-history (accessed on 15 March 2017).
35. Hein G. Kiessling, *Faith, Unity, Discipline*, p. 130.
36. K. Natwar Singh, *One Life Is Not Enough: An Autobiography*, New Delhi: Rupa & Co., 2014, p. 209.
37. Lt Gen. V.R. Raghavan, *Siachen: Conflict without End*, New Delhi: Viking /Penguin Books, 2002, p. 40. Details regarding Siachen are largely derived from Gen. V.R. Raghavan's book.
38. Ibid.
39. Humayun Khan and G. Parthasarathy, *Diplomatic Divide*, New Delhi: Roli Books, 2004, p. 13. The volume is part of the series 'Cross Border-Talks' (series editor, David Page). The references that follow to Humayun Khan's recollections are from the essay by him titled 'Reflections of an Ambassador'.
40. Ibid., p. 17.
41. Speech of President Zia-ul-Haq to the Majlis-e-Shoora, Islamabad, 10 July 1984, in Avatar Singh Bhasin (ed.), *India Pakistan Relations, 1947-2007: A Documentary Study*, Vol. IV, p. 2801.
42. Humayun Khan and G. Parthasarathy, *Diplomatic Divide*, p. 23.
43. Ibid., p. 24.
44. Abdul Sattar, *Pakistan's Foreign Policy*, pp. 214–15.
45. General K.M. Arif, *Working with Zia*, pp. 362–63; Abdul Sattar, *Pakistan's Foreign Policy*, pp. 214–15.
46. *The Times of India*, 31 October 1984.
47. Sartaz Aziz, *Between Dreams and Realities: Some Milestones in Pakistan's History*, Karachi: OUP, 2009, p. 64.
48. Humayun Khan and G. Parthasarathy, *Diplomatic Divide,* p. 27.
49. Ibid., p. 31.
50. Ibid.
51. Ibid., pp. 27–28.
52. Ibid., p. 40.
53. 'Pakistan opens private trade to India', *The Times of India*, 11 January 1986.
54. Avatar Singh Bhasin (ed.), *India Pakistan Relations, 1947-2007: A Documentary Study*, Vol. IV, p. 2906; Inder Malhotra, 'Parleys with

Pakistan: Harsh Realities vs Soft Options', *The Times of India*, 28 February 1986.

55. Avatar Singh Bhasin (ed.), *India Pakistan Relations, 1947-2007: A Documentary Study*, Vol. IV, p. 2911.
56. J.N. Dixit however writes: 'Curiously, Junejo did not raise the question of Operation Brasstacks in any significant manner'. *India-Pakistan: In War & Peace*, p. 259.
57. Dilip Bobb and Inderjit Badhwar, 'A.P. Venkateswaran: An avoidable blunder', *India Today*, 15 February 1987.
58. See also *The Times of India*, 21 January 1987 where the two prominent front-page stories are 'Venkateswaran quits' and 'Concern at Pak troop moves'. The lead editorial of the same day is entitled 'Utter Disgrace'.
59. Humayun Khan and G. Parthasarathy, *Diplomatic Divide*, p. 52.
60. K. Natwar Singh, *One Life Is Not Enough: An Autobiography*, p. 276.
61. Kuldip Nayar. *Beyond the Lines: An Autobiography*, New Delhi: Roli Books, 2012, p. 304.
62. Ibid., p. 305.
63. Ibid., p. 308. For a Pakistani variant of this episode see Feroz Hassan Khan, *Eating Grass: The Making of the Pakistan Bomb*, New Delhi: Cambridge University Press, 2013, pp. 215-17. Mushahid Hussain was to lose his job as editor of the *Muslim* newspaper.
64. See editorial 'Propaganda Coup', *The Times of India*, 25 February1987; Press Conference of President Zia-ul-Haq, Islamabad, 23 February 1987, in Avatar Singh Bhasin (ed.), *India Pakistan Relations, 1947-2007: A Documentary Study*, Vol. IV, p. 3031.
65. K Subrahmanyam, 'Pakistan's Nuclear Message: A Well Calculated Exercise', *The Times of India*, 7 March 1987.
66. 'Tension Without Reason', *The Times of India*, 26 January 1987; See also Girilal jain, 'Confused Signals to Pakistan', *The Times of India*, 28 January 1987.
67. Humayun Khan and G. Parthasarathy, *Diplomatic Divide*, p. 38.
68. *The Times of India*, 17 August 1988, p. 9.
69. Ibid., 18 August 1988, p. 9.
70. Ibid., 19 August 1988, p. 8.
71. Letters to the editor, *The Times of India*, 30 August 1988.
72. Iqbal Akhund, *Trial and Error: The Advent and Eclipse of Benazir Bhutto*, Karachi: OUP, 2000, p. 42.

73. Mani Shankar Aiyar, *Pakistan Papers*, New Delhi: UBSPD, 1994, pp. 53–54.
74. Ibid., p. 55.
75. Iqbal Akhund, *Trial and Error*, p. 95.
76. Ibid., p. 97.
77. *The Times of India*, 3 January 1989, p. 12.
78. Banquet Speech of Prime Minister Rajiv Gandhi, 16 July 1989, Islamabad, MEA, Foreign Affairs Record. http://mealib.nic.in/?pdf2577?000 (accessed on 15 March 2017).
79. Abdul Sattar, *Pakistan's Foreign Policy*, p. 211; Iqbal Akhund, *Trial and Error*, pp. 102–07.
80. Lt Gen. V.R. Raghavan, *Siachen: Conflict without End*, p. 142.
81. *Outlook*, 31 December 2007.
82. I.K. Gujral, *Matters of Discretion: An Autobiography*, New Delhi: Hay House, 2011, p. 270.
83. A.S. Dulat, *Kashmir: The Vajpayee Years*, Noida: HarperCollins, 2015, p. 59.
84. Harinder Baweja, 'Mufti Sayeed's dark hour: Militants released for kidnapped daughter', *Hindustan Times*, 8 January 2016.
85. Iqbal Akhund, *Trial and Error*, p. 206.
86. I.K. Gujral, *Matters of Discretion*, p. 279.
87. *The Times of India*, 22 January 1990.
88. Ibid., p. 280.
89. P.R. Chari, Pervaiz Iqbal Cheema and Stephen Philip Cohen, *Perception, Politics and Security in South Asia: The Compound Crisis of 1990*, New York: RoutledgeCurzon, 2003, p. 72.
90. J.N. Dixit, *India–Pakistan: In War & Peace*, p. 273.
91. I.K. Gujral, *Matters of Discretion*, p. 282.
92. Ibid.
93. Iqbal Akhund, *Trial and Error*, p. 225.
94. I.K. Gujral, *Matters of Discretion*, p. 283.

7: Hopes for the Future in a Troubled Decade

1. See for instance Khurshid Mahmud Kasuri, *Neither a Hawk Nor a Dove: An Insider's Account of Pakistan's Foreign Policy*, Gurgaon: Penguin Random House, 2015, pp. 421–22.
2. Iqbal Akhund, *Trial and Error: The Advent and Eclipse of Benazir Bhutto*, Karachi: Oxford University Press, 2000, p. 209.

3. J.N. Dixit, *Anatomy of a Flawed Inheritance: Indo-Pak Relations, 1970-94*, New Delhi: Konark, 1995, pp. 129–30.
4. 'VP urges nation to be ready and Pak troops move to border', *The Times of India*, 11 April,1990.
5. Shuja Nawaz, *Crossed Swords: Pakistan, Its Army, and the Wars Within*, Karachi: Oxford University Press, 2008, pp. 419–21.
6. P.R. Chari, Pervaiz Iqbal Cheema and Stephen Philip Cohen, *Perception, Politics and Security in South Asia: The Compound Crisis of 1990*, New York: RoutledgeCurzon, 2003, pp. 81–88.
7. Iqbal Akhund, *Trial and Error*, p. 213.
8. Ibid., pp. 207–08.
9. Howard B. Schaffer, *The Limits of Influence: America's Role in Kashmir*, New Delhi: Penguin Books, 2009, p. 128.
10. Gautam Adhikari, 'War Threat Recedes', *The Times of India*, 27 April 1990, p. 1.
11 Seymour Hersh, 'On the Nuclear Edge', *The New Yorker*, 29 March 1993.
12. Iqbal Akhund, *Trial and Error*, p. 229.
13. See P.R. Chari, Pervaiz Iqbal Cheema and Stephen Philip Cohen, *Perception, Politics and Security in South Asia: The Compound Crisis of 1990*, pp. 111–13, although this analysis veers to the view that the Gates mission and the US diplomacy preceding it was a major factor in diffusing the crisis.
14. J.N. Dixit, *India–Pakistan: In War & Peace*, New Delhi: Books Today, 2002, p. 285.
15. P.R. Chari, Pervaiz Iqbal Cheema and Stephen Philip Cohen, *Perception, Politics and Security in South Asia: The Compound Crisis of 1990*, pp. 2–3.
16. '3 JKLF men die in Pak firing', *The Times of India*, 13 February 1992, p. 1.
17. J.N. Dixit, *India–Pakistan: In War & Peace*, p. 282.
18. Sunil Narula, 'Pakistan shocked at demolition', *The Times of India*, 8 December 1992, p. 1.
19. 'Ishaq crossing limits: India', *The Times of India*, 26 December 1992, p. 13.
20. For instance, 'ISI behind J&K standoff: Bhatia', *The Times of India*, 24 October 1993, p. 10; 'Kashmir tension mounts', *The Times of India*, 24 October 1993, p 1; Swapan Dasgupta, 'Hazratbal not the

last: Heralding the Capitulationist Clamour', *The Times of India*, 27 October 1993, p. 16.

21. J.N. Dixit, *India-Pakistan: In War & Peace*, p. 295.
22. Howard B. Schaffer, *The Limits of Influence: America's Role in Kashmir*, p. 141; Abhay Vaidya, 'Kashmir disputed territory: US', *The Times of India*, 30 October, 1993, p. 1.
23. A.S. Dulat, *Kashmir: The Vajpayee Years*, Noida: HarperCollins, 2015, p. 179.
24. Krishnan Srinivasan, *Diplomatic Channels,* New Delhi: Manohar Publishers, 2012, p. 37.
25. Ibid., p. 36.
26. Shekhar Gupta, 'Triumph of Diplomacy', *India Today*, 31 March 1994.
27. Krishnan Srinivasan, *Diplomatic Channels*, p. 37.
28. Ibid., p. 36.
29. Quoted by Shekhar Gupta, 'Triumph of Diplomacy'.
30. Jamsheed Marker, *Quiet Diplomacy: Memoirs of an Ambassador of Pakistan*, Karachi: OUP, 2010, p. 413.
31. Ibid., pp. 413–14.
32. Krishnan Srinivasan, *Diplomatic Channels*, p. 38.
33. Ibid., p. 41.
34. Ibid.
35. Umer Farooq, 'The Mast Gul Factor', *Herald,* Karachi, 10 August 2016.
36. Howard B. Schaffer, *The Limits of Influence: America's Role in Kashmir*, p. 150.
37. Belusa group is an influential lobby headed by US-based Shireen Tahir Kheli. Other members in the Belusa group include senior journalists from India, Pakistan and retired bureaucrats.
38. Mubashir Hasan, 'Nikhil Chakravarty and the Momentum of Peace', Keynote address delivered at the India International Centre, New Delhi on 3 November 2003. http://www.sacw.net/peace/mubahirHasanNov2003.html (accessed on 15 March 2017).
39. Ibid.
40. I.A. Rahman, 'Finding Roots and References in South Asia', in Smitu Kothari and Zia Mian (eds), *Bridging Partition: People's Initiatives for Peace Between India and Pakistan*, Hyderabad: Orient BlackSwan, 2010, pp. 103–06.

41. Ibid., pp. 104–05.
42. Ibid., p. 106.
43. J.N. Dixit, *India-Pakistan: In War & Peace*, p. 261.
44. Mukul Kesavan, 'I, the Nation', *Outlook*, 21 May 2007. See also Meenakshi Bharat and Nirmal Kumar (eds), *Filming the Line of Control: The Indo-Pak Relationship through the Cinematic Lens*, New Delhi: Routledge, 2008.
45. I.K. Gujral, *Matters of Discretion: An Autobiography*, New Delhi: Hay House, 2011, p. 380.
46. Swapan Dasgupta, 'Betraying the Doctrine', *India Today*, 31 May 1997.
47. Saba Naqvi Bhaumik, 'Fogeys in Arms', *India Today*, 31 May 1997.
48. 'The Foreign Office has proved stronger than PM', Interview of Bhabani Sengupta by Ramananda Sengupta, *Outlook*, 21 May 1997.
49. I.K. Gujral, *Matters of Discretion: An Autobiography*, pp. 407–08.
50. Ibid., p. 415.
51. Kuldip Nayar, *Beyond the Lines: An Autobiography*, New Delhi: Roli Books, 2012, p. 353.
52. Jaswant Singh, *A Call to Honour: In Service of Emergent India*, New Delhi: Rupa & Co, 2006, p. 135.
53. Avatar Singh Bhasin (ed.), *India Pakistan Relations 1947-2007: A Documentary Study*, New Delhi: Geetika Publishers, 2012, Vol. V, p. 3596.
54. Shashi Tharoor and Shaharyar Khan, *Shadows Across the Playing Field: Sixty Years of India Pakistan Cricket*, New Delhi: Roli Books, Kindle location 1817.
55. Ibid., Kindle location 1852.
56. https://sports.ndtv.com/cricket/incidents-of-fan-brawls-that-shamed-the-gentleman-s-game-1492963 (accessed on 15 March 2017).
57. Abdul Sattar, *Pakistan's Foreign Policy 1947-2012: A Concise History*, Karachi: OUP, 2013, p. 242.
58. Humayun Khan and G. Parthasarathy, *Diplomatic Divide*, New Delhi: Roli Books, 2004, p. 109. G. Parthasarathy's contribution to this volume is titled 'Memories of Pakistan'.
59. Jaswant Singh, *A Call to Honour*, p. 202.
60. Sartaz Aziz, *Between Dreams and Realities: Some Milestones in Pakistan's History*, Karachi: OUP, 2009, p. 269.
61. Jaswant Singh, *A Call to Honour*, p. 211.
62. Abdul Sattar, *Pakistan's Foreign Policy*, p. 245.

63. Sartaz Aziz, *Between Dreams and Realities*, p. 281.
64. Jaswant Singh, *A Call to Honour*, p. 211.
65. Shuja Nawaz, *Crossed Swords: Pakistan, Its Army, and the Wars Within*, p. 510.
66. Abdul Sattar, *Pakistan's Foreign Policy*, p. 247.
67. Sartaz Aziz, *Between Dreams and Realities*, p. 285.
68. Shamshad Ahmad, 'The truth about the Kargil episode', *Dawn*, 15 October 2006.
69. A.S. Dulat, *Kashmir: The Vajpayee Years*, p. 44.
70. Jaswant Singh, *A Call to Honour*, pp. 230, 232.
71. Ibid., p. 230.
72. A.S. Dulat, *Kashmir: The Vajpayee Years*, p. 56.
73. Jaswant Singh, *A Call to Honour*, pp. 235, 240.
74. Zahid Hussain, 'The demon we created', *Dawn*, 20 January 2016. http://epaper.dawn.com/DetailImage.php?StoryImage=20_01_2016_008_002 (accessed on 21 March 2017).
75. Zafar Abbas, 'Terror on Indian Airlines Flight 814', *Herald*, Karachi, January 2000.
76. Prime Minister's Address to the Nation, 31 December 1999, http://archivepmo.nic.in/abv/speech-details.php?nodeid=9171 (accessed on 21 Month 2017).

8: A New Century but An Old Terrain

1. These were the themes pursued in Meghnad Desai and Aitzaz Ahsan, *Divided by Democracy,* New Delhi: Roli Books, 2005, in the series 'Cross-border talks' edited by David Page.
2. Akbar Zaidi, *Issues in Pakistan's Economy: A Political Economy Perspective*, Karachi: OUP, 3rd ed., 2015, pp. 724–25.
3. Ibid.
4. Nadeem Farooq Paracha, *Eyewitness Pakistan: End of the Past,* Lahore: Vanguard Books, 2016, p. 174.
5. Ibid., p. 175.
6. Akbar Zaidi, *Issues in Pakistan's Economy*, p. 522.
7. Jaswant Singh, *A Call to Honour: In Service of Emergent India,* New Delhi: Rupa & Co., 2006, p. 320.
8. Ayesha Jalal, *The Struggle for Pakistan: A Muslim Homeland and Global Politics*, Cambridge, Massachusetts: Harvard University Press, 2014, p. 319.

9. *The Economist*, 30 March 2000.
10. Kuldip Nayar, *Beyond the Lines: An Autobiography*, New Delhi: Roli Books, 2012, p. 361.
11. http://pib.nic.in/focus/foyr2001/fojan2001/fo020120011.html (accessed on 15 March 2017).
12. L.K. Advani, *My Country My Life*, New Delhi: Rupa &Co., 2008, p. 696.
13. Ibid., p. 697.
14. *India Today*, 4 June 2001.
15. Abdul Sattar, *Pakistan's Foreign Policy 1947-2012: A Concise History*, Karachi: OUP, 2013, p. 252.
16. Pervez Musharraf, *In the Line of Fire: A Memoir*, London: Simon & Schuster, 2006, p. 299.
17. Ibid., p. 251.
18. Ibid., p. 258.
19. Ibid., p. 259.
20. Jaswant Singh, *A Call to Honour*, p. 266.
21. Manoj Joshi, 'December 13 & After: Angry India Disengages from Pakistan', *The Times of India*, 4 January 2002, p. 8.
22. Brig. (Retd) Gurmeet Kanwal, 'Military Dimensions of the 2002 India-Pakistan Standoff: Planning and Preparation for Land Operations', in Zachary S. Davis (ed.), *The India-Pakistan Military Standoff: Crisis and Escalation in South Asia*, New York: Palgrave Macmillan, 2011, p. 81.
23. Jaswant Singh, *A Call to Honour*, p. 268.
24. *Dawn*, 3 March, 2002.
25. Jaswant Singh, *A Call to Honour*, p. 347.
26. Ibid.
27. Howard B. Schaffer, *The Limits of Influence: America's Role in Kashmir*, New Delhi: Penguin Books, 2009, p. 177.
28. Jaswant Singh, *A Call to Honour*, p. 348.
29. A.S. Dulat, *Kashmir: The Vajpayee Years*, Noida: HarperCollins, 2015, p. 166.
30. Jaswant Singh, *A Call to Honour*, p. 349.
31. Vilani Peiris, 'Pakistan's sham referendum endorses Musharraf as president', https://www.wsws.org/en/articles/2002/05/paki-m07.html (accessed on 15 March 2017).
32. Pervez Musharraf, *In the Line of Fire: A Memoir*, p. 299.

33. Brigadier Gurmeet Kanwal, 'Lost Opportunities in Operation Parakram', *Indian Defence Review*, Net ed., 13 December, 2011. http://www.indiandefencereview.com/spotlights/lost-opportunities-in-operation-parakram/ (accessed on 15 March 2017).
34. K. Subrahmanyam, 'Containing Pakistan: Talk First, De-escalate Later', *The Times of India*, 15 October 2002.
35. 'Shun guns for brotherhood, says PM in J and K', *The Times of India*, 19 April 2003, p. 1; 'Stop terrorism, begin talks, PM tells Pak', *The Times of India*, 24 April 2003, p. 5.
36. Simon Denyer and Sanjeev Miglani, 'India, Pakistan edge back from the brink', Reuters, 6 January 2004. http://www.smh.com.au/articles/2004/01/05/1073267971118.html?from=storyrhs (accessed on 15 March 2017).
37. James Astill, *The Great Tamasha: Cricket, Corruption and the Turbulent Rise of Modern India*, London: Bloomsbury, 2013, p. 130.
38. 'India's glitterati go to Lahore', *The Times of India*, 24 March 1996, p. 11.
39. 'It's Only a Game', *The Times of India*, 12 March 1996, p. 14.
40. 'Googly for goodwill', *The Times of India*, 17 March 1996, p. 13.
41. The expression 'whiff of grapeshot' is from Mukul Kesavan, *Men in White: A Book of Cricket*, New Delhi: Penguin Books, 2007, p. 226. See also, Shashi Tharoor and Shaharyar Khan, *Shadows across the Playing Field: Sixty Years of India Pakistan Cricket*, New Delhi: Roli Books, Kindle location 2008.
42. Ibid., Kindle location 2001.
43. Abdul Sattar, *Pakistan's Foreign Policy 1947-2012: A Concise History*, p. 231.
44. K. Natwar Singh, *One Life Is Not Enough: An Autobiography*, New Delhi: Rupa & Co., 2014, pp. 196–97.
45. Afzal Mahmood, 'BJP Defeat and Its Fallout', *Dawn*, 15 May 2004.
46. Rajeshwar Dayal, *A Life in Our Times*, New Delhi: Orient Longman, 1998, pp. 290–92.
47. J.K. Galbraith, *Ambassador's Journal: A Personal Account of the Kennedy Years*, London: Hamish Hamilton, 1969, p. 278.
48. Kuldip Nayar, *Beyond the Lines*, p. 122.
49. George Verghese, *Our Neighbour Pakistan*, Bombay: Yusuf Meherally Centre, 1965, p. 79.
50. Kuldip Nayar, *Beyond the Lines*, p. 122.

51. Rafi Raza, *Zulfikar Ali Bhutto and Pakistan 1967-1977*, Karachi: OUP, 1997, p. 201.
52. Ibid.
53. Pervez Musharraf, *In the Line of Fire: A Memoir*, p. 303.
54. Khurshid Ahmed Kasuri was the foreign minister of Pakistan during the period 2002–07. His account of what purportedly transpired in the 'back channel discussion' can be found in *Neither a Hawk Nor a Dove: An Insider's Account of Pakistan's Foreign Policy,* Gurgaon: Penguin Random House, 2015. S.K. Lambah the designated representative of India in this discussion gave a briefer account in a speech in May 2015. http://www.outlookindia.com/website/story/a-possible-outline-of-a-solution/290718 (accessed on 15 April 2017). Tariq Aziz, secretary to President Musharraf was the designated Pakistani representative during the Musharraf era. He has not spoken about what transpired in the discussions. Although there are numerous analysis of what conclusions and recommendations the backchannel had arrived at, the full details and the story of the discussions remains to be told.
55. Salman Ahmad (with Robert Schroeder), *Rock and Roll Jihad,* Mumbai: Jaico Books, 2010, p. 168.
56. Ibid. See also Shehryar Ahmad, 'Changing the Paradigm', in Smitu Kothari and Zia Mian with Kamla Bhasin, A.H. Nayyar and Mohammad Tahseen (eds), *Bridging Partition: People's Initiatives for Peace Between India and Pakistan*, Hyderabad: Orient BlackSwan, 2010.
57. *Ghoom Tana,* https://www.youtube.com/watch?v=6ah9zEc8HQM, (accessed on 15 March 2017).
58. Madeeha Gohar, 'Changing Hearts through Theatre', in Smitu Kothari and Zia Mian with Kamla Bhasin, A.H. Nayyar and Mohammad Tahseen (eds), *Bridging Partition,* p. 284.
59. Kuldip Nayar, 'People to People Contact', in Smitu Kothari and Zia Mian with Kamla Bhasin, A.H. Nayyar and Mohammad Tahseen (eds), *Bridging Partition: People's Initiatives for Peace Between India and Pakistan*, Hyderabad: Orient BlackSwan, 2010, p. 90.
60 Balraj Puri, 'Pakistan India Interactions', in Smitu Kothari and Zia Mian with Kamla Bhasin, A.H. Nayyar and Mohammad Tahseen (eds), *Bridging Partition*, p. 311.
61. Ibid., pp. 310–11.
62. https://www.youtube.com/watch?v=MUNQgXtl36M (accessed on 15 March 2017).

63. Oral History Transcript, B.F.H.B. Tyabji, Nehru Memorial Museum and Library (NMML), Accession No. 312, p. 61. Badruddin Faiz Hasan Badruddin (B.F.H.B.) Tyabji has been referred to, all through this book, as Badr-ud-Din Tyabji.

Epilogue

1. Prime Minister Manmohan Singh's address to the FICCI Annual General Meeting, 8 January 2007. http://archivepmo.nic.in/drmanmohansingh/speech-details.php?nodeid=437 (accessed on 15 March 2017).
2. Tariq Fatemi, 'The Peace Process Revisited', *Dawn*, 25 November 2006.
3. Abdul Sattar, *Pakistan's Foreign Policy 1947-2012: A Concise History*, Karachi: OUP, 2013, p. 310.
4. Amir Mir, *The Bhutto Murder Trail: From Waziristan to GHQ*, Chennai: Tranquebar, 2010, p. 18.
5. 'There is a bit of India in every Pakistani: Zardari', *Hindustan Times*, 23 November 2008, www.hindustantimes.com/india/there-is-a-bit-of-india-in-every-pakistani-zardari/story-gB4zET8PlhmNHGZOxYYugP.html (accessed on 15 March 2017).
6. For details see Shivshankar Menon, *Choices: Inside the Making of India's Foreign Policy*, Gurgaon: Penguin Random House, 2016, pp. 89–90.
7. Ibid., pp. 92–98.
8. Iqbal Akhund, *Trial and Error: The Advent and Eclipse of Benazir Bhutto*, Karachi: Oxford University Press, 2000, p. 68.
9. K. Natwar Singh, *One Life Is Not Enough: An Autobiography*, New Delhi: Rupa & Co., 2014, p. 187.
10. Stephen Cohen, *Shooting for a Century: Finding Answers to the India–Pakistan Conundrum*, Noida: HarperCollins, 2013.

Acknowledgements

I AM GRATEFUL TO numerous colleagues and friends in India and Pakistan who have spoken to me about various aspects of India–Pakistan history over the years and pointed me to different sources and readings.

I am grateful to the following for reading drafts of the book at different stages or in providing specific details:

T.C.A. Achintya, T.C.A. Anant, Ashish Ray, Devendra Singh, Indivar Kamtekar, K.S. Bajpai, Laila Sumpton, Mahendra Vyas, Mukul Kesavan, Rachel Dwyer, Radhika Chopra and T.C.A. Ranganathan. Of course, the usual disclaimers apply. Anyone who works in this field will remain grateful to Avatar Singh Bhasin and his ten-volume collection of official documents on India–Pakistan Relations. Pallavi Raghavan was most generous in sharing her unpublished work on India–Pakistan diplomacy in the 1950s.

I am grateful to the Ministry of External Affairs and the ARM Division for facilitating my access to some files of the 1950s. The great collections of the Nehru Memorial Museum and Library, the Indian Council of World Affairs Library and the India International Centre Library were my mainstays in the writing of this book. I am most grateful to them and their staff.

Antara Raghavan edited and reorganized the early drafts of this book.

I am grateful to my publishers: to Ananth Padmanabhan for suggesting this book and V.K. Karthika for very useful initial discussions. I am especially grateful to my editor Udayan Mitra for his unfailingly patient guidance and support and to Antony Thomas for his meticulous editing.

Finally, my thanks to Ranjana, Pallavi and Antara for their unflinching and uncomplaining support and encouragement all through the writing of this book.